Manufacturing Catastrophe

Manufacturing Catastrophe

Massachusetts and the Making of Global Capitalism, 1813 to the Present

SHAUN S. NICHOLS

OXFORD
UNIVERSITY PRESS

OXFORD
UNIVERSITY PRESS

CIP data is on file at the Library of Congress

ISBN 978-0-19-766532-9 (pbk.)
ISBN 978-0-19-766531-2 (hbk.)

DOI: 10.1093/oso/9780197665312.001.0001

In memory of my grandparents:
Mémé, Pépé
Vovó, Vovô

Contents

Preface   ix

Acknowledgments   xi

Introduction   1

PART I. *From Farm to Factory, from Ship to Loom*

1. The Irrational Revolution: The Failure of Early Massachusetts
   Industrialization   13

2. Economies in Motion: Crisis and Industry in the Whaling City   30

3. Labor in Motion: The Peopling of Industrial Massachusetts   51

PART II. *From Cloth to Clothes, from Crisis to Prosperity*

4. Un-Making Industrial Massachusetts: Labor and Capital in an
   Age of Deindustrialization   81

5. Cut from the Same Cloth: The Remaking of Industrial
   Massachusetts   107

6. Toward Free Migration: The Reopening of Industrial
   Massachusetts   128

PART III. *From the Needle to High Tech, from Massachusetts to the World*

7. Toward Free Trade: Globalization from the Ground Up   153

8. Reconstructing Industrial Ascendance: Massachusetts and the
   Reordering of American Capitalism   167

9. Industrial Twilight? Massachusetts and the Reordering
   of Global Capitalism   186

10. The "New" Economy: Making High-Tech Massachusetts   208

Conclusion   229

Notes   237

Bibliography   311

Index   345

Preface

IT HAS BEEN a decade since I started this book. Looking back on the years spent researching, reflecting, and writing, I can see clearly that there was more at stake for me than unearthing some neglected chapter in the making of the global economy. If the old cliché that we are products of our history is true, then it is especially true for me in regard to this particular history.

As best I can tell, Andrew Jackson Nichols, born in 1840 to a Norwell shipwright, was the first of my ancestors to make his way to the factory. He moved to New Bedford's West End and became a shoemaker. My paternal grandmother's first language was French. Her parents immigrated to New Bedford from Prince Edward Island sometime in the early twentieth century. Her father, who had a sixth-grade education, worked as a mechanic. Her mother (with an eighth-grade education) was a stitcher in a pajama factory. My mother's parents were Azorean farmers. The family immigrated to Fall River in 1969 so my uncle could avoid being drafted to fight in a war against African independence. My grandfather became a janitor in a textile mill, and my grandmother became a stitcher in a local men's clothing factory. Ensconced in Fall River's vibrant Portuguese community, neither ever learned English.

Growing up in New Bedford, it was hard to miss the sense of frenetic desperation that seemed to suffuse the city. Decent jobs were scarce. Seemingly empty factories abounded. The only national news the city ever made was uniformly negative. All the while, Massachusetts policymakers constantly spun tales of how they could fix the "problem" of communities like ours. Life in New Bedford was punctuated by the ever-present sense that this was a city in crisis.

But residents could at least take comfort in the widespread understanding of why things seemed so bleak. It could be summarized in just one word: "deindustrialization." When I returned to the city as an adult, it seemed to me that "deindustrialization" served as a sort of catch-all for the city's pervasive sense of resignation and powerlessness. It was talked about as a sort of virus, a plague the city had caught somewhere and could not quite shake. "Foreign competition," or its less-than-savory variants, was an equally popular explanation—but it functioned as a sort of explanation of an explanation, a shorthand for how the city got infected in the first place. The empty factories downtown stood, in this telling, as tangible memorials to the slow, grinding decline that all of us were caught up in.

A product of generations of migrants who made their way to southeastern Massachusetts in search of a better life, I always felt that something was amiss about this foundational mythology. After all, how could one square that long-held narrative with the thousands of immigrants who had made their way to these cities throughout the nineteenth and twentieth centuries? My grandparents, after all, arrived in 1969—certainly well past the late nineteenth-century heyday of industrial triumph. Why immigrate to a place in the throes of long-standing decline?

And then there was the 2007 Immigration and Customs Enforcement raid of a downtown factory making backpacks and vests. Weren't those factories supposed to be empty? Perhaps there was something more to this narrative of deindustrialization—a narrative so central to my understanding of our nation's past, and of my own past. That vague sense of historical dissonance became the foundation for *Manufacturing Catastrophe*.

Acknowledgments

I AM NOT very good at writing acknowledgments. It is not (I hope) because I am lacking in gratitude. Rather, the problem is that the whole exercise feels so asymmetric. I could have never imagined—when I entered adulthood—that I would ever write a book like this. The people listed here (and many others I surely forgot to include) helped make that possible. To give a quick "shout-out" in a brief prefatory section thus feels a bit hollow. But—alas—we live in a society of rules. So, I will just say, beyond what is written here, I hope all of you who helped make this work possible know how much your support has meant to me.

I would be remiss if I did not begin by thanking my undergraduate professors. My four years at Western Washington University in Bellingham, Washington, were truly transformative. When I first arrived at college, I was the very model of the disaffected and disinterested high-schooler. It was the kindness and endless generosity of my undergraduate mentors that revealed a whole different path for my life, helping this directionless college student become (dare I say it?) "Harvard material." George Mariz never gave up on me; I would not be where I am today had he not encouraged me to actually take college seriously. Chris Friday was unbelievably giving with his time; so much of my approach to labor history was developed during our conversations. Johann N. Neem taught me what it means to be a thinker and a scholar, and he continues to serve as my model of an academic with a true awareness of the ethical obligations that come with a life of the mind. Finally, A. Ricardo López not only served as my first introduction to global history but has also remained a constant reminder that great history can be revolutionary.

I was also unbelievably lucky to work with a group of equally incisive and kind-hearted advisors at Harvard University. Sven Beckert has been, and continues to be, an unparalleled friend and mentor. He has always pushed me to expand my research further and further out—in time, space, and methodology—and I owe him an incalculable debt for his unflagging enthusiasm for a Massachusetts project that, at times, seemed to have nothing to do with Massachusetts. Lizabeth Cohen remains one of the most discerning and brilliant scholars with whom I have ever had the honor of working. Her influence is apparent on almost every page of this book. James Kloppenberg was both a perceptive reader and an endlessly cheery voice of reason in the development of this project. My approach to this work was also enormously influenced by the advice of Nancy Cott, Christine Desan, Deborah Levenson, Erez Manela, and Scott Reynolds Nelson.

Since moving to Idaho, my newfound friends and colleagues at the Boise State University Department of History have been a consistent source of camaraderie and inspiration. In a more just world, I would call out all the ways each of my colleagues has helped make this book possible, but I would have to publish another book for the acknowledgments alone.

In finishing this manuscript, I have also benefited enormously from the help of the editorial staff and anonymous readers I worked with at Oxford University Press. Everybody I spoke to in choosing an editor could not stop singing the praises of Susan Ferber; I now see why. Susan's sharp eye was invaluable at every step of the publication process.

I was also lucky to receive financial support from a number of sources. Early on, scholarships from the UNOVA Foundation and the Western Washington University History Department, including the Bernard L. Boylan Scholarship and the Carl and Evelyn Schuler Scholarship, helped keep me afloat during a very precarious time in my life. I also owe a great debt to the Harvard University Graduate School of Arts and Sciences for funding my graduate studies. In addition, my research was generously funded by the Thomas Cochran Dissertation Fellowship in Economic and Business History, the Charles Warren Center for American Studies, the Canada Center at Harvard University, the Weatherhead Center for International Affairs, and the Boise State University Department of History.

I have also been assisted by many kind and accommodating archivists and librarians in researching and gathering materials for this project. The staffs of the New Bedford Free Public Library and the New Bedford Whaling Museum Research Library—in particular, Mark Procknik and Paul Cyr— were a tremendous help. I also received a lot of patience and assistance from librarians at numerous Portuguese archives: Maria Margarida S. M. Almeida of the Biblioteca Pública e Arquivo Regional de Ponta Delgada in particular. I also owe a special thanks to the International Institute of Social History in Amsterdam—especially Marcel van der Linden, Jaqueline Rutte, Anja van der Lee, and Willeke Tijssen. I am also thankful for the assistance of Libby Lipin at the French Institute of Assumption College, the librarians at the Schlesinger Archive of the Radcliffe Institute, as well as the fantastic staff at the University of Massachusetts Dartmouth Ferreira-Mendes Portuguese American Archives. Two research assistants, Matthew Gordon and Bryan Robert Paradis, deserve a special note of thanks for sending me digital copies of material I could not view in person.

There are so many friends who kept me going over my years of graduate work; I cannot possibly name them all. Marco Basile, Rudi Batzell, Aaron Bekemeyer, Casey Bohlen, Joan Chaker, Eli Cook, Elizabeth Cross, Clair Dahm, Claire Dunning, Alicia Harley, Erin Haynes, Louis Hyman, Eva Payne, Samantha Payne, Solé Prillaman, Mircea Raianu, Caitlin Rosenthal, Becca Scofield, Liat Spiro, Rachel Steely, Michael J. Taylor, Heidi Tworek, and Benjamin Waterhouse all offered invaluable feedback and friendship in the making of this project.

Numerous other colleagues offered critical feedback on the manuscript. Members of the Harvard University Twentieth-Century Dissertation Reading Group (especially Lisa McGirr and Andrew Jewett), the Weatherhead Center Graduate Student Associates Program, the Harvard Program on Capitalism Dissertation Workshop, the Business History Conference (especially Pamela Laird, Barbara Hahn, and Jennifer Delton), the Labor and Working Class History Association (Jefferson Cowie, in particular), the Charles Warren Center for Studies in American History, and Harvard's Workshop on the Political Economy of Modern Capitalism were all immensely helpful in the making of this book.

I must also thank the members of my family who put up with my increasingly erratic (perhaps declining) mental state over the course of these years of intense writing and research. My parents, Steve and Nalia (along with my brother Adam and the rest of the Nichols family), as well as my in-laws—Donald, Ronda, Jennifer, and the sorely missed Susan Thoren—were all frequent sources of moral support and encouragement. I cannot thank them enough. The entire Johnson family—Roland, Joan, Dylan, and Annie—has always been there for me. Sean, Jeni, Vander, and Phin McCullough also helped get me through these last few years of research.

I owe a special debt of gratitude to my grandparents: Ron and Joan Nichols, and Luis and Ermelinda Borges. Not only did my grandparents house (and feed!) me over the many weeks I spent researching in Southeastern Massachusetts—but, more important, their stories, struggles, and successes served as a constant reminder of why these almost totally forgotten industrial cities still really mattered. They inspired this project. For that reason, I dedicate this work to them and their memory.

In closing, I cannot help but acknowledge the immense love and support of my wife, Kathryn. If these years of research and writing have taught me anything, it is that every piece of (hopefully) great scholarship is a fusion of creativity, research, and escalating neuroticism. I sometimes fear that the latter may be the totality of her memory of this project. I took a wonderful girl on a date driving down the Mountain Loop Highway, we danced to "Sugar Magnolia" in a pumpkin patch, and, somehow, she ended up getting skirted all over the world chasing the economic history of Massachusetts. I still find myself amazed that such a lovely person has stayed by my side at each step of the way. I am thankful for every day I have spent with her.

Manufacturing Catastrophe

Introduction

IN 2014, GUATEMALAN migrant Samuel Aj described to local anthropologist Lisa Knauer how he had made his way to New Bedford, Massachusetts. "His landless family was virtually enslaved by a wealthy landowner, or finquero," and their lives were under constant threat of collateral violence as a result of the raging Guatemalan civil war. Aj vividly recalled his village being stormed by the Guatemalan army, leaving him and his family "huddled in a ditch . . . while the armed forces carried out a bloody massacre above them." In Aj's eyes, Knauer realized, his decision to leave Guatemala "did not begin in the early 2000s when he started to plan his journey, but over two decades earlier," amid a life of rural poverty, unrelenting bloodshed, and economic turmoil.[1] Like countless immigrants before him, Aj decided to seek a new life in Massachusetts.

Today, cities like New Bedford are often viewed as economically moribund monuments of rust-belt obsolescence. And yet, since the late 1980s, thousands of Guatemalans like Aj—mostly ethnic Mayans—have made their way to the city. Following in the footsteps of migrant Brazilians, Puerto Ricans, and other South American and Caribbean nationals, they have together set up a thriving Latin American district in New Bedford's North End, taking up work in the city's remaining garment, fish-processing, and electronics factories.[2] New Bedford may not have the highest wages in the state, but, for these migrants, it has other important virtues, cheap housing foremost among them. As Earl Chase, president of a local Maya assistance organization, pointed out in a 2001 interview, they "can rent a reasonably good-sized apartment . . . sometimes for as low as $300 or $400 a month," allowing migrants "to send back at least $200 to $300 per month to their families."[3] As of 2011, Latinos make up 15 percent of the city's population and nearly a third of its public school students.[4] The stretch of North Front Street that bridges New Bedford's docks and the North End is colloquially known as "Maya Alley."[5]

Workers are not the only ones attracted to a place like New Bedford. For capitalists too, the city still has its draws. Francesco Insolia, born in southeast Sicily in 1956, originally began his career as a sea captain for the Carnival Cruise Lines in the 1970s before marrying a Quincy, Massachusetts, native. Insolia eventually founded an export business in Italy before he and his wife relocated to Pembroke, Massachusetts, where they set up an Italian goods retailer. In 1985, he also founded the Michael Bianco company. With eighty-five employees, it manufactured handbags and purses for major labels such as Coach, Fossil, G. H. Bass, and Mark Cross. Not surprisingly, Insolia chose to open the plant not in suburban Pembroke, but in the factory town of Lawrence, before relocating to New Bedford in 1990.[6] As the company grew in the early 2000s, Insolia considered moving to South Carolina or Puerto Rico—but city and state government aid helped convince him to simply move from the North End of New Bedford to the South End—reaping $57,000 in tax breaks through the Massachusetts Department of Workforce Development.[7] Insolia eventually won an $82-million contract from the United States Department of Defense to sew military clothing and equipment for the army.[8]

On the face of it, the mix of workforce development tax breaks proffered by the state worked exactly as intended: Michael Bianco Inc. stayed put in Massachusetts and quickly grew to 500 employees. Conditions rapidly deteriorated, however. Workers were docked fifteen minutes of pay for every minute they were late; they could be fined or fired for spending too long in the bathroom; and $20 fines were issued to employees for infractions ranging from leaving work early to simply talking to one another.[9] Relying on recent migrants, including Samuel Aj, Insolia's factory became, for all intents and purposes, a modern-day sweatshop.

Insolia's and Aj's fates became forever entwined when, on March 6, 2007, both were arrested after more than 300 Immigration and Customs Enforcement (ICE) agents stormed the Michael Bianco factory. Some 362 undocumented workers, including Aj, were rounded up; most had emigrated from Guatemala, El Salvador, and Honduras.[10] While Insolia would be released on bail the next day, his workers were spread out and detained all over the country, from Massachusetts and New Mexico to Texas and Florida.[11] As one immigrant recalled of the raid, "they were trying to grab everybody and people just started running like crazy. They panicked, they fell down.

You found that they were pursuing people just like you were an animal."[12] Attempting to deflect criticism, US Attorney for the State of Massachusetts Michael Sullivan stated that although "it is understandable that many from around the globe would want to come to live, work and raise families here in the greatest democracy in the world . . . this must be done in compliance with US immigration laws—not in violation of them."[13]

Many in New Bedford were surprised by the raid. Few had any clue that the city even had a backpack factory. Most residents assumed the old mills that crowded the city shoreline were largely empty.[14] After all, as political scientist John Tirman pointed out, the Michael Bianco plant sat in "an unremarkable four-story red brick factory building that has housed enterprises long forgotten . . . unremarkable because so many buildings of that kind still stand in this legendary whaling town."[15] The factory's home was the former Kilburn textile mill—first opened in 1905, eventually acquired by Henry L. Tiffany of the famed New York jewelry family, and liquidated in the 1940s.[16] Once a site that famed photographer Lewis Hine captured in his cataloging of child labor in the United States, the building was one a passerby could be forgiven for seeing as just another victim of twentieth-century deindustrialization.[17] Like many of the city's mills, it looked more or less abandoned.[18]

But appearances can deceive. After all, generations of capitalists before Insolia had also found opportunity in these empty mills and crisis-stricken cities. New Bedford's Wamsutta Mill building no. 4, built in 1868, may similarly appear mostly vacant—save for a few cars and a smattering of random signs—but inside the 190,514 square foot building sits a custom welding shop, a small technology company, a social club for West Africans, a machine shop, and the base of New Bedford operations for The Maids cleaning service, among others.[19] Even former talk show host Maury Povich had his clothing line, Mother Freedom, made in New Bedford, in keeping with his mission to "demonstrate that our products—like our country—are number one."[20] The tale of New Bedford—and the tale of American industrial supremacy more broadly—is often told as a story of industrious elites, brawny artisans, and the slow but steady growth of American enterprise. But a more accurate portrayal begins with people more like Aj and Insolia, and the unexpected ways industrial growth has thrived on the constant churn of humans and capital across the globe.

FIGURE I.I The Massachusetts South Coast/ Southeastern Massachusetts (light gray) with New Bedford and Fall River highlighted (dark gray).

Manufacturing Catastrophe offers a reappraisal of a seemingly familiar story—the origins of industrial growth in the United States as told through the paradigmatic case of southeastern Massachusetts—by showing how the changing global geographies of migrant labor and mobile capital defined the making of the Massachusetts economy and, with it, American economic ascendance. It was in New Bedford and Fall River, Massachusetts, that the United States found, at various points in time, its most productive whaling center, its leading producer of cotton cloth, its largest dress manufacturer, and the progenitor of massive (though often little known) conglomerates like AVX, the globe's leading producer of tantalum capacitors.[21] There are, simply put, few cities in the United States (or the world) that offer such an extended timeframe through which to examine both industrial creation and destruction.

Despite these places' centrality to American economic history, they are now shrouded in relative obscurity. As some of the poorest cities in Massachusetts, there is little public support for historical preservation.[22] Consequently, the records of many of these earliest textile mills, garment plants, and electronics factories have been permanently lost.

Faced with this lack of obvious archival material, many historians and popular commentators have simply projected the master narrative of American industrial development onto the economic trajectory of Massachusetts: namely, the oft-repeated story of how nineteenth-century

FIGURE I.2 Wamsutta Mill building no. 4, April 2023. © Kelly Smith Studios, 2023.

industrialization, urbanization, and capitalist expansion collapsed into twentieth-century deindustrialization, globalization, and urban decay.[23] Industrial Massachusetts has become just another example of "rust-belt" decline: a place that flowered in America's industrial heyday only to be left to rust as the industrial epicenter of the United States shifted southward and, ultimately, out of the United States altogether. The state's infamous industrial collapse is even used as an example of why "deindustrialization" must be decoupled from late twentieth-century "globalization."[24] Massachusetts, after all, is said to have begun "deindustrializing" as early as the 1880s, as textile mills were coaxed away not by so-called Third World countries, but by the cheap labor, anti-union American South.

This book tells a very different story. It shows that industrial Massachusetts did not simply "rise" and "fall" but was made and re-made over and over again. Tracing the succeeding rise and fall of the Massachusetts whaling, textile, garment, electronics, and high-tech industries over the past 200 years, *Manufacturing Catastrophe* explores how Massachusetts business, labor, and political leaders repeatedly mobilized the lure of crisis itself—in everything from cheap workers and slashed tax rates to low rents and high manufacturing subsidies—to pull and push both capital and workers across the continents. In other words, it demonstrates how economic crisis—with its unique power to upend prevailing geographies of migrant labor and mobile capital—has served as a potent weapon in the battle for industrial ascendance.[25]

Global capitalism was constructed from the ground up. It was a process in which myriad local economies, like Massachusetts's, each sought to outflank and outcompete one another in the struggle to ensnare precious reserves of capital and labor. It can be all too easy to see these tactics of capitalist seduction as a relatively recent strategy pioneered by the "state-led" development programs of late twentieth-century Asian and Latin American states—nations that eagerly exploited desperate workers and enormous business subsidies to induce industrial growth. But these schemes have a much longer history. The mad scramble for mobile capital is not some unique new problem that affluent nations alone face. It was part and parcel of the global spread of industrial capitalism, stretching back to the nineteenth century.

This book shows how the continuously shifting geography of capitalist development has provoked chronic economic instability and crisis. It is also a story of how crisis itself has been leveraged into renewed industrial expansion and growth. Importantly, the point is not to reiterate existing narratives of how cities, states, and nations do often find ways to creatively (or not so creatively) adapt to economic calamity.[26] Similarly, Massachusetts's story cannot simply be reduced to the claim that economic elites have often shrewdly capitalized on crisis to gain political leverage in fostering self-serving policy changes—although that certainly occurred at key moments.[27] Neither is the point to rehash economist Joseph Schumpeter's central insight that, in the forward march of innovation, new economic regimes come to undermine old ones, ensuring that capitalist destruction for some is inevitably predicated on capitalist growth for others.[28] In fact, in Massachusetts, Schumpeter's dynamic operated in reverse. From the very beginnings of industrialization in the nineteenth century, it was crisis that served as the critical engine of creation—not the other way around. Although it has not been a major facet of scholarly study, this aspect of industrial capitalism was obvious to local leaders, who frequently advertised the advantages of "crisis" as a way to reorder the global economy to their benefit.

This is precisely why this book examines Massachusetts's economic history through a global lens. Only by investigating Massachusetts as just a single node in a complicated web of capital and labor in constant motion can one see how and why crisis was such a singularly regenerative force in the state's history. Over and over again, the state's store of desperate workers, desperate governments, and desperate investors made it look like a haven for factories, firms, and multinational subsidiaries searching the globe for the cheapest and most profitable sites of investment. In Massachusetts, it was economic catastrophe that, somewhat paradoxically, fueled capitalist expansion and consolidation. Crisis was instrumental in making Massachusetts one of the great industrial centers of the United States.

Manufacturing Catastrophe is divided into three parts. The first part, "From Farm to Factory, from Ship to Loom," traces the emergence of the South Coast textile industry by looking at how economic crisis drove mass industrialization in Massachusetts. Chapter 1 highlights the oft-forgotten constraints and failures of early nineteenth-century Massachusetts manufacturing. With the state's agricultural and mercantile economies still relatively robust—making capital scarce and labor itself a pricey commodity—early Lowell and Lawrence mills underperformed compared to their British counterparts. Worse yet, after the Civil War, capitalists and financiers, tempted away by new (and more profitable) opportunities in the American West, rapidly abandoned Massachusetts's textile mills, leaving the state's first industrial cities to stagnate. In other words, Massachusetts's early attempts at industrialization failed precisely because the state was too prosperous to maintain either adequate reserves of industrial capital or a labor force cheap enough to sustain mass production.

What changed? As chapter 2 shows, it was a massive technological and environmental crisis in the whaling industry that brought the city of New Bedford, once widely regarded as the richest city in the nation, to the brink of economic collapse—paving the way for industrial revolution.[29] Indeed, as capital and labor fled the city's whaling ships and wharves, desperate municipal leaders sought to transform their city into a textile manufacturing center. Economic catastrophe in the Whaling City not only fostered local governments eager to do almost anything to spur industrial development—slashing taxes, cutting welfare rolls, and building infrastructure—but it also gifted textile capitalists with the massive labor force that whaleships had helped carry to Massachusetts a generation earlier. In the 1870s, urban crisis midwifed industrial expansion.

Chapter 3 delves into how the economic and political crises of the late nineteenth-century Atlantic world helped consolidate Massachusetts's industrial workforce, bringing throngs of workers from Britain, French Canada, and the Azores to cities like New Bedford and Fall River. The first generation of South Coast Massachusetts industry arose from these crises; the area transformed from the nation's whaling center to its largest producer of cotton cloth.

Part II, "From Cloth to Clothes, from Crisis to Prosperity," traces the origins and consequences of textile deindustrialization. Deindustrialization, chapter 4 suggests, was no inevitable product of industrial maturation, widening wage differentials, or global competition. Instead, certain workers (and certain business leaders) made deliberate choices that led to industrial collapse. Labor and capital never spoke with one voice. The internal conflicts among them would prove decisive in causing industrial catastrophe.

Chapter 5 examines how the desperation and working-class suffering left in the wake of textile collapse in the 1930s was itself packaged, marketed, and ultimately exploited by local capitalists' "development programs" in their efforts to again attract mobile capital to the area. As a result, just as textile mills were fleeing the Massachusetts seaboard en masse, they were replaced by a wave of equally mobile garment and electronics firms from cities such as New York, Philadelphia, and Chicago. Lured by promises of newly unemployed immigrant women willing to work for rock-bottom wages, generous funding packages from local elites desperate to see the economy revived, and a host of incentives from state leaders ranging from free rent to tax clemency, these invading sweatshops turned local desperation into industrial development.

As industrial Massachusetts expanded anew, its ballooning appetite for labor began to bump up against the inflexible strictures of early twentieth-century American immigration law. Chapter 6 interrogates how Massachusetts workers—in particular, Azorean immigrants—worked throughout the 1950s and 1960s to erode these barriers to labor migration. Their success would transform Massachusetts. With surging rates of immigration and a plentiful labor pool, the state's small manufacturing economy flourished. The textile crisis, in short, did not spell doom for industrial Massachusetts, as is so often argued; instead, it was leveraged into an entirely new economic regime. Labor migrants and runaway garment firms effectively re-made the Massachusetts economy at mid-century.

Part III, "From the Needle to High Tech, from Massachusetts to the World," traces the globalization of garment and electronics production, its grinding decline in Massachusetts, and the eventual rise of "high-tech" industry in its place. Too often, globalization is imagined as a conspiracy concocted by high-flying capitalists and power-hungry financiers who surgically targeted the world's cheapest sources of labor. As chapter 7 shows, in Massachusetts, such a story must be flipped on its head. While manufacturers clung to protectionism and economic insularity, it was Massachusetts's workers, immigrants, and budding global labor unions that sought to enthrone free migration, free capital mobility, and free trade as the linchpins of a peaceful and stable global economy. Economic globalization was, if anything, more a working-class than business-class conspiracy.

But, as the final chapters reveal, "free trade" and "free migration" yielded unexpected results. Chapter 8 examines how the loosening of America's immigration laws became a tremendous boon to Massachusetts manufacturers, bringing immense growth to the state's industries. Prosperity transformed Massachusetts in unanticipated ways. As manufacturing thrived on new sources of immigrant labor, local industry re-emerged as a profitable capital investment opportunity, catalyzing the oft-forgotten merger wave of the 1960s. Emerging conglomerate multinationals hungrily swallowed up local manufacturing firms. Proprietary capitalism collapsed; local plant owners became mere middle managers. Massachusetts manufacturing plants became cogs in the vast machinery of corporate conglomeration.

As chapter 9 shows, these newly forged multinational conglomerates had little interest in these local plants beyond using their immediate profitability to help fund further corporate acquisition. In a sort of parasitic industrialism, the profits of local plants were—time and time again—funneled into further conglomerate expansion abroad, leaving the area's factories to be run into the ground and shuttered once their infrastructures had been exhausted. Ultimately, then, the seeds of economic collapse in the 1970s were sown in the prosperous 1950s and 1960s. In fact, it was the very profitability of Massachusetts's manufacturing firms that helped launch the multinational conglomerates that would unceremoniously shut them down in the last decades of the twentieth century.

Chapter 10 tells the story of how Boston-area capitalists leveraged the 1973 crisis into renewed commitments of state investment toward the creation of an entirely new economic regime: "high-tech" Massachusetts. Neither a story of "creative destruction," nor sudden shock, nor long-term deindustrialization, the global restructuring of the Massachusetts economy in the 1970s was once more a story of how prosperity fueled crisis, and crisis fueled subsequent accumulation. Fittingly, since the 1970s, South Coast leaders have again sought to leverage the attractions of economic calamity in an attempt to re-make the area once more—trying to entice everything and everyone from casinos and Amazon centers to hip artists and offshore windmills. As in past moments of industrial transition, their endeavors have certainly resulted in new jobs, but they have brought little relief in terms of these cities' stubbornly elevated rates of poverty and unemployment. The result has been simmering—at times boiling—moments of discontent.

This is not a surprising result. In fact, this seemingly puzzling mix of unfilled jobs and rising unemployment has been a persistent feature of industrial Massachusetts. After all, employers lured by desperation and economic crisis rarely come to town with attractive jobs in tow. Development through catastrophe has often yielded new industries, but it has rarely resulted in stability or affluence. If history is any guide, then, it would seem that these last few decades simply represent the most recent undulation in the interminable drama of succeeding economic regimes in the state of Massachusetts.

PART I

From Farm to Factory, from Ship to Loom

I

The Irrational Revolution

THE FAILURE OF EARLY MASSACHUSETTS INDUSTRIALIZATION

NEW BEDFORD NATIVE William Allen Wall's painting of the city's first successful textile factory, the "Wamsutta Mill" (1853), presented New Bedford as a sort of apotheosis of the industrial-pastoral sublime. The Wamsutta, looking more like a Roman temple than some "dark, satanic mill," is no domineering industrial giant; it stands almost peripheral to the scene. A train zooms rightward, but its minuscule frame hardly consumes the landscape. It is easy to miss. In New Bedford, cattle apparently dwarf locomotives in size. Cows, factories, and smartly dressed Victorians peacefully commingle. The painting reassures the viewer that nature and commerce are in harmony—that there is still a place for both culture and agriculture in industrial New Bedford. Although the industrial revolution was a crucial turning point in world economic history, most people on the ground wanted something much more like Wall's halcyon scene—not the mass industrial regime that eventually overtook Massachusetts.

The Wamsutta Mill was originally viewed with suspicion, if not disdain, by most citizens of New Bedford. In fact, when Thomas Bennett Jr.—newly returned from a three-year tour of the American South to learn the ins and outs of the cotton industry—first approached local Quaker merchant Joseph Grinnell about bankrolling a textile factory in the 1840s, the plan was to build the mill in Georgia, where both land and labor were cheaper.[1] Grinnell believed New Bedford a less profitable but "much more reliable" site of capital investment and made his money contingent on a New Bedford location, to which Bennett hesitantly acceded.[2] The mill faced other obstacles as well. Even though New Bedford was likely the wealthiest per capita city

FIGURE 1.1 William Allen Wall, painting of the Wamsutta Mill, ca. 1853. Image courtesy of the New Bedford Whaling Museum.

in the nation, raising capital proved remarkably difficult. Although Grinnell sported no shortage of wealthy connections, his hopes of raising $300,000 in investment capital for the Wamsutta were soon dashed; he had to settle for about half of that.[3] As a result, capacity plans for the first mill had to be reduced by about a third.[4]

If local capitalists were not convinced that the Wamsutta Mill represented a viable future for New Bedford, local workers were outraged by the very notion. "The general sentiments of the citizens were in opposition to the introduction of manufacturers by incorporated companies.... Particularly so were the mechanics who regarded the organized and disciplined labor and the longer hours of mill work as inimical to the labor interests," Bennett later reflected on the beginnings of the mill.[5] Even among New Bedford's elite, a near consensus emerged that the city had much to lose in industrialization and its attendant need for a settled working class. "New Bedford now is the best city in the State to live in," one concerned citizen wrote to the local newspaper in 1865. "Its neatly kept streets . . . its abundance of shade trees, its French Avenue for a summer evening drive . . . and last, but not least, its freedom, comparatively speaking, from the laboring classes of society, makes it all that anyone can ask for to reside in."[6] In short, the Wamsutta was celebrated only insofar as it conformed to Wall's fabulist conception. Otherwise, its construction faced either indifference or outright hostility.

Despite these limitations, the new mill achieved some degree of success. Opening its doors in 1849, its first twenty-five years of operation returned an average 12 percent annual dividend to its investors.[7] A second mill building was constructed in 1855; another followed in 1860.[8] By the end of the American Civil War, the Wamsutta boasted 45,000 spindles and 1,100 looms.[9] Despite all this, the Wamsutta remained something of an anomaly. Another mill did not come along in New Bedford until 1871, some thirty years later.[10] Soon thereafter, industry positively boomed in the city. In the fourteen years after 1882, a new mill was incorporated, on average, every year in New Bedford. Existing mills added buildings, spindles, and looms at a furious pace as New Bedford lurched forward into the industrial era.

By the end of the nineteenth century, many Americans would revel in their nation's mounting industrial supremacy. But, at its inception, the gospel of industrial revolution garnered few converts. For its part, the Wamsutta project was buffeted by an endless stream of seemingly insoluble problems, namely, a lack of capital, labor, and local support. Why, thirty years later, was industry suddenly surging ahead in Massachusetts?

The answer, ironically, lies in a series of propitious economic catastrophes. The mass industrialization of the late nineteenth century was enabled by a series of economic crises that catalyzed labor and capital concentration in the factories of the Massachusetts South Coast. Three crises particularly drove local industrialization. First, a mounting industrial crisis drained labor and capital away from northern Lowell and Lawrence mills, paving the way for insurgent textile industrialization on the South Coast. Second, a far-flung environmental and technological crisis brought irreversible calamity to the state's whaling industry, releasing the reserves of labor and capital these whaling ships had originally brought to Massachusetts. Finally, a global agricultural crisis, part and parcel of the industrial transformation overtaking the Atlantic world, helped send a veritable army of soon-to-be industrial workers to the state.

Massachusetts's earliest mills—including the famous Lowell mills of the early nineteenth century—were all desperate for labor and capital in an era in which so many other economic pursuits competed for these scarce resources. The obstacles these early factories confronted were not somehow transcended by the mills that followed; instead, they were annulled through processes of

capitalist destruction and geographic realignment. Crisis made the mass industrialization of the late nineteenth century possible.

Working-Class Reluctance

The first glimmers of industrialization in the United States were not spared the
problems the early Wamsutta confronted. The first factory ever constructed in
America—the first building constructed primarily to quarter machinery, not
simply house human labor—was hardly the result of organic commercial development or economic maturation.[11] The origins of the American factory are
generally credited to British spinner Samuel Slater. Knowing of the interest
in America in textile production (and equally aware of the laws that barred
skilled textile workers from emigrating, lest Britain lose its vaunted global
monopoly on industrial textile production), he illegally left Britain with a
head full of memorized factory designs and dreams of wealth.[12] Through a
combination of stolen technology, illegal migration, and the investment
dollars of Newport merchant Moses Brown, Slater erected America's first factory: Slater's Mill in Pawtucket, Rhode Island, about seventeen miles northwest of Fall River, in 1793.[13]

The problem, though, was that Slater simply could not offer wages high
enough to recruit local farmers without endangering the factory's profitability. After all, no self-respecting, independent American yeoman would
ever deign to take a position of industrial servitude. Slater's solution, ostensibly, was to hire entire families; his real target, however, was working-age
children.[14] Recruitment advertisements made Slater's goal abundantly clear.
"WANTED. At the Factory of Samuel Slater . . . one or two large FAMILIES,
to work in the mill."[15] "Large" was the operative word. Another advertisement for a nearby Dudley factory called for "12 Weavers and 2 Families with
5 or 6 children."[16] Fathers, crucially, were promised work in decidedly non-
manufacturing pursuits, such as construction, transportation, overseeing, or
simply farming.[17] Consequently, the first mass-production factory labor force
ever assembled in America was composed entirely of children: seven boys and
two girls, all twelve years old or younger.[18] With adult labor too expensive in
a time and place in which landlessness was decidedly not the norm, this was,
simply put, the best workforce early American industrialists could afford.[19]

Such difficulties in attracting labor stemmed, in part, from the surprising
resilience of New England agriculture. Although northeastern soils left much
to be desired, in a market still only regionally integrated, it mattered little
that northeastern soils were rocky and poor, provided only that they were

universally so.[20] Although early nineteenth-century New England farmers did not entirely align with the stereotype of the rough and self-subsistent yeoman agriculturalist, transportation constraints nevertheless limited their capacity to engage fully in global agricultural markets. The average distance of selling trips by New England farmers, even armed with wagons and oxen, was only twenty to twenty-five miles in the early national period.[21] Even as the construction of the Erie Canal in 1825 accelerated national market integration—bringing to New England competing produce from the far more fertile farms of the American West—local farmers simply responded by moving away from disadvantaged products (like wheat) and toward crops and commodities that could little withstand long canal journeys, mainly, milk and meat.[22] With no widespread agricultural crisis driving desperate farmers into the arms of manufacturers, workers had to be enticed to these factories, often from great distances and with promises of relatively high wages.[23]

Early mill investors were similarly frustrated by the long-standing American hostility to manufacturing itself. Many of America's founders had abhorred the prospect that the nation's virtuous stock of yeoman farmers could one day be degraded to the status of landless wage workers. As Thomas Jefferson famously put it in his 1781 *Notes on the State of Virginia*, "Those who labour in the earth are the chosen people of God." They alone, Jefferson surmised, possessed the necessary independence, equal status, and lack of private interests to effectively promote the common good as citizens of a democratic state. By contrast, Jefferson saw those who relied on either bosses or customers for their livelihood as neither truly independent nor free, and such "dependence," he feared, would only foster "subservience and venality, suffocat[ing] the germ of virtue." "While we have land to labour then, let us never wish to see our citizens occupied at a work-bench," he concluded: "let our work-shops remain in Europe."[24] Many Americans shared Jefferson's revulsion for the drudgery of factory labor. His ascension to the presidency on a wave of popular support in the so-called Revolution of 1800 was heralded by both him and his supporters as a devastating rejection of the pro-industrial, pro-growth, and pro-corporate policies of Alexander Hamilton and the American Federalists.[25]

In support of their anti-industrial proclivities, Americans like Jefferson needed only to point to the horrors of old England's "dark, satanic mills"—to quote England's great industrial critic, William Blake.[26] The "scourge" of industrial Manchester threw an unshakable pall over all debate on American manufacturing in the early nineteenth century. Even supporters of industrialization had little good to say about the English factory town. A decade before he emerged as one of the key founders of the early textile mills of Waltham and Lowell, Nathan Appleton assured his younger brother during an 1802 trip to England that although more consumer conveniences were available across the Atlantic, it came at a terrible price: "the debasement of the lower classes of society." "For the happiness of our country at large," he added, "I could wish it long without them."[27] At the very moment Francis Cabot Lowell was across the Atlantic executing his covert plan to follow in Slater's footsteps and smuggle industrial textile machinery designs into the United States, he still could not help but remark on how much he despised these industrial centers.[28] "We found the manufacturing towns very dirty," he wrote in 1812, pointing to the "great corruption of the highest and lowest classes, and the great number of beggars and thieves."[29] Even as Lowell was conspiring to bring industry to America, he still had little good to say about it.

Lowell had misgivings about British factory towns, but many Americans saw in them something even more insidious. By the 1820s, a sub-genre of travelogues had come into vogue in the United States, exposing the horrors that would greet the American visitor to a place like Manchester.[30] One author, James Paulding, simply pretended to have visited England in his denunciatory 1822 *A Sketch of Old England, By a New England Man*: "No one, that has not seen [it]" firsthand, he declared—somewhat ironically—"can conceive the squalid and miserable looks of these people . . . the ignorant worthlessness of their characters."[31] Crucially, these writers repudiated industrialization not simply because it was ugly, environmentally toxic, or entailed harsh work regimes, but because it presaged the inexorable debasement of the American people themselves. "Heaven forbid that America should ever be cursed with such a manufacturing system as that which is now the curse of England," another nineteenth-century author concluded: "May the day never come" when "the labouring classes of America shall be taken from her broad fields and rich soil."[32] Industrialization was feared not for what it would unleash upon America, but upon Americans.

Consequently, when the first Massachusetts textile mills began humming to life in the nineteenth century, millowners were forced to jump through extraordinary hoops to circumvent industry's foul reputation. America's first water-powered spinning and weaving factory, the Boston Manufacturing Company of Waltham, Massachusetts, organized in 1813 by a group of wealthy Boston merchants (often referred to as the "Boston Associates"), faced major obstacles in securing both its economic legitimacy and its labor force.[33] Deciding that the complexity of power-loom technology foreclosed the possibility of child labor, the Associates scrambled to find some way to affordably lure adult workers into the mills.[34] Their solution—targeting local farmers' teenage and young adult daughters for labor recruitment—proved a fraught enterprise.

The Associates were ultimately forced into a remarkable public-relations campaign to convince Americans of the merits of industrialization and persuade local farmers that sending their daughters to the factory for a temporary bout of industrial toil would not corrupt their progeny.[35] To that end, the Associates concocted a complex system of moral codes and boardinghouses to attract, contain, and regulate their workers. Boardinghouses were policed, as Appleton put it, by "respectable women . . . at the cost of the Company," in order to oversee the moral maintenance of their young preserves.[36] Church attendance was made mandatory; liquor was banned entirely; a 10:00 P.M. curfew was strictly enforced.[37] Boardinghouse keepers were instructed to essentially act as substitute parents and would be, as the agent of the Middlesex Mills put it, "considered answerable for any improper conduct in their houses."[38] In this way, the Associates strove to assure local fathers that sending their young daughters to the factory would not interfere with their maturation into honorable, republican mothers and would serve as but a temporary stage before each moved on to "a reputable connection in marriage" and "the higher and more appropriate responsibilities of her sex."[39]

The Associates thus had to absorb costs that future industrialists would have found laughable. The directors of the Merrimack Manufacturing Company—the first major textile mill in Lowell, founded in 1823—had to put aside monies "not exceeding" $9,000 to build a church more than a year before declaring its first dividend.[40] Although there is no exact record of how much was expended on the construction of the Merrimack's many boardinghouses, they were valued at around $18,000 in 1826.[41] Schools, boardinghouses, and churches were all erected at the company's expense.

These expenditures were hardly philanthropic. After all, churches, schools, and boardinghouses all functioned as part of an explicit campaign of pro-industrial persuasion. The famed *Lowell Offering* magazine was a similar masterwork of pro-industrial propaganda. Funded by its 6½-cent cost to the consumer and, more important, regular cash infusions from Boston capitalist Amos Lawrence, it showcased to a skeptical public the moral and intellectual progress of these young women under textile tutelage through "original articles on various subjects written by factory operatives" (such as "Woman's Proper Sphere" and "Divine Love").[42] All these efforts served in the tense battle to conscript Americans (and especially the fathers of potential workers) into the ideological project of industrialization.

Industry's heinous reputation in America also forced Lowell millowners to shell out relatively high wages to attract these migrant farm daughters. It was not, after all, mass impoverishment that pushed these "farm girls" into the factory. Instead, citing the expanded freedom and pre-marriage earnings a spell of textile work might yield, these young women largely chose to go into the mills and required decent wages to make such employment worth their while.[43] All told, mill owners were left forking out 84 percent over prevailing British pay scales.[44]

Nonetheless, mill owners received a sizable discount on their female laborers compared to their American male compatriots. At the Lawrence Manufacturing Company in Lowell, built in 1833, the first extant payroll records reveal that the company's twenty card room drawers (of which nineteen were women) averaged 48 cents a day in the five weeks ending December 14, 1833; its thirty-seven filling spinners (all women) averaged 59 cents a day; and the factory's fifty-two piece weavers (all women) took home 77 cents a day.[45] Although men were few and far between (in a factory of over 300 workers, there were only ten male workers, most in oversight positions), their presence nevertheless testifies to the massive gender gap that existed in wages and bargaining power.[46] One male operative, a drawer in the carding room, earned 22 percent more than the average wage in his department.[47] The nearby Hamilton Company looked much the same: of 1,030 workers, 86 percent were women, and they earned about 57 percent of what their male peers made.[48] Thus, although Lowell mills certainly had to expend more than their British counterparts, they still yielded substantial savings by taking advantage of the lesser bargaining power of these young women.

The Associates, having no personal knowledge or experience in textiles, were also forced to compensate their mill managers with—by nineteenth-century standards—relatively exorbitant salaries. John D. Prince, the overseer of the Merrimack Printworks, took home $5,000 yearly.[49] By comparison, in 1830, Francis Cabot Lowell's unmatched $80,000 investment in the Boston Manufacturing Company yielded him only $600 more than Prince's annual income.[50] Across the board, Boston capitalists had to pay dearly for their labor force.

Thus, although the Massachusetts countryside possessed some important advantages over its competitors in the global race for industrialization, in other ways, it was an unlikely site for one of the globe's crucial cradles of industrial transformation. Given Americans' proliferating hostility to factory work and the state's limited supply of available labor, it might be wondered why these capitalists decided to open a textile factory in Massachusetts at all.

Irrational Revolutionaries

It may seem odd that Massachusetts capitalists did not decide to chase potentially much greater returns with enslaved labor in the US South or the far cheaper sources of labor available virtually anywhere else in the world. After all, had these Boston capitalists been "rational," profit-maximizing economic actors, Massachusetts would have been low on their list of possible manufacturing locations. Simply put, the state's economy was far too healthy to allow for the creation of a sufficient class of pliable industrial laborers. So—why Massachusetts? The answer lies at a curious (and, crucially, temporary) confluence of culture, politics, and risk.

Most immediately, these Boston capitalists were not simply looking to maximize profits. If anything, their experiences in the hurly-burly world of global finance and trade had left them yearning for security and stability, not outrageous capital returns.[51] While the profitability of the Boston merchant trade was certainly not plummeting in this era, many of these capitalists were nonetheless growing frustrated with the trade's increasingly "feast or famine" character.[52] Fortunes could be gained or lost with remarkable speed; ocean tempests, market fluctuations, or international hostility could make or break an enterprise overnight. Fittingly, the most immediate cause of the sudden interest in mass American textile manufacturing was the 1807 embargo against France and Britain, which starved American consumers of imported cloth and American merchants of maritime profit.[53] When Amos Lawrence was asked by a friend for investment advice in 1833, he, not surprisingly, pointed him away from more lucrative real estate or mercantile pursuits and toward "manufacturing stocks," where one would have "*reasonable* assurance" of dependable returns.[54] Although many Boston elites continued to engage in mercantile affairs after the sea trade resumed in 1815, manufacturing investment represented, in their eyes, a secure and conservative bedrock for their financial portfolios.

Some Boston merchants simply retired from the maritime trade altogether, citing the stress and anxiety saved by eschewing the frenetic world of nineteenth-century global commerce as just compensation for the lackluster profit returns of manufacturing. Few of these merchant-turned-textile investors had anything good to say about the life of global commerce. In fact, it appears that Lowell's plan to steal British weaving technology while abroad was a side benefit of a trip that was essentially planned as a two-year medical leave for Lowell to deal with health issues resulting from his mounting anxiety over his business affairs.[55] "The hazards of business are much greater now than they even were in my day," he wrote after the failure of the mercantile firm of Joseph and Henry Lee wiped out his brother-in-law's entire fortune.[56] Commerce, as Boston merchant Amos Lawrence never tired of complaining, had a seemingly insatiable appetite for time and attention. In 1826, he grumbled over his "*overengagedness* in business," adding that "the quiet and comfort of home are broken in upon by the anxiety arising from losses and mischances of a business so extensive as ours. . . . Property acquired at such sacrifices as I have been obliged to make the past year costs more than it's worth."[57] After developing what appears to have been, in retrospect, a psychosomatically induced ulcer, Lawrence withdrew from his mercantile pursuits altogether and simply lived off the dividends from his numerous manufacturing investments, spending the next two decades giving thousands of dollars to rural colleges and academies.[58] The life of a merchant was one of unremitting anxiety and stress; the life of a manufacturing investor was one of collecting quarterly dividend payments. Even if the profits were lower, the appeal was undeniable.

Other benefits came alongside passive investment in manufacturing, including the potential to invest more time in political and cultural pursuits. As historian Robert Dalzell Jr. has pointed out, part of what likely drove Francis Cabot Lowell to embrace manufacturing so wholeheartedly was his gnawing apprehension of the fact that the unwavering attention nineteenth-century commerce commanded kept him away from the political, cultural, and philanthropic pursuits that had made his family's name so prominent in Boston in the first place.[59] With his days finally freed from the tyranny of the merchant trade, he dreamed that he too could finally live up to the Lowells' rarefied legacy as Massachusetts's political and cultural elite.

The Associates' desire for cultural and political prestige might also help explain their determination to open mills in Massachusetts. Nathan Appleton and Amos Lawrence became key figures in the Massachusetts Whig Party.[60] Appleton and his brother William both became congressmen, as did Abbott Lawrence.[61] Locally situated economic achievement, in other words, could be leveraged into locally situated political power, which could then be leveraged into economic assistance.[62] Federal support—in everything from protective tariffs to direct subsidies—would be a key aspect of how these industrialists initially found success, despite the severe headwinds they faced.[63]

The Boston Associates largely achieved what they sought for their efforts. The original 1813 Boston Manufacturing Company in Waltham, 90 feet by 45 feet, rising a little over three stories tall and loaded with 3,000 spindles, was succeeded by a cavalcade of followers: the Hamilton (1825), the Lowell (1828), the Appleton (1829), the Middlesex (1830), the Suffolk (1832), the Tremont (1832), the Lawrence (1833), the Boott (1835), and the Associates' last major corporation, the Massachusetts (1840).[64] By then, the Massachusetts Manufacturing Company was capitalized at $1.2 million (three times the value of the Boston Manufacturing Company), had 64 boardinghouses, 4 mills, 28,288 spindles, 904 looms, and a workforce of 750 women and 60 men.[65] The Associates certainly reaped the steady, modest returns they desired—at least at first.

The motivation of these Boston capitalists was hardly one of pure economic self-interest. Instead, it was a more slippery concoction of culture, politics, and a mounting personal desire for safety and security over maximal economic return. Despite its limitations, Massachusetts industrialization advanced their personal goals of security and social renown. While capital may be infinitely mobile in the abstract, capitalists are human actors with real connections to real places. Although extra-economic concerns convinced these entrepreneurs to ignore the many, obvious obstacles to putting up factories in Massachusetts, such concerns would be of much less importance to the next generation of Massachusetts capitalists.

Facing Capitalist Resistance

Seeing the limits of manufacturing, the Associates' sons hatched entirely different plans. The next generation of Boston elites would largely shun manufacturing for the wild (but potentially very lucrative) world of western real estate and railroad investment. By the time the Lowell mills entered the period of economic tumult that followed the Panic of 1857 and the Civil War, a generation had effectively passed. Most of the original Associates had either died or retired. Lowell had been dead forty years. Amos and Abbot Lawrence died earlier in the decade. Appleton passed in 1861.[66] Despite Amos Lawrence's counsel that his son not enter commerce—"I have no wish that you pursue trade. I would rather see you on a farm, or studying any profession," he advised him in 1829—Amos Adams (A. A.) Lawrence remained undeterred.[67] He was determined to become, as he put it in his senior year at Harvard College, "a merchant," though he endeavored not to be "a plodding narrow-minded one pent up in a city, with my mind always in my counting room."[68] As sons succeeded fathers, they often inherited titular posts in the mills their fathers had founded, but they generally knew or cared little about them. They had their sights set elsewhere.

The problem was twofold. While new business ventures in the nation's vast western hinterland seemed to promise both profit and excitement, Massachusetts industry already appeared to be in decline. The Associates' strategic focus on maintaining steady dividend payments had virtually ensured that profit returns would tumble as earnings were funneled into investor pocketbooks at the expense of reinvestment. The Boston Company, the oldest of the cohort, was a case in point. After 1828, Boston Company dividends both fell and became more erratic. Investors earned nothing in both 1842 and 1858.[69] Throughout the 1850s, the directors had to repeatedly vote to increase the mill's debt-carrying capacity, as well as the ability of the agent and treasurer to take out loans independent of directorial authority.[70] By 1857, the company carried a debt of nearly $400,000.[71] That same year, five Lowell mills failed completely, while several others slid to the brink of bankruptcy.[72] Although quick sales of stockpiled cotton at inflated prices helped investors rack up enormous profits and cut debts amid the Civil War (even though the mill was completely shut down), mill debt again skyrocketed in the postwar era. By 1881, the Boston Company's $530,000 debt equaled two-thirds of its paid assessments.[73] Despite even this dire situation, the company still pushed 60 percent of its profits into dividend payments.[74] By the end of the century, the Boston Company had racked up $800,000 in debt.[75] The directors had no choice but to split the company up and sell it off.[76]

Across the board, Massachusetts textile profitability slid in the 1840s. Steady returns became increasingly unpredictable and then declined over the course of the nineteenth century.[77] Peaking in the early 1820s at an average 28 percent annual return, Waltham-Lowell dividends on the Boston stock exchange slumped thereafter. Although from 1824 to 1831 they still averaged 17 percent annually, they dropped to 12 percent for the next seven years before dropping to 5 percent annually from 1838 to 1846.[78]

As textile profits drooped, alternative opportunities abounded. Over the course of the nineteenth century, even respectable textile returns were eclipsed by the enormous money-making potential of a wave of new financial instruments and economic opportunities in the West.[79] As historian John T. Morse Jr. reflected in 1920 on the Boston of his youth, "One had not to look back far to see one or two brokers running about State Street and trying to get someone to buy or sell a few shares of a cotton mill or one of the little New England railroads. . . . But within a few years a new situation had developed. The lavish outpouring of bonds and stock by the new Western railroads . . . the issues of Government bonds with tempting fluctuations in price, the speculation in gold . . . all combined to make a stock exchange which would have dazed the old-time broker."[80] "Why does Boston not grow like New York and Chicago?" historian Henry Adams similarly mused to his brother in 1867: "The truth is Chicago rose as a colony of New England. . . . New England is depleted. Her wealth and life are drawn irresistibly towards more promising markets."[81] As was all too clear to these Bostonians, an astounding wave of capital mobility was taking place in mid-nineteenth-century America.[82]

The sons (and sons-in-law) of the Boston Associates were at the forefront of this remarkable capital migration. There is perhaps no better example of this than the life and career of Thomas Jefferson Coolidge. Having graduated from Harvard College and deciding that "money . . . was the only real avenue to power and success both socially and in regard of your fellow-man," Coolidge made a smart and well-timed marriage to textile magnate William Appleton's daughter in 1852, catapulting him into the Associates' inner circle.[83] When the Boott Cotton Mills found itself teetering on the edge of bankruptcy, Appleton offered to bail the company out on the condition that his new son-in-law was made treasurer.[84] The directors acquiesced, and Coolidge took control of the mill's finances. The inexperienced Coolidge had to seek outside help for even the most rudimentary management decisions. When he left the Boott, it was in about as abysmal financial condition as when he had arrived.[85]

As his ledgers show, Coolidge nevertheless became a wealthy man. In 1858—the year he got his first executive position—he took out eight shares of the Amoskeag Mills (valued at $6,900), eleven shares of the Stark Mills ($7,177.50), five shares of the Hamilton ($4,262.50), three shares of the Dwight Mills, 100 shares of the Lyman Mills, five shares of the Boston Company ($2,500), and nineteen shares worth $8,887.50 in his own Boott Mills.[86] With striking swiftness, he liquidated his textile interests. His shares in the Hamilton were sold off in 1861, his shares in the Dwight Mills were sold off by 1863, all but one of his shares in the Stark Mills were sold by 1872, and his 100 shares of the Lyman Mills were gone within four years.[87]

Not coincidentally, a new set of interests absorbed Coolidge's attention: the Northern Railroad, the Chicago Burlington Quincy Railroad, the Hannibal & St. Joseph Railroad, the Union Land Co. of St. Paul, Missouri State bonds, the Union Stockyard and Transit Co., the New England Telephone Co., the Chicago Cattle Yard, International (Guam) Telegraph, the Mexican Telegraph Co., the Oregon Transcontinental Railroad, lands all over the South and West, and a nearly $100,000 investment in the Lake Shore and Michigan Railroad.[88] He also became president of the Atchison,

Topeka, and Santa Fe Railroad as well as director of the Chicago, Burlington and Quincy Railroad.[89] In effect, Coolidge transformed himself from mediocre textile manufacturer into a leading figure in the transport and telecommunications revolution overtaking the United States.

Amos Lawrence's son, A. A. Lawrence, also made good on his promise to escape provincial mercantile pursuits. In 1854, he became treasurer of the Massachusetts Emigrant Aid Society.[90] Founded to push anti-slavery northerners into Kansas to shift political power away from pro-slavery voters, it was no accident that the company happened to push migrants onto lands owned by (and with implements sold by) the railroad companies of its originators, Boston magnates Eli Thayer, Nathaniel Thayer, John Murray Forbes, and Lawrence.[91] Nathaniel Thayer's investment firm—John E. Thayer and Brother—followed suit. By the early 1860s, it too had wiped all textile investments from its ledgers, turning its attention and its capital to its countless western railroad ventures.[92]

As mills underperformed due to deterioration and high labor costs, investors divested, repairs were foregone, and directors increasingly focused on maintaining profits in the short term. The reaction of Lowell-area mills to the Civil War illustrated this destructive feedback loop all too well. Most mills responded to raw cotton's sudden paucity by simply shutting down and selling off stocks of cotton at inflated prices, taking advantage of the chance to siphon bonus earnings into investors' pockets. The Lawrence Company treasurer sold off some 3,256 bales of cotton in late 1861 for a quick return of $200,000.[93] At the same time, textile production was slashed from 6.34 million pounds of cloth for the year ending February 1861 to 1.36 million for the year ending 1863.[94] No cloth whatsoever was produced during the year ending February 1864.[95] Nevertheless, over the course of the war, $585,000 was distributed to stockholders—yielding a 15-percent return in 1863 alone, a year in which no actual cloth was produced—while only $200,000 was reserved for repairs.[96] This left the Lawrence Company in an unenviable position at the war's end, struggling to refurbish machinery, re-attract a now dispersed labor force, and re-enter a cotton market forever transformed by the events of the 1860s.

Almost every Lowell-area mill found itself in deplorable condition after the Civil War, having all issued balloon payments to investors while saving little for updates or repairs. As an 1881 report from the Boston Manufacturing Company put it, the company's "condition in 1872 was a very low one.... The machinery, and the buildings were all insufficient, and the concern could be run only at great Expense. The styles of goods were all bad, neither popular in the market, nor Economical to make."[97] The Boott mill, as Coolidge put it in 1865, was "old, having been run very hard . . . the goods produced cost high, the waste is too large, the yarn uneven, the cloth not what it should be."[98] One turn-of-the-century consultant determined it best to simply demolish the mill and start anew.[99] The machines in the Suffolk Mills had been repaired so many times, a mill agent wrote in 1862, they were "more than worthless for use by the improvements introduced into modern built machines."[100] Some mills attempted to forge ahead with long, costly conversion plans. The Lawrence switched from making cloth to hosiery (from 1865 to 1870, dividends averaged only 2.17 percent annually). Three other mills switched over to woolens; the Lowell Mill eventually became a carpet company.[101]

The final straw for these elite Boston investors, however, was the increasing organization (and power) of outside shareholders. Although the original Boston Associates had maintained tight control over their investments, as many of their heirs liquidated their textile holdings, these mills found themselves saddled with a new, more diverse group of owners. The Merrimack Mill, for instance, went from a mere five stockholders at its 1823 founding to nearly 400 by 1842.[102] As these new shareholders sought to investigate why these mills were performing so horribly, they often uncovered the incompetence and indifference of Boston's elite, only redoubling their desire to dethrone them from their perches of power.

In particular, local doctor J. C. Ayer—infuriated after losing a fortune when two mills in which he was a major investor collapsed—assembled his own circle of "anti-Boston" shareholder "reformers" to directly take on Boston's community of capital.[103] Ayer generated a number of humiliating reports exposing the ineptitude, disinterest, and heartlessness of these scions of the Boston Associates. He first exposed Coolidge's clumsiness in managing the Boott Mills with his incendiary 1863 pamphlet, *Some of the Uses and Abuses in the Management of Our Manufacturing Corporations*.[104] He similarly skewered the appointment of the Hamilton Company treasurer's son to purchase cotton in the South. The "inexperienced youth" bought "a quantity of miserable trash filled with sand [and] stones . . . which was piled up in a heap by the side of the picker-house at the mill" at a loss of $50,000.[105] The handling of the Civil War—and the concomitant dismissal of nearly 10,000 operatives—was a particular point of outrage.[106] "How would the great men who founded the factory system of Lowell regard this ruthless dismissal of hundreds and thousands of operatives, dependent on their day's wages for their day's bread?" asked one of Ayer's colleagues, historian Charles Cowley, in 1868.[107] These "brainless cousins and nephews" of the original founders,

Cowley fumed, soon discovered that "this crime . . . this blunder, entailed its own punishment. . . . When these companies resumed operations, their former skilled operatives were dispersed, and could no more be recalled than the Ten Lost Tribes of Israel."[108]

Incensed and well organized, Ayer's group leveraged their shareholder power to take the reins of management in many local mills. After getting elected president of the Tremont and Suffolk Mills in 1869, Ayer embarked on a major merger and renovation plan.[109] As a *Boston Traveller* editorial summarized, "Those who originally gave [the mills] birth" and "controlled and made them subservient to their own ends," had "become too puny to control the giants they [had] begotten," left to be "crushed" by the organized many.[110] The specter of humiliation by (or acquiescence to) Ayer and his cohort, combined with sinking profits and failing factories, diminished the attraction of Massachusetts manufacturing for Boston capitalists. Whereas mill ownership had once been a route to passive income and political prestige, it had become a harbinger of embarrassment, loss, and public disgrace.

―――

Early industrial textile manufacturing in Massachusetts was, in some sense, an odd and ill-fitting phenomenon. Starved for both capital and labor, the mills were founded by men who sought neither profit maximization nor long-term stability, but security and the entrenchment of their own cultural and political power. But the mounting weight of floundering capital returns, an increasing lack of control, and relentless attacks on these capitalists' competence combined to smother any lingering justification for continuing to invest in Massachusetts. As Nathan Appleton summed up the situation at the dawn of the Civil War, it was "inadequate capital" that spelled the decline of Lowell-area mills.[111] Investors simply lost interest.

Laborers had always been reluctant to embrace industrialization; capitalists increasingly joined these choruses of disapprobation. Had subsequent events not intervened, industrial Massachusetts might well have simply burned out at the end of the Civil War.

But these constrained enterprises would ultimately pale in size and scope to what came next. Between 1836 and 1860, spindle capacity had tripled in Lowell.[112] In Fall River, by contrast, spindle capacity quintupled in the single decade after 1865. While Lowell stagnated, Fall River amassed over three times Lowell's pre-war productive capacity by 1875; Fall River spindleage again doubled by 1900.[113] Just as Fall River mills were later outcompeted by cheaper labor mills in places like Gastonia, North Carolina, and Macon, Georgia, in the 1920s, Lowell mills were out-gamed by South Coast textile factories in the late nineteenth century.

To understand why the South Coast's manufacturers were so flush with capital and labor—the very things Lowell mills so desperately lacked—it is necessary to understand the collapse of its own particular industry, the first one in which the United States unquestionably dominated the world.

2

Economies in Motion

CRISIS AND INDUSTRY IN THE WHALING CITY

WHALING-ERA NEW BEDFORD little resembled its future as a gritty industrial center. As Herman Melville described the city in *Moby-Dick*, it was "perhaps the dearest place to live in all New England." "Nowhere in all America will you find more patrician-like houses; parks and gardens more opulent, than in New Bedford."[1] It was "a city of palaces," in the words of one nineteenth-century travel handbook, "lined with stately old residences of the marine aristocracy."[2] The city had "a cosmopolitan air always blowing over its strata," another writer put it. "On the vessels fitting out for their long and adventurous cruise you may hear all the modern languages spoken.... You will distinguish Portuguese or French descent in the smart black-haired girl.... Dutchmen, Frenchmen, Spaniards, Norwegians, and Scotch have also pitched their tents here."[3] Whaling made New Bedford one of the richest cities, per capita, in the world, turning it into an exemplar of American cosmopolitanism and high culture.[4]

The industry's collapse over the course of the 1860s would launch New Bedford into a spiraling crisis. As panicked workers, religious leaders, municipal policymakers, and capitalists sought to reconstruct the city's economy on some new foundation, they fomented an industrial revolution on the Massachusetts South Coast.

Industrialization, however, catalyzed immense consternation among those who deplored the drudgeries of factory labor, feared the specter of a massive working-class presence within the city's limits, or simply saw wage labor as running counter to the American ideals of freedom and self-sovereignty. Industry was no natural outcome of economic progress. Instead, it was a hard-fought political project that initially generated nothing but controversy in the Whaling City.

Economic crisis was critical to eroding this public opposition. As economic catastrophe threw account books into disarray and harried former whaling workers onto the streets of New Bedford, it laid the groundwork for something revolutionary: the rise of industrial Massachusetts.

Making Whaling Hegemony

Like its rise to textile manufacturing prominence some fifty years later, New Bedford's ascent to whaling hegemony was similarly founded on the misfortune of others: in this case, the island of Nantucket. As early as the mid-seventeenth century, American colonists had begun shoreline whaling along Long Island and Buzzards Bay, using small, six-men crews to harpoon and drag whales back to shore, and then boiling down the blubber harvested from their catch to produce oil for candles and lubrication.[5] Nantucket was particularly well situated for coastwise whaling. But securing labor remained a vexing issue.[6] Early whalers, finding it difficult to lure English colonists off their landed independence, instead depended on local Wampanoag Indians, whom they quickly sought to chain in place through coercive labor contracts underpinned by cycles of indebtedness.[7] As eighteenth-century London—the often described "best-lit city in the world"—developed a nearly insatiable appetite for whale-derived illuminants, Nantucket emerged as the center of the American whaling industry.[8] By the late eighteenth century, Nantucket whale oil brought in half of all sterling earned in New England through its exports to Great Britain.[9]

But as voyages increasingly left the Massachusetts coast for destinations throughout the Atlantic, Pacific, and, by the 1820s, Indian Oceans, Nantucket's location became more of a hindrance than convenience. As early as the 1760s, Nantucket's shallow harbor and low labor supply began to push whalers back onshore.[10] Joseph Rotch, a prominent Nantucket merchant, was first to make the move. In 1764 he purchased a ten-acre parcel of land on Buzzards Bay, outside of Dartmouth, Massachusetts, at the foot of a large farm owned by Joseph Russell. Rotch suggested the name "Bedford" for the new community—after the Duke of Bedford, who shared Russell's surname.[11] Upon discovering another "Bedford" village northwest of Boston, "New" was added to the name and "New Bedford" was formally incorporated in 1787.[12]

Although members of the Russell family were already engaged in whaling, Rotch brought business acumen and, more important, capital to the fledgling

town, establishing New Bedford's first formal whaling firm.[13] The area grew
rapidly thereafter. By 1771 New Bedford had 321 homes, 123 barns, and 30,684
feet of wharfage for the use of 71 shipowners.[14] By 1807, some 90 to 100 ships
called Buzzards Bay home.[15]

By contrast, Nantucket whaling steadily declined in the early nineteenth
century, a process only exacerbated by the depredations of the War of 1812. As
an 1813 petition for relief to the federal congress by the "Town and County of
Nantucket" lamented, the island had "realized losses by war in a very extensive
degree; a number of valuable ships with full cargoes of oil have been captured
and totally lost. . . . Several of the owners, that were heretofore in opulent
circumstances, are now reduced to indigence."[16] "The whale fishery, which
has constantly been considered the staple of Nantucket," the missive added,
"must inevitably decline . . . [compelling] hundreds of people to remove to
the continent."[17] Nantucket's collapse was New Bedford's good fortune. As
Nantucket receded in importance, by 1823, New Bedford dominated the
American whaling industry, and America dominated the world in whaling.[18]
By its peak, just before the Civil War, New Bedford had amassed 320 ships,
generating $4.8 million in earnings and nearly 200,000 barrels of whale and
sperm oil each year.[19]

Manning these voyages was not necessarily any easier than staffing the
mills of Lowell, but New Bedford whalers had some crucial advantages over
their labor-market competitors. Foremost, mirroring processes that had formerly been used to recruit local natives in Nantucket, they used coercive labor
contracts to bind workers to particular voyages. Through a system known as
the "lay," prospective mariners were not paid in wages but instead were promised a share of a voyage's net return, generally ranging from 1/15 for the captain
to 1/90 for midshipmen (harpooners, boatsteerers, and watchmen) to 1/189
for unskilled "foremast hands," the last of which did everything from greasing
masts to cleaning.[20] Not only did the "lay" keep workers committed to the
city's increasingly lengthy whale hunts (average voyage duration increased
from 2.6 years to 3.6 years in the twenty years after 1840), it also used the
voyage's potential payout to discourage idleness.[21] Under the lay, potential
windfall earnings at the end of the journey (along with a system of harsh shipboard discipline, fines, and state-backed jail-time for desertion) were designed
to insure a captive and diligent workforce.[22]

For shipowners, the "lay" system of labor foisted a considerable amount
of whaling's risk onto its laborers. A failed voyage would bring ruin not just
to investors, but to seaworkers of all classes. When seaman Richard Boyenton
set down his earnings to date in his diary in February of 1834, for instance,

he could not help but muster a bit of dark humor. After months at sea with little to show for his labors, Boyenton's careful accounting recorded only 6¼ cents in earnings: "I have not yet concluded," he mused sarcastically, "whether to give this as a donation to the sabath school union or to the education foreign mission or temperance society."[23] Higher-ranking workers were not spared. From 1840 to 1858, New Bedford captains yielded an aggregate average monthly income of $98.31 in 1880 dollars. Such neat averages, however, obscure whaling's prodigious volatility. In reality, their incomes ranged from a high of $345 to a low of 66 cents for a month's work.[24]

On the flipside, the potential for bonanza payouts was an important lure in attracting labor, making whaling work seem less like "wage labor" drudgery and more like a potential stepping stone to bigger and better things. Stories abounded among sailors of cash cow voyages, such as the 1853 thirty-two-month excursion of the *Montreal*, which netted $136,000.[25] Some indeed got very lucky. Azorean Frank Joseph took in $518.20 for his 1/120 lay on New Bedford's *Golconda* in 1832. Promoted to boatsteerer, his 1/80 lay on his next journey brought him $797.66 after only eleven months of service.[26] It would have taken an average Lowell spinner of the same era more than four years to earn that amount, not including the saved room and board costs that came with shipboard labor.[27]

Thus, in a society that still abhorred the prospect of a life of wage labor servitude, a whaling voyage might have seemed a fair and temporary trade for a potential future of landed independence. Such dreams loomed large in sailors' fantasies of what their lump-sum earnings might bring.[28] One 1841 sailor was "quite shure that I shall get enuf . . . to turn my attention to farming"; another left shore in 1847 with the ambition of "bying A farm."[29] The men of the 1859 voyage of the *Gratitude*, one sailor recorded, similarly forestalled boredom with tales of what their whaling work might bring them: "All hands . . . are going to either Turn farmers or Storekeepers the latter seems to be the Favorite if they ever do land in [sweet] Amerika."[30] Finding independence and securing wives often went hand in hand in sailors' minds. "There will be more marriages take place and more farms bought than was Ever heard of before," one whaleman fantasized, imagining the coming payday he and his friends were expecting.[31] Whaling seemed, with luck, a truly transitory stage to an independent "competence."

Consequently, one of the crucial legacies of the whaling industry was that it turned the city of New Bedford (and, to a similar extent, Fall River) into labor magnets, bringing in workers from around the country. "Shipping Agents," located all over the United States, funneled young men to local whaling outfits.[32] The correspondence of New Bedford whaling agent Jonathan Bourne Jr. is replete with letters from worried parents from all over the country—Virginia, Maryland, New York, and towns throughout New England—inquiring after (or seeking the contractual release of) sons on Bourne's vessels.[33] Although a "few Deaths occur," Bourne reassured one apprehensive father, "these voyages are as a general thing very healthy"—though he also made sure to mention that if this father did succeed in recalling his son back to Richmond, he would perforce "[forfeit] all his interest" in the voyage and be liable for $64.55 to "pay for his outfits."[34]

In addition, the long and distant journeys demanded by New Bedford whaling work—alongside the racially progressive proclivities of its mainly Quaker proprietors—made the city an attractive destination for runaway slaves.[35] As one former slave put it, he entered the whale trade after finding he "could not sleep . . . so near the slaveholding country. I thought I could not be safe until I had gone to the other side of the globe"—a desire whaling agents were all too happy to satisfy.[36] Most famously, Frederick Douglass, assured that New Bedford "was a safe place," settled there in 1838 to seek work as a ship caulker—though he was furious to discover his race still relegated him to common-labor status.[37] Nevertheless, Douglass's decade among New Bedford's Quaker radicals gave him his first introduction to anti-slavery ideology.[38] All told, some 3,000 African Americans sailed on New Bedford ships during whaling's heyday.[39]

Even the well-known sea shanty "Blow Ye Winds, Heigh Ho" testified to the centripetal forces that brought throngs of laborers to New Bedford: "'Tis Advertised in Boston/ New York and Buffalo/ Five hundred brave Americans/ A whaling for to go. . . . They'll send you to New Bedford town/ That famous whaling port/ And hand you to some land-sharks there/ To board and fit you out."[40] All told, about 41 percent of New Bedford crews in 1837 came from outside New England.[41]

Moreover, the global reach of whaling ships themselves ensured fresh labor supplies for New Bedford whalers. In particular, the Azorean and Cape Verde islands of Portugal emerged as a frequent stop for both supplies and people. An Azorean stopover appeared as a sort of foregone conclusion, for instance, in Elisha Dexter's memoir of his time on the *William and Joseph*: "On the 2nd of September [1840] we ran into Fayal . . . for the required complement of men, and for the purpose of obtaining the usual supply of vegetables, which are there very cheap."[42] Another sailor on the *George and Mary* noted that an 1852 stop in Cape Verde yielded them "18 pigs a lot of fouls Pumpkin Bananas and oringes, and 2 Portugues."[43] One sailor made the connection between supplies and men all too cruelly explicit during an 1855 stop at the island of Fogo: "In an hour came off with 10 hogs, 4 goats, a dozen chickens and a bunch of bananas—capt. came back at 10 p.m. bringing three new Portuguese, to be added to the rest of the live stock!"[44] By 1838, ships were even leaving New Bedford under Portuguese command. A thriving Portuguese district soon marked New Bedford's waterfront, containing four Portuguese-operated boardinghouses, as well as a variety of Portuguese shops, cigarmakers, and outfitters.[45] Thousands of Portuguese sailors would come to make up a little over a quarter of New Bedford's whaling crews.[46]

Whaling ships from Fall River similarly helped turn southeastern Massachusetts into something of a labor sink. Almost half of all Fall River whaling voyages after 1840 picked up sailors from foreign ports while at sea (generally the Azores, Cape Verde, or Hawaii), and about two-thirds sailed with recognizably Portuguese sailors on their crew lists.[47] The 1851–1852 voyage of the *Aerial* accumulated a mix of nationalities for whaling workers typical of the era: the United States, the Azores, Scotland, St. Croix, and Wales were all represented onboard.[48] Not all of these recruits would have gone on to settle in Fall River or New Bedford on a permanent basis—but many certainly did. For instance, about 60 percent of the *Aerial*'s sailors born outside of Fall River had officially relocated to Southeastern Massachusetts by the time the ship set off, and it is not improbable that many others relocated thereafter.[49]

Whalers did not have to look far for a captive workforce. Their ability to trawl the continents for workers, lure them with promises of a lucrative path to landed independence, and lock them into coercive labor contracts ensured they would not struggle like their labor- and capital-starved Boston peers. Moreover, the ability of whaling to bring throngs of laborers to the Massachusetts South Coast made certain that whaling's decline would eventually help New Bedford capitalists do what the Boston Associates could not: namely, assemble a mass industrial labor force.

Fortune, Risk, Collapse

With a secure labor force and a near hegemony on the seas, South Coast whaling was a tremendously profitable affair. But, like the Boston sea trade, it was also a largely feast-or-famine enterprise.[50] The life, career, and correspondence of famed New Bedford whaling agent Jonathan Bourne Jr. illustrate the factors that made whaling such an attractive outlet for capital in the nineteenth century, as well as the many frustrations and forces that pushed whaling owners, quite suddenly, out of the sector altogether.

Born tenth of eleven children in 1811 on a farm of only about twenty-three acres of arable land in Sandwich (present-day Bourne), Massachusetts, the younger Jonathan Bourne was never likely to follow in his father's yeoman footsteps.[51] He left home at seventeen to move to New Bedford and work in a grocery store, where in 1834 he married Emily Summers Howland, the daughter of Captain John Howland and a member of one of the city's most prominent whaling families.[52] The following year, he invested $750 to claim a 1/16 stake in the whaler *General Pike*.[53] The year after that, he acquired a 4/16 stake in the 235-ton *Roscoe*.[54] Within a decade, he had acquired interests in (or outright ownership of) ten local vessels, becoming the richest of New Bedford's whaling agents.[55]

As a fixture of the city's class of elite whalers, he was elected director of the New Bedford Merchants Bank in 1853 and president in 1876. He was a five-time delegate to the Republican National Convention, and in 1855 purchased an entire city block on which to erect a stately mansion at the cost of $38,000.[56] From his first investments in 1836 to his 1889 death, he netted an average annual salary of $41,518. By the time of his passing, his estate was appraised at $2.5 million.[57]

Though a decidedly wealthy man, Bourne was not immune to the ups and downs of one of the most chaotic of extractive industries; 1837, 1851, 1857, 1858, the entire Civil War era, 1869–1871, and 1876 were, for all intents and purposes, terrible whaling seasons across the board.[58] "Considerable news has come from the Arctic Fleet which is *bad! bad!* . . . Many of the first class ships have taken nothing the whole season," Bourne fretted in 1851.[59] Unfortunately for agents, whaling's erratic character derived from the capriciousness of both mother nature and man-made markets. Incidents such as the sudden whale scarcity Bourne faced in 1851, or the two Arctic ice disasters of 1871 and 1876 (the first left 1,200 men stranded on thirty-four iced-in ships; the second destroyed twenty ships and took the lives of some fifty men) exposed the ways in which whalers were always at the mercy of the sea in their search for riches.[60] Yet whalers were also subject to all the same economic swings that plagued any merchant or manufacturer. In 1858, for instance, the falling price of oil and bone left Bourne scrambling. "Not one ship in ten that is to arrive this year can make a dollar to their owners," he wrote the wife of one of his captains, adding "many I fear . . . will be left nearly destitute."[61] His fears were realized. Of the sixty-eight ships that returned to New Bedford that year, forty-four arrived in the red, with losses estimated at about $1 million.[62]

Like many other whaling shipowners, Bourne was no stranger to total loss. His ship, the *Kingfisher*, bought in 1853, sailed only once before getting run into by another ship and sinking near St. Helena with 1,700 barrels of oil onboard.[63] A new *Kingfisher* was built in 1856, but its second journey saw the captain cut down by a "foul line" and killed; it returned only 225 barrels of oil.[64] Bourne gave up and sold it off in 1861. His 381-ton *Alex Coffin* was completely lost on only its third journey in the Okhotsk Sea off the coast of Russia in 1856.[65] Safe returns (in both senses of the word) could be hard to come by for New Bedford whalers.

Shipowners staked their capital and sailors staked their lives on an industry in which freak accidents could wipe away profits and people with the thrash of a fifty-ton whale or the slow and steady decay of a ship's life at sea. Of the 763 traceable whaling vessels that called New Bedford home during the industry's heyday, 297 were forever lost to the sea, while an additional seventy were condemned at foreign ports—adding up to a nearly 50-percent loss rate.[66] Even on a per-journey basis, the average total loss rate for New Bedford whaling ships hovered somewhere around 7.4 percent, with slightly better odds for smaller barks.[67] Such losses came in a variety of forms. The 81-ton *Agate* vanished in a storm off Cape Verde in December 1844 on its sixth voyage; the 421-ton *Alexander* sank on a reef near Sydney in 1858 with 1,300 barrels of sperm oil on board; the *Kathleen* and the *Ann Alexander* were both demolished by whales.[68] The 166-ton *Marcella* was condemned at St. Helena in 1879 after departing New Bedford in 1876 on its fifteenth voyage.[69] Perhaps to help ward off questions from an angry shipowner, the US consulate officer in St. Helena gave the captain an affidavit swearing his logbook "a true and faithful log" of the journey to take back with him to New Bedford.[70]

The *Marcella*'s consular affidavit underscores the lack of information or control whaling owners had over their ships. Shipowners had to put a remarkable amount of trust in their captains, and, if Bourne is any guide, they were frequently left disappointed. Bourne was horrified, for instance, by the news that one of his captains had arrived in the Azores in 1860 "so much intoxicated as to be for some time wholly unfit for the duties of master of [the] ship."[71] "Fearing my property (haveing a large interest in the ship) . . . was to be sacrificed through misplaced confidence," he covertly conscripted the ship's second mate to act as a sort of proverbial man on the inside, commanding him not to "for one moment entertain thought of leaving my ship" and ordering that "if Capt Weld takes rum at sea . . . remonstrate with him strongly and [if] he still continues, throw it overbord in my name."[72]

Although Bourne's drunken captain was perhaps an extreme case of misconduct, the more quotidian aggravations of dealing with a global industry in a world before telecommunication remained a wellspring of frustration and risk. Even rumors of loss could send prices skyrocketing or investors panicking, much to his chagrin.[73] Bourne frequently reminded captains to "write every opportunity" and was quick to admonish them if they did not.[74] Through countless irate letters and furious missives, Bourne endlessly harangued his captains for actions that did not adhere to his high standards of conduct and communication.[75] In 1850, for example, the ever-feisty Bourne wrote a long, defensive letter to one captain who complained his "feelings was hurt" by Bourne's salty demeanor.[76]

Moreover, striking a matter close to Bourne's heart, whaling required an immense amount of financial trust in captains. No issue was more irksome to the agent than that of taking "drafts" while at sea to pay for supplies—in essence, captains acquiring supplies using a sort of third-party check (issued by Bourne) to be sent back to him in New Bedford for payment. Bourne frequently upbraided profligate captains he found too spendthrift with his money.[77] In one particularly flagrant incident in 1849, he became convinced that one of his captains was simply gallivanting around the Pacific on his dime. Captain Finch, he complained, left with a ship fit for forty months at sea "but before she was 15 [months] out the Captain commenced drawing [taking drafts] & has continued at every Port I believe since where a draft could be negociated."[78] "With great mortification," Bourne refused to honor payment for the third and fourth drafts, forcing him into a somewhat awkward standoff with a Hawaiian merchant.[79] He ended up firing the captain after he racked up some $10,000 in foreign drafts.[80] "As soon as the ships arrive into the Sandwich Islands, the *Devil* is to pay with the crew and officers," Bourne later complained, "consequently upon that follows Drafts the worst of all evils in this business."[81]

His quickness to anger was visible in a long stream of letters complaining of captains who too frequently docked at ports for breaks from sea, spent too much on supplies, shipped oil without his explicit permission, or paid off workers who needed to leave during the voyage. All the while, Bourne constantly implored captains to stay out at sea as long as possible ("now is the time to make a voyage and a year lost in comeing home is lost forever," he often reminded them).[82] Simply put, while whaling may have generated great wealth, it was also an industry awash with risk, loss, and lack of control, much to the frustration of New Bedford capitalists.

Captains, for their part, did not necessarily ignore the pleas of their agents out of indolence or impudence. An angry agent would have to be dealt with in a few years, once the ship docked back home; angry workers could make shipboard life miserable day after day. Workers could slow down or stop work (sometimes by literally slowing the tempos of the shanties they sang while at labor).[83] All-out mutiny or desertion were real possibilities.

Not surprisingly—considering the nature of so much of Bourne's correspondence—one consistent demand workers made on their captains was for more frequent port stops and better supplies. The captain of the *Reaper* complained in 1839 that his crew had nearly complete control of his ship, forcing him to stop at port in the Indian Ocean for rest and even sleep onshore so they could bring women onto the ship. "I have tried to reason the case with them," the captain lamented, "but it is no use they have combined togeather."[84] Working-class resistance was itself a crucial source of risk and potential loss to whaling capitalists.

For whalers like Bourne, bad seasons, freak accidents, or unresponsive captains could cost them thousands of dollars. Although every owner wanted their captain to be like Samuel Winegar of the *Julian*, who justified nearly wrecking his ship and losing his crew in the Arctic to save a freshly caught whale by claiming that he would rather "go to the Devil with a whale . . . than go to New Bedford without one," captains generally bore little resemblance to their Ahab caricatures.[85] Other forces beyond the prospect of returning to a fuming agent back in New Bedford guided their decision-making, much to the frustration of whaling capitalists.

Ironically, then, just as Boston capitalists were fleeing the relative stability of local manufacturing to enter the risky (and potentially very lucrative) world of westward expansion, New Bedford capitalists were beginning to anchor their chaotic and risk-prone whaling investments in textile manufacturing.[86] As early as the 1820s, whaling capitalists began investing in water-powered mills in neighboring Fall River as a way to diversify their holdings with safer returns.[87] One of Fall River's first mills—the Pocasset—was built in 1821 by New Bedford whaler Samuel Rodman.[88] Such early investments set a precedent for how whalers responded to the increasing riskiness of whaling over the course of the nineteenth century.

As seasons got worse and returns increasingly perilous, whaling agents slowly withdrew from the business altogether. "The present prospect of the whaling business together with the general prostration of all kinds of trade in the Country cast a gloom over the minds of those engaged in so precarious an enterprise as the whaling business," Bourne wrote one of his captains as early as 1858.[89] By the 1870s, even New Bedford's *Whalemen's Shipping List* had concluded that "the continued purpose to sell whalers . . . shows the judgement of those who have long and successfully been engaged in the business, viz: that it has become too hazardous, and its results too uncertain to continue it, when capital is promised a safer employment, and surer rewards in enterprises on the land."[90]

The industry's troubles came from multiple directions. First, an increasing scarcity of whales forced shipowners to pursue longer journeys, increasing both the costs and risks of whaling, while only exacerbating the control and information problems that so frustrated them.[91] Second, the Civil War (the "great Commotion at the south," which Bourne unconcernedly predicted would fizzle out and "end up in smoke") and the destruction it laid upon New Bedford ships brought tremendous losses to the industry.[92] Half of all whaling ships were withdrawn from service during the war. Additionally, the federal government took some forty New Bedford ships and loaded them with stones in order to sink them outside Charleston harbor in a largely unsuccessful attempt to block Confederate trade.[93] Confederate raiders intentionally sought out Northern whaling vessels and destroyed some twenty-five New Bedford ships over the course of the war, inflicting some $2 million in economic damage.[94] "For a time," local historian Leonard Ellis wrote in 1892, "it seemed as if the city was to experience the fate of Nantucket" and be left an "abandoned seaport."[95]

Whaling's fate was sealed by the advent of modern petroleum drilling and refining, beginning with Edwin Drake's 1859 Pennsylvania well, which sent prices and demand for whaling illuminants and lubricants spiraling downward.[96] An ideal whaling voyage of three to four years might have yielded around 4,000 barrels of oil, but that much oil could be pumped from a single Pennsylvania well in just over a day.[97] All told, by 1861, Bourne could not help but "confess" a "gloomy" view of the future of whaling.[98] "All those that have not tried the Kerosine or petroleum must do so," he advised a friend, adding, "and of course that very much prevents the consumption of whale, which is poor stuff at best as you know."[99] Some simply embraced the competition. In a brazen act of economic betrayal, Weston Howland—who, like Bourne's wife, was a member of one of the city's oldest and most illustrious whaling dynasties—built a refinery for Pennsylvania petroleum off the coast of New Bedford in 1860.[100]

Seeing the writing on the wall, New Bedford capitalists rapidly abandoned the whaling industry. From its peak in the late 1850s, with over 300 ships, the New Bedford fleet declined continuously thereafter. From 1855 to 1906, some 4 percent of ships were shed every year, leaving only twenty-three still operating by the turn of the century.[101] The value of the city's whaling catch was nearly halved in the decade after 1855, and by 1885 it was worth about a quarter of its 1865 valuation.[102] While Bourne's favorite ship, the *Lagoda*, had netted him massive returns before 1873 (at one point bringing him a 363 percent profit on a single voyage) it too became an increasing disappointment.[103] After 1873, it reaped a whopping $18,300 loss over its next three voyages.[104] Sold in 1886, it ended its days hauling coal in Japan.[105]

Reconstructing the South Coast

Whaling decline quickly metastasized into full-fledged economic crisis on the Massachusetts South Coast. As one local historian summed up the state of postwar New Bedford, "Our idle wharves were fringed with dismantled ships. Cargoes of oil covered with seaweed were stowed in the sheds . . . waiting for a satisfactory market that never came. Every returning whaler increased the depression. Voyages that in former times would have netted handsome returns . . . resulted only in loss."[106] The number of New Bedford residents on poor relief increased by nearly 80 percent from 1861 to 1870.[107] From 1865 to 1880, the city was consistently first or second among Massachusetts cities in relief expenditures.[108] One frantic 1861 city report bemoaned the fact that in the wake of the whaling crisis, "many houses are vacant, and shops and stores in great number are standing empty, and our mechanics and citizens are seeking employment elsewhere."[109] As Mayor Isaac Taber put it bluntly in 1862, whaling was "no longer profitable," demanding new measures to counteract the city's surging unemployment and relief costs.[110] Taber's successor, George Howland Jr. (son of one of the city's wealthiest whalers), could not help but grieve the "stagnation of the usual business of our city, and the general depression and gloom which overhang our land" as he was forced to slash $21,000 from the city's budget.[111]

Whaling's collapse was both an emotional and economic blow to the people of New Bedford. The city's residents were, in a nation already preoccupied with the deleterious effects of industrialization, particularly worried that manufacturing would undo the basis of what had made them so attached to New Bedford in the first place—namely, that whaling's "underclass" never truly resided in the city. Perpetually at sea in search of flukes and riches, New Bedford's "working class" only breezed through town between voyages, keeping the city's streets, in the eyes of many locals, free of the slums and urban misery they saw as endemic to "factory towns" like Manchester.[112] The origins of New Bedford's early wealth mark its urban geography to this day. Unlike so many other industrial towns, the mansions of New Bedford's elite run right through the middle of the city center, not some quaint outskirt. With no resident working class to speak of, New Bedford citizens saw their city as a uniquely prosperous cultural center unparalleled on the American continent.

Anti–working class and anti-manufacturing sentiment ran strong among New Bedford's whaling elite. In fact, the largest riot in New Bedford's antebellum history was not an uprising of disquieted sailors or rebellious workmen, but an "organized mob" of the wealthy, who, in 1856, invaded a neighborhood "infested with a dangerous class of citizens"—as one nineteenth-century historian recorded—and torched two houses in New Bedford's small working-class "vice" district along Howland Street. Three thousand strong, the mob then proceeded to prevent the fire department from extinguishing the flames.[113] With the rich attempting to protect New Bedford as a unique oasis of affluence, its future as a mass industrial city was far from foreordained.

As economic crisis overtook the city, this public consensus began to tear apart. Policymakers and local elites increasingly fractured into pro-whaling "conservatives" and pro-industry boosters.[114] While the conservative George Howland Jr. sought to use his mayoral tenure from 1862 to 1865 to fight potential industry, his two successors took a different tack.[115] Andrew G. Pierce, a clerk at New Bedford's Wamsutta Mill, taking office in 1868, repeatedly called on the city council to "encourage the investment of capital in new enterprises" through tax cuts and pro-business infrastructure projects.[116] George Richmond was even more ardent in his industrial advocacy. "There was a time, fresh in our memories . . . when all the enterprise and capital of New Bedford was centered in the whaling interest," he lectured the city council in 1870, but, "for reasons beyond our control the fleet has been rapidly dwindling, and the profits of the fishery do not . . . tempt to new investments."[117] Whaling decline left these councilors with but one choice, Richmond contended: to embrace "the music of the spindle and shuttle, the cheering sound of the hammer and anvil, and the noise of countless artisans" and make New Bedford "as thrifty in manufacturers, as it was in its palmiest day in whaling."[118] Political contests in New Bedford rapidly devolved into struggles over the issue of industrialization.

The campaign to construct a citywide water system became a particular lightning rod of controversy. In the context of thirsty steam-powered textile industrialization, the municipal conveyance of water became something of a public referendum on whether New Bedford should encourage its own industrial revolution.[119] A significant contingent of New Bedford residents, including Mayor Howland, opposed the creation of a water system for precisely the same reason its supporters championed it.[120] "A No Water Man," for instance—a local capitalist who claimed to have "made all [his] money" in New Bedford—wrote to the local newspaper in July 1865, arguing that creating a water system would mean giving up a whaling-economy New Bedford of evenings of "hundreds of young ladies, fully arrayed in silks and flowers, and the equally fashionably dressed young gents on our streets" for an industrial city "full of mechanics and operatives, which no humane mind would desire to introduce among us."[121] Another writer, "Main Street" ("a native citizen of the primitive stock" who "identified with the growth of the place from its early history"), opined that New Bedford would do best to forget the water issue altogether and instead concentrate on the "cultivation of our tastes in the pursuit of useful knowledge, the fine arts, and the sciences."[122] Besides, "Main Street" added, "there are many objections also to becoming a manufacturing people," foremost among them, "the evils from poverty and degradation among the poorer classes of operatives."[123] Wealthy whalers proffered a curious ideological concoction of aristocratic anti-industrialism.

Economic turmoil, however, forced the issue. While "old time men" of the "*old school*" held the city back, "Amor Patrie" wrote the local newspaper in regards to the water issue, "We can't live here now. There isn't anything for us to do in our native city." "Amor Patrie" mocked those who feared introducing "the poorer classes of operatives" to the city, suggesting that New Bedford could perhaps erect "a boarding netting around the town" to "keep from 'betwixt the wind and our nobility,' these *poor, degraded operatives*."[124] As Mayor Isaac Taber put it in 1862, "We have ceased in a great degree to be a producing people," leaving "laborers, cut off from their accustomed sources" of income, with no other choice but to appeal to the "army or navy, or public charity" for support.[125] For Taber, the water issue, though it would "undoubtedly call for an apparently large expenditure," promised the "encouragement of industrial enterprise" and nothing less than the "future prosperity of our city."[126] Another pro–water system report similarly argued that the water system was necessary if the city would "desire and intend to prosper."[127]

Proponents framed the choice as an existential question. In one 1861 city report on introducing water to the city, its "sanitary" benefits took a backseat to the argument that it was a "great *mechanical necessity*." Citing the "stagnation and decay" of whaling, the report bluntly stated it "useless to wink the great fact out of sight,—our city is in a critical position." It was, the report claimed, thus the duty of city government to take the reins of economic revitalization: "Cities, like men, flourish and prosper only by their own exertions." Those who could "comprehend the present crisis in our affairs" would see the solution: "Encourage the introduction of machinery,—foster manufacturers and the mechanical arts. . . . Water! water!! is our great desideratum, an ample supply we must have or cease to prosper."[128] New Bedford's economic crisis of the 1860s was fast amassing popular support for an industrial transformation.

One of the city's leading ministers, Unitarian William J. Potter, used the pulpit to provide a spiritual undergirding for such a transformation. In a series of published sermons on the "Business Interests of Our City," delivered in January 1863, Potter urged the faithful to act: "Three years ago, when I first came to your city, I found everywhere depression and gloom. . . . Your ships were lying idle. . . . A large class of working people were out of employment; poverty and beggary were increasing; homes were vacated . . . laborers were beginning to move away."[129] "What was to become of New Bedford?" Potter asked, rhetorically.[130] The answer, he insisted, was industrialization: "All commercialization, all improvement in the arts . . . all commerce and manufactur[ing] . . . in short, all material interests [and] prosperity [and] progress," Potter argued, "have for their object the welfare of the soul, [and] culminate in the development of this, . . . [the] spiritual part that [is] called the laws of political economy."[131] Turning opponents' arguments on their heads, Potter contended that industry was not antithetical to virtue. It was, in fact, "the prop of all the virtues," and "stagnation in the business of a community" was the cause of "intellectual [and] moral stagnation."[132] Finally, Potter claimed that if "water is wanted before new business can be further introduced," then the city need only tap into its "vast sleeping ponds" in the north, "which are only waiting to be touched with the spirit of the age in order to fly into steam [and] be set to lifting hammers or humming spindles. They are sleeping now, like our city, in violation of the law of the nineteenth century."[133] For Potter, arguments that industry would herald the spiritual and moral decline of the city had it all wrong. Crisis and stagnation were the true progenitors of social collapse.

When a vote was finally taken on the issue in April 1864, 781 outvoted 594 in favor of the new water system.[134] It took five years and $500,000 to complete the project.[135] Although it cost a massive sum for the era, the water system did help to encourage a rapid increase of steam-powered mills. The Wamsutta brought in a Corliss steam engine the very next year.[136] A cavalcade of new mills followed, beginning in 1871.[137]

A series of new municipal enactments also helped push the city headlong into the industrial era. The city issued grants to establish a street railway in 1872, revamped the city charter in 1875, and continued to rack up debt—skyrocketing to $854,000 by 1870—in order to cut taxes and fund improvements.[138] Although the city's debt situation, one mayor argued in 1876, was "sanctioned by our own experience of nearly twenty years, and highly commended by many experienced capitalists and bankers," he was nonetheless dismayed that an anxious Massachusetts legislature rebuked New Bedford by passing a cautionary "Act to Regulate and Limit Municipal Indebtedness" in 1875.[139]

Regardless of the actions of the legislature in Boston, by the 1880s, the city was slashing relief rolls to balance the books on its pro-industry, low-tax crusade. In 1885 alone, it completely severed relief payments to 54 percent of families and reduced allowances for an additional 28 percent of recipients.[140] Welfare cutbacks and pro-industrial development policies marched in lockstep.

The threat of capital mobility also helped create a sense of urgency among city leaders. After all, early on, many New Bedford capitalists had followed Bostonians' lead and had begun looking to the country's West. Henry Howland Crapo invested in western railroads and was eventually elected governor of Michigan.[141] Whaler Charles Morgan bought an iron works in Pennsylvania.[142] Members of the Rotch family invested in railroads, toll roads, banks, insurance companies, and real estate.[143]

This movement of capital terrified local leaders. As Mayor George Richmond warned in his 1870 inaugural speech, New Bedford needed to face the fact that its whaling days were over. "Capital," he reminded the city council, "has sought other investments," but it had "found most of them, I regret to say, abroad.... I am by no means inclined to despair of our commercial prosperity, but the great hope for the future must rest upon the multiplication and growth of manufacturing enterprise."[144]

Luckily, the changes the city enacted, paired with the railroad panic of 1873, ultimately helped convince New Bedford capitalists that their investments might be safest close to home. As men like Bourne pulled their investments out of whaling, they established a new industrial regime on the ruins of whaling's former prosperity. As early as 1851, whaler Charles Morgan invested $20,000 into New Bedford's first (failed) textile concern. The Wamsutta was funded by a whaling merchant, two whaling captains, a West Indian rum merchant, and an oil broker.[145] The Potomska Mill, erected in 1871, had James Robinson (oil merchant) as its first president, and William Rotch (whaler), Charles L. Wood (captain), Matthew Howland (whaling shipping agent), William Watkins (whaler and candlemaker), and Andrew Pierce as directors: only Pierce had no connection to New Bedford's maritime past.[146] The Acushnet Mill, organized in 1881, had whaler Horatio Hathaway as president, acting alongside directors William Crapo (an admiralty lawyer), Francis Hathaway (merchant trader), Loum Snow Jr. (whaler), Gilbert Allen (whaler), Thomas Brayton (a Fall River textile manufacturer), and none other than Jonathan Bourne Jr. as directors.[147] These savvy capitalists helped transform New Bedford from the globe's largest whaling port to its largest producer of fine cotton cloth.[148]

Bourne, for his part, threw himself wholeheartedly into the world of textile industrialization. Although Bourne continued to invest in whaling voyages after the war, these interests clearly took a back seat to the investments he was making in mills all over New Bedford and Fall River, including the "Bourne" Mill on Fall River's southern border, built in 1881.[149] As whale oil prices continued to fall, Bourne's instructions to Captain Fisher in 1887 were typical: "Sperm oil is now selling at 60 cents. . . . I would advise selling at very low prices [to] pay bills, rather than making drafts."[150] By then, Bourne was by no means panicking: "Although the whale fishery is declining," Bourne reminded Fisher, "manufacturing has taken its place . . . and there never was more [business] doing in New Bedford than now."[151]

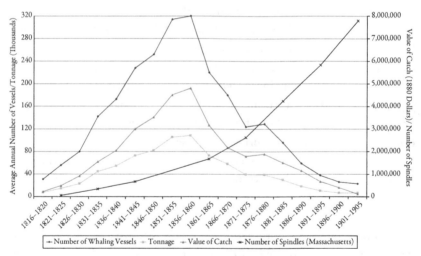

FIGURE 2.1 The Rise and Fall of the New Bedford Whaling Industry and the Rise of Massachusetts Textile Production, 1816–1905.

Note that textile spindleage in the state of Massachusetts grew slowly until the postbellum era, at which point it re-centered in southeastern Massachusetts and took off. The whaling industry is measured here in the annual average of New Bedford ships and tonnage (*left* y-axis scale) and the dollar value of its catch (*right* y-axis scale). The rise of the textile industry is measured in spindleage (*right* y-axis scale). Data derived from Davis et al., *In Pursuit of Leviathan*, 6–7; Clark, *History of Manufactures in the United States*, 544; United States, *Reports of the Immigration Commission*, 7.

Indeed, Bourne's ships were mostly withdrawn over the course of the following decades. His bark *Pantheon* was sold off in 1853; his ship *Stephania* was condemned in Sydney in 1868; the 478-ton ship *Marengo* was sold in San Francisco in 1874; the 453-ton *Hunter* sailed its last journey in 1882, bringing back only 120 barrels of oil; and his barks *Northern Light* and *Napoleon* were both sold off in 1883.[152] As whaling ships were offloaded, Bourne transformed himself into a whole new type of capitalist. By the time of his death in 1889, Bourne was the director of eight local textile mills, president of the local bank, and the director of three local utility companies.[153]

Desperate Capital, Desperate Labor

Beyond freeing up local reserves of capital and coaxing pro-industrial state policy, the collapse of the whaling industry "liberated" the large workforce it had amassed over the course of some five decades. Unlike earlier Lowell mills, South Coast firms would not have to pay to bring workers to them; whaling did that for them, uprooting workers from all over the globe. Whaling's collapse ultimately left behind unemployed, desperate workers—one of the most important ingredients in the making of the South Coast's industrial revolution.

As a result, South Coast textile firms would be staffed by far more male (and far more foreign) workers than any competing American mill. On its own, this demographic fact would mean little, except that the production of "fine" textiles on mule spinning machines—a water frame and spinning jenny hybrid that produced stronger and finer yarn than the water frame machines used in Lowell—required great strength to operate and was considered unfit, at least by the mores of the nineteenth century, for women.[154] Consequently, whereas Lowell machinery (operated by women) produced only coarse yarns and fabrics in this era, only mule-spinning men could produce the fine cloths that gave Britain hegemony over the global textile market.[155] Not coincidentally, the first mule-spinning machines successfully brought to the United States came by way of Bradford Durfee and William Davol of Fall River for use in their Annawan Mill.[156] "From this date forward the progress of mule spinning in the 'Southern district' of Massachusetts and Rhode Island was very rapid," one historian of the cotton industry noted in 1879, and it was decades before these mills faced any serious American competitors.[157] Arguably, few other factories in America would have been able to afford male labor on such a massive scale. In effect, the whaling crisis helped give the South Coast of Massachusetts a near hegemony in America on fine cotton-cloth production, allowing the American textile industry to finally compete with British producers.

Not surprisingly, an analysis of the payroll of Fall River's Annawan Mill reveals a very different labor profile than that which prevailed in Lowell. In April 1858—the first month for which full records exist—the Annawan spinning room had only four women out of twenty-five workers. Even in unskilled departments like carding, men made up more than a third of the workforce. Whereas many Lowell women worked inconsistent or part-time schedules to complement their other economic and agricultural activities, only two Annawan spinners worked fewer than 24.5 days that month (a 26-day month meant working full days, every day, except Sundays).[158]

And—most important to mill owners—these spinners made only 54 cents a day. For comparison, the Lowell female spinners twenty-five years earlier had earned more than the male spinners of the Annawan Mills in 1858.[159] Moreover, those workers who lived in corporate-owned houses found an average of $4.60 taken from their monthly paychecks for rent, leaving one male carder—who earned an average of 47 cents a day—with just $7.15 to show for a month of twenty-five days of work.[160] Even by nineteenth-century standards, these were paltry wages, less than a third of what American artisans like blacksmiths or carpenters generally took home each month.[161]

Postbellum Lowell mills sought to adapt, but New Bedford and Fall River mills remained uniquely staffed with largely male, immigrant, and comparatively low-wage workers. Although the Irish potato famine contributed to more immigrants entering the doors of Lowell's Lawrence Manufacturing Company in 1860 than ever before, the factory still maintained a majority female workforce.[162] For the month ending September 1860, Lawrence Manufacturing Company warp spinners—all of whom were women—earned about as much as Fall River's male spinners.[163] In the carding department, women made up over half the operatives and earned an average daily wage of 64 cents, 36 percent higher than the male workers in Fall River's Annawan carding department.[164] Almost across the board, Lowell millowners had to shell out more for their (female) workers. And, as (male-produced) fine cloth became the new standard in textiles, Lowell's inability to access cheap male labor only exacerbated the city's industrial downfall.

These factory labor systems slowly hardened into their most enduring form, with a few skilled male workers dominating payrolls and labor systems, backed by armies of unskilled, subservient, usually immigrant operatives. In the Fall River Metacomet Mill, for instance, twenty-two skilled spinners (all male) earned average daily wages of $1.42 for the week ending January 8,

1881.[165] That same week, the mill's male doffers (workers who changed out full bobbins for empty ones) took home an average of 67 cents a day, its roving hoisters (who moved cotton roving on and off the machines) earned 55 cents daily, its "back boys" (child laborers who assisted the mule spinners) made about 50 cents, and its "tubers" (those who oversaw the cloth-winding machinery) made a measly 25 cents.[166] In the Annawan Mills, experienced mule spinners like William Holmes could take home as much as $62.10 for thirty days of work—producing 4,296 pounds of cloth at 1.45 cents a pound—while unskilled spoolers made about a third as much, some 75 cents a day.[167] South Coast mills reaped tremendous financial rewards from the immense pool of unskilled, immigrant laborers they had on tap. Cheap labor made mass industrialization possible, and the whaling crisis made cheap labor plentiful.

The immigrant workers brought to these cities by whaling—Azoreans and Cape Verdeans, primarily—were thus critical to the rise and success of the South Coast textile industry. As New Bedford's Portuguese newspaper noted decades later, when "the use and commercialization of petroleum . . . launched New Bedford into a worsening crisis," there was "great apprehension" among the Portuguese of "the maritime classes" concerning this "irreparable blow" to the New Bedford economy. But, the paper noted, the city's strength remained its labor force. After all, New Bedford offered "an abundance of arms, and well-used arms that did not hesitate in the face of the gravest difficulties of life."[168] The South Coast would continue to amass thousands of laborers from abroad over the course of the late nineteenth and early twentieth centuries based on the networks established during whaling's heyday.

———

"In a more perfect manner, probably than any other American seaport, New Bedford connects the commercial era that . . . has passed away, with the manufacturing era that now is," the *New Bedford Semi-Centennial Souvenir* proudly announced in 1897. "These two great phases of industrial life have been manifested in her experience during the past fifty years, and she has thereby been . . . an epitome of the industrial progress of the times."[169] This industrialization was no natural outgrowth of economic or institutional evolution, but a grueling and hard-fought transition between two very different economic regimes. From the perspective of the South Coast, neither Americans' "popular culture of enterprise" nor the unique New England "synergy between the skill of industrial leaders and of the educated, hard-working machine operators" drove mass industrialization.[170] Instead, it was economic crisis that furnished its cities with the reserves of low-wage labor that allowed them to undercut competing mills in the north, whose investors were fast being lured away by far-flung opportunities. Lacking, for most of its early history, a comparable labor pool of relatively cheap, migrant labor, Lowell mills long remained enterprises of coarse-goods production, unable to challenge British textile supremacy.

Crisis also helped crack the bedrock of popular opposition to industry in Massachusetts. As whaling decline threw former seamen onto New Bedford's streets, popular anti-industrial sentiment rapidly disintegrated. Desperate city leaders felt they had little choice but to embrace the new industrial order.

Tangled up in the odd genealogies of crisis and capital, nineteenth-century New Bedford seems eerily close to the present. Indeed, auguring larger developments in industrial America a century later, New Bedford responded to economic crisis in the 1870s by cutting taxes and running up debts to encourage industry—only to have to slash welfare rolls in the 1880s in order to balance budgets. Then, as now, astute industrial and political leaders knew that crisis, properly employed, could act as midwife to capital re-accumulation.

The "industrial revolution" in the South Coast was no endogenous productive boom nor the natural evolution of a "maturing" economy. Even in the nineteenth century, so much of what marked the industrial transition in cities like New Bedford came from the very mobility of industrial production and its factors. Rather than simply a story of flourishing productive growth based on new, capitalist ideologies, state power, or innovative technology, the rise of the textile industry in South Coast Massachusetts was a tale of labor and capital in motion.

3

Labor in Motion

THE PEOPLING OF INDUSTRIAL MASSACHUSETTS

"WHY IS IT that the working people of Fall River are in constant turmoil, when at Lowell and Lawrence they are quiet?" This question, posed by a member of the Massachusetts House of Representatives in 1881, launched the Massachusetts Bureau of Statistics of Labor on a full-scale, multi-city investigation. Six months and hundreds of interviews later, the answer was clear: the British were to blame. When the Fall River mills had gone through an abrupt burst of growth in the aftermath of the whaling crisis, their labor needs fast outpaced their reserves of unemployed whalers, forcing millowners to make wholesale importations of English and Irish help. This, the bureau concluded, was an enormous miscalculation.[1]

What made British immigrant workers so problematic? To the bureau's investigators, the issue was obvious: they carried stubborn, "old world" antipathies—particularly toward industrial capitalism—that proved difficult to dislodge. As one Fall River manufacturer bluntly put it, "The whole trouble consists in the fact that they brought their habits with them." "The one great trouble with Fall River," another interviewee reported, "as compared with Lowell and Lawrence, is the existence of so much English help. . . . They come here with air of their old English ideas, which they had best leave behind them." One mill treasurer was even more forthright in his assessment: "We have the scum of the English and Irish in our midst; they brought their antagonistic notions with them." Whereas Lowell hired a "better class of help"—namely, American farm girls from the rural hinterland—Fall River's increasing reliance on "antagonistic" British workers had doomed the city to relentless industrial turmoil.[2]

Not only did these workers disdain their bosses, but they also constantly battled against an array of other immigrant working people, most notably, the French Canadians. As the bureau summed up the situation, Fall River's interminable industrial warfare was a result of the conflict of "the American and the English style of accomplishing work" and the "mixture of English, Irish, and French help" that "so confuses matters as to keep antagonistic feeling uppermost about all the time." French Canadians, in particular, "were ostracized by all," because "they would accept the lowest wages for their work . . . and also because they would not join strikes."[3]

If the British worker was too radical, the French Canadian represented an equally problematic extreme. Only a year earlier, the labor bureau had cited the "presence of the Canadian French" as a major obstacle to getting meaningful ten-hour reform legislation passed in Massachusetts. The French Canadians, after all, were "the Chinese of the Eastern States." "Docile" and "indefatigable," they were "a horde of industrial invaders, not a stream of stable settlers." They had but one mission: "To earn all they can by no matter how many hours of toil, to live in the most beggarly way so that out of their earnings they may spend as little for living as possible, and to carry out of the country what they can thus save."[4] In other words, ten-hour reform could never take root with such lowly and desperate workers present in high volumes. In the eyes of the bureau, it was this infelicitous amalgamation of belligerent British workers and pliant French transients that ensured Fall River's factories would be forever at war with themselves.

Thankfully, "assimilation," the labor bureau pointed out, was just on the horizon.[5] British, French, and Portuguese workers, under the sway of Americanization, were beginning to work together. As immigrants became Americans they would drop their "antagonistic" attitudes and "socialistic" ideas. The bureau foresaw eventual labor unity and, with time, labor peace.[6]

Epic stories of conniving manufacturers seeking to exploit the ethnic or racial divisions among their workers to extinguish any possibility of working-class solidarity have made for some of the oldest and most well-worn narratives in American labor history.[7] "Americanization" as a potential path to labor unity has similarly become a common trope.[8] There is much truth to this narrative, but it implicitly reproduces the idea that racial and ethnic conflict must somehow inexorably divide and encumber working-class activism.

Rather than beginning with the problem of industrial conflict, this chapter asks a more foundational question: what forces brought these migrant workers to Massachusetts in the first place? How and why did so many workers, from all over the world, come to populate Massachusetts factories and factory towns in the late nineteenth and early twentieth centuries? At the most superficial level, it was the global crises of the nineteenth-century Atlantic world that pushed a generation of peasants and migratory workers into the factories of the Anglo-American core.[9] Crisis—and the subsequent realignment of the global economy—catalyzed mass labor migration.

Yet, these British, French Canadian, and Portuguese migrations across the continents and oceans to the factories of Massachusetts were hardly reducible to an impoverished periphery venturing to a rapidly industrializing core. Each group came from a very specific set of social and economic circumstances—and were thus freighted with very different goals and ideologies—setting the stage for the ethnic conflict that made cities like Fall River such havens of industrial turmoil. Ultimately, an analysis of immigrant politics in Massachusetts from the perspective of these immigrants' sending states helps illuminate the character of American working-class politics. Rather than some primordial ethnic antagonism acting to dash any hope of class solidarity, it was actually the mechanics of global labor migration and the role of British, French-Canadian, and Portuguese institutions—hundreds or thousands of miles away—that would define working-class development in industrial Massachusetts.

"Antagonistic" British Immigrants

As the disruptions of the American Civil War rippled across the world, the shattering of the international cotton trade fundamentally reordered the global economy. The American South spiraled into economic obsolescence as new opportunities for mass cotton cultivation emerged (or were consciously created) in places like India, Brazil, and Egypt.[10] As New Bedford whaling collapsed, America's remaining whaling fleet relocated to San Francisco and the safer waters of the Pacific.[11] And the British cotton industry, which relied on the US South for nearly three-quarters of its cotton, was plunged into chaos.[12]

This so-called cotton famine upended British industry. By the outbreak of the war, the industrial districts of Lancashire, Derbyshire, and Cheshire had accumulated 2,270 factories with over 440,000 workers—a little over eleven times the size of Massachusetts's textile workforce.[13] It took only a year of disrupted American imports to see two-thirds of these mills shut down, leaving nearly half the population of cotton towns like Preston on poor relief.[14] As the chief medical officer of one Lancashire poor house put it in 1862, "I have daily experiences of the prevailing misery and want. . . . The poor people have neither money nor credit, and are destitute of the common necessaries of life."[15] This crisis—and the sluggish recovery that followed—spelled opportunity for Massachusetts manufacturers.

The "cotton famine" helped cut down some of these Massachusetts industrialists' most potent competitors on the global stage while offering them an entirely new source of labor. Notified by a state department circular that numerous unemployed English workers were available for recruitment ("in consequence of [the] want of employment . . . which prevails among [them]"), Massachusetts manufacturers founded the so-called Foreign Emigrant Society to raise money to send recruitment agents to Europe. These agents were empowered to extend the upfront costs necessary to import British workers on labor contracts.[16]

Not surprisingly, manufacturers found their biggest successes in the hardest hit locales. One recruitment agent, John Williams, made this clear in letters he sent back home for publication, in an attempt to stoke support for the investment of public funds into immigration. "Here in Manchester I have excited quite a lively interest amongst the mechanics and mill hands," he reported. Unlike other English towns, where "all was bustle, employment, and comparative prosperity," Manchester overflowed with "groups of men walking about in listless idleness; stout boys hanging around the street corners, with vacant, hopeless countenances . . . eagerly rushing in famished crowds for the slightest chance of a penny job."[17] These workers, Williams argued, could help ameliorate the complaints he was getting "every day" from American manufacturers, faced with demands for "increased rates of payment . . . by some special class of operatives."[18]

The number of workers specifically recruited by these agents was modest, but the long-term impact was incalculable. In part spurred by the 1864 Act to Encourage Immigration, which promised federal enforcement of labor importation contracts, numerous groups followed in the Foreign Emigrant Society model.[19] The American Emigrant Company (AEC), for instance, brought in some 400 foreign workers over the course of the war.[20] Among them were some 120 Scottish operatives bound for the American Linen Company of Fall River, which eventually signed a long-term recruitment contract with the AEC.[21] Comparatively, this was hardly a mass migration. But these early experiences taught American manufactures that they had an unlikely partner on the other side of the Atlantic, willing to take up the cause on their behalf.

The British union movement quickly put its considerable organizational strength behind the emigration cause. This may seem somewhat curious. Most unions do not actively encourage (or pay) members to leave their organization. But British unions had long theorized that the root cause of the textile industry's instability was, as the Bolton Spinners put it in 1886, "over production"; the "cure" was "reduced output."[22] "The theories of the political economists have been completely falsified," the union declared in 1892. "Hitherto we have been taught that cheapness stimulates consumption, but the experience of the cotton trade proves that for once the reverse has been the case. With falling rates for both the raw material and the manufactured article, the demand for the latter likewise contracted, and stocks gradually accumulated to an uncomfortable extent which nothing but a serious curtailment of production could hope to rectify."[23] Future labor economists might have suggested that inadequate aggregate demand or anemic purchasing power was the cause of falling prices for finished cotton cloth, but in the eyes of these British union leaders, there were, simply put, too many cloth producers and they were producing too much cloth.

Emigration, then, made sense as a political goal. "As capital seeks the most profitable investment wherever security for life and property is guaranteed," the Lancashire spinners reflected in 1870, "it is a matter of comparative indifference to investors [whether] it be employed in Great Britain, Australia, the United States of America, or in fact any other part of the world."[24] As a result, they proposed that "a portion of our funds be applied, when necessary, to the removal of the really surplus labourers connected with this Association."[25] Similarly, just as the Power-Loom Carpet Weavers saw their paramount goal as achieving "a fair remuneration for labour," the goal of "help[ing] members to emigrate" stood alongside other, more traditional union goals like "the regulation of the supply of hands and hours of work" and giving "assistance in cases of sickness, accident, infirmity, or death."[26] Incentivizing emigration was just another means of regulating wages and production in workers' favor.

By the late nineteenth century, countless British unions were sponsoring emigration programs. The Bolton Spinners offered members an emigration allowance through at least the 1920s. An 1864 meeting of the Associated Operative Cotton Spinners of Lancashire, Cheshire, Yorkshire, and Derbyshire likewise ordered each "individual member of this association . . . to promote to the utmost of his power the emigration movement [amid] this important crisis," and that "each locality" must develop "its own system of emigration, experience having proved that it is only by emigration that the position of the working classes can be improved."[27] In 1879, the Lancashire unions disbursed about £170 in emigration assistance, nearly five times what they paid in sick benefits.[28] By 1882, spending on emigration had doubled.[29] Blackburn's spinners similarly funneled £500 into their own emigration society; 1,000 workmen applied for benefits in its first month.[30]

Although these sums may seem modest, cheap steerage transportation rates ensured that these efforts could yield thousands of new emigrants. Most unions disbursed anywhere from £2 to £7 per successful applicant for emigration, generally enough to cover passage to the United States.[31] With transportation rates so low, even a single union could send off hundreds of workers. For instance, the Lancashire spinners disbursed some £3,106 in emigration benefits from 1879 to 1893 to send more than 1,000 workers to the United States.[32] By 1869, emigration had become a standard benefit of almost every British textile union.[33]

As a result, British emigration to Massachusetts surged during the Civil War and the postbellum era. From 1862 to 1885, about 10,000 spinners left the United Kingdom destined for the United States.[34] Correspondingly, the decade after 1865 saw a fivefold increase in the number of English residents in Fall River, from 1,800 to 8,700.[35] By 1875, Fall River had the most foreign-dominated workforce in Massachusetts, with over 50 percent of its workers coming from Britain alone.[36] About 65 percent of New Bedford's population at that time had immigrated from the United Kingdom.[37] In popular discourse, Fall River soon became widely known as the "Manchester of America" and New Bedford as its "Bolton"—a reference to both these cities' industries and their people.[38] Both soon sported numerous English fraternal clubs and societies, such as the Odd Fellows and the Foresters.[39] There were eighty-eight such clubs in Fall River by the end of the nineteenth century.[40] So thorough-going was the British takeover of the city that one Lancashire writer felt himself immediately transported back home during a visit in the 1880s. In his recounting of a semi-fictionalized night of barroom carousing at the local Foresters' hall, "I soon forgeet wheere I wur, an' fancied I're i' England, an' wur th' only Yankee i'th' company. I towd 'em I wouldno' forget 'em when I geet back to Ameriky."[41]

Because British unions played such an outsized role in structuring British American emigration, their influence privileged the movement of only their most militant members. Many unions allowed only blacklisted workers, those on strike, or those fired for union activism—that is, "victims"—to take benefits.[42] The Oldham spinners, for example, originally allowed only strikers and victims to take advantage of the union's emigration benefits.[43] By 1880, they changed the rules so that any member could receive emigration funds but still set aside 40 percent for those blacklisted for union activism.[44] The Lancashire spinners similarly only allowed victims and strikers to draw on emigration funds.[45] Beginning in 1866, the Hyde Spinners set aside an emigration benefit equal to three months' pay for any member "discharged through visiting his master or defending his shopmates' rights."[46] Even those unions that did not privilege "victimized" workers generally had rules that allowed only long-standing members to access emigration funds, or, at the very least, disbursed money based on the worker's years of service (as did the Ashton, Bolton, Bradford, Brighouse, Halifax, Lees, Manchester, Pendlebury, Preston, Rochdale, and Stockport unions).[47] Overall, then, the emigrants sent to America tended to be militant, older, and well versed in union principles. Unsuspecting New Bedford and Fall River millowners were gaining workers with unexpected ideological baggage.[48]

It is no exaggeration to say that almost every late nineteenth-century South Coast labor leader cut his or her teeth within the British trade union movement, often having been forced out for their radical activities. Thomas Evans (widely known around Fall River as "the old labor agitator," a moniker that even marks his grave) was the Chartist secretary of the Bolton weavers before getting blacklisted after an 1853 strike; he migrated to the United States, where his penchant for debate, labor reform, and attempts to organize the Fall River weavers got him again blacklisted in 1888.[49] John Norris, eventually indicted by a Fall River grand jury for his strike activities, was forced to admit that he had also "incurred the displeasure of the manufacturers" back home in England, which had caused his departure for Fall River a few months earlier.[50] Thomas Webb had to flee Ireland due to his involvement in the Irish independence rebellion of 1848; he eventually became a leading figure of the Fall River weavers, founded the *Trades Union and Fall River Weavers' Journal*, and was elected state senator as part of the Fall River "Labor Campaign Club" in 1879.[51] John Golden, blacklisted in Lancashire, left for Fall River in 1884; he eventually became treasurer of the Fall River Mule Spinners' Union before becoming president of the United Textile Workers, a position he held for nearly two decades.[52] Robert Howard, an officer of the Stockport Spinners' Society in England, was blacklisted and forced to emigrate in 1873; he worked as a spinner at the Flint Mills before becoming secretary and de facto leader of the Fall River Mule Spinners' Union, a position that catapulted him to eight terms as state senator from 1886 to 1892.[53]

British emigrant workers quickly developed a well-deserved reputation for union radicalism. It was British workmen who led the Fall River strikes of 1868, 1870, 1875, and 1879, as well as the New Bedford strikes of 1867 and 1877.[54] Similarly, the successful 1874 struggle for a ten-hour law in Massachusetts was widely credited to British activism. "Were American agitators for this measure[?]," labor reformer Jennie Collins wrote shortly after the bill's passage. "No! I am ashamed to confess it. The men who have

worked and struggled for this law . . . were of British birth, born under monarchy," adding, derisively, "no graduates of Harvard came to help these men."[55]
Rumors began to fly around mill offices and boardrooms that perhaps it
was actually their manufacturing competitors in Britain (and not Britain's
unionists) that had conspired to send them their most belligerent and obsti-
nate workers.[56]

Such complaints were rampant in the report the Massachusetts labor
bureau eventually filed on Fall River. "We built many mills in 1871–72,
and imported operatives rapidly," one Fall River manufacturer told the bureau, adding that "it is with this unassimilated material that all the trouble
originates."[57] A Fall River clergyman similarly complained of "foreigners"
bringing "their Old World ideas and prejudices . . . laboring under a hered-
itary feeling of discontent . . . filled with communistic notions" and never
"satisfied with fair wages."[58] Indeed, as historian Mary Blewett has noted,
when Fall River's Lizzie Borden was first confronted by police over her possible role in the infamous 1892 murder of her parents, she quickly fabricated a
story about a recent argument between her textile magnate father and one of
his English workmen. Although Lizzie later dropped this lie, the Lancashire
penchant for labor radicalism gave the young murder suspect an easy potential scapegoat.[59]

British workers imported many of the labor protest methods they had effectively deployed back home. Amid the Fall River "Long Vacation" of 1875,
workers put on an old-fashioned "bread riot," marching down the street
bearing bobbins and stolen loaves of bread tied to poles (a Lancashire tradition), shouting "Bread!" and "Tyranny!" One "vacationing" woman struck
Fall River's mayor in the head with a loaf of bread.[60] The British penchant for
public mockery was certainly on display in an 1878 parade of 20,000 workers,
which saw one of Fall River's principal mill agents denounced as another
"Lord Leitrim"—an infamous English landlord in Ireland—and featured
signs that ranged from "if cheap labor be the basis of prosperity, why is China
not the head of civilization?" to "[Fall River] Board of Trade—Qualifications
for membership: Fools in business management, asses in statesmanship, idiots
in political economy and traitors to Republican institutions."[61]

Bursts of real and mock violence toward strikebreakers and owners were
also widely cited as representing another classically "Lancashire" method
of enforced labor solidarity.[62] During an 1889 strike, unionists burned mill
superintendents in effigy and, confronted with a group of strikebreakers,
"followed the [fleeing] weavers," a newspaper reported, "surrounded
[them] . . . and proceeded to pound [them] unmercifully."[63] Fall River

unionists also attempted to shame strikebreakers by sending their names to their former unions and old friends back home in England.[64]

Even organizationally, Massachusetts textile unions were self-consciously modeled on their "sister" unions back in England.[65] New Bedford textile workers, for instance, set up a cooperative store on the English "Rochdale" model. Its annual meetings took the form of "old fashioned English tea meetings" with food, entertainment, and rousing choruses of "God Save the Queen."[66]

This distinctly "British" approach to labor activism also made these unions notoriously insular and unyieldingly xenophobic. Years later, New Bedford worker Jack Rubinstein recalled this particular aspect of British labor activism, relaying an especially egregious conversation he overheard from a group of British operatives. "They were talking about the bloody foreigners, the bloody this and the bloody that. . . . They were talking about the French Canadians who had probably . . . been living in and around New Bedford for several generations . . . whereas these people themselves had not even acquired American citizenship[,] 'cause the English didn't readily give up their citizenship."[67] Moreover, the hierarchical division of mill labor itself, with skilled British mule spinners and weavers possessing the best jobs, helped reinforce these xenophobic predilections. As Rubinstein noted, "The general attitude that skilled English speaking [workers] have to non-skilled foreigners, [is] as an inferior group," adding "their whole group was made up primarily of Anglo-Saxons" with "better jobs."[68] Job hierarchies—as well as the very different goals and ideologies with which French Canadian and Portuguese workers arrived—would make inter-ethnic harmony a herculean task for South Coast workers.

As Rubinstein's observations attest, British workers' commitments to trade union radicalism had little to do with a more thoroughgoing commitment to being "stable settlers," to use the Massachusetts labor bureau's terminology. During strikes—or if wages in America dipped—emigrant British workers were quick to return home.[69] In fact, amid labor struggles, American unions often explicitly offered provisions that "if any discouraged persons . . . wish to return to the old country, we can find a way to send them back."[70] During an 1875 Fall River strike, workers decided "the best system of fighting the battle was by thinning the labor market by emigration," resolving to spend surplus strike-fund money on "sending home to England such persons as are willing to go."[71] Observers often castigated French Canadian or Portuguese immigrants for their "sojourner" status, but British immigrants were not terribly different in this regard.

For these British immigrants, labor migration remained just another tactic workers had at their disposal to exact as much as they could from their circumstances. Rates of British emigration were thus incredibly volatile, rising and falling with the ups and downs of the British and American economies.[72] Information on prevailing wages, labor conditions, and unemployment was ceaselessly sent back and forth between Fall River and Lancashire workers.[73] When conditions in America worsened, emigration was halted; workers returned to Britain.[74] Thriving American productivity had the opposite effect. As one Fall River weaver (formerly of Darwen) explained to an English visitor, "This is the right side of the water." Although "I would sooner live in England," he added, "and if I can save enough to keep me out of the mill, I'll go home before I die," Fall River was, simply put, "better for making money," at least for the moment.[75]

British workers were deeply committed to labor reform and trade unionism. But their commitment had little to do with "the antagonistic spirit that is in [their] blood," as one millowner put it, nor any unique dedication to staying on American soil.[76] Nevertheless, their militancy would have crucial consequences for the development of the state's textile industry. It also ensured that British laborers would face off against another group of workers who came from an entirely different social context and with entirely different ideas about how to go about reshaping industrial Massachusetts.

"Docile" French Canadians

There is no clear consensus on any single event or factor that triggered the massive influx of French Canadians to New England in the late nineteenth century. Key precedents were likely set by the Acadian expulsions of the 1750s, in which Britain—apprehensive over its seemingly tenuous hold on the former French colonies of Canada—forcibly scattered the people of Acadia (covering the Gaspé Peninsula as well as present-day New Brunswick, Prince Edward Island, and the northern fringes of Maine), dispersing them all over North America.[77] About a quarter of these Acadian resettlements took place in Massachusetts.[78] The Canadian government, for its part, would point to the fallout of the failed independence rebellions of 1837 and 1838 as first pushing French Canadians southward.[79] The most proximate cause, however, were the attempts of Massachusetts manufacturers to import struggling French Canadian farmers as strikebreakers in order to undercut British union organizing efforts.[80]

It is no coincidence that French Canadians would become the target of ceaseless English vitriol: they were imported precisely to serve as a foil to their pugnacious workmates. The origins of "French Village" in Fall River, for instance, date to the first major importation of French Canadians to the city, when Fall River's American Linen mills put migrants up in tenements on Broadway, Division, and Bay Streets to break an 1879 strike.[81] As one agent of the Boston and Albany Railroad testified at an 1881 Massachusetts Bureau of Labor hearing, the past two years had seen "no less than one hundred superintendents or agents of mills" apply "for French help, one mill asking for as many as fifty families."[82]

Coming largely as strikebreakers, these migrants made few friends among their working-class peers. When the Stafford and Crescent Mills of Fall River imported some seventy to eighty French Canadians in 1879, the new workers were greeted at the train station by, as the local newspaper reported, "a crowd of women, children, and a few men. . . . Rocks were thrown in perfect showers, and one of the men . . . was so roughly assaulted that a man who witnessed the whole affair said he did not expect to see him come out of it alive."[83] By the late nineteenth century, the word "knobstick," originally a Lancashire term reserved for strikebreakers, had become simply another word for "French Canadian" in Fall River.[84]

British hatred for French Canadian immigration found its match in Canadian hatred for French Canadian emigration. Whereas British workers emigrated via supportive sending institutions, Canadian state and local officials roundly condemned the practice.[85] As early as 1849, the Canadian legislative assembly had convened a special committee to investigate the "calamity" of emigration.[86] It was a "mutilation of the homeland," Canadian journalist and future senator Laurent-Olivier David grieved in 1871.[87] Catholic leaders were even more vehement in their opposition to emigration: "How many of our compatriots will have lost their language, perhaps even their faith, to become Canadian in name only[?]," the bishop of Trois-Rivières, Louis-François Richer Laflèche, asked in 1866.[88] Instead, Laflèche suggested it better to encourage farmers to simply be "contented with what they have. And if there is not enough, let us suffer—suffering has its merit."[89] As the premier of Canada East, George-Étienne Cartier, reputedly (and infamously) put it, "C'est la canaille qui s'en va"—"it is the scoundrel that goes."[90]

Emigration cut at the heart of what so many Franco-Americans saw as their abiding mission on the North American continent: ousting the English in order to reclaim a French national territory in the New World.[91] Such feelings of betrayal were even more acute for Acadian leaders who dreamed of retaking the lands from which they had been forcibly expelled. "How I regret, how I feel my heart beat with pain," the Reverend M. F. Richard declared at the first National Acadian Convention in 1881, "seeing our Acadian youth," upon "reaching the age they could render such grand services to the father-land, voluntarily take the path of exile, and turn their backs to the church."[92] "If Acadians worked half as hard on their farms as they have to in a foreign land," Father Camille Lefebvre put it dismissively in 1889, "they would soon become rich and independent.... Why then emigrate to the United States?"[93]

Despite the immense social pressure to stay in Canada, most serious observers already knew that, more often than not, French Canadians left pre-cisely so they could preserve their farms back home. The economic changes of the mid-nineteenth century forced Canadian farmers into competition with the far more productive farms of the American West, whose produce could be daily taken to the industrial East on the very same railroads the children of the Boston Associates had bankrolled in the 1850s and 1860s.[94] New England farmers adapted by specializing in products that could little withstand long rail or canal journeys on their way to nearby urban centers; farmers on iso-lated Prince Edward Island or the Gaspé Peninsula did not have that luxury.[95]

The American Civil War, too, had an enormous impact on the Canadian countryside. As secession brought pro-industrial American Republicans to power, it catalyzed the passage of a number of stiff new tariffs designed to encourage domestic industry. Consequently, Canada's reciprocal trade treaty with the United States was quite suddenly quashed in 1866, leading to a col-lapse in agricultural prices and a sharp economic contraction.[96] Poverty be-came endemic on Canadian farms. "My parents talked about how little they received in Canada for a barrel of potatoes or fish," one Massachusetts French Canadian remembered in 1983. "When they would come to sell it they were paid so little that it was hardly worth selling, so they put it on the ground to use as fertilizer on their farms. They never made much of a living there because they were always working for nothing."[97] In a world of interconnected capital, the market for Canadian agricultural goods was undermined by the very same transformations that had devastated textile production in Lowell while simul-taneously catalyzing the buildup of the South Coast textile industry.

Such market disruptions only compounded the challenges of French Canada's poor soils, cold weather, lack of arable land, and inadequate access to markets.[98] When the Canadian government paid to tour a delegation of potential British farmers throughout the nation's countryside in an effort to induce them and their compatriots to immigrate, they had little good to say about Québécois farmland.[99] As one farmer tersely reported back, the journey from New England to Canada took them "through the great cotton manufacturing towns of America, and also through a very miserable farming country."[100]

Not only were soils poor, but the narrow plotting of French Canadian farms also made it nearly impossible to divide land among inheritors.[101] As one state report found, a significant class of emigrants consisted of "young people from good farming families" who were forced to leave due to the "difficulty for the parents in procuring land with which to establish their children."[102] This was a recurrent issue given the size of most Catholic French Canadian families. Elmire Boucher would later recall that her family ventured to Fall River in 1899 because their farmland in Bic, Québec—"rather rocky, in the mountains"—was "too small for the family": two parents and a modest cohort of sixteen children.[103]

Overcoming these constraints required capital, and with little to go around, most farmers found themselves quickly locked into cycles of debt and poverty. Credit through local storekeepers and merchants became the source for everything from mechanical equipment and land to seeds and livestock.[104] With a captive audience, moneylenders often attached brutal terms and unworkable schedules to credit. "What do you want a farmer to do with your money, due in three months?" a local by the name of "M. Ossaye" wrote to the Québec *Gazette des Campagnes* (Countryside Gazette) in 1861. "The land does not pay us for a year. . . . How can we pay when we have nothing to sell?"[105]

Interest rates were injuriously high. The "ruin" of the farmer was ensured "by his falling into the greedy hands of men whom the love of profit drives to dishonest speculations," Samuel Gendron complained to the Canadian assembly. "How can a farmer pay 10%, 15%, or 20% interest[?]," he asked, adding that it was "the plague of usury which gnaws at the countryside . . . [forcing] the *habitant* to leave the field . . . and take the road to the United States."[106] Many early migrants to the United States came under just these circumstances, hoping a brief bout of factory work might help settle debts back home before the new harvest.[107]

Despite the best efforts of Canadian authorities, once French Canadians developed social connections in the United States, a process of chain migration set in, constantly drawing migrants southward.[108] The classic 1913 French Canadian novel *Maria Chapdelaine* evoked the lure of emigrant connections in America. "When I was a girl," young Maria's mother tells her, "pretty nearly everyone went off to the States. Farming did not pay as well as it does now, prices were low, we were always hearing of the big wages earned over there in the factories, and every year one family after another sold out for next to nothing and left Canada."[109] One oft-repeated migration story told of a baker, Napoléon Lord, of St. Hilaire, who, after noticing that all his customers were gone, decided to simply give up and follow them to Massachusetts.[110] Oral histories of French Canadian immigrants almost always record the presence of receptive families and friends waiting in New England as an important pre-condition for the emigration process.[111]

During the last four decades of the nineteenth century, some 327,000 French Canadians left for New England.[112] In 1860, Fall River and New Bedford together had ten French Canadian residents; by 1900, New Bedford had 24,800 and Fall River had 33,000.[113] By the early twentieth century, Fall River had become, with the exception of Montréal, the largest concentration of French speakers on the American continent.[114] All told, from 1840 to 1930, nearly 1 million French Canadians emigrated to the United States.[115]

Driven as they were by the vagaries of agricultural indebtedness, French Canadians remained a peripatetic bunch. Immigration to New England spiked in moments of prosperity, such as the eras of 1865–1873, 1879–1882, 1885–1888, and 1891–1893. Similarly, moments of recession sent migrants packing back home, such as the panics of 1873, 1884, 1890, and 1893.[116] As Jos Morin, an eighty-one-year-old emigrant, recalled in a 1978 interview, "[French Canadians] would make a little bit of money to pay their debts, then return. . . . They moved for three to four years in one direction, three to four years to the other; they practically had no place to call home."[117] Joseph Maltais's childhood displayed this affinity for constant motion all too well. Born in 1876 in a small village on the Gaspé Peninsula, Maltais's family left Canada for the United States when he was five years old before returning to Québec the following spring. He again returned to Fall River to work at the Kerr Mill at age seven; his family then moved to New Hampshire to work at another mill for three years before moving to New York, returning again to Fall River by the time Maltais turned ten.[118]

The relative proximity of French Canada to New England enabled this frequent relocation. Demographic studies of French Canadian emigrants have shown turnover rates in certain communities as high as 50 percent every three years.[119] It was this characteristic that the Massachusetts labor bureau was attempting to highlight by calling French Canadians the "Chinese of the Eastern States." For the bureau, the comparison was not actually about race. Instead, it was because the French Canadians' "purpose is merely to sojourn a few years as aliens, touching us only at a single point, that of work, and, when they have gathered out of us what will satisfy their ends, to get them away to whence they came."[120] For this reason the bureau classified them as "invaders" rather than "stable settlers." Despite the racialized language, the bureau was not entirely incorrect.

Although few records are left to illuminate these early migrations from the perspective of emigrants themselves, oral histories of older French Canadians taken in the 1980s confirm how frequently these migrants zigzagged back and forth across the American continent. As always, the ultimate goal was to achieve landed independence. Beatrice Mandeville was brought by her parents to the United States in 1900, "because they were poor and there was no way to escape their lives. . . . My parents had a farm, but it was not large enough to support the whole family."[121] When she was twelve, her parents brought her back to Canada. After her marriage, Mandeville and her husband obtained a farm, but soon found themselves $11,000 in debt. By 1922, they had emigrated back to Massachusetts, only to again return to Canada in 1925 to reestablish their farm.[122] Similarly, Alma Ouelette's parents came to Massachusetts in 1908 because "they were not able to make a living on their land," with her father insisting that "in four years . . . we will find enough money to [come back and] repair the house. Then we will work on the earth"—a promise he eventually made good on.[123]

Such narratives also highlight the ways in which return migration was a distinctly male affair. Women, preferring the freedom that came from working alongside their husbands as relative equals in the factory, were generally far more reluctant to head back to the hardscrabble life of Canadian agriculture. Évelyne Desruisseaux, for instance, emigrated as a child in 1901. After marrying, her husband insisted they return home.[124] "He always had the idea of returning to Canada. He was born in the land of his father and he loved Canada. Myself, I never understood working the earth and I loved the United States . . . but I thought 'He must have his turn.' We came back to Canada [in 1923]."[125] Béatrice Mandeville similarly "liked the United States, better than Canada," because it "was easier to make a living," but found her husband of a totally different mind. "His profession was to be a farmer. He liked that. When you are in the cities . . . you are not your boss. . . . My husband was Canadian and he liked to have a farm."[126] Like generations of Jeffersonian yeomen and Azorean whalers before them, for these migrants, true independence was only available back home on the farm.

The penchant for French Canadians to return to Canada during moments of American economic depression was not merely a manifestation of their dreams of agricultural independence or their thin investment in the United States, but a product of explicit Canadian state policy. Since the very beginnings

of the "emigration menace," the Canadian government had engaged in a vigorous campaign of "repatriation." In 1870, the provincial government of
Québec created three "repatriation" offices, giving state agents a broad mandate to tour cities all over New England, offering emigrants various incentives
to return.[127] The Canadian government passed its own repatriation act in 1873,
dispersing numerous agents all over New England in order to, as the chairman
of the Commission on Immigration and Colonization put it, "bring back to
our country a population so justly entitled to our affection and esteem."[128]
Another repatriation act was passed in 1875, setting up a special colony—"La
Patrie" (The Homeland)—reserved for returning French Canadians.[129]

Ferdinand Gagnon, a prominent Worcester journalist turned Canadian
repatriation agent in 1875, led the charge. When Gagnon came to Fall River
that year, he was greeted by "a large and enthusiastic" crowd, as he offered "each
head of a family who have emigrated from Canada, and who will return and
become permanent settlers, one hundred acres of land, with house thereon,
and betterments of the land to the amount of $200."[130] Following Gagnon's
visit, 182 French Canadian migrant families left for the new colony.[131] Gagnon
later reported that, "without exaggeration," he had repatriated 2,000 French
Canadians with just a year of work.[132] When a group of furious local French
Canadian leaders convened an official hearing to challenge the Massachusetts
labor bureau's damning assertions that the French Canadians were mere
sojourning "industrial invaders," they were nonetheless forced to sheepishly
confess that many of them had been, or still were, on the Canadian government payroll, touring Massachusetts to offer emigrants "great inducements"
to return home.[133]

Appeals to French nationalism frequently joined offers of material assistance in repatriation pitches. Citing God's scattering of man after Babel
at an 1871 convention in Worcester, Gagnon argued that it was no less than
the Almighty who "forced [man] to separate and form nations" and "[gave]
to each people [their] part of the globe." Gagnon thus reminded French
Canadians of their duty to "love the soil of the motherland," and to "keep intact
our institutions, our morals, our faith, our language." And, in a happy coincidence, he was quick to remind audiences that, thanks to new state programs,
it was now easier than ever to fulfill God's will. "Colonization . . . demands
strong arms," Gagnon exhorted. "The government [of Canada] offers real
benefits. Land is cheap and conditions of sale and obligatory use are easy."
Simply put, "patriotism" made it a "duty to repatriate."[134]

Tactically, the Canadian government smartly bulked up repatriation
programs whenever economic crisis struck the United States. Canadian

authorities, for instance, shut down their repatriation efforts in the prosperous early 1870s only to restart again after the 1873 panic.[135] After the 1893 panic, Canadian authorities again rekindled their repatriation efforts, in the hope that, as a Montréal immigration officer explained in 1894, emigrant "experiences in recent times" had helped "these people realize their mistake as they never did before. . . . They will find the plow and the harrow less irksome and more certain of reward for their labor than either lathe or loom."[136] Even private colonization societies could receive government funds; they sprang up everywhere in late nineteenth-century Canada. There were so many that they had even convened their own congress by 1898.[137] Some were wildly successful. *La Société de rapatriement du Lac-Saint-Jean*, working with a $14,000 annual grant from the Canadian government, ultimately distributed 18,658 colonization tickets.[138]

But French Canadians remained difficult to pin down, much to Canada's constant chagrin. Gagnon's earliest repatriation efforts, for instance, were only half successful, as 50 percent of those repatriated eventually returned to the United States.[139] Canadian authorities fretted constantly about these migrants "using" Canada as a mere way-station to endure cyclical economic crisis rather than a place of permanent settlement.[140] As one annual immigration report lamented three years after the 1902 recession, "When the crisis came to the United States . . . a larger number than one would believe of our emigrated compatriots returned to Canada," but, "in spite of attempts to retain them, a larger number of those who had come back to us returned . . . to take advantage of the reopening of the American [manufacturers]."[141] Whether or not they bought the nationalist rhetoric, French Canadian migrants smartly used these "repatriation" programs to navigate the recurrent swings of the Massachusetts economy.

Available evidence suggests that this inherently migratory outlook was in large part responsible for much of what infuriated British communities and native populations about these French migrants: namely, their insularity, their lack of concern for local politics, and their infamously anti-union outlook. British workers complained endlessly about the French failing to educate their children properly and faking documents in order to put them to work below the legal age minimum.[142] But for many French Canadian immigrants, this "family" labor strategy made sense in the context of their long-term dreams of returning to Canada. "We are here for two or three years at most and we shall send our children to school in Canada when we return home," was a constant refrain.[143] As one Massachusetts factory owner put it, "We have considerable Canadian-French help," but "many families [come] . . . with the intention [to] remain only a few years at most, and then [return] to their homes in Canada, and they regard it as time thrown away to send their children to school, as they . . . do not understand our language, and do not want to learn it; as they will not use it when they return to Canada."[144]

The infamous anti-union stance of these Canadians likely sprang from the same source.[145] Drawn-out labor conflicts probably seemed of little benefit to migrants eager to return home. Since they were generally excluded from local unions anyway, French Canadians had little investment in these organizations and no institutional access to strike funds.[146] Instead, most French Canadians simply left town during strikes.[147] During a major 1898 strike in New Bedford, one observer was shocked by "the exodus of French Canadians," seeing "hundreds . . . going back to Canadian farms."[148] As one French Canadian explained during that same 1898 strike, "I am poor. I cannot stay idle. I do not belong to any union, and therefore cannot expect them to look out for me. . . . I am not a citizen of New Bedford . . . [but] I can go home now and get work."[149]

Even the French penchant for ethnic insularity seems to have been in part driven by the demands of priests and community leaders who were, more often than not, either Canadian repatriation agents or repatriation sympathizers.[150] French Canadian ecclesiastical leaders preached an ideology of "la survivance"—survival—encouraging French Canadians to resist assimilation and maintain French culture and language at all costs.[151] French Canadian emigrants took this rhetoric very seriously and developed a vibrant, albeit intentionally insular, community.[152] As Thérèse Bealieu of New Bedford, a machine inspector whose family emigrated from St. Hyacinthe, reflected on her childhood during a 1983 oral history, "We sang French songs and read French newspapers. . . . Franco-American community life was close and heart warming. Everything was in French—plays—parish entertainment, whist [card game] party—bazaara—etc."[153] It was also no coincidence that many of the most ardent advocates of "survivance" ideology were doubling as agents of the Canadian government, working in the background to encourage repatriation.[154]

Such cultural practices had very real consequences for these workers' incorporation into the mills of Massachusetts. While millowners lavishly praised their French Canadian recruits as "steady," of "general good behavior," and "not given to drunkenness" (a swipe at their British workmates), they faced interminable harassment and exclusion from their fellow workers.[155] Violence against French strikebreakers was a frequent occurrence.[156] Skirmishes (sometimes violent) over access to Catholic Church services broke out constantly between Irish and French immigrants.[157] Everyday bursts of animosity often devolved into violent bouts of conflict. In 1894, a local paper reported that twenty-five Fall River families were advised not to send their children to the Eastern Avenue School "for fear they would be injured in a race war," after a schoolyard squabble degenerated into a massive stone-throwing fight involving 200 students. "Clannish and apt to entertain race prejudices... each side took refuge behind its own pile of rocks, and the air was full of missiles," leaving multiple children and onlookers injured.[158] In another horrifying incident, a group of textile doffers decided to haze Alphonse Farland, just arrived from Canada, putting him on "trial" for "being a greenhorn," convicting him of "being too green to live among civilized people," and ultimately carrying out the penalty of hanging.[159] Tying Farland by the neck to a mill elevator, they raised the elevator until he was "black in the face" before cutting him down.[160] Although arguments about French nationalism and ethnic insularity may seem remote from the activity of the factory floor, they could have very real consequences for these migrant workers.

In sum, British and French Canadian conflict was not simply a natural outgrowth of ethnic hostility, racial prejudice, or an elaborate conspiracy of divisiveness orchestrated by manufacturers. A mix of divergent migratory experiences, the close proximity of French Canadians' homeland, and the continuing involvement of Canadian authorities helped catalyze ethnic conflict and suppress interest in union activism or local politics. Not coincidentally, only when frustrated Canadian authorities and local leaders largely abandoned their repatriation efforts did French Canadians—especially women, who had long felt most committed to lives in industry—begin to manifest a much more thoroughgoing desire to reshape the politics of industrial Massachusetts.

The "Poorest" Portuguese

The Azores and Massachusetts have long existed in a peculiarly close economic orbit, dating back to the beginnings of the whaling industry in the 1760s.[161] Despite these long-standing migratory connections, Portuguese workers would not numerically dominate textile workforces in the South Coast until the early twentieth century, for reasons that had much more to do with events in Portugal than in Massachusetts.[162]

As in French Canada and Britain, Azorean emigration emerged from local crisis. By the nineteenth century, Portuguese self-rule had effectively collapsed. A series of French invasions in 1807 sent the royal family packing for Brazil, leaving Portugal a British dominion until the 1820s.[163] A protracted civil war followed the royal family's return to Portugal in the 1830s, which was in turn followed by a chaotic seventy-year period of "Rotativismo"—roughly, government by constant rotation. Portugal's parliament was formally "dissolved" some thirty times.[164] By the early twentieth century, the Portuguese economy was in shambles, illiteracy hovered around 80 percent, and the state was forced to declare bankruptcy in 1892 and again in 1902.[165] Dissent and disorder, paired with the 1908 assassination of the Portuguese king and his son in the streets of Lisbon, led to the collapse of the Portuguese monarchy and the rise of the First Republic.[166] Stability was fleeting. During its sixteen-year tenure from 1910 to 1926, the First Republic would see nine presidents, forty-four ministries, twenty-five uprisings, three interludes of military dictatorship, and some 325 bombings.[167]

Interminable instability drove ceaseless waves of migration. Annual Portuguese emigration rose from 14,000 in 1886, when the first emigration statistics were recorded, to an annual average of 28,000 in the 1890s, cresting at 301,000 annually throughout the 1910s and 40,000 in the 1920s, not counting the additional, unrecorded numbers of emigrants who escaped official appraisal.[168]

As in Canada, "the emigratory problem" emerged as one of the most vexing social issues of late nineteenth- and early twentieth-century Portugal.[169] Most Portuguese policymakers viewed this trend as a cause, rather than an effect, of national crisis.[170] The state passed a series of emigration restriction laws in 1873, 1880, 1886, 1892, 1895, 1896, 1898, and 1903, ultimately creating a nineteenth-century "border patrol" of sorts: the Polícia Repressiva da Emigração Clandestina, or the Police of Clandestine Emigration.[171] As illegal emigration emerged as a critical issue for Portuguese policymakers, a near universal consensus emerged for using the power of the state to restrict or re-channel emigrant flows.[172]

For state leaders, restriction promoted key policy goals, first among which was the furthering of Portugal's imperial ambitions. The hope was that emigration restriction might re-route potential emigrants to Portuguese colonial Africa. Almost as soon as Portugal began restricting emigration abroad, it also began offering potential African colonists "free tickets," land grants, and "a subsidy, paid at time of boarding" of 30,000 réis "in cash, to the head of the family and 5,000 [réis] more for each [added] person."[173]

Similarly, restrictions were explicitly crafted to crack down on those who might use migration to evade Portugal's mandatory military conscription laws. A feeble nation attempting to keep an overextended global empire from unraveling, the Portuguese state required an exceptionally onerous eight years of military service from each Portuguese male.[174] As one English traveler put it in 1886, "the Azorean islander flies from the recruiting sergeant as he would from the Evil One."[175] Consequently, many of Portugal's emigration restriction laws were thinly veiled conscription edicts. One 1880 law required all emigrants to deposit the equivalent of £40 into state coffers before they could be permitted to leave the country so as to hire a military substitute in case they did not return before turning thirty-six.[176]

Behind the inevitable paeans to Portuguese national pride that accompanied almost all anti-emigration exegeses, most observers understood that there were material interests at stake. For the Azores's powerful agro-export interests, emigration threatened the one advantage that helped offset the many disadvantages that came from producing agricultural goods out in the middle of the Atlantic Ocean, namely, that the very "captivity" of the Azorean people ensured a ready supply of cheap labor with few alternative sources of employment.[177] Agro-business operators were thus hardly enthralled by the prospect of mass emigration. Interest in emigration "repression," one Azorean writer seethed in the early twentieth century, was driven by the desire to maintain "cheap arms for their fields, for their crops" by keeping "[Azoreans] chained down for very little money." "The property owner, especially the greedy one, makes war without truce against emigration . . . because it benefits him to have at his service a super cheap worker or operative."[178]

Despite Portugal's best efforts, the nearly insatiable labor needs of New Bedford whaling ships made clandestine emigration an alluring option. Countless Azorean and Cape Verdean men were fleeing every year, using New Bedford whale ships as a covert means to escape emigration restrictions and obtain free passage to the United States.[179] As one defeated state official noted in 1880, the stationing of emigration police at Brava, Cape Verde, had ultimately solved nothing. "Not even the police are a guarantee as agents of authority in these matters," he pointed out, "because it has already happened that they have been the first to embark, leaving their swords on the beach as a souvenir."[180] Typical became stories like that of Antonio Fortes, born in São Nicolau in Cape Verde in 1890, who shipped out on the New Bedford whaler *Pedro Varela* in 1908. After nine months at sea, he settled in New Bedford and got a job at a local factory until he landed a spot on the same whaler in 1910. He continued shipping out on various vessels until 1921.[181] Manuel Sylvia of Faial similarly stowed away on a whaling ship at age twelve to make the journey to Massachusetts in 1905.[182] Although most personal accounts such as these come from oral histories of those who entered the whaling industry in the early twentieth century, clandestine emigration via whaling labor likely peaked even earlier—around the 1850s and 1860s.

While most Americans had lost interest in the harsh discipline and long durations of whaling voyages, for these landless peasants, whaling work was a welcome escape from Portugal's declining island economies. The Azores was initially settled in the fifteenth century as a profitable wheat outpost to feed mainland Portugal, but the economy cooled in the face of competition from cheaper and more productive sources of wheat agriculture in the New World.[183] While a retreat toward self-sufficiency might have been warranted amid increasing food shortages and commercial decline, Portuguese policies forced the islands to channel two-thirds of Azorean grain to the mainland and its colonies throughout the eighteenth century.[184] Even when local authorities tried to restrict the export of agricultural products off the islands during periods of famine, merchants and landowners simply took advantage of the Azores's proliferation of small, hidden bays to chase larger profits through illicit trade.[185] The Azores was forced down a path of self-destructive dedication to market export rather than self-sufficiency.

For a time, the Industrial Revolution in Britain gave Azoreans a way to sustain their agricultural economy without relying on cereal crops. Growers produced oranges as a cheap export food for industrial workers.[186] By the 1850s, nearly 200,000 boxes of oranges were exported each year, constituting the cargo of about half the ships leaving the Azores's largest port.[187] The orange craze, however, only exacerbated the monopolization of the island's lands by a wealthy elite, leaving the archipelago dependent on global markets for its economic livelihood and a net importer of cereal and food crops.

The reverberations of the American Civil War sent the Azorean economy tumbling again. War in America meant closed-down factories in Britain, which soon meant empty ports in the Azores.[188] As one Azorean newspaper reported with a bit of dark humor in 1862, "The news coming through Lisbon from England is a little terrifying, in respect to the profits obtained from sales of our orange," causing a "scarcity of almost everything" except "poetry," which could be found at a "negligible price . . . perhaps due to its poor quality."[189] A series of poor harvests, storms that interrupted travel and hurt crop yields, and a fatal orange blight that hit the island of São Miguel in 1877 only exacerbated the island's economic woes.[190] Hunger, riots, and misery followed.[191]

Portugal, for its part, seemed determined to maintain the Azores as a point of resource extraction for supplying the rest of the empire. Azoreans fumed to no avail over Lisbon's lack of concern in promoting Azorean economic growth.[192] A particular bone of contention was the high tariffs and alcohol production prohibitions that appeared designed only to lock the Azores in pseudo-colonial servitude.[193] Low-quality poetry indeed reflected the hopelessness that came to blanket the islands. In the Azorean "popular" almanacs of the late nineteenth century, uplifting selections of local poetry such as "Misery" ("Defeated children, homeless . . . / Room without light, table without wheat/ Who knocks at my door?—The snow!") and "Abandoned" ("Without bread and without shelter! Bewildered! / Through the streets, walking pensively . . .") were packaged alongside informative investigations into the spreading scourge of suicide.[194]

Due to the prevailing land tenancy regime, landless farmers were hit particularly hard by the crises of the mid-nineteenth century. By 1840, the islands' lands were controlled by a tiny minority—less than 3 percent—of the population.[195] As a result, farmland was largely distributed via the system of "arrendamento," a vicious regime of rural land tenancy in which poor farmers had to rent land, cattle, and equipment from local elites.[196] Unlike sharecropping systems, in which risk is shared between owner and cropper, the cash tenancy system inherent in "arrendamento" foisted almost all risk on to the farmer. To take one example, an 1862 income tax assessment of the areas around Lagoa, São Miguel, revealed how local farmers were systemically exploited by the paired forces of economic crisis and "arrendamento." On hundreds of slips of paper, the state assiduously recorded the crops planted, their yields, and the rent paid by each farmer, painting a somewhat disturbing picture. J. Carreiro grew 100 alqueires (alq.), roughly 7–20 acres, of wheat, taking in 27,000 réis on property he rented from Luis Rebello for 30,000 réis.[197] Another of Rebello's tenants grew 40 alq. (3–8 acres) of beans, earning 7,600 réis—not nearly enough to cover the 10,000 in rent owed. Another grew 20 alq. of beans, earning 3,800 réis, but paying 4,000 in rent.[198] Over and over, the Lagoan tax assessment showed elite farmers, possessing extensive holdings, offering lands to tenants that did not produce nearly enough to make rent. After all, for landowners, the story was quite different. J. Michael de Medeiros Borges grew 80 alq. of corn, 80 alq. of fava beans, and 150 alq. of oranges, taking in 313,200 réis, while he rented out no less than fifteen other properties, whose rents were, on average, about 30 percent more costly than the incomes they produced.[199] Amid the darkest days of the American Civil War's disruptions to trade, agriculture was effectively bankrupting landless Azorean farmers.

Unlike French Canada, the Azores's problem was not that its soils were poor or that it suffered from adverse climate conditions. On the contrary, most observers fawned over the lushness of the island's fields and the richness of its soils.[200] The problem was that the islands' sizable class of landless farmers was being squeezed on one side by the strictures of Portuguese imperialism and the vicious iniquities of "arrendamento," while being squeezed on the other by the bitter capriciousness of the international export trade. As one local writer noted in the early twentieth century, "little by little," this "blissful and blessed island ... famed for richness (but only for one or two dozen men)" was being "converted into a land of hunger and misery, due to unbridled greed."[201]

As a result, much like the French Canadians, most Azorean migrant men came to Massachusetts with an abiding faith that they were simply sojourning to the United States to gain the capital necessary to return to the Azores and establish their own landed independence. Although return migration statistics were not recorded until 1908, the financial impact returnees had on the Azorean economy certainly testifies to their importance long before that date. As early as 1871, military captain Francisco José da Silva Jr. declared in "The Emancipation of the Azores" that the "enrichment of the island ... is mainly due to its fabulous export, both regular and clandestine, of men for North America aboard American ships ... and the not insubstantial reimportation of the fortunate ones, who at the end of many years of exile, return to the fatherland, bringing [savings], that will successively enrich [the island]."[202] Similarly, one Portuguese newspaper article from the 1890s invidiously compared those emigrants returning from Brazil ("utterly devoid of good instincts ... the embodiment of laziness") to the returning "Americano": "a man strengthened in frame ... his modest capital ... consecrated to the honest transactions of industry and commerce."[203]

Not surprisingly, then, emigrants left the Azores "with big dreams of returning rich," as one daughter characterized her emigrating father's mindset.[204] From 1908 to 1910, while 19,072 Portuguese entered the United States, 3,163 left for home (of which 72 percent had been in the United States for less than five years), adding up to a 6 to 1 return ratio. Overall, the period from 1911 to 1921 would see nearly 30,000 Portuguese return to their homeland.[205]

A number of forces thus restrained any mass movement of Portuguese workers into the Massachusetts textile industry. Portugal's restrictive emigration laws ensured that whaling represented one of the only avenues available for the average male farmer to even venture to the United States, tying Portuguese emigration rates to the health of the failing industry. Since workers' sights were set on eventually returning home, these Azorean migrants initially had little interest in establishing themselves outside the movement of whaling ships.

Consequently, to the extent the Portuguese are mentioned in conjunction with the Massachusetts textile industry in the nineteenth century, they are either referenced for providing an initial labor supply at the dawn of textile industrialization or for simply holding down wages as a result of the fact that they "can do only the poorest work," and thus "naturally get the poorest wages," as described by one 1895 state report on unemployment.[206] Even into the twentieth century, one English worker would complain that "these Portagee workers . . . don't know what a union means. We couldn't get them to pay dues to the union after the strike is over unless we used guns."[207] As Fall River's John Golden, president of the United Textile Workers of America, put it in 1909, the inevitable effect of bringing in workers from "parts of Europe and the Western Islands [Azores]" was to "[keep] down the standard of the whole industry so far as wages, hours of labor, and working conditions are concerned," especially since Portuguese workers "have not taken, nor can they be expected to take, any active part in the . . . agitation of the older employees for shorter hours and better wages."[208] Although their inability to be quickly imported to break strikes ensured that Portuguese workers were never treated quite as venomously as their French counterparts, they were generally portrayed as poor unionists with little understanding of the possibilities of labor activism.

Once these first whaling workers established a masthead in Massachusetts, it set the stage for future Azorean migrants of a very different sort. As the social connections between Massachusetts and the islands deepened—as kin connections overspread the Atlantic Ocean, as economic and social news from Fall River and New Bedford became ordinary features in Azorean newspapers, and as numerous steamship companies began offering regular transatlantic services between the islands and Southeastern Massachusetts—emigration grew increasingly attractive and much less risky.[209]

As it turned out, Portugal's conscription-focused emigration laws had little effect on one segment of Azorean society. By the last two decades of the nineteenth century and into the early twentieth century, women made up an increasing share of Portugal's emigrants.[210] In 1886, for instance, of the 4,791 emigrants who left Portugal's islands, about half were women. Moreover, these were not simply wives venturing out to join husbands; 60 percent of these women migrants were single.[211] Extant administrative records from the processing of emigrants in remote rural hamlets paint an even starker image. Emigration records from the town of Povoação, São Miguel, taken in 1917, record 70 percent of its emigrants as women (and about half of those as single women).[212] In fact, the most common emigrant grouping leaving Povoação was not entire families, but groups of young women (especially sisters).[213] For instance, Maria (age eighteen) and Rosalina Cabral (age seventeen) left Lomba do Loução on January 20, 1917; it was probably not a coincidence that Emilia de Lousa (age eighteen) and Maria Jacinto da Camara (age fourteen), from the same tiny village, happened to depart the same day.[214] Like their French Canadian counterparts, these increasing numbers of female emigrants to Massachusetts had little interest in returning to the Azores, thanks in no small part to the repressive, patriarchal culture that prevailed there.[215] For every three men who returned to the Azores from 1908 to 1919, only one woman went back.[216]

All told, nearly 250,000 Portuguese arrived in the United States between 1880 and 1929.[217] Although women were by no means a majority of those who migrated, compared to other ethnic groups, their numbers were impressive. From 1899 to 1910, 41 percent of Portuguese immigrants were women, in contrast to only 5 percent of Greek immigrants or 21 percent of Italian immigrants in the same period.[218] In 1924, a full 68 percent of incoming Portuguese were women.[219] Portuguese women also tended to engage in much higher rates of labor participation than other ethnic groups. In 1920, a Portuguese immigrant woman was twice as likely as her Italian peer to work.[220]

Portuguese workers—especially women—eventually came to dominate South Coast textile workforces. With their sights set on making their permanent home in Massachusetts, these Portuguese women would begin to play a major role in shaping the politics of textile production and the coming garment trade.

———

By the start of the twentieth century, South Coast mills looked very different from the Lowell mills of the early nineteenth century. An investigation by the Massachusetts labor bureau in 1912 revealed that native-born workers were a distinct minority: only 35 percent of Fall River's workforce and only 26 percent of New Bedford's (and, most likely, a significant number of these "native born" workers were themselves the children of immigrants). A substantial number of these workers were women: about half of Fall River's foreign workers, and about 60 percent of New Bedford's. Almost equal numbers of French Canadian, Portuguese, and British laborers worked side by side on the shop floor.[221] Nevertheless, cooperation remained hard to come by, and ethnic conflicts were legion.

Such tensions had deep roots in the cultures and ideologies of these various groups, but they were by no means inevitable. In fact, they emerged from the conditions of their very migration to Massachusetts, especially the ways in which their sending states and institutions shaped how and why these migrants ventured to the South Coast in the first place. British immigrants, often conveyed by their powerful and tightly organized home unions, arrived with a strong commitment to reshaping the politics of industrial Massachusetts. French Canadians, under the sway of the persistent pleas (and incentives) of various Canadian authorities urging them to remain in Canada—and repatriate quickly if they had already made the mistake of leaving—had much less investment in shaping the political economy of textile industrialization. Portuguese men, with most emigration options foreclosed to them by the Portuguese restriction regime, had no choice but to use whaling ships to make their way to and from Massachusetts. Factory work for them became but a mere stopgap means of subsistence between voyages (and the hope of a potential journey home). Their willingness to work for the "poorest" wages and do the "poorest" work was in part a reflection of this social reality.

Changing conditions abroad were equally responsible for the increasing interest in trade unionism and collective action immigrants began to display in the early twentieth century. As the Canadian government, frustrated by the fleeting successes of its repatriation programs, largely gave up on the effort, French Canadians began organizing a more robust union presence in Massachusetts's mills. Similarly, as Portugal began sending more and more women migrants—women who had much less interest in returning to the repressive and hardscrabble role of farming wife—a generation of vocal female Portuguese laborers would make their presence known in Massachusetts.

PART II

*From Cloth to Clothes,
from Crisis to Prosperity*

4

Un-Making Industrial Massachusetts

LABOR AND CAPITAL IN AN AGE OF DEINDUSTRIALIZATION

BY THE LAST two decades of the nineteenth century, the South Coast was the center of the American textile industry, a position it would hold for nearly half a century. English workers, at the helm of powerful, tightly organized craft unions, exercised immense influence over Massachusetts's state and shop floor politics. When the state labor bureau canvassed workers and manufacturers in preparation for its 1882 report on Fall River's "constant turmoil," few probably realized that both the city's textile interests and its unions were in a short-lived peak of influence and power.

The days of textile prosperity and craft union hegemony were numbered. After a wave of factory closures and liquidations devastated the local cotton industry in the 1920s and 1930s, Northeastern University conducted a similar study of the (now former) textile workers of the South Coast. Its results made for a stark contrast to what the state labor bureau had found in the 1880s.

Working-class expressions of radicalism had transformed into cautious conservatism and a bitter disillusionment with the union establishment. As one fifty-eight-year-old Fall River worker told the university's researchers, "Textiles have been very bad lately. There are no jobs here with any security. Unions have forced the mills out with their demands." Another worker lamented the loss of their former mill in similar terms. It "was a grand company to work for. . . . Don't think we'll ever have a nice concern like that to work for again. . . . Surely was a sorry day for us when they moved out of town." As one thirty-eight-year old worker summed up the situation, "The union became too powerful" and "the workers got away with murder." Over and over again, unions took the blame for deindustrialization. Pushy union leaders and their reckless demands had apparently conspired to send the Massachusetts textile industry packing for the more favorable climate of the American South.[1]

This is not the standard interpretation of industrial decline, which tends to shift the blame away from workers. Some have decried cloth manufacturers' insatiable thirst for profit at the expense of overproduction and market saturation; others have underscored workers' (generally unsuccessful) attempts to preserve local industry; others have highlighted the larger, structural changes in the national and global economy that incentivized the flow of capital to locales with lower wages, lower taxes, and less regulation.[2] Northern workers are usually portrayed as more hapless victims than progenitors of northern textile collapse.

Neither extreme tells the whole story. While it is certainly not the case that unions undermined northeastern textile production with their out-of-control demands, absolving them of all blame diminishes the militancy of those workers who asserted their rights in the face of potential factory closures, knowing full well the risks they ran. It also downplays how detestable workers found factory labor; it assumes that no rational actor would have chosen "no job" over "terrible job." But workers, like capitalists, were not simple, money-maximizing automatons. Equally concerned over intangible prerogatives—dignity, fairness, and respectability, in particular—they rarely operated in such a cold and calculating way. Workers, especially those in the highest echelons of the labor hierarchy, almost certainly made deliberate decisions that helped to enable industrial decline.

Business leaders did not possess unlimited power and leverage in this moment either. While a certain class of elite textile mill operators undoubtedly realized that they could readily liquidate their mills or move South, disincentivizing them from tackling thorny problems like market saturation or outdated technology, these business leaders represented a distinct minority. A much larger group of business operators—including both smaller millowners and local utility, retail, and merchant capitalists who were far more fixed to the local community—remained dedicated to Massachusetts manufacturing. In their own eyes, they were being squeezed in the vise of elite mill operators' intransigence, the vocal demands of their workers, and the growing threat of southern textile production. These middling business operators often seem much more like stereotypical hapless victims than the assertive, organized textile workers who dominated the labor movement in industrial Massachusetts. Workers and business owners were not homogenous groups; the divisions between them helped enable this era of industrial cataclysm.

Life on the Mill Floor

It might be hard to believe that activist workers really understood the existential threat that capital mobility posed. After all, why would they continue to go on strike and continue to press their demands if they knew their jobs—as well as the jobs of almost everyone in their communities—were at stake? Answering this question requires understanding how these workers experienced daily life on the factory floor. Working long hours in dangerous mills for unsteady pay with capricious employment terms, it is perhaps not quite so surprising that textile workers were willing to challenge their employers in the name of gaining something better.

For any young worker entering the mill, it would become instantly clear that "textile work" did not mean any one thing. Jobs came in a swirling variety of hierarchically (and ethnically) divided forms, pays, and duties.[3] An incoming French Canadian worker in the 1890s, for instance, would likely have been slotted into one of many unskilled or semi-skilled positions, such as warper, drawing tender, stripper, scrubber, or ring spinner, all of which varied in pay.[4] In this era, warpers took home around $7.09 weekly, strippers $6.54, and ring spinners $5.05.[5] Portuguese workers often found themselves slotted a bit lower: doffing, assisting spinners, or working as "picker hands"—the lowest paid adult male job in a textile mill. Picker hands earned about $5 a week, constantly moving "laps" (flattened rolls) of cotton, each weighing anywhere from thirty-five to seventy-five pounds, between machines.[6]

Picker hands were not at the bottom of the mill hierarchy. Below them were children, who were left with dangerous and low-paid work as back boys and other machine assistants.[7] William Isherwood, whose parents emigrated from England in 1910, began work in New Bedford at fourteen as a "wireboy," stringing stop-motion wires into weaving machines. Paid by each thousand wires he strung, Isherwood earned only $4.39 for his first week of labor.[8]

Even such small sums of money became a crucial part of overall subsistence for many textile families, as confirmed by an 1875 survey conducted by the Massachusetts Bureau of Statistics of Labor. One English family of seven, whose unskilled father earned only $395 annually, had its income supplemented by a twelve-year-old daughter who earned $184.75. The family, not surprisingly, lived in an "out of repair" tenement of five rooms, "situated in the worst part of the city. . . . The drainage from the sink is choked up, causing a stench which is almost unbearable in wet weather." They were in debt, and the only sliver of potential salvation was that "another one of the children will be able to work this summer, so the family is in hopes of doing better."[9] This was not uncommon. Among French Canadian families in early twentieth-century textile mills, children's wages made up around one-third of the average family income; for Portuguese families, it was 22 percent; for the Irish, it was almost half.[10] As early as 1867, only 60 percent of Fall River youth aged five to fifteen were enrolled in any type of schooling.[11] The rest were already in the mills.

Even as new legislation clamped down on the age children had to be to enter mill work, such laws were easily evaded by French Canadian and Portuguese families, who could simply doctor or misrepresent birth documents written in foreign languages.[12] French Canadian Joseph Maltais began work in Fall River's mills at age ten, earning $8 a month by using his father's school card to circumvent Massachusetts's 1866 law requiring children ages ten to fourteen to "attend at least 6 months of school each year."[13] Despite the fact that Maltais's school card did not actually match his name, his boss was unfazed, simply instructing him that "when you see somebody come in . . . he dressed up nice . . . don't let him see you . . . get under the frame and watch the feet . . . when they are across on this side, you cross on the other side."[14] Even for those who followed the letter of the law, extant oral histories reveal that for the area's working-class youth, there was every expectation that at age fourteen, school would end and life in the mill would begin.[15]

At the other end of the labor hierarchy, English-dominated crafts like mule spinning and loom fixing offered much more money and far less danger. Mule spinning was not necessarily an easy job. The average spinner traveled thirty miles a day walking back and forth in place, endlessly pushing the 1,400–1,800-pound mule carriages five feet in and out, over and over again, some 4,400 times a day.[16] But mule spinners had one of the best organized unions and, at nearly $18 a week in the 1870s, some of the highest rates of pay.[17] Joining mule spinners at the top of the labor hierarchy was each factory's small number of loom fixers, who earned up to $14 a week—nearly double the wages of picker hands—and had an equally powerful union behind them that aggressively policed workplace abuses such as unauthorized overtime, arbitrary promotions, and unwarranted job terminations.[18]

While loom fixers may not have earned as much as the spinners, there were other, less tangible reasons workers coveted loom-fixing positions. As one Portuguese operative made clear in describing his own journey from lunch carrier to loom fixer over the course of the 1920s, what made the job so attractive was hardly just its material rewards: "All they did was sit down go to sleep and wait for a thread to break. And all the mothers were trying to marry their daughters off to a loom fixer because it was the highest paying job in the

weavers['] room."[19] It is perhaps not surprising that loom fixers made attractive husbands; unlike doffers or picker hands, they earned enough to generally keep their children out of the textile mill. From lifting heavy cotton rolls
or crawling under dangerous machinery to sleeping on the job and waiting
around for threads to break, there was much more than one "textile operative"
experience in Massachusetts's mills.

Decent wages did not necessarily ensure a life of ease, of course. The capriciousness of the cloth market, in particular, affected the highly paid and
poorly paid alike. Textile work was beset by constant production interruptions
and concomitant bouts of joblessness. As mule spinner Thomas O'Donnell
testified at a congressional inquiry in 1883, although his earnings of $1.50 a
day (with only $6 due in rent each month) should have made for a decent
living, the problem was that "since that strike we had down in Fall River about
three years ago I have not worked much more than half the time, and that
has brought my circumstances down very much." O'Donnell estimated that
he had made $133 over the course of the year—meaning he was unemployed
two-thirds of the time.[20]

Although O'Donnell's case was likely somewhat extreme, extant production records from area mills reveal that his story was by no means entirely unique. In the decade spanning 1885 to 1894, for instance, Fall River's
Metacomet Mill was open a full schedule of 311 days only one year. It averaged
285 annual operational days over the course of the decade, and some years it
ran as few as 245.5 days, entailing nearly three months of lost wages for its
operatives.[21]

Other unpredictable events, such as sudden curtailments, strikes, or fires
could similarly kick workers off shop floors and onto city streets. A fire at
Fall River's American Print Works in 1867 left 500 workers unemployed; an
1874 fire at the Granite Mill left 400 workers idle; another thirty operatives
(mostly children) jumped to their deaths trying to escape the flames; an 1876
fire at the American Linen Mill left 1,100 unemployed; and an 1877 fire at the
Border City Mill left 450 jobless.[22]

Even amid normal conditions, textile work was extremely dangerous, especially for the young children whose small stature often relegated them to
jobs crawling in and around machinery.[23] Stories of industrial accidents in the
mills were a constant feature of local newspapers. There was eight-year-old
Katie Lyon of Fall River, who, despite having "just been beaten for careless-
ness," got her dress caught in the gears of the Linen Mill's mule room, drawing
her arm in: "the flesh was stripped from her arm in some places to the bone,
and many of the arteries and sinews were severed."[24] Emmanuel Taylor of the

Azores got his arm similarly broken and skinned only ten days into his first job in 1873.[25] Annie McNeal, a fifteen-year-old doffer, got her hair wound into a speeder machine in 1879, and found "her hair and portions of her scalp . . . [wound] around the machine. . . . A piece of the skull two inches long . . . was also missing and the brain was laid bare though uninjured."[26] A tired, young French Canadian operative, Regis Verzina, walked into an empty elevator shaft and fell forty-five feet to his death one early morning in 1880.[27] Portuguese immigrant Joseph Pacheco, only four months into his American sojourn, was killed in 1903 after his clothing got caught in a machine: it was almost instantaneously stripped from his body and wrapped around his neck.[28] The list of such incidents goes on and on.

FIGURE 4.1 Lewis Hine, "General view of the spinning room, Cornell Mill [Fall River], showing some of the young boys and girls employed there." January 1912. Courtesy of the National Child Labor Committee Collection, Library of Congress, Prints and Photographs Division, LC-DIG-nclc-02494.

Beyond freak accidents, layoffs, and catastrophic conflagrations, everyday life in the mills left much to be desired. Working hours were long. Fall River's earliest mills often kept their workers at their machines from 4:00 A.M. to 7:30 P.M. each day.[29] After a fourteen-year-old girl died of what a local physician diagnosed as "overwork," Fall River millowners voluntarily agreed to reduce summer working hours to 5:00 A.M. to 7:00 P.M. Although hours had been again reduced by the 1840s, they still ranged around twelve hours daily.[30] By 1874, workers' strenuous political efforts resulted in a sixty-hour law for women and minors, with 10½-hour weekdays and 7½-hour Saturdays becoming the standard schedule in area mills until the passage of fifty-eight-hour legislation in 1892.[31] Much to workers' chagrin, however, manufacturers often responded to legal cuts in maximum workdays by simply speeding up machines or increasing the number of machines workers had to tend.[32] Whereas weavers had once been expected to run two looms for over twelve hours each day in the early nineteenth century, by the 1880s, although operatives were working two hours less, they were tending four times as many machines.[33] Paired with the hot and humid conditions in the mills—around 86 degrees Fahrenheit, summer and winter—working conditions were certainly less than ideal.[34]

Housing conditions were not much better. The working-class tenement districts of Fall River and New Bedford were often hastily constructed, tightly packed, and lacked basic amenities such as sufficient plumbing and drainage.[35] One Fall River journalist took readers on a vivid tour of the city's filthy living conditions in 1867, inviting his audience to "take a short walk . . . through certain portions of our city." "We would suggest, however, that gentlemen whose stomachs are weak and nasal organs moderately acute, take the precaution to burden their pockets with a few bottles of volatile salts. . . . Pig-pens, cesspools, privies, stagnant pools, puddles of slops, dish-water, and a thousand other things, all productive of the most sickening stenches, are scattered around in profusion." In particular, the "filthy, green, stagnant puddles" and the "army of rats" of 6½ Street were marked as some of the worst in the city, though this journalist was quick to admit that "seventh street is only an improvement as far as [the] puddles in the street and the size and tameness of the rats are concerned."[36]

Company-built housing was singled out as some of the worst in the city. One investigation of the tenements of the Borden Mills described "operatives [living] in bedrooms and kitchens," with as many as ten people packed into each apartment. In the yards, where both water spigot and water closet stood side by side, "the air is pestilential and the place revolting to every sense." Perhaps most egregious was the discovery of one company-owned bedroom with three cots for fifteen men and children, one of whom was a young boy dying of typhoid fever.[37] Tenements, often overcrowded with impoverished French Canadian and Portuguese immigrants, defined the South Coast landscape.[38]

It is perhaps not surprising, then, that Fall River and New Bedford became viewed as almost uniquely wretched industrial cities by observers locally and beyond. In fact, one of the most surprising findings of the Massachusetts labor bureau's 1882 investigation was that Lowell's workers were not only in better circumstances, but they were also manifestly aware of their superior status. Whereas "the agents in Fall River . . . found much misery, rarely meeting with happy, contented people," in Lowell, the workers they interviewed proudly defined themselves as, in the words of one laborer, "the best paid and the best treated class of help in Massachusetts . . . a better class of operatives than you will find in Fall River."[39] As one Fall River millowner summed up his city to the Bureau's investigator, "Fall River is a large manufacturing city, and the central stopping-place for operatives from the other side. . . . We manufacture cheap goods, and have cheap help to make them."[40] In 1898, one journalist even went so far as to bring ex-slave Joseph Copeland to New Bedford to compare his former enslaved condition to the city's textile operatives. "I never liked being a slave, and would not like to be one again" he apparently told reporters after touring the city, "but if I had to take my choice between being a slave again and living like those people I have just seen in New Bedford[,] I would prefer being a slave again for sure."[41]

Objectively, such comparisons must be taken with an enormous grain of salt. But subjectively, they help explain the growing consensus among New Bedford and Fall River textile workers that they had little to lose in labor activism. As the leader of the New Bedford weavers said in the midst of an 1898 strike, "The weavers in this city are the worst paid mill help in the United States. . . . They are desperate, I can assure you." Having decided it was "a question of starvation anyway," their decision to strike was partly motivated by the conviction that they "might as well starve in idleness."[42] This sense of desperation was equally reflected in the reminiscences of one leader of the New Bedford strike of 1928, recorded some fifty years after the strike concluded: "I don't think you could get a group of workers to go through with what they did today, to go on strike for six months. . . . They have something to lose now, no matter what their status is. In those days, they had nothing to lose."[43]

An understanding of working-class politics in this era must begin with this sense of desperation and collective suffering. Although it might be easy to imagine confident and assertive unions standing up for the virtues and prerogatives of "manliness" and "skill"—as is often claimed—this was the reality for only a fraction of the highest paid and best organized workers. For the vast majority, unionization, strikes, and labor activism were much more reactive responses, prompted by sudden wage cuts and stoked by the daily sense of desperation that came from the precariousness and the drudgeries of lives spent on the textile mill floor. This explains two of the most surprising aspects of early twentieth century labor activism on the Massachusetts South Coast: workers' generally half-hearted and erratic organizational work was also paired with occasional bursts of bold and radical direct activism.

Labor in a Deindustrial Era

The specter of textile deindustrialization cast its shadow over almost all facets of early twentieth-century South Coast labor activism. These cities' laborers were always and everywhere acutely aware of the competition they faced from their southern brethren. As early as 1873, Robert Howard, the leader of the Fall River spinners, had begun correspondence with "all the new mills being built in Georgia and Alabama," discovering that spinners' wages in "those Southern states were only about $1.25 a day."[44] Operatives were also kept abreast of southern working conditions by those who traveled north in search of higher wages. One group of workers who migrated to Fall River in 1900 told a local newspaper that although "work in the South was easier than it is here," the pay was lower and "the hours range all the way from 66 to 72 a week."[45] There was, simply put, no way of ignoring the growing southern textile industry.

More to the point, manufacturers used the southern threat as a bargaining chip in almost every early twentieth-century labor conflict. Amid hearings on whether to limit women's and children's hours to eight hours daily in 1901, for example, a member of the Arkwright Club—a political organization for New England's textile interests—suggested that it was just this sort of legislation that explained "the fact that during the last two years there were only three mills built in Massachusetts, while in the state of South Carolina 43 mills were built."[46] Fred Waterman, treasurer of Fall River's Cornell Mills, was even more blunt in his assessment, predicting that, in light of growing southern competition, "grass will be growing on the streets of Fall River in ten years."[47] "Northern spinners," a New Bedford newspaper reported in 1903, were already "convinced that southern competition is something more than a mere bugaboo."[48]

In fact, workers were remarkably attuned to the fluctuations of the cotton and textile markets. "They have as good a knowledge of the markets as anyone," one Fall River reporter commented on the city's workers in 1875. "They know the sources of supply and the costs of the materials, transportation and working machinery, and of course . . . the average profits."[49] "Talk with a mill agent for five minutes and he will paralyze you with an array of figures he presents to show you that the mills are almost bankrupting themselves by paying 19 cents a cut for weaving," another reporter noted in 1889. By the same token, one could "give a weaver a piece of paper and a pencil, and in a twinkle he will have it covered with figures, which he claims will convince any sane man that the mills are making nearly a cent a yard profit on cloth and one-third their capital stock in a year."[50] As the secretary of the local slasher tenders' union justified his own position in 1901, "The secretaries watch the markets," keeping up on the dividends and quarterly statements of the mills, and are thus "always willing to argue their claims and if they make a claim they are always willing to submit to arbitration."[51] Just as this sort of market savvy defined textile operatives' experiences as labor migrants, it similarly structured their activism as workers and unionists.[52]

Moreover, rather than looking to extricate themselves from the hegemony of market forces—like so many other late nineteenth and early twentieth century unions—Massachusetts textile unionists often argued that fair wages were those that simply reflected the overall health of the industry.[53] As a result, workers could be surprisingly quiescent if they believed a poor market truly warranted wage cutting. As one textile worker explained to the Massachusetts labor bureau in 1882, "The market is very low now, and the profits are small, so, happily, the help are contented." But he made sure to add in a crucial corollary: "We [also] think, and I think rightly, that when the profits are large we ought to share in them."[54] Another Fall River operative agreed: "Whenever the market is dull, and the mill is not making money, the operatives have to be reduced, and, as a rule, they swallow the fact, and accept the situation."[55] Curiously, these workers largely accepted the supremacy of market forces.

This was not mere rhetoric. In 1897, Fall River unionists, after a series of citywide negotiations, agreed to a 10 percent wage cut in order to maintain the mills' competitiveness.[56] When another 10 percent cut was announced in 1903, Fall River's unions—aware of the meager market, cotton's high price, and the mills' cloth stockpiles—simply accepted the cut under protest.[57] Strikes were sometimes formally "deferred," waiting for precise market benchmarks. In 1881, a planned strike was delayed until the price of print cloth returned to 4½ cents a yard.[58]

In fact, unions increasingly began fighting to enforce precise mathematical wage determinations that depended directly on the health of the textile market, as measured by the price of cotton subtracted from the selling price of cloth. It was this very formula that was codified as the ruling wage agreement between mule spinners and the mills of New Bedford, Fall River, and Lawrence in 1886.[59] With regularly negotiated revisions, it would continue to structure spinners' wages until the First World War.[60] Fall River weavers established a similar, though shorter-lived "sliding scale" wage agreement in the wake of a 1904 strike.[61] Unions effectively fought to pin their own economic futures on the very same market forces that both sustained and endangered local mills.

Motivated by this "just wage" market ideology, some unionists even began to argue that the role of unions was to restrain strikes in deference to prevailing sliding scale agreements. As labor leader Robert Howard boasted in 1875, "I have been congratulated a good deal within the last three years for keeping the men quiet and getting little grievances rectified without trouble."[62] For James Tansey of the Fall River carders, "unions are beneficial" precisely "because they prevent 'impulsive strikes.' "[63] In other words, these union leaders little resembled their eventual caricatures as aggressive and uncompromising stalwarts. They sought a relationship of relative harmony between worker and millowner, leaving wages to simply fluctuate alongside the health of the market, vitiating any need for either strikes or sudden cuts.[64]

This is what essentially played out in 1906 when Fall River's workers—responding to reports that three local mills declared dividends of 50 to 75 percent—asked for wages to be restored to their 1903 levels.[65] The mills countered with a 5 percent advance, a deal the workers rejected. The full wage increase was eventually granted, along with another 10 percent increase in 1907.[66]

Although this "just wage" ideology sometimes pushed workers to accept cuts in light of a floundering textile market, it was by no means inherently conservative. After all, if workers felt that manufacturers were violating their end of the bargain, this desire for the "just wage" could also come to animate massive labor protest. One of the first textile strikes in New Bedford—an 1877 strike of 1,500 workers at the Wamsutta Mill—was prompted by workers' sense of "astonishment" at a 7 to 10 percent wage cut that seemed incongruous with "the improved state of the market."[67] The New Bedford strikes of 1898 and 1928 were similarly catalyzed by a sense that announced wage cuts did not reflect market conditions.[68] Motivated by their abiding faith in the market itself, workers were quick to launch strikes if convinced that manufacturers were trying to solve problems of overproduction by cutting wages rather than curtailing production in order to adjust to new market realities. At a time when many American workers were rejecting the sway of market forces in their lives, Massachusetts workers actually saw the market as a neutral arbiter of economic justice.

These mill workers would even sometimes launch work stoppages in the name of restoring market "equilibrium." Indeed, this faith in market supremacy ultimately inspired one of the most unique labor actions in these textile workers' protest repertoire: the so-called vacation. In contrast to strikes—rooted as they were in class antagonism and the desire for concessions—vacations were walkouts that came with no explicit moral critique or oppositional claim: they were merely a means to forcibly halt production and help equalize the market. Fall River's "Great Vacation" of 1875, for instance, involving 15,000 workers and entailing a nearly mile-a-minute total production loss, was launched explicitly on the premise that a production curtailment would end the textile supply glut and raise wages.[69] Workers were not waiting on any particular act of compromise from manufacturers. They simply decided to withhold their labor (and thereby halt production) for four weeks (hence the "vacation" moniker).[70] Another, similar vacation was launched in 1894.[71] To the extent there was any critique of millowners in these sorts of protests, it was in their inability to band together for their own rational self-protection. In the words of an 1877 Fall River letter to the editor, "The cotton manufacturers are not an entirely reliable source of support, from the very evident fact that the business in that line is overdone already; and still the cry comes 'more mills.' "[72] Workers thus used the vacation to take production management into their own hands and force the mills into behaving like "rational" market actors.

Contrary to later popular opinion, the southern migration of textile production was not a result of overactive northern labor unions or a never-ending cavalcade of working-class demands. In fact, motivated by their "just wage" ideology, workers sought to pin their own economic futures to the very same forces that endangered and sustained local mills, using their unions, more often than not, as a bulwark against wildcat activism.

But there was certainly one way in which some South Coast workers' strategies, especially among union leaders, did help catalyze southbound capital mobility: namely, their refusal to extend organizing efforts across the lines of geography and craft. These failures became lessons future generations of workers would not soon forget.

Like millowners, workers rarely provided a united front on any issue, thanks to both craft and ethnic segregation. Weavers, card room workers, spinners, and loom fixers all had their own exclusive unions throughout the late nineteenth and early twentieth centuries. New Bedford's first textile strike at the Wamsutta Mill—engaged on behalf of gaining the ten-hour day—ground to a halt when skilled union leaders accepted a compromise deal obtaining their demands at the expense of a pay cut to the mill's unskilled workers (a cut that had no effect on those involved in the negotiations).[73] Such craft exclusivity was only compounded by the inter-ethnic animosity that often defined local labor politics. In 1884, when the Knights of Labor attempted to organize an amalgamation of all local textile operatives, it only took two years for the union to fragment into spinners, weavers, card room employees, and a separate French ethnic union.[74]

This unyielding refusal to incorporate both women and new immigrants into the labor movement became a recurrent feature of Massachusetts's most skilled and well-organized textile unions.[75] Even unions like the Fall River "Yarn Finishers," which organized a majority female workforce, were still firmly controlled by men, who ran the union and even called strikes on behalf of the "girls."[76] Local textile unions similarly made few efforts to organize unskilled immigrants. Years later, when Mary Alves, a former doffer at New Bedford's Whitman Mills, was asked whether she was a union member in the early twentieth century, her answer was quite telling: "No, there was no such thing. Only a few of the English people . . . belonged to the union."[77] Alves's take on the situation is not surprising. Despite its outsized influence on local labor politics, the Fall River mule spinners union numbered a mere 380 in 1908, making it just a tiny fraction of the city's overall textile workforce.[78] On the whole, the vast majority of Massachusetts textile workers remained unorganized.

Facing these headwinds, efforts to expand organization and amalgamate the textile crafts never made it far. In 1875, Fall River mule spinners refused to join a labor amalgamation proposed by the city's weavers because it would have meant co-organizing with female ring spinners.[79] Even successful labor combinations often remained ephemeral concoctions, prone to fragmentation. The Fall River weavers seceded from an 1894 amalgamation of the city's five main textile unions after the other workers refused to strike a 10 percent wage cut.[80] In turn, the striking weavers were incensed when Robert Howard, acting on behalf of the spinners, accepted a "compromise" 5 percent reduction for the spinners that stuck all other workers with the full 10 percent cut.[81] The spinners effectively sold out their fellow workers; the strike was doomed. Even the delegates to the eventual creation of the United Textile Workers in 1901 reported that "they never took part in a harder fight than this one" because, despite "a feeling on the part of all that the textile workers of this country should be united," nobody, especially the "national mule spinners and loom fixers," was willing to give up their own union.[82] Over and over again, skilled unions—with the fullest coffers and the most political sway—were loath to sacrifice their prestige and power by allying with (or incorporating) the unskilled, women, or immigrants.

Making matters worse, local craft exclusivity increasingly bled into regional insularity. South Coast textile unions developed a habit of abruptly trying to cobble together state and national union organizations when the economy soured, only to discard them when conditions improved, as they worried their own earnings would get siphoned away to support weaker organizations.[83] The example of the United Textile Workers (UTW) is particularly instructive. Amid the fallout of the national 1893 economic panic, Fall River and New Bedford weavers decided to form a "Massachusetts State Federation of Weavers" in 1895, which morphed into a regional organization, then banded together with the National Union of Textile Workers to form the UTW in 1901, carrying an explicit mandate to organize the American South.[84] But, amid the prosperity of the first decade of the twentieth century, local unionists began to chafe at the UTW's attempts to use their money to organize new unions elsewhere. In 1908, following on the heels of major across-the-board wage increases in 1906 and 1907, the UTW raised its levies on union dues, and both the New Bedford and Fall River weavers exited the organization. After the UTW moved its headquarters from Fall River to New York City in 1915, all remaining South Coast textile unions abandoned the confederation.[85] In other words, at the very moment these unionists could have been using their flush treasuries to strengthen and expand their organizations outward—especially in the South, where the threat of cheaper labor loomed so large—they were leaning ever more inward.

These union leaders were hardly without their critics. Fellow unionists back in England were perhaps the most damning in their analysis of the situation. As English weaver William Birtles told one New Bedford newspaper in 1898, the city's operatives were "a quarter of a century behind the times. . . . They used to get good wages which suited them, and I am afraid they did not pay that heed to the future which they ought to have done." He advised New Bedford unionists to create "a wide and extensive combination" in order to "approximate conditions of capital and labor" across space, vitiating the need for endless labor struggles that devolved into "a mere cutting of each other's throats."[86] English unionists had always taken a global approach to trying to shape the textile market to their advantage. It was baffling to them that so many American unions failed to follow suit.

Women were, not surprisingly, among the most critical of the union establishment's exclusivity and insularity. Following one 1875 wage cut months before the start of the Great Vacation, Fall River's weaving men assembled and voted—in light of the unfavorable business conditions—not to strike.[87] In response, Fall River's weaving women organized their own meeting, and, "being more spunky than the men," as one local observer described it, decided to call their own strike (the men, hoping not to lose face, sheepishly followed suit).[88] Moreover, the women explicitly dedicated their strike to, as one laborer put it, "[sinking] all national differences in the one great question of [our] preservation."[89] The women similarly concluded their successful strike by further offering a pledge to be "mindful of our brethren and sisters in other places who are struggling against the domination of capital" and to "put forth our united effort and purpose for the emancipation of downtrodden and oppressed labor."[90]

Precisely because of their outward radicalism, it was often the outspoken women of these cities who became the "leaders" of strikes in the public eye. As one Fall River operative confessed to the Massachusetts labor bureau, "strikes are rarely caused by the men: they dare not strike; but the women may strike, and the only result will be that they gain their point."[91] Lancashire widow, weaver, and self-described "Christian Socialist" Harriet Pickering became the inflammatory celebrity of New Bedford's 1898 strike.[92] Labor reformer Eva Valesh dubbed her New Bedford's "Joan of Arc."[93] Pickering fought hard to make sure the strike committee did not ignore issues of particular import to women (such as the fining system, which disproportionately impacted them) and pushed for "the thorough amalgamation of all trade unionism."[94] Similarly, in the 1928 strike, radical Portuguese women like Eula Mendes, Mary Valente, Maria Botelho, and Mary Costa would join communist organizers, pushing a larger campaign to create one big industrial union spanning the genders, races, and crafts, from New England to the United States South.[95]

Workers did not simply "get away with murder," pushing Massachusetts textile mills out with their excessive demands. In fact, labor activists sought, more often than not, to handcuff wages to the very same market forces that governed Massachusetts mills. Workers knew what was at stake in shop floor activism in the face of southern competition; in light of what life was like on the mill floor, the risk seemed worth it. But this does not mean workers were totally blameless. While some workers pitched broad organizing strategies that would have attempted to incorporate all workers together—North and South, skilled and unskilled—in the hope of undercutting the advantages of southern production, a powerful minority chose insularity, prestige, and local autonomy in the face of global capital mobility. This critical division would prove devastating.

Business in a Deindustrial Era

Workers obviously had their own variegated strategies for confronting the increasing threat of southern competition, but the South was, first and foremost, a threat to Massachusetts textile operators. While much scholarship has focused on either implicating or excusing workers from blame for textile deindustrialization—comparatively less has been written about why northern business owners were so thoroughly unable to measure up to the threat of southern competition.

Partly, this is a result of the enduring strength of the "deindustrialization" narrative itself. As economist Seymour Harris confidently put it in 1947, explicitly comparing New England's decline to the British precedent, "any region that depends heavily on manufacturing is almost certain to lose ground in the late stages of industrial development."[96] By this reading, "deindustrialization" was hardly a consequence of any human choice; it was simply an upshot of the inevitable dynamics of economic growth. And yet, many manufacturers did make choices that hastened industrial decline. They too were internally divided, racked by constant inter-competition, and left struggling to wrestle with emerging southern competitors. While some clamored for business readjustment, production cuts, and technological upgrades, most established textile producers became convinced that they were structurally incapable of overcoming southern competition. A growing sense of the inevitability of the relocation of textile production to the South became a self-fulfilling prophecy.

The fact that Massachusetts textile interests were so thoroughly divided may seem surprising given that one of the most outstanding facts of textile management in this era was its overwhelmingly incestuous nature. In what became denounced by reformers and workers alike as an "interlocking directorate," a mere seven Fall River families controlled the vast majority of the city's mills.[97] Similarly, the average late nineteenth-century New Bedford mill executive had interests in five different corporations, and about 60 percent had either been involved in whaling or had fathers who had.[98] When Col. Richard Borden of Fall River died in February of 1874, he was the president and director of the Fall River National Bank and served in some executive capacity in a local furnace company, two railroad corporations, a waterworks, a toolmaker, and seven textile mills.[99] His oldest son, Thomas, was equally ambitious. He served as manager and agent of the Bay State Print Works, treasurer of the Troy Mills, president and agent of the Mechanics Mills, chief organizer of the Richard Borden Mills, president of the American Printing Company, president of two local banks, and an executive for the same railroad, steamboat, and water corporations his father originally oversaw.[100] Most textile industrialists sported similar pedigrees.[101]

Economic oligarchy was reproduced across the generations through rampant intermarriage between elite families. Deviation from the norm was swiftly punished. For instance, after M. C. D. Borden discovered that his son Matthew secretly married a struggling actress while attending Yale University, he conspired to have a doctor convince Matthew that his poor health necessitated removal to the gentler climates of Europe.[102] With his son out of the country, Borden then paid Matthew's wife $15,000 to obtain an out-of-state divorce.[103] It was all for naught. Upon Matthew's return, the couple remarried, and Matthew instead found himself written out of his father's will.[104] Few sons or daughters followed the impertinent path blazed by the young Matthew Borden.

Nonetheless, the "interlocking" nature of textile management ultimately did little to diminish local competition. While the connections between textile families were legion in the city, textile management was essentially divided into two core groups, a "western" and an "eastern" alliance, roughly corresponding to the original landholdings that defined Fall River.[105] Moreover, Fall River and New Bedford millowners felt themselves constantly under siege from the Boston area's remaining textile interests—concretized by the formation of the Arkwright Club—as well as emerging textile concerns in New Hampshire, Rhode Island, Connecticut, and Maine.[106] More to the point, executives' very interconnection also made it easier to share notes on production returns and relative labor costs. This allowed them to directly compare how much each mill was able to extract from its workers, and enabled them to work even harder to cut costs and maximize production.[107] Incestuous management actually had the peculiar effect of exacerbating, not diminishing, competition.

Long before the threat of southern mills had crystallized, local mills ruthlessly competed with one another to minimize costs. In a system denounced by workers as the "grind," manufacturers developed strategies that would later define their response to increasing southern competition. As spinner Robert Howard reminded Congress in 1875, "the keen grind of competition . . . is going on against each other by the manufacturers. . . . It is not a competition against the foreigner at all; it is manufacturer against manufacturer, each trying to undersell the other, that is creating the trouble."[108] The reason workers felt the pull of the "grind" most acutely was because, as New Bedford textile capitalist Andrew G. Pierce pointed out in 1901, labor was basically the only cost "mills have any control over."[109]

Pierce was not being entirely hyperbolic. Balance sheets from one of his own mills, the Pierce Manufacturing Company, show that wage payments typically made up around 40 to 50 percent of total costs.[110] Not surprisingly, then, millowners first sought to reduce this part of their expenses whenever their other, immutable costs increased. For instance, as Pierce faced a twelvefold increase in the price of cotton between 1895 and 1908, mill wage payments were squeezed downward.[111] With no real recourse to manipulate the price of cotton, it was laborers who would have to make up the difference. In other words, long before the rise of mass southern cloth production, these cities' interrelated textile magnates were already locked in a vicious race to the bottom against one another.

As early as the late nineteenth century, millowners developed a common set of strategies to mitigate the baleful forces of local competition—almost all centered on their workers. Most infamous was the sudden wage "cut" itself.[112] Other common "efficiency" tactics included the "stretch-out"—making workers run increasingly more machines—and the "speedup," the increase of the machinery's overall pace.[113] Beginning in the 1920s, Massachusetts's textile manufactures also began a vigorous and hotly contested political campaign to overturn the state's labor legislation, especially the law banning women and children from working at night.[114] Labor, in other words, became a key part of the textile industry's competitive strategy.

Unfortunately, strategies to wring more from their workers had a crucial unintended consequence: overproduction. There fast emerged a near universal consensus that Massachusetts mills "overproduced" cloth and oversaturated global markets. But most textile industrialists, locked into the competitive logic of the market itself, felt powerless to do anything about it. When Fall River textile capitalist S. B. Chace defended an 1884 wage cut, his answer spoke volumes about why millowners simply accepted overproduction as a fact of life. "We [Fall River manufacturers] produce a little over one-half of the print cloths made in this country," Chace explained. While the goal was "to produce no more goods than the people want and are willing to pay a fair price for," the reality was that overproduction existed and there was little manufacturers could do about it. "Suppose we assume that the overproduction as a whole is . . . the output of all New England for two weeks. Allowing Fall River to have one-sixth of the spindles in New England . . . it would take us twelve weeks of absolute idleness to correct the evil."[115] All the while Fall River's stoppage would "be hailed with delight" by the owners of the other "thousands of looms in New England."[116] In other words, Fall River simply could not curtail production, lest it lose its competitive edge and hegemonic sway over the global cloth market.

To Chace's credit, overproduction was hard to detect (and even harder to avoid). After all, producers produce for future markets; they have no idea what those future markets will look like. As a result, for millowners, the line separating "overproduction" from "wise market readiness" could be frustratingly elusive. Sales, after all, tended to come in large, volatile spurts. In 1882, for example, Fall River's Annawan Mill faced a dearth of sales that spanned July, August, and September. The mill responded with only a modest production cut; otherwise, the looms continued at their furious pace. As summer turned to fall, with no sales to speak of, the mill amassed a spectacular surplus of unsold cloth. By October, the Annawan had stockpiled enough cloth to stretch from Fall River to Detroit with fifty miles of slack. While this might seem like overproduction of the most egregious variety, time ultimately validated the mill management's strategy. With a sudden spate of sales in October and November, the Annawan's massive surplus evaporated.[117] In other words, amid a market of unpredictable demand, millowners likely preferred to hazard overproduction rather than risk missing out on a sudden surge of orders. Overproduction was in some sense built into the system itself.

At first, South Coast millowners were confident the rise of southern industry would pose little threat. After all, unlike their coarse-goods producing brethren across much of the rest of New England, these industrialists felt reassured that their specialization in fine goods would protect them from the rise of unskilled, coarse-goods production in the South.[118] "There is no probability that the mills of the South will for many years to come be able to produce the finer qualities of goods now furnished by the looms of the Eastern States," the *New-York Times* declared in 1881.[119] Most northern industrialists agreed.[120] But, with astonishing speed, southern millowners surpassed the skill and capital barriers that had formerly blocked fine goods production—all the while paying wages that ranged anywhere from 70 percent to only half of the prevailing rates in Massachusetts.[121] By 1897, gloomy Fall River manufacturers confessed that the city had "lost its control of the market for goods of the sorts made here."[122]

Ultimately, very little separated how manufacturers handled local competition in the late nineteenth century and southern competition in the twentieth. Wages were cut, machines were added and sped up, and production was relentlessly ramped up in an attempt to maintain solvency amid shrinking profit margins. Unfortunately for millowners, such tactics only tended to exacerbate problems of overproduction and market saturation. Following the

collapse of cloth prices after the First World War, the problem of overproduction became widely recognized as something of a plague on the American textile industry.[123] Plans for collective curtailments were cooked up occasionally,
but such efforts rarely succeeded.

This is not to say that the emerging threat of capital mobility had no impact
on the management of Massachusetts's textile mills. Importantly, it catalyzed
two new techniques millowners could adopt to contain competition. One
was the option of simply moving south. Southern industrial boosters, after all,
worked tirelessly to advertise the area's limited protective labor legislation, alluring tax incentives, and "docile" labor force ready to submit to the whims of
northern capital.[124] The Massasoit Mills of Fall River spent $200,000 to open
a plant in the town of Lake Charles, Louisiana, in 1926; Beacon Manufacturing
of New Bedford moved its machinery to its new mill in Swannanoa, North
Carolina; and Fall River's giant American Printing Company moved much of
its machinery to its new mill in Kingsport, Tennessee.[125]

Nevertheless, the overwhelming choice of textile capitalists and
stockholders was to simply liquidate, eventually causing another massive economic catastrophe in the area.[126] From 1922 to 1933, ninety-three
Massachusetts mills shut down; only eleven were owned by corporations with
extant southern factories.[127] The transformation was impossible to miss. By
1927, 67 percent of American cloth originated from below the Mason-Dixon
Line.[128] Massachusetts was plunged into economic turmoil.

The sudden flood of shutdowns may have partly been a product of generational change. The children of these South Coast textile magnates—like
the children of the Boston Associates before them—showed little interest in
the life of mill management. M. C. D. Borden's sons, for instance, went on to
become fixtures of the resort community of Rumson, located on the Jersey
Shore. Bertram Borden became something of a professional philanthropist,
and Howard Borden transitioned to land development (building more than
150 houses in Rumson) as well as taking on work in local law enforcement,
becoming the town's "millionaire police officer," as the local press colorfully
described him.[129] Matthew—written out of his father's will for his unor-
thodox marriage—assumed a life of labor as a lowly New York City doctor.[130]
Of Fall River magnate John S. Brayton's four children, only one went into
textiles.[131] His two other sons went into investment banking, and his one
daughter became a philanthropist, managing local food relief operations in
crisis-torn 1930s Fall River.[132]

Crucially, those left behind to either resurrect or fight to preserve the
local economy were largely not the descendants of these original whaling and

landholding families. After 1910, few of the mills incorporated in New Bedford had descendants of the city's whaling elite on their executive boards.[133] Local industry was increasingly dominated by newer entrants, lacking the old-money lineage of the previous generation of New Bedford capitalists. Thus, as the textile industry collapsed over the ensuing decades, those who would fight to revive New Bedford would be local capitalists who had relatively recently joined the ranks of textile mill ownership, as well as the sizable class of allied utility, real estate, retail, and banking interests who depended on the economic vitality of these cities for their livelihood.

Falling Apart in the Strike of 1928

New Bedford's massive strike of 1928, in which more than 30,000 textile workers walked off their jobs, was in some sense a fitting denouement for this long period of protracted labor-capital struggle in the context of the constant threat of capital mobility. Fittingly, it too was justified by workers' "just wage" ideology; it too resulted from manufacturers' failure to uphold a voluntary production cut; and it too was in some sense doomed by the divisions that roiled local unions, torn between craft-based exclusivity and ethnic and geographic inclusivity.

Like so many strikes before it, this one began with a cut. Manufacturers announced a 10 percent wage cut on April 9, 1928, citing the "extremely critical" situation of high operating costs, "unfair conditions" of competition, and the "handicap" of hours and wage restrictions.[134] The next week, the day the cut was to take effect, 2,571 union members outvoted 188 in favor of the walkout, taking with them another 25,000 or so unorganized workers.[135]

The argument put forth by unionists remained the same as in previous contests: wages should reflect profits. Although the price of cloth may have plummeted in the early 1920s, textile firms had continued to reap massive profits by selling off surplus cotton left over from the First World War.[136] Rather than investing these earnings into updating outmoded production technology, New Bedford mills had pushed profits back into investor pocketbooks through a campaign of massive dividend payments.[137] While the 1920s are routinely identified as "lean years" in the textile industry, dividends from New England textile firms averaged some 12.2 percent through 1924.[138] After local mills had suffered setbacks in 1926, 1927 proved to be a year of recovery; New Bedford mills made profits in excess of $2.5 million.[139] In the months leading up to the strike, the local newspapers were chock full of good news about the mills' substantial profits.[140] Four months before the wage-cut

announcement, the chairman of the New Bedford Boosters Club enthusiasti-
cally announced that the city's textile industry had "emerged from the world
wide depression in the cotton industry," and that "the fine textile industry [is]
here in New Bedford to stay" with "nothing to fear from the South."[141] It is
not surprising that workers remained unmoved by manufacturers' claims of
distress.

Further compounding workers' sense of righteous grievance, wages had
been in a steady decline since 1920, despite the mills' recoveries. Immediately
following the war, New Bedford workers had to accept both a wave of layoffs
and a 20 percent wage cut. Wages continued to fall an additional 15 percent
over the next six years as manufacturers attempted, as they had so many times
before, to address the problem of overproduction by cutting labor costs.[142]
In fact, the wage cut leading up to the 1928 strike was itself the result of the
local Manufacturers' Association's failure to uphold a voluntary 20 percent production cut instituted that January.[143] Despite the agreement, most
manufacturers quickly broke ranks and boosted production, thus further
lowering the price of cloth and exacerbating profit instability.[144]

Armed with these data, unionists worked tirelessly to prove to the people
of New Bedford that local mills could indeed pay fairly and compete effectively. Local unionists repeatedly pointed out that one of the few mills in the
city that refused to institute the wage cut, Walter Langshaw's Dartmouth
Mill, was also the city's most profitable factory. It did not help that Langshaw
was something of an outsider himself—an English immigrant who worked
his way up from factory floor to industrial capitalist—and he took immense
pleasure in publicly denouncing local millowners for their "greed and in-
tolerance" as well as their unwillingness to address the real issue at stake,
"overproduction."[145] "The cause of the depression in the textile industry had
nothing to do with wages," one local newspaper confidently declared. "The
reason for the situation was known and admitted by every manufacturer and
student in the land. It was due to the overbuilding of mills. . . . The remedy
was obvious. It lay in curtailment of production."[146] New Bedford unionists
even commissioned a twelve-part series of articles by famed labor economist
Norman Ware in an effort to demonstrate empirically that the manufacturers'
wage cut was unnecessary.[147]

In workers' eyes, the manufacturers had failed to uphold their end of the
"just wage" bargain. It was this combination of rising profits, an unwillingness to curtail production, and declining wages that inspired the strike of
1928. A poem by weaver Thomas Spellmen, addressed to his fellow workers,
described these feelings of frustration: "In the industrial depression/ you did

take a noble part/ And ungrumbling shared the leanness/of the floundering textile mart. . . . By your courage and your patience/ Toiling in the uphill rut/ You've deserved a commendation/ Not the stinging lash—the cut."[148] As in the nineteenth century, unionists saw the just wage as a function of the same market pressures manufacturers faced. These understandings of the political economy of textile manufacturing would continue to guide their angry protests throughout the strike.

Partly as a result of the local union's efforts to prove the justice of their cause, the strike of 1928 enjoyed tremendous community support. Local newspapers, clergy, merchants, and even national trade magazines criticized local millowners for their short-sighted business strategy and voiced support for the strikers.[149] Even the *American Cotton and Wool Reporter* found mill management to blame: "The whole world has changed. Everything is different now than it was 50 years ago—except the selling methods of these and other cotton mills."[150] A local minister recounted to a reporter all the headlines he wished he would have seen in the local newspaper instead of reading of the wage cut: "MILLS ADJUST [MANAGEMENT] ALONG PROGRESSIVE NEW LINES!" or "MILLS DROP EVERY USELESS OFFICIAL FROM THEIR STAFFS." For him, it was millowners' "LACK OF FAITH in their own ability to grow" that undergirded the strike.[151] A local businessman similarly cited millowners' "lack of courage" as the issue, adding that millowners needed "a 'Mussolini' to take them over and make them do the things they're afraid, or too inert, or too locked in their old ways of doing things, to attempt for themselves."[152] Across the board, millowners were shocked by the vicious public backlash to the wage cut.[153]

For those long denied a place or a voice in New Bedford's unions, the strike also presented an opportunity to create an entirely new kind of working-class organization. Portuguese, Polish, and French Canadian workers began to flock to New Bedford's newly organized Textile Mill Committee (TMC), founded by two Communist Party operatives, Fred Beal and William Murdoch.[154] "On Pleasant street," at the craft union Textile Council headquarters, one journalist noted, "You will hear the cadence of Lancashire tongues predominating over every other accent," but at TMC headquarters, "the tongue is Portuguese and Polish for the most part."[155] TMC rallies regularly featured speeches in English, Portuguese, French, and Polish.[156] Although many local residents looked on the TMC with deep discomfort—it was, after all, organized by out-of-town "red agitators" attracted to New Bedford by the massive strike—its promise to bring all textile mill operatives under one umbrella union, regardless of skill or ethnicity, was deeply compelling to unskilled immigrants long

deprived a place on the local Textile Council.[157] At one of the earliest TMC
rallies, Juliet Poyntz declared "this strike in New Bedford" to be "the greatest
ray of hope to workers that has come out of New England in years." She urged
"the non-unionists to organize," making "an especial appeal for the women
to join in the movement."[158] At another rally, "Miss Irene" urged "workers to
make one, great, big union" and to not "be afraid of the bosses."[159] Fred Beal,
a former textile operative of Lawrence, urged workers that no strike is won by
"a group of little unions," but by "one big union."[160] Fittingly, after the close of
the 1928 strike, Beal would move on to organizing in North Carolina, where
his activism would get him thrown in jail. He eventually skipped bail and fled
to the Soviet Union.[161]

FIGURE 4.2 Textile Mill Committee (TMC) picketers hold signs advocating the
union's anti-discriminatory, egalitarian vision, 1928. Courtesy of Spinner Publications,
New Bedford, MA.

The TMC became a haven for women, who not only made up the majority of New Bedford's strikers but also took on crucial roles as leaders and
organizers.[162] Portuguese immigrant Eula Mendes became a prominent TMC
organizer, struggling to create, as she put it, "a union that would take in all of
the textile workers . . . not only for the . . . so-called cream of the textile workers,
not highly skilled workers but for the unskilled and for all the workers."[163]
Mendes was later arrested and deported for her activities "as a member of
an organization that advocates the overthrow of the U.S. Government"
and was forced to seek asylum in Poland.[164] Picket lines were dominated by

women, often with their children by their sides, much to the dismay of local authorities. No less than sixty-five women were arrested over the course of the strike for either intimidating strikebreakers or fighting back when police violently sought to disperse picket lines.[165] Arrestees included Greek immigrants Christina Simores and Angilina Tsoupreas, the latter of whom, witnesses claimed, kept strikebreakers from entering a mill by "brandishing [a] brick above her head" and screaming "I kill. I kill."[166] Portuguese operative Mary Valente threatened a police sergeant, claiming that "we broke [Officer McCarty's] head and we're going to split yours open too."[167] Issues like equal pay for women—and equal freedom for wives in the household—became recurrent themes in TMC speeches.[168] Women immigrants—in particular Portuguese, Polish, and Greek workers—became crucial agents of radicalism in the strike of 1928.

In short, the TMC represented the institutional consolidation of the alternative organizing ideologies that unskilled workers had been cultivating for decades. As non-union Portuguese operative Alfred Botelho wrote to a local paper in April 1928, in the war of conflicting ideologies, "It is the manufacturers who are wrong and the unions partly so." He blamed manufacturers for their stubbornness and unions for their exclusivity.[169] For workers like Botelho and the thousands of unskilled workers long excluded from New Bedford's formal union establishment, the TMC's call to organize both North and South, skilled and unskilled, women and men, and immigrant and non-immigrant was immensely attractive.

The results of the strike were nonetheless anticlimactic. After six months of joblessness, a series of hearings conducted by the State Board of Arbitration brought the strike to a close. Millowners sat on one side, Textile Council leaders on the other. No women, TMC members, Portuguese, French Canadian, or Polish workers were included in the negotiations.[170] For those who had the privilege, the agreement reached was pointedly non-radical: a 5 percent (rather than 10 percent) wage cut. It was cold comfort after six months of joblessness. The mills reopened on October 28, 1928.[171]

———

It may seem puzzling that workers would call such a massive strike at a moment that, in retrospect, seems defined by far-reaching economic decline. Workers, though, were acutely aware of the threat of southern competition, the state of the cotton and textile markets, and the ways in which northern mills were manipulating the price of cloth. Having stressed that the just wage was a function of the health of the global economy, New Bedford unionists were adamant in their belief that it was possible for New Bedford mills to compete effectively and pay fairly.

But neither workers nor millowners necessarily spoke with one voice. Whereas these cities' craft unions had little interest in expanding the benefits of unionization across the lines of skill and geography, others, like Eula Mendes and the TMC, fought for just this sort of expansive working-class organization. While some millowners, such as S. B. Chace, hoped that wage cuts would buy them ever-soaring production levels from a stable, ever-competitive position, others, like Walter Langshaw, relentlessly criticized these mills' self-destructive path. The strike of 1928 saw these economic visions clash in the streets of New Bedford. As the textile crisis deepened, the failure of these alternative visions of political economy to gain traction would devastate these cities.

5

Cut from the Same Cloth

THE REMAKING OF INDUSTRIAL MASSACHUSETTS

THE COLLAPSE OF the New England textile industry in the 1920s wrought almost unimaginable suffering on the people of Massachusetts. "I had not ever lived through such a rough time as I did in those days," one Portuguese immigrant worker remembered in the 1980s. "I gave birth to seven children in the thirties. Three of those children died. One boy was stillborn, and another died at two months due to health. Her lungs had been affected due to the air I breathed in the mill. Another little girl died at the age of three from malnutrition."[1] As unemployment and poverty overtook Massachusetts, children could be seen in the streets stripping wood from abandoned tenements to burn for heat; others scrounged through local trash dumps looking for cloth rags to sell at one-and-a-half cents a pound at the cotton waste plant. By the early 1930s, the city of New Bedford was literally paying the travel expenses for unemployed Azoreans to return to Portugal, provided they promised never to return.[2] Oral histories of the era are harrowing tales of starvation, families in disarray, and the exhaustion of local sources of relief, leaving workers simply penniless.

It was economic crisis on an unthinkable scale. Whereas in 1920, Fall River boasted some 111 mills and one-eighth of the nation's total spindles, by 1931, more than half those mills had been liquidated and a state-appointed board was managing the bankrupt city.[3] In New Bedford, the story was little different. Having once employed some 35,000 workers in 1928, the next ten years saw the evaporation of some 27,000 jobs from local mills.[4] When the city attempted to institute a jobs program in 1930 in an effort to connect the unemployed with potential employers, it simply ended up with lines of unemployed workers and few jobs to offer. In the first two days alone, the city

FIGURE 5.1 Fall River as the "Spindle City," ca. 1910s. Barnard Mills, Quequechan River, Fall River, Mass. Detroit Publishing Co. Courtesy of the Library of Congress, LC-DIG-det-4a24924.

received nearly 1,000 applications for aid, with only one morning of work for forty to offer in return.[5] The collapse of an industry that had once provided over 80 percent of local employment was simply not an obstacle easily overcome.[6] As the president of the United Textile Workers of America lamented in the fall of 1931, these former centers of New England's industrial ascendance had become places of "destitution . . . misery and degradation." Filled with hungry workers and empty factories, these were "sad, sad places."[7]

For those who weathered the ordeal, it is little wonder that the 1930s became regarded as the end of an era in Massachusetts. Such stories of acute suffering and the angry grievances of policymakers who saw their state as a victim of economic forces they could neither see nor control have only reinforced the notion that the collapse of the Massachusetts textile industry was but a bitter prologue to the imminently unfolding drama of American deindustrialization.[8] Most works on Massachusetts industrialization end precisely at this moment of far-flung capital mobility and economic depression.[9] Yet focusing on the movements of capital rather than people misses the critical question of what workers do once all the jobs are gone. The operative assumption, it seems, is that once industry leaves, workers depart, and all that is left behind is rust, degradation, and crisis. Labor history typically ends where unemployment begins.[10]

Yet industrial Massachusetts proved more phoenix-like than many observers expected. Just as its textile factories fled for the non-union South, they were replaced by a wave of equally mobile garment shops from the union strongholds of Philadelphia, Chicago, and New York. Looking to capitalize on the area's seemingly endless pool of newly unemployed immigrant women, open factory space, and monetary incentives from local elites, these garment factories leveraged textile deindustrialization into the creation of an entirely new economic regime.

In 1930s Massachusetts, migrant labor, mobile capital, and state power collided in spectacular fashion. The desperation left in the wake of the textile crisis was exploited by local elites in their struggle to lure mobile capital back to the state. In turn, workers and middle-class pressure groups would counter-organize, seeking to reform an economy of "fly-by-night" sweatshops into something more stable and prosperous. Out of this complicated entanglement of crisis and rebirth—creation and defiance—the next generation of industrial Massachusetts emerged.

Desperation and Development

Unskilled Portuguese laborers, who made up the majority of the area's mill workers, suffered terribly from the mill liquidations of the 1920s and 1930s. For these workers, the Great Depression in South Coast Massachusetts felt more like the compounding of a longer-developing depression in wages and employment stretching back to the end of the First World War. Even a decade after the stock market crash of 1929, nearly half the local Portuguese population remained unemployed.[11] Municipalities were in similar disarray. Cities that had traditionally encouraged industrialization through low taxation suddenly found themselves in financial ruin.[12]

Already strained local relief agencies broke down quickly. Unemployed workers learned to survive by whatever means necessary.[13] Many Portuguese immigrants lived off the small gardens they kept behind their tenement houses.[14] In fact, one of the few successful welfare programs instituted in New Bedford was managed by a local gardening club. The organization gave out hundreds of 2,500-square-foot plots of unused land to the local unemployed for the purposes of small-scale farming. It was a perfect fit, given that most Azoreans had spent their pre-migration years as farmers. Within months, more than 600 plowed plots had been distributed and successfully farmed.[15] For a brief moment, the industrial era seemed to be genuinely over in New Bedford, as workers returned to the land for their subsistence as if a century in the past. Yet no matter how creative, few saw New Bedford's resourceful "garden program" as much more than a stopgap solution.[16] Simply put, the city needed something to replace its eviscerated textile infrastructure.

Not coincidentally, almost as soon as New England mills began shutting their doors, local capitalists began an ambitious program to attract new industry to the area. In New Bedford, the Board of Commerce—a group dominated by local utility, retail, and real estate interests—set up an Industrial Development Fund in May of 1927, into which local business owners poured tens of thousands of dollars.[17] The parallels with the similar transition undertaken by whaling capitalists some half-century earlier were not lost on them. "Many of us can go back and remember the lull after the city's whaling industry died out," one of many Development Fund circulars read. "From the whaling industry we went into the manufacture of textile goods, using the capital that had been earned in whaling . . . [but] for the future, even if textiles come back within the next two years to what they were ten years ago, it certainly would be the height of folly not to persist in bringing other industries to our community."[18] Just as whaling agents were forced to become lords of the loom, they too would have to reinvent both themselves and their community.

Frank J. Leary, head of New Bedford's new Industrial Development Commission (IDC), made sure to strike an attractive bargain with potential industrialists. Constantly touring outside capitalists around abandoned mills, he offered low rents, low taxes, and free money for moving and machine costs.[19] Fall River boosters promoted a similar array of tax breaks and free use of abandoned mill space for new factories.[20] At least one corporation moved its factory fifteen miles from New Bedford to Fall River just to take advantage of such temporary inducements.[21]

The state of Massachusetts, equally desperate to attract manufacturers, also jumped into the fray. In 1937, the newly formed Massachusetts Development and Industrial Commission produced a gold-bound, hardcover volume, addressed to all "manufacturers who desire to relocate existing manufacturing plants or establish new industries," entitled *In Black and White: The Facts Concerning the Industrial Advantages in Massachusetts.*[22] In the introduction, the department commissioner proudly declared it "a curious, yet easily understandable fact that the ebb and flow of economic factors have again placed striking advantages in the old Bay State" and that "MASSACHUSETTS, pioneer industrial state . . . again spells OPPORTUNITY to the ambitious and far-sighted manufacturer."[23] A quick perusal of the "striking advantages" Massachusetts offered mobile capital made clear the state's "curious" yet "easily understandable" attractions: an "unexcelled labor supply," "freedom from labor unrest," and "a State Government, mindful of industry's needs, friendly and helpful towards its manufacturers."[24] Massachusetts had 275,738 residents seeking new employment as of April 1937, *In Black and White* boasted, constituting an estimated 70 percent of the state's labor pool.[25] The Fall River and New Bedford metropolitan area remained the seventh largest manufacturing area in the country, but wages there were lower than every other city in the top twenty. Both cities sat in rock-bottom positions on cost-of-living charts.[26] Manufacturers were likewise assured that although Massachusetts was once "known throughout the country as the leader in the adoption of so-called liberal labor legislation," those days were long gone. Workers understood that "labor cannot enjoy good wages and steady employment without a prosperous industry," and manufacturers took responsibility for their employees' contentment without the need for state interference.[27] The state of Massachusetts continued to distribute these kinds of books and booster materials throughout the late 1930s and the 1940s, always emphasizing the desperate condition of labor and the friendly posture of the state.[28]

These efforts were, at least on paper, remarkably successful. The list of incorporated shops in the New Bedford City Directory offers a glimpse of the massive transformation these "industrial development" schemes initiated. Whereas in 1930, New Bedford had twenty-six officially incorporated cotton mills and no garment shops, by 1936, the city had nineteen cloth manufacturers and nine clothing makers; by 1941, the city had fourteen textile mills, but fifteen garment shops.[29] By 1945, there were only twelve cotton manufacturers left, but twenty-one garment shops called the city home.[30] As textile mills fled, garment makers seemed to fill the gaps.

The number of officially incorporated factories told only half the story. New Bedford and Fall River were frequently home to "runaway" shops that simply came for a period of months—sometimes weeks—in order to escape the hold of the clothing workers' unions on New York and to reap the profits of cheap, non-union labor.[31] The costs were low and the profits potentially huge. A contractor needed only to set up an agreement with a New York shop, receive cuts of cloth ready for sewing, put up a few machines in an empty factory loft, and bring the finished clothing back to New York for a handsome profit.[32] New York garment production had long been based on subcontracting out batches of work to various subsidiary producers in order to minimize costs and maintain flexibility amid a constantly shifting industry; the only difference was that shop operators were starting to contract outside of New York City altogether, in search of the lowest possible wages.[33]

To remain profitable, the whole process depended on plentiful labor and pitiful wages. Indeed, when Frank Leary gave a local congressional representative a personal tour of the former Fairhaven Mill complex, a reporter noted that at least ten manufacturers were operating in the "vacant" mill, although no garment shops were officially incorporated in New Bedford. In one firm, young women shirt-makers were getting paid 75 cents a day.[34] Similarly, when Edwin Smith, Massachusetts's Commissioner of Labor and Industries, investigated wages in New Bedford and Fall River garment shops, he found that in New Bedford, 90 percent of workers in women's apparel and 74 percent of those in menswear earned less than $1.50 a day. In Fall River, he found "rates as low as ten cents and even in one case five cents an hour, and hundreds of girls with weekly earnings under $5.00."[35] For the time being, the desperation left in the wake of textile deindustrialization left workers in no position to bargain for much better.

Even when factories did officially incorporate, this did not necessarily stop them from taking shrewd advantage of these cities' situation. One of the largest shops in the area, the Har-Lee factory of Fall River—relocated from Chicago—was well known for hiring workers at a special "learner's wage" with promises that future raises would eventually buoy their wages to the state-mandated minimum, only to fire them after six months.[36] Like many other local garment shops, Har-Lee also took specific "deductions" out of workers' pay to fund various, sometimes non-existent programs. For example, one worker made only $3.51 after her first six-day week at Har-Lee, in large part because of mandatory deductions to fund a fictional "social club" and to buy a Christmas gift for the forelady.[37]

Working conditions in these sweatshops were similarly deplorable. Recalling their experiences in the early garment trade decades later, workers vividly remembered the brutal hot and cold of the factory floor, their tyrannical bosses, and the deafening noise and unrelenting rush of the machines. One worker, having worked in an underwear factory in New Bedford for 66 cents a day throughout the 1930s, could still remember the name of her menacing foreman, "Sam," fifty years later. "It was a real sweatshop. I'm telling you, boy, it was," she reflected. "It was in turmoil all the time. It was this rush, rush, rush; Bring bundles there, put them over here, and hurry up we need this." She would continue to work in various local garment firms for another forty years.[38] Another worker remembered the constant fear of machine breakage: "If the machine broke, we would almost be in tears. We were afraid to tell the boss. . . . He would get mad. He called us 'God damned Portaguees'. . . . 'Go back to your country,' he would say."[39] Workers had little recourse. Jobs were scarce, and these jobs were the sole source of support for many of these women and their families.[40]

Sweatshops ran on low wages, low wages ran on desperation, and desperation ran on economic crisis. Hard at work turning working-class desperation into renewed industrial ascendance, enterprising capitalists invested thousands of dollars into bringing these kinds of shops to New Bedford and Fall River. Much to their chagrin, however, not everyone celebrated the coming of the garment shop as a harbinger of the next era of New England industrialization. Workers may have been forced to take jobs in the expanding garment trade, but it did not stop them from challenging the legitimacy of these elites' visions of Massachusetts's economic future.

Defining Recovery

Almost as soon as garment factories began rolling into Massachusetts, their presence set off a fierce debate over their legitimacy as heir to the state's dethroned textile industry. While local capitalists extolled the garment shop as promising a rebirth of industrial Massachusetts, others decried its low wages and abysmal conditions as recovery's very negation. In hindsight, garment making may seem to be a natural successor to textile production, but by no means was this the way it seemed to people on the ground.

Motivated by their sense of being "public mothers" with a duty to safeguard those who required special protection, the middle-class women of the Consumers' League of Massachusetts helped turn these invading sweatshops into a statewide concern.[41] For instance, the group generated plenty of publicity after it sent three Boston University seniors to engage in undercover work at a Fall River garment shop. One lurid *Boston Daily Record* article based on the Consumers' League investigation authored by Joan Lowell—a former silent film star as well as a member of one of Massachusetts's most prominent families—recorded how these "girls" were "regularly shamed and ridiculed in Fall River by unscrupulous New York sweatshop operators."[42] "I have walked and talked with the girls who are the victims of sweatshop wages," Lowell wrote. "Bent-shouldered youngsters, 40-years old before they are 16," they knew that any possibility of protest would be "muted by threats of unemployment."[43] Another article printed two workers' weekly paystubs—one for $3.20 and the other for $3.60—as proof of the low pay in these shops.[44]

What is most surprising about League activism is the degree to which it centered not on the shocking and the lurid, but on the more prosaic argument that these sweatshops were actually an impediment to real economic recovery. "The consumer has a right to expect a responsible guarantee that his or her dollar will expedite and not undermine recovery," declared one of many League press releases and internal memos from the early 1930s addressing the sweatshop issue.[45] Convinced that high wages and well-spent consumer dollars were the soundest path to economic reconstruction, the League saw little merit in local policymakers' plans to reconstruct the Massachusetts economy on the basis of sweatshop garment production.[46] As the Citizens' Committee for the Ladies Garment Industry put it in 1936, although "the papers are full of talk of recovery, of return to prosperity . . . shall we have recovery at the human cost involved in wages of $8.00 a week[?]" It concluded, pessimistically, "Indeed, *can* we have recovery under such conditions?"[47] For the Consumers' League, the sweatshop was as much a menace to women's dignity as it was to the future prosperity of Massachusetts.

In New Bedford, local textile unionists also began to mount an ideological battle against the notion of "recovery" through industrial seduction. During a March 1931 legislative hearing in Boston, local workers personally condemned Frank Leary for the effect his "industrial development commission" was having on New Bedford. As one worker put it, "It seems to me that our Board of Commerce and city officials are condoning a bad thing by throwing out bait in the way of low rents and other privileges to these concerns." Although the Board of Commerce might be pleased to see new shops in the area, "we'd be far better off without them," he argued, adding "you know $5 a week doesn't help much in making good citizens."[48] From union resolutions to editorials, city councilmen to the state commissioner of labor, few were reticent to express their deep disdain for Leary's so-called development plan.[49]

Frank Leary—director of a recently arrived rayon company in addition to his existing duties as the leader of New Bedford's industrial development commission—remained equally vocal.[50] He publicly upbraided local unionists and state representatives alike as self-interested opportunists, attacking their ideas as both impractical and retrograde. He lost no time in pointing out that the complaints of local labor leaders "[were] not helping out employment any." In fact, such agitation made recovery all the more difficult by driving businesses out and making it increasingly hard to attract new industry to the area.[51] "Idleness, want, hunger, and labor agitation breed Communism," he declared during a 1931 state legislative hearing. "There are some people who do not want to work so long as New Bedford pays $70,000 a month to welfare and landlords can live without rents."[52] Moreover, after a city councilman suggested in July of 1932 that Massachusetts should encourage national forty-eight-hour legislation instead of abolishing its own forty-eight-hour requirements—as the Board of Commerce had suggested the previous month—Leary took it as a personal attack. He shot back that New Bedford workers were "more interested in jobs [than] political bologna."[53] For Leary, labor agitation and inflexible labor laws had not just caused New Bedford's economic crisis in the first place: they also threatened to prolong it indefinitely.

Leary was no one-dimensional capitalist autocrat, but neither was he the pragmatic humanitarian he often envisioned himself to be. Taking on the Massachusetts Commissioner of Labor's derisive report about the appalling state of wages in the New Bedford garment industry, Leary put forth what would become a familiar defense of low wages. "We wish we could put everyone in New Bedford to work at fair living wages," Leary told a local reporter, "but we are facing facts, not theories."[54] Although he confessed that the commissioner was technically right in pointing out that some factories were paying below the state minimum, Leary remained unmoved. While the commissioner had done nothing to address the "troubles of our older industries," Leary argued, he himself was actually spurring real economic development and bringing factories back to Massachusetts. "We are concerned about low wages. We do not like them but our civic problems are many and varied."[55] While others merely complained about the nature of the business he was bringing in, Leary felt he was the only one actually generating new business activity and working to solve New Bedford's economic woes. For many New Bedford capitalists, like Leary, the resurrection of local industry would have to be built from the same formula that had propelled industrial greatness in generations past: low wages, plentiful labor, and an unyielding refusal to grant either personal or municipal welfare provision.

Noticeably absent from these debates were the women whose labor actually fueled Massachusetts's growing sweatshop economy. Although textile unionists may have claimed to be speaking on behalf of these women workers, the unionists' past activism against any involvement of women in industry made their sincerity questionable.[56] Like many craft unionists around the nation, they had shown themselves firmly dedicated to the ideal of a "living wage" high enough to keep women out of the factory.[57] During an 1898 state hearing, for example, New Bedford union weaver James Green called for a law that would permanently ban married women from working in textile mills. When asked what kind of hardship he thought this might cause multiple-income families, his reply was simple and curt: "My wife don't work in the mill and it don't work any hardship on her."[58]

Similarly, in its support for garment unionization throughout the 1930s, the local New Bedford Textile Council continued to highlight the superiority of (male) textile work over (female) garment work. During an anti-sweatshop rally held in 1937, for instance, a journalist noted one textile unionist who "went at some length" about "the contrast between the textile industry requiring large capital, in which there are many owners, and with a management that is responsible to both [employees] and to stockholders . . . while the garment shops he declared are under no such responsibility."[59] In other words, dedicated as they were to the prerogatives of skilled, male workers, the eradication of the sweatshop was likely just a means through which to gain political clout in rebuilding the city's broken textile economy.[60] Skilled textile unionists too may have claimed the mantle of humanitarianism, but their conceptions of a male-dominated household economy equally limited the reach of their activism.

Nonetheless, the unskilled women largely left out of these debates were beginning to form their own visions of a new economic order. Rather than merely eliminating the garment factory or returning to some halcyon era of textile hegemony, they campaigned to re-make the garment industry of New Bedford and Fall River along entirely different lines. They organized not to abolish, but to fundamentally reinvent the sweatshop.

Reforming the Sweatshop

In January of 1936, a somewhat odd photo appeared in the *Boston Evening American*. Seven women—clad in stereotypical, knightly Arthurian dress, bearing shields and chainmail armor—stood shoulder-to-shoulder. "TO ALL COTTON GARMENT and UNDERWEAR WORKERS," their shields read, "THE CRUSADE IS ON!"[61] The message of this publicity stunt was clear: The International Ladies' Garment Workers' Union (ILGWU) was planning its crusade into the Massachusetts sweatshop economy.[62]

The ILGWU had begun organizing in Fall River as early as 1934 but found it exceedingly difficult to make progress. Although the New Deal's ill-fated National Recovery Administration (NRA) was originally charged with protecting the right of workers to organize as well as setting minimum wages and maximum hours in the garment trade, small employers easily evaded these codes.[63] NRA provisions were especially difficult to enforce in a place like Fall River, as most employers were minor contractors for major shops in other cities. As a result, if workers attempted any kind of organized protest, the head office could simply close shop and shift production to some other shop in some other city.[64]

These tactics repeatedly frustrated ILGWU efforts. Even more embarrassing for early unionists, the ILGWU was simply not strong enough to exact fair wages from the small number of shops it did manage to organize. By May 1935, the ILGWU had unionized some of the smaller shops in Fall River and New Bedford, but these efforts had not even earned them NRA mandated wage minimums. As the ILGWU's main Fall River organizer, William Ross, lamented in January 1935, whereas most union members in smaller firms were making $11.70 a week, large, unorganized firms were shelling out the full $13 minimum mandated by the NRA codes.[65] Unionized workers were actually getting less than their non-union peers. "In view of the fact that the employers [we are] dealing with are contractors," he wrote, "there is not much we can do about it at this time."[66]

Garment unions were in an unenviable position. When union organizers in New Bedford called on local sweatshop laborers to write them letters describing their workplace conditions in 1937, some decried their low wages and long hours while others denounced the local unions for their inability to do anything about it. "We have a union but they don't do us any good.... All they want is our quarters.... I really believe they were bought by the boss," one local worker at an underwear factory fumed.[67] The combined effects of poverty, limited bargaining power, and contract production made effective unionization seemingly impossible.

The NRA's termination in May of 1935 created new, unexpected openings for organization at firms like Har-Lee, which, because of their size and status, had formerly been forced to follow the NRA codes, beating out prevailing union wage scales in the process.[68] Almost as soon as the NRA expired, Har-Lee instituted a forty-four-hour week and cut its wages far below what workers were making in unionized shops.[69] When Har-Lee workers began to organize in response, the factory reversed its policies, restoring wages and cutting work schedules back to forty hours a week. Nevertheless, as a letter collectively addressed from the workers of Fall River to those at Har-Lee's parent Chicago plant put it, it was a lesson in the power of organization: "Today, we want union recognition and a living wage."[70] The fear the union inspired in Har-Lee's bosses had shown these workers its potential power.

Har-Lee, though, had a number of anti-union strategies at its disposal. Its slash-and-burn labor recruitment and expulsion policies maintained both high rates of turnover and low wages, leaving the ILGWU's Fall River organizer to conclude that it might never be possible "to have anything like a majority . . . join the union in a reasonable length of time."[71] Har-Lee also remained affiliated with its powerful Chicago parent, B. Sopkin & Sons Company, leaving many organizers fearing that if they attempted a strike, production would simply be shifted back to Chicago.[72] Har-Lee had also started its own, internal "company union" in June of 1934 in an effort to undercut demands for organization.[73]

Other obstacles were less tangible. Although, in retrospect, it may seem only natural to assume that workers would be rallying behind the industrial union movement of the 1930s, ILGWU organizers discovered that local workers' experiences with the old, exclusionary textile unions had left them deeply disenchanted with, if not openly hostile to, union organization.[74] As the ILGWU's Fall River organizer put it in 1936, the local labor movement was in a "deplorable" condition as a result of the apathy and insularity of the local textile union establishment. The fact that Fall River's dying textile union continued to call strikes despite having organized only 10 percent of the workforce only compounded local, anti-union attitudes.[75] "It is ever necessary for us," he wrote, "to state that we are 'another union.' "[76]

If workers were suspicious of unionization, it was nothing compared to the hostility of employers and community leaders. In sharp contrast to the general support strikers had received during the 1928 strike, garment unions initially made few allies. One French Canadian priest personally denounced the ILGWU organizer, declaring "it took the Almighty six days to make the world and this blasphemer has the devilish effrontery to promise you a week of only five working days."[77] Employers, not surprisingly, also assured workers that the ILGWU simply wanted to drive business out of the area.[78] Precisely because so many locals saw the unions as the main culprit in the collapse of the textile industry, clothing unions like the ILGWU and the Amalgamated Clothing Workers of America (ACWA) would need to convince a new generation of workers of the merits of labor unionism.

Organizers quickly discovered that workers were not necessarily anti-union; they had simply developed a deep distrust of the union institutions that had traditionally dominated these communities. In fact, the initial groundswell of union activism in the South Coast actually came from local workers themselves. One of the first garment walkouts in the area, for instance, occurred after two women were fired from the Shelburne Shirt Company for organizing activity. The solidarity walkout that followed became the beginning of the Fall River chapter of the ACWA.[79] Similarly, in February of 1934, after two women were fired from the Harwood Underwear Company in New

Bedford for their union activity, some 100 workers marched off the factory floor and into the ACWA headquarters.[80] Some women went straight from serving as radical TMC leaders to organizing for the garment unions. Former textile operative and 1928 strike leader Eula Mendes, by the 1930s a dressmaker at the M and M manufacturing firm in New Bedford, led her shop's ILGWU organizing drive.[81]

Even when New Bedford organizers began to collect and publish garment workers' letters, describing their terrible working conditions and pay in order to generate public support for unionization, the idea was inspired by the actions of a local worker. When President Roosevelt toured New Bedford in 1936, a lone, young garment worker ambushed his motorcade, insisting he take her letter.[82] "We are working in a garment factory[;] a few months ago our minimum wages were $11. Today they have been cut down to $4 and $5 and $6. Please send someone from Washington to restore our minimum wages so that we can live," she pleaded. Roosevelt used the letter to illustrate wage cuts since the end of the NRA during a subsequent press conference.[83] Organizers were inspired to build off this same strategy. Consequently, New Bedford unionists would end up using a series of real letters from local garment workers for a pamphlet entitled "Thirteen Letters Addressed to You— From Thirteen Unlucky Girls" to garner national press attention for their cause.[84]

In searching for a concrete victory, the local Har-Lee factory, the area's largest garment plant, with 2,000 employees, became a major target. Clothing worker organizers found themselves having to reach out to groups of workers who had been routinely ignored by the craft union establishment: French Canadian, Polish, and Portuguese women. To that end, union organizers used every cultural resource available, placing advertisements in the local Portuguese newspaper, putting on radio broadcasts, and ultimately writing and performing a pro-union play, "Sit Down Sister!"[85] Regardless of method or media, the aim was to convince workers that industrialists did not have their best interests at heart and that only self-assertion would win them better working conditions and fair pay.

For example, the play "Sit Down Sister!"—set on the factory floor of the not so subtly named "Far-Lee Dress Co."—was a veritable paean to the virtues of self-determination, self-dependence, and union solidarity. First, it urged workers to see the ultimate hollowness of the humanitarianism of their bosses. Throughout the production, the forelady tries to lure the "girls" into company loyalty by offering a number of inane promises and gifts—candy, a baseball team, and gold medals for the fastest worker—to show them that the boss is "always thinkin' of youse girls." The workers, of course, see through the false humanitarianism of their employer: "You keep the candy. Give us a raise!," they shout, and "We'd rather have beer!" Similarly, when the forelady, on behalf of the boss, offers the workers "protection" to keep "Bolshevik agitators" from bothering them, she is met with a sharp rebuke. "We're not babies. We can talk to anybody we feel like," one calls back. The writers even noted that the actual enticements were less important than what they represented. In the production notes, they encouraged potential actors to change the specific promises offered by "Far-Lee" to match the "different kinds of 'sops' or paternalistic stunts" their own local employer "may have used to prevent organization."[86]

Most important, the play extolled the power of solidarity. When, in a last-ditch effort to secure the workers' loyalty the forelady decides to give out a "gold medal" to the fastest worker ("Miss Florence Speed-Up"), she is met with quick admonishment: "Cool off, sister—you'll get heartfailure that way!" The forelady is finally left questioning the workers' loyalty and company spirit:

> Listen saps, you don't sound loyal to me. . . . What's got into you? Maybe ya think ya wanna strike too? . . . Well, listen, dopes . . . The Big Shot [boss] he told me if there was any trouble to give you a dose of our sure-fire remedy—the old Far-Lee Spirit. Listen if ya got a complaint we can straighten 'em out later—that is, provided of course ya never lose that old Far-Lee spirit.[87]

The workers remain unimpressed. "Sit down, sister!," one says. "We work for pay—not sex appeal," calls back another. "Far-Lee spirit don't buy groceries!" calls out the third. Finally, the fourth declares, "And what's more, I'd rather have union spirit!"[88] The message was clear: workers no longer needed to depend on the humanitarianism of others. They could now depend on themselves and their union.

The ILGWU even brought in playwright Peter Frye—newly returned from fighting fascism in the Spanish Civil War—to help the local union put on what became a radio show titled "Rita Quill, Union Member."[89] Emphasizing the problems these laboring women experienced at work alongside the domestic problems they faced at home, "Rita Quill" showcased the democratic nature of the ILGWU as well as the methods through which a reluctant husband or boyfriend could be converted to the union cause.[90] After all, hostile husbands and ambivalent boyfriends were a frequent problem for the women unionists of the ILGWU.[91] In fact, after the Fall River radio show's main star—a seventeen-year old French Canadian operative by the name of Dorothy Brière—complained about her boyfriend's uneasiness over her involvement in both the union and the radio show, Frye simply wrote him into the following week's program.[92] Thus "Rita" ended up assuaging the doubts of her unhappy boyfriend, "Mickey," over her involvement in the union, explaining how the union gave her a sense of self-empowerment. Thankfully, Mickey understood.[93]

Just as important, the women of the ILGWU used the power of their votes to erode the structural advantages that had made Har-Lee so difficult to organize. Like workers around the nation, they were vocal organizers for President Franklin D. Roosevelt.[94] When he visited Fall River shortly before the election of 1936, 50,000 people greeted him at a local rally. Unionists waved signs declaring that "Garment Workers Want Roosevelt and More of the New Deal."[95] The importance of such changes cannot be overstated. The ILGWU could face off against Har-Lee on a far more level playing field thanks to a host of new federal protections: the Norris-LaGuardia Act of 1932, curtailing the ability of employers to level debilitating court injunctions against unions; the National Labor Relations Act (Wagner Act) of 1935, protecting workers' rights of self-organization; and, most important of all, the Fair Labor Standards Act of 1938, which set national wage minimums, helping to undercut the appeal of the "low-wage" South.[96]

No longer could Har-Lee's parent company move production back to Chicago in case of a strike. In the summer of 1933, a union of Black and white garment workers, organized by the Needle Trades Workers' Industrial Union, had successfully struck for higher wages, non-segregated restrooms, and a shorter workweek at Har-Lee's parent firm in Chicago.[97] The Sopkins eventually liquidated their Chicago plant and moved all production to non-union Fall River.[98] Har-Lee became the nation's largest cotton dress factory.[99]

The cultural and political efforts of the ILGWU ultimately paid off. In February 1941, the ILGWU won a National Labor Relations Board election at Har-Lee by a 5 to 1 margin.[100] Over the coming months, a delegation of workers and ILGWU union leaders worked out a contract for the new union. In sharp contrast to the highly exclusive negotiations that had ended the 1928 strike, the ILGWU's delegation included nine women workers. Judging by last names, it also included a diverse mix of American, French Canadian, and Portuguese operatives.[101] By March, the ILGWU had reached a contractual agreement with Har-Lee, promising a $15-a-week minimum wage, a closed union shop, and provisions for wages to go up automatically based on changes to the federal minimum wage.[102] Almost instantly, wages in other Fall River garment shops shot up to match the new Har-Lee standard.[103] By August, Har-Lee workers' salaries had gone up to $16 a week.[104] It was an incredible victory considering that just five years earlier, one Har-Lee employee had been fired after she had brought her "learners' wage" of $3.51 up to $10.06 a week.[105] The garment workers of Fall River had achieved a remarkable, industry-altering victory.

Over the next half-century, both the ILGWU and the ACWA continued to score victories in the New Bedford and Fall River area, becoming a fixture of community life. By the end of the Second World War, the two unions had together achieved collective bargaining agreements with most of the area's major garment manufacturers.[106] The newly founded industrial textile workers' union—the Textile Workers Union of America—similarly organized ten of New Bedford's eleven remaining cotton mills.[107]

Other benefits, beyond wage increases, accompanied successful unionization. In 1944, the ILGWU opened a union health center in Fall River. In 1954, the Northeast Department of the ILGWU even acquired a "Mobile Health Unit" truck to provide periodic medical services to workers living too far away from local ILGWU clinics.[108] And, on December 6, 1952, the ILGWU opened a new Fall River health center with an elaborate ceremony—attended by workers, government officials, and industry representatives—held in the newly minted "Garment Workers' Square," right in front of the city hall. As a symbol of this new era of cooperation between community and labor, the old street signs were taken down and replaced with new ones emblazoned with the ILGWU logo. With garment workers enjoying a fully functioning health center, prescription drug program, paid vacations, death benefits, seniority rights, and union representation, perhaps recovery had finally come to Massachusetts.[109]

The Missing Industrial Revolution

Despite the gains of the garment industry in the 1930s and 1940s, commentators continued to see the economy of Massachusetts as one defined by decline.[110] Partly, this was a function of who these apparel factories hired: namely, unskilled, largely immigrant women. By the early 1950s, New Bedford's still expanding garment industry contained an impressive seventy-five shops and 7,500 workers, but 98 percent of these workers were women.[111] The rebirth of industrial Massachusetts primarily benefited its clusters of new immigrant women and unskilled workers. For many skilled men, and even for many working women who abhorred the drudgery of the garment factory, the benefits of re-industrialization were far less tangible.

What happened to the men? Some skilled male workers simply moved. As in the strikes of 1898 and 1928, many likely left town or returned to England, French Canada, or Portugal. Others, mainly those who worked in the ancillary machine shops the original textile mills had spun off, faced less economic upheaval than the average textile worker. Many of these shops survived by simply embracing the opportunity of exporting their wares to the emerging markets of the American South.[112] Other men became commuter workers for the jewelry factories of the nearby town of Attleboro.[113] Still others found themselves pushed back and forth from textile job to textile job amid the swings of a dying industry.[114] All told, as captured by extant oral histories, the collapse of the textile industry often launched the working lives of local men along a confusing and chaotic trajectory: from working in textiles to installing telegraph poles to gravedigging to painting interiors; another went from textiles to construction to telephones to construction planning to power plant foreman; another from textiles to machinery to zipper factory mechanic to oil burner serviceman to navy carpenter to gas station operator.[115]

Ultimately, it is impossible to understand the "diversification" of the Massachusetts industrial base without understanding the unease the problem of "men's employment" created, as well as the ability of local capitalists to exploit that problem in the name of industrial gain. After all, for contemporaries, the lack of "manly" employment was a serious problem in these cities. Following the Second World War, the New Bedford Textile Institute and a Fall River partnership between the federal government and the ILGWU both independently attempted to train returning veterans for stitching work. Both projects, however, proved widely unpopular and summarily failed. Sewing clothes was not men's work, apparently.[116] As one Lawrence priest complained as late as 1954, Massachusetts needed more "hard-core industries" and less garment firms: "If we bring in many more we are going to have men walking the streets and women working."[117] Prevailing gender norms made women breadwinners and male dress stitchers seemingly unthinkable, leaving these cities caught in the lurch.

The repeated re-organization of the New Bedford Industrial Development Commission was inspired by the desire to finally attract an industry for men. In 1938, the New Bedford City Council formed a municipal Industrial Development League (IDL), composed of local textile and machine-production capitalists, as well as one textile trade union representative, charged with bringing a new, "stable" industry to the area.[118] The League officially incorporated, and then, in a bizarre twist, began a vigorous fund-raising drive to get donations from workers to help industrialize the city. "The Industrial Development Legion Needs Your Help—Give Your Contribution Today," was the headline of New Bedford's newspaper for weeks.[119] From February to March 1938, IDL fundraisers took in $55,363.[120] Capitalism was seemingly turned on its head in midcentury New Bedford: workers were paying employers for their jobs.

Like its progenitor, Frank Leary's Industrial Development Commission (IDC), the IDL was, at least on paper, remarkably successful. Playing off the controversy that surrounded Leary's moribund IDC, the IDL emphasized that it was searching for something better than a mere "fly-by-night" industry. T. A. Haish, the IDL's managing director, underscored that the businesses he sought would be "investigated thoroughly and approved by a committee from the Industrial Legion" and would employ "both men and women."[121] The IDL ultimately spent $42,000—about three-quarters of its entire fundraising—to lure one electronics company, Aerovox, from New York City to New Bedford.[122] Although many local citizens were outraged to discover that so much of the money raised was given away to a single firm, Haish was unapologetic.[123] As he put it to a gala of local capitalists and Aerovox executives, "the acquisition of this outstanding industry . . . will be the beginning of bringing New Bedford back into the industrial limelight of this country." Paired with a vigorous national advertising campaign, Haish was sure New Bedford would soon have a "stream of industrialists looking for happier manufacturing environments."[124]

The movement of electronics firms into Massachusetts differed little from the collective journey of their garment-producing co-conspirators. Both industrial migrations were animated by generous funding packages from local capitalists and promises of cheap, unemployed labor. As the years went on, New Bedford's apparently disproportionate store of unemployed male workers became an increasingly important selling point for the city.[125] When the IDC was again resurrected in 1949, for instance, William Zink, manager of the local employment office, noted that there were still "considerably more men unemployed and available for work here than there are women," which gave New Bedford a "a golden opportunity . . . to bring new industries here which will employ these men."[126] Like mobile garment firms, then, electronics factories were lured to New Bedford to employ those left unemployed by the southern march of textile firms.[127] And like mobile garment firms, many of these Massachusetts electronics factories had their workforces eventually organized by inter-ethnic industrial unions.[128]

Importantly, these local capitalists were not necessarily out to take advantage of the desperation of workers. Many members of these development groups were simply retail or utility-owning capitalists who were frankly concerned about—and directly invested in—the area's economic prospects.[129] Others, like Hathaway Mill owner Seabury Stanton, seemed to have genuinely felt a strong, emotional connection to the local community. Once Stanton took control of the business in the 1930s, rather than caving to calls to liquidate the firm, he put his own money toward gaining majority control and proceeded with a $10 million modernization plan.[130] Neither "moneybags" caricatures nor self-abnegating "job creators," capitalists also found their agency constrained by the dictates of an unforgiving global market. Regardless of whether or not local elites pursued the development of the electronics industry for civic-minded or totally self-interested reasons, the structures of the global economy channeled their desires into specific forms of industrial-regime building.

The electronics industry never quite became the haven of masculine labor for which boosters had hoped. While these first shops emerged out of a familiar combination of cheap labor and enterprising elites, massive federal investment during the Second World War and the Cold War would help transform them into productive behemoths.[131] As these plants ballooned in size and scope, they too began to increasingly rely on cheaper, female labor. By the early 1950s, an estimated 72 percent of New Bedford's 5,500 electronics operatives were women.[132] While this was a slightly more even gender balance than would have been found in the area's garment shops, electronics factories were hardly hotbeds of skilled, male work.

As a result, these cities often found themselves in the seemingly contradictory position of facing both elevated levels of unemployment and recurrent labor shortages. Backbreaking garment or electronics production work was easy to find, but skilled, more "masculine" jobs remained scarce. This situation in part explains the odd results of Northeastern University's 1953 survey of former textile workers. On the one hand, the survey conductors found serious rates of unemployment among displaced textile workers—nearly half, in fact. At the same time, the one-third of displaced workers who had managed to secure new jobs reported having a "choice of jobs" when taking their current occupation.[133] How, the surveyors wondered, could unemployment be so high if so many workers enjoyed a choice of jobs upon re-entering the workforce?

As in past eras, the answer revolved back to what kinds of jobs workers would be getting. After all, the study noted that "many . . . women said they

had been offered employment in garment factories . . . which they refused,"
and men "frequently turned down jobs which paid the legal minimum wage
on which, they said, they were unable to support their families."[134] Grueling
factory jobs were easily secured; anything better remained more elusive.
Unsurprisingly, for those displaced textile workers who had taken new jobs,
job satisfaction was abysmally low. In a sample of 241 displaced and re-
employed Fall River textile workers, 58 percent of males and an astounding
71 percent of females found their new job worse than their former employment in textiles.[135]

A combination of workers' ideology and the kinds of employers attracted
to economic crisis thus created a paradoxical situation of high unemployment
and labor shortage, precisely because workers did not want just any job. They
wanted a job worth having, and they were often willing to go jobless rather
than put up with less. Unlike those who had worked so hard to bring the
"sweatshop" to Massachusetts, workers did not see "recovery" as simply a process of re-accumulating jobs, no matter how ill-paying or degrading. Crisis
could attract capital, but it did not necessarily attract prosperity. Although
the ILGWU was working to organize factories like Har-Lee, its benefits did
not extend to all women, and they certainly did not extend to many men.

Southeastern Massachusetts workers and capitalists inaugurated a new industrial moment. In an act of mutual historical re-imagining, workers and elites
had come to see the collapse of the Massachusetts economy in the 1920s as
the product of an over-reliance on a single industry, and they had embraced
"mixed" manufacturing as the appropriate recipe for permanent stability.[136] In
reality, textile firms had simply been traded out for apparel factories and electronics plants, lured by promises of massive returns based on the prevailing
economic crisis. By the early 1950s, Massachusetts apparel factories employed
almost 60,000 workers, while cotton and synthetic textiles employed fewer
than 30,000.[137] By the 1960s, New Bedford's garment factories were growing
so rapidly that they were actually encountering labor shortages, a remarkable
turnaround for a city once plagued by starvation and crisis.[138]

Industrialization and deindustrialization worked in tandem in midcentury
Massachusetts, but it was no sterile process of capitalist evolution or maturation. There was no real innovation—no "creative destruction"—no changing
out of older productive regimes for newer, more efficient ones.[139] Textile
mills moved south; British and French-Canadian workers moved almost

every direction but south; garment factories moved inward from western and southern locales; Azoreans continued their cross-Atlantic migrations to the ebb and flow of the Massachusetts economy.

Mobile capital had escaped the house of labor, lured by crisis on the Massachusetts South Coast, only to find that its very movement ironically engendered a recovery that ignited the activist spirits of workers and middle-class citizens concerned for the future of their community.[140] A process of industrialization that began in the throes of crisis thus resolved in a stasis remarkably similar to its predecessor. Prosperity and decline, recovery and crisis, and industrialization and deindustrialization were all cut from the same cloth.

6

Toward Free Migration

THE REOPENING OF INDUSTRIAL MASSACHUSETTS

ON THE AFTERNOON of March 23, 1924, some 6,000 Portuguese immigrants gathered in New Bedford's Grove Park to protest. They were incited by—of all things—the publication of an academic dissertation.[1] Donald Taft, a Columbia University–trained sociologist, had just published his first book. The product of eight years of research on the Portuguese populations of Fall River, Massachusetts, and Portsmouth, New Hampshire, *Two Portuguese Communities in New England* revealed volumes about the suspect place immigrants held in the American psyche.[2] His primary interest, Taft explained, was determining the cause of the "notoriously excessive" rates of infant mortality that prevailed among Portuguese immigrants and to inquire as to whether these infants "died because of racial or nationalistic traits" or simply "because the Portuguese chanced to be exposed to peculiarly adverse surroundings."[3] Although he confessed that he had started "with a considerable prejudice in favor of the economic and non-personal causes of infant mortality," his eight years of research had apparently changed his outlook.[4]

Taft ultimately concluded that these high rates of infant mortality were rooted in Portuguese immigrants' extraordinary ignorance and inferior racial makeup. The Portuguese, by his analysis, were a "semi-negroid type."[5] For Taft, it was an unavoidable social fact that "this infusion of negro blood" adversely affected "their own social welfare and . . . the influence they exert in America." Racial characteristics were not the only culprits. Taft was also excruciatingly careful to detail the minute ways in which these immigrants were an astonishingly base people. While higher incomes might help reduce Portuguese infant mortality, he remained doubtful as to whether material improvement would have any meaningful impact. In his view, wage increases would be useless without somehow altering "the personal causes of infant deaths": "ignorance on the part of mothers, improper spacing of pregnancies which accompanies ignorance, and certain other," presumably racial, "characteristics of the nationality."[6]

Taft's book was well received by the scholarly community. It eventually landed him a position at Ohio State University and a positive review from famed University of Chicago sociologist Robert Park. According to Park, it was a "careful and cautious" study that showed the Portuguese to be, "by all the accepted standards, a low-grade people, and one that responds very slowly to supposedly better economic and living conditions of the American environment."[7]

Portuguese immigrants, however, did not share in the scholarly consensus. The local Portuguese immigrant newspaper, *A Alvorada*, published two livid reviews, side by side, on the front page of their March 19, 1924, edition. Local Azorean Alipio C. Bartholo defended his countrymen against Taft's calumnies: "There is, of course, amongst [us] a great number of illiterates, but illiteracy does not mean stupidity, but rather a lack of intellectual culture, and poverty is not, nor has it ever been, synonymous with stupidity or ignorance."[8] The other editorial blasted Taft's book as "statistics without basis, assertions without formal evidence, and absurd conclusions; nothing more."[9] Curiously, both editorials condemned Taft for failing to visit the Azorean islands.[10]

Nevertheless, the conclusions were already rendered, the book was already published, and Taft himself was halfway across the country. So, what was the point of protesting? What were these angry demonstrators in Grove Park actually trying to achieve? The answer is somewhat surprising: the protests targeted neither Taft nor the American intellectual or political establishment more generally. Instead, their primary audience was their homeland. As one speaker at the New Bedford rally put it, their purpose in gathering was to show the "Portuguese Colony of New Bedford's desire that our government" take on the responsibility of "responding to the book in question . . . in whatever way the Portuguese government considers most convenient and dignified for restoring prestige and lifting the Portuguese name."[11] The event itself was led by a dignitary of the Portuguese consulate in Fall River, Dr. Castro Madureira.[12] Moreover, at the demonstration's conclusion, all agreed to send copies of Taft's book to "each of the Portuguese Universities, namely, Lisbon, Coimbra, and Porto, so that all of the great professors and doctors in sociology can respond scientifically to this hypothetical work by Dr. Donald R. Taft."[13] It is not altogether improbable that future Portuguese dictator

Dr. Oliveira Salazar—then head of the Social Science department at the University of Coimbra—may have gotten wind of the furious reception of Taft's book.

Portuguese Americans never built themselves into a political force akin to the Irish of Boston, but, as the fallout from Taft's incendiary work demonstrates, they were indeed capable of mass collective action and political engagement.[14] However, their sights were not set toward Washington, DC, or Boston, but toward Lisbon.

It is not surprising that Portuguese Americans were searching for political allies in the 1920s. For American immigrants, the early twentieth century was an era of rapidly escalating xenophobia and racism. The Johnson-Reed Immigration Act, signed into law about two months after the Grove Park protest, was a fitting capstone to these decades of growing anti-immigrant sentiment. Allocating immigration "quotas" to the various nations of the world, the act erected a system of immigration restriction based on a hierarchy of racial desirability. Nations like Great Britain were given annual immigration quotas as high as 65,721, while "undesirable" migrants from nations in Eastern Europe, Asia, and Africa were either barred from entering the United States altogether or limited by minuscule quotas, generally not larger than 100 annually for each country.[15] Portugal was allocated a mere 440 immigrants each year.[16] The legislation inaugurated some forty years of migratory stagnation in Massachusetts.

The eventual overthrow of quota restriction by the reformist 1965 Hart-Celler Act did help "open" the doors to American immigration, but Hart-Celler was never intended as a means of increasing immigration or even eliminating the concept of quotas.[17] Instead, the 1965 reforms sought to transform a system of immigration restriction based on nationality and race into one based on economic need and familial connection. Portuguese emigrants, lacking any real skills unavailable within the American working population, thus depended almost wholly on a transatlantic community of kin and fellow Portuguese migrants to open up the possibility of immigration in the post-1965 era.

By the late 1960s, capitalizing on the reforms introduced by Hart-Celler, a tremendous surge of Portuguese immigration to Massachusetts would transform the state's industrial economy. Riding a rising tide of immigrant labor, Massachusetts factories prospered. As other eastern manufacturers found themselves beset by tight labor markets and rising wage rates, Massachusetts manufacturers had found a constant source of immigrant labor at their disposal.

Why, despite decades of migratory stagnation, did the connections between Portugal and Massachusetts remain so strong? It may seem only natural that for immigrant families who arrived in the late nineteenth and early twentieth centuries, the link between them and their brethren back home would remain strong after some 50 to 100 years; but immigrants to the United States faced heavy pressures to assimilate into American culture, particularly during the decades of war and global crisis spanning the 1920s to the 1950s.[18] Other ethnic groups developed decidedly frosty relations across the generations. It was not uncommon for other immigrant groups to see the arrival of their "unwashed" brethren as less an opportunity than a threat to their hard-won American respectability.[19] The entrenched Portuguese communities of Massachusetts, however, remained closely linked to their home country, fighting hard to bring their compatriots to the United States.

For Portuguese immigrants, these midcentury years certainly did not see a rush toward Americanization and assimilation.[20] Portuguese immigrants instead blazed a somewhat exceptional path, due in large part to the machinations of a fascist dictatorship in Portugal determined to foment Portuguese nationalism in its emigrant colonies abroad, including its "colony" in America. While other immigrant groups drifted toward new, more thoroughly American identities, fascist Portugal used its might—manifested through often covert mechanisms—to make sure Portuguese Americans stayed deeply connected to their homeland. Through the circuitous connections of a global capitalist system, the Portuguese state was in part responsible for reopening the doors to migration for Portuguese immigrants and, by extension, the prosperity of 1960s Massachusetts manufacturing.

Being Portuguese in Midcentury Massachusetts

The nearly 250,000 Portuguese who arrived in the United States from 1880 to 1929 left a nation in disarray—a fact that many seemed to understand innately.[21] Portuguese intellectuals had long ago conceded that their nation had become ensnared in some sort of inexorable decline following the close of the so-called marvelous century of 1415–1515.[22] Portugal's vigorous emigration restriction edicts were one result of this consensus; the state's emigrants often took the blame for national and imperial decline. Migrant Azoreans were thus acutely aware that they were, more often than not, viewed by their compatriots as betrayers of Portuguese progress and perhaps even the root cause of Portugal's decline.[23]

Yet Portugal's antipathy toward its emigrants paled in comparison to the outright hatred many Americans harbored for these incoming migrants. As Taft's book showed all too well, early twentieth-century America was riddled with xenophobia and anti-immigrant nativism.[24] One of the most vocal anti-immigrant groups of the era, the Immigration Restriction League, was based in Massachusetts, founded by three Harvard College graduates in 1894 to keep those "elements undesirable for citizenship" and "injurious to our national character" away from America's shores.[25] Immigrant Azoreans—and especially their "Black" Cape Verdean compatriots—were quickly branded as racially suspect.[26] The Restriction League would spend the next thirty years lobbying Congress on various immigration control bills. The notion of using literacy tests to restrict immigration, for instance, began as a pet project of the Restriction League before it was formally enacted into law in 1917.[27]

Although the Portuguese of Massachusetts were very much aware of the bigotry they faced in America, their diagnosis of its cause often had less to do with American racism or xenophobia than with their frustrations over Portugal's inability to adequately promote its apparently massive global power. If only Americans understood Portugal's true imperial might—the argument frequently went—then they would have no choice but to accept that nation's illustrious progeny as equals. In the pages of New Bedford's Portuguese newspaper, discussions of even the most banal problems in the local community frequently devolved into diatribes against the Portuguese state's ineptness in protecting its emigrants abroad. One article on the lack of Portuguese wine consumption in the United States, for example, went on to lament that "the reality of the Luso-American colony is this: we have all been excellent people, we have all complied with caring, zeal, intelligence, and patriotism to our duty. . . but the colony of the United States" still remains "an 'unknown colony' to Portugal."[28] In fact, the author enviously compared the direction and guidance Portugal gave to its African holdings with the cool indifference it bestowed upon its "American" colonies.[29] Facing hostile nativism in a foreign land, Portuguese Americans saw themselves as an embattled people who searched for support from their government in Lisbon.

Thus, the rise of António de Oliveira Salazar and his unique brand of Portuguese fascism in the 1930s—bent on "restoring" Portugal's global power and imperial might—was nearly as compelling to the Portuguese of Massachusetts as it was to their friends and family back home. Born in 1889, Salazar's training in economics and law catapulted him to a position as head of the University of Coimbra's Economic and Social Science Department, giving him a bully pulpit from which to criticize the policies of the Portuguese

First Republic. As the republic crumbled, Salazar became something of an intellectual prophet. Following the ascension of a right-wing military government in 1927, General Óscar Carmona made Salazar Portugal's head of finance.[30] By 1932, as the nation's prime minister, Salazar began to consolidate his dominion over Portuguese politics through the formation of the fascist "Estado Novo" (New State) regime, formally inaugurated in March of 1933.[31] Envisioning himself as a true, modern-day philosopher king, he candidly accepted his title as "dictator."[32]

Yet there was always an imperial, globally expansive edge to Salazarist regeneration. The First Republic had created a whole array of unifying national symbols to shore up public support. Salazar took a very different tack.[33] His rhetoric of national regeneration was unapologetically and unwaveringly framed in global terms. He aimed to convince his people that, although they may have been small in Iberia, they were downright enormous when seen as a true, global empire.[34] For Salazar, and increasingly, the Portuguese public at large, Portuguese nationalism and Portuguese imperialism became ever more deeply entwined.[35] By staking his legitimacy on his mission to rebuild

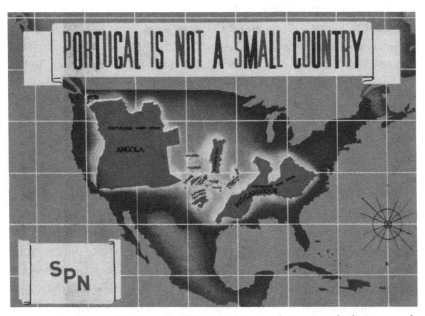

FIGURE 6.1 "Portugal Is Not a Small Country," Portugal, Secretariado da Propaganda Nacional (National Propaganda Secretariat). Postcard depicting Portugal and its colonies superimposed over a map of the United States to compare land area, extolling Portugal's apparently massive global reach and power, ca. 1951. Map reproduction courtesy of the Norman B. Leventhal Map and Education Center at the Boston Public Library.

Portugal's power and character on the global stage, Salazar emerged as a compelling figure to Portuguese on both sides of the Atlantic.

Salazar's administration would come to see the Portuguese communities of the United States as critical allies in its drive to rebuild Portuguese global legitimacy and power. For instance, Portugal sought to use the 1939 New York World's Fair, and the press and propaganda it generated, to formally reach out to "our colony in America," as Salazar put it.[36] The Portuguese state would come to deploy all of its engines of propaganda—neatly consolidated in 1933 into the National Propaganda Secretariat (SPN) under the leadership of fascist ideologue António Ferro—in preparation for the World's Fair.[37] Portugal ultimately constructed a prominent pavilion at the fairgrounds, adorned with oversized Portuguese flags, coats of arms, and an imposing statue of Prince Henry the Navigator. António Ferro would personally guide reporters from almost all the major New York newspapers, as well as New Bedford's *Diário de Notícias*, through the Portuguese complex, including the "Room of Industrial Arts," the "Room of Discoveries," the "Columbus Room," and the "Room of Portuguese Expansion throughout the World."[38] The SPN would also produce and disseminate a series of pamphlets among the American public. One pamphlet in particular, *Portugal: The New State in Theory and in Practice*, was circulated to major colleges and universities nationwide (a surprising feat, considering its highly tendentious content, such as its opening "fundamental principle" that all "democratic constitutions of the French kind," founded on the "rights of man," have "no economic or social content" whatsoever).[39]

Moreover, Salazar would use the main event of the Portuguese Pavilion's tenure at the World's Fair—his June 12, 1939, "Portugal Day" address in the "Room of Honor"—to finally concede to Portuguese Americans their long-standing demand for a place in Portugal's global empire.[40] The point of Portugal's presence at the world's fair, Salazar assured his audience, was "to pay homage to the American people and their work," to "reclaim for Portugal its fair share . . . in the formation of the United States of America," and to "give the Portuguese and the Americans an idea . . . of the force of the reconstruction realized in these last years in Portugal." "Our whole policy can be reduced, after all," Salazar declared, "to making it so that the Portuguese are proud of the traditions of their fatherland and to show them that the homeland is going through a resurgence operating in all fields worthy of the love and dedication of its children," including its American colony.[41]

If Salazar only hinted at the Estado Novo's emerging emigrant nationalist and community-building project, his chief propaganda agent made it a central theme in almost every speech he delivered at the World's Fair. It was Salazar,

Ferro told a New York reception in 1938, who insisted that Portugal make a strong showing at the World's Fair; it was Salazar who had "remembered the thousands of Portuguese who toil in America," and "with his vision always fair," saw their "moral desolation" and "deep discouragement . . . in the absence of our colors in this competition of nations."[42] Delivering a message to the Portuguese American community, Ferro proclaimed that "if you, so despised and humiliated in other times, can now walk with your head up, without fear that they will confuse your nationality, it is Salazar who has done it!"[43]

The ways in which Portugal's Pavilion might directly aid emigrant struggles for respectability became one of the most prominent themes in Ferro's speeches. The Estado Novo, Ferro reminded audiences, represented a regeneration for all who belonged to Portugal's "great moral imperial nation," including its "colonies" in the United States.[44] As if directly addressing Taft's book, Ferro observed that "the Portuguese of the United States have organized their economic life within the possibilities that are offered in this great nation. That which they expected, therefore, of the government of their native land was only moral support and prestige . . . to be released from this inferiority complex that has thrived lately; and for us to bring to the United States—so ignorant of our past and our present—this image of Portugal reborn and of Portugal forever" so that American Portuguese could "hold their heads up proudly alongside the descendants of other major nations."[45] As always, Salazarist emigrant community building went hand-in-hand with resurgent Portuguese nationalism and imperial power.

For many Massachusetts Portuguese, stung by decades of marginalization, this was exactly what they had long demanded from the state of Portugal. Salazar's collected papers make it all too clear how closely his administration followed the Portuguese American press; the archive is filled with countless clippings of articles denouncing Portugal's failure to adequately advertise its power and prestige abroad.[46] He used the World's Fair as a chance to fight back. Pamphlets like *Portugal: The New State in Theory and in Practice* were celebrated by the editors of New Bedford's *Diário de Notícias* as a triumph for the constantly denigrated Portuguese community. In fact, in November 1939, it printed a full page of letters sent to Portugal by professors and librarians around the United States, thanking the Portuguese state for its generous propagandist donations.[47] It was an especially curious choice, as most of the newspaper's readers would have been unable to read these English-language letters. The content of these messages was likely less important than the prestige conferred by thank-you notes from grateful Yale and Macalester professors and librarians.

Letters and editorials from local Portuguese similarly attest to how immigrants re-appropriated Salazarist rhetoric in their own struggles for prestige. For instance, Gil Stone, who appears to have emigrated from the Azores sometime in the first decade of the twentieth century, submitted his own "review" of the Portuguese pavilion. For Stone, the pavilion represented a new era for the Portuguese of America: "The colony cannot ignore that it was not long ago that Portugal was almost totally unknown in America... [often] mistakenly seen as a dependent of Spain or England! And then we all screamed for Portuguese propaganda in this country, as we felt a deeply hurt national pride, a deeply hurt Portuguese pride."[48] Thankfully, Portugal's presence at the World's Fair, Stone argued, "declares loudly that Portugal is an independent nation, sovereign, of noble scrolls and covered in glory through the courage and valor of its people. . . . The Portuguese Pavilion is the payoff and the eloquent response to the humiliations we have suffered."[49] In another editorial printed two months later, Stone would argue that it was "the duty of the GOOD PORTUGUESE: the GOOD PATRIOT" to push "our government to take the lead in this Portuguese propaganda crusade" as to "increase our prestige in this country."[50] Stone's loyalty would not go unnoticed, nor unrewarded. After getting a job as the personal secretary of the Portuguese ambassador, he would eventually be put in charge of one of Portugal's main propaganda hubs in New York City in May 1945.[51]

Luiz Gomes, president of New Bedford's Portuguese American Club, expressed similar appreciation for the Portuguese government. "If 80%, today, of people, know us then they thus know," he wrote in November 1939, "that Portugal is an independent nation; that the Portuguese people are an apostle of civilization; and that Portugal maintains vast overseas dominions in five parts of the globe, so vast and rich that we can call ourselves a COLONIAL EMPIRE—we owe it to HIM!"—meaning Salazar, of course.[52]

Portugal mustered vast institutional resources in its campaign to foment just this sort of emigrant nationalism. It apparently funneled some $200,000 into the Portuguese Radio Club in 1935 to build broadcast towers in Asia, Mozambique, Brazil, and North America to disseminate, as Portugal's head of propaganda put it, "political propaganda" through this "uncommon and patriotic initiative."[53] Through its Casa de Portugal in New York City, the Portuguese state worked to covertly inject pro-fascist messaging into New Bedford's Portuguese newspaper, *Diário de Notícias*.[54] By October 1947, the Portuguese government had also created an Emigrant Board that peppered migrants with both practical advice and political indoctrination.[55] One 1954 pamphlet began with the declaration that "WE, THE EMIGRANTS, have aspired, for quite a long time, for a BOOK that made us feel the HOMELAND with us ... to comfort us with the imperishable certainty that—*in any part of the world*—[the fatherland] sees us and loves us as children."[56]

The Portuguese state also cultivated a personal contact in the New Bedford community through journalist João Rocha. After Rocha was fired from the *Diário de Notícias* for, in his own words, "the links I maintained with the consulate ... tackling the onerous task of defending the [Portuguese] political station against a well-organized minority," in 1932 he bought out the newsweekly *O Independente* (The Independent), in an attempt to turn it into a mouthpiece for pro-Portuguese propaganda.[57] Although it is not clear what "links" exactly bound Rocha to the Portuguese state apparatus, he was clearly a close contact of the propaganda secretariat, and he certainly felt comfortable appealing to the state (and Salazar personally) in the hope of receiving $7,500 to distribute a pro-Portuguese English-language pamphlet in 1939.[58] After a member of the Portuguese embassy, Laurinda Andrade, successfully lobbied the City of New Bedford to begin teaching Portuguese in the local high school, Rocha would help her co-found the Portuguese Educational Society of New Bedford, Massachusetts, in 1944 to "promote the learning and teaching of the Portuguese language" by giving out college scholarships to students who chose to learn Portuguese in high school.[59] Through everything from ordinary subsidies to elaborate fetes, the Portuguese state apparatus continued to work in the background to keep Portuguese identity and national pride alive among its emigrants in Massachusetts.

António Ferro even came up with a broader "Campaign of 'Lusitanidade' in all of America" that entailed "guiding through a distance ... the Portuguese press in Brazil and all of Portuguese media throughout the New World," subsidizing local libraries to include more Portuguese books, setting up Portuguese primary schools across the United States, and putting on Portuguese music concerts to help "[keep] alive within these emigrants the pride of their origins and elucidating them on the progress of Portugal these past years."[60] Ferro planned a larger media offensive, including the creation of "a Portuguese weekly covertly linked" to Portugal's National Propaganda Secretariat and the creation of a Los Angeles consulate with the sole purpose of infiltrating Hollywood to foment the production of more pro-Portuguese cinema.[61]

Although these Hollywood dreams likely fizzled out, Portugal's more immediate goals in New Bedford certainly bore fruit. Throughout the 1940s and 1950s, the Portuguese-American Club and the New York–based Casa de

Portugal would throw lavish Portugal Day celebrations. Both also continued to print propaganda advertisements in local newspapers. Some expounded the great progress made in Portugal under Salazar's leadership; others urged Portuguese residents of America to continue to keep their Portuguese identity alive.[62] After the Portuguese state declared Portugal Day an official international holiday in 1956, the *Diário de Notícias* took the initiative of launching an annual celebration in New Bedford—"in conformity with the desires expressed by the Portuguese government."[63]

Even as Portuguese immigrants joined the patriotic fervor surrounding the United States' involvement in the Second World War, they did not adopt some sort of homogenized Americanism. Wartime pamphlets from the Associação Beneficente Aliança Portuguesa (Portuguese Mutual Aid Society) of Fall River, for instance, show how easily Portuguese immigrants could fold Portugal and the United States together as intimate allies in the struggle against Nazism.[64] This was no easy task, considering that Portugal was itself both fascist and officially neutral during the conflict. Salazar, terrified of a German invasion of Iberia, remained officially uncommitted throughout the war. He even called for a formal "half-day" of mourning following Hitler's suicide, hoping to demonstrate Portugal's only "half" commitment to either side.[65] Nevertheless, the establishment of American air bases in the Azores, as well as the fact that Portugal was apparently the victim of the "first act" of Japanese "treason"—a reference to the killing of forty-eight Portuguese missionaries in Japan in 1639—became points of pride among local Azoreans during World War II.[66] Even with a neutral homeland, Portuguese American wartime patriotism had a distinctly Portuguese hue.

What exactly did Salazar want from his American colony? The official state position was that it was merely answering these emigrants' frequent calls for aid, but it is hard not to speculate about other, more self-interested goals.[67] After all, Salazar likely recognized the crucial role that both emigrant remittances and American dollars played in supporting the Portuguese economy. His papers reveal a desire to use these "colonies" as an opening wedge to increase American consumption of Portuguese goods. Americans were, as Ferro assured Salazar, basically "kids that always want new toys" and, with their ideology of "joy, artless joy, not immoral but amoral, joy for joy's sake," they could easily be sold on Portuguese culture. "If [Americans] were intelligently understood in their infantile psychology, their love of flashy news, they could solve our economic problems, becoming the best market for our products." The United States was, he concluded, "a continent of big kids, and to understand it is to dominate it."[68] Portuguese emigrants, by projecting

Portuguese nationalism within their new national settings, could perhaps be exploited to shore up the national economy.

Regardless of Portugal's underlying motivations, the Portuguese of Massachusetts took the state's emigrant community–building project seriously. For these migrants, so embittered by the experiences of the early twentieth century, the ability to claim the mantle of empire for the Portuguese people was a crucial ingredient in their claims to respectability as equals in the American nation. Rather than distancing themselves from their ethnic heritage to gain the hallmarks of American respectability, immigrant thinkers instead argued that respectability came from their affiliation with a powerful Portuguese empire. Consequently, Salazarist efforts at building emigrant nationalism countered trends toward assimilation, strengthening these immigrants' connection to both their homeland and their identities as Portuguese emigrants. In contrast to the common experience of wartime and postwar immigrant Americanization, Portuguese Americans remained distinctively connected to their homeland and never fully part of the American mainstream.

Making Migration Free

The efforts of the Portuguese state apparatus to keep its American "emigrant colonies" in the Portuguese orbit would yield unexpected benefits when the doorway to free migration began to slowly reopen in the 1950s and 1960s. After a series of eruptions in 1957 and 1958 from the Capelinhos Volcano on the western coast of the Azorean island of Faial left nearly 25,000 Azoreans homeless, the relocation of displaced Azoreans to the United States became a major goal for both the Azorean government and the Portuguese of Massachusetts.[69] What they succeeded in achieving—a series of congressional Azorean Refugee Acts that ultimately allowed some 5,000 Portuguese to immigrate to America beyond Portugal's quota allocation—owed its existence to the political activism of Portuguese Americans, the Portuguese government, and the connections between the two.[70]

Local Portuguese immigrants and their descendants took an outsized role in lobbying for the Refugee Acts. They took letters received from kin in Faial and submitted them to local newspapers ("it looks like the end of the world," one letter read; "we are here trusting in God, crying and hungry") to drum up awareness of the crisis.[71] Portuguese groups in both California and Massachusetts also ran fundraising drives to help those affected.[72] Perhaps most important, groups like the Portuguese-American Civic League, the

União Portuguesa Beneficente, the Portuguese-American Democrats of Rhode Island, and the Clube Social Português bombarded local congressional offices with demands for a temporary suspension of American immigration law to ameliorate the crisis.[73] Particularly targeted were representatives such as Joseph Martin Jr.—re-elected to Congress on a wave of Portuguese support based on his past struggles to raise the Portuguese immigration quota—and the recently elected Senator John F. Kennedy, who had also received tremendous support from the Portuguese community.[74]

Officials in the Portuguese government also worked behind the scenes to alleviate the Azorean crisis, depending heavily on the organized might and unity of Portuguese American communities. Officially, Salazar favored relocating displaced Azoreans to Africa, not to the United States. Salazar, after all, was both fiercely pro-imperialist and highly suspicious of America's global hegemony. He had long suspected (somewhat accurately) that the United States harbored annexationist intentions with the Azores.[75] Nevertheless, in the aftermath of the eruption, Freitas Pimentel, governor of Horta (the Azorean island to which Faialense refugees were removed), began directly lobbying American lawmakers while also encouraging Portuguese Americans to agitate for immigration reform.[76]

Pimentel was able to use Portugal's own logic of emigrant community building to legitimize American relocation. When confronted by a critic who claimed that Faialense relocated to America would be "irremediably lost to Portugal," the governor fired back that this "fresh crop of Azoreans" would instead ensure that the Portuguese community of America did not "[disappear] within one or two generations . . . [bringing] it new blood, which will guarantee its survival for a century."[77] Fittingly, the Portuguese state rewarded those American Portuguese who raised money for these refugees and lobbied for the Refugee Acts with an official trip to Faial and Lisbon in August of 1958 to meet with top-ranking officials, including Salazar himself.[78] As one consular official noted, the trip would be "another step in the direction of what can be our only policy toward the colony: to create among its leaders the unity, whose lack has been the major obstacle to the fair social improvement of our community."[79] The Portuguese secretary-general of the Ministry of Foreign Affairs even considered giving Kennedy a formal Portuguese decoration until he was reminded that the senator had revealed himself as too "uncomprehending and hostile" toward Portugal's imperial policies.[80] The Portuguese state continued to encourage, manipulate, and selectively diminish the connection between Azoreans and Azorean Americans to suit its own purposes.

Nevertheless, these connections were instrumental in making Portuguese immigration a political and legal possibility. In supporting the Azorean Refugee legislation, Congressman John Fogarty of Rhode Island assured Congress that he was "certain that the good Americans of Portuguese descent . . . will provide refuge for their relatives and friends and greet them with open arms." Congressman Aime Forand promised that his constituents "are ready and anxious to provide all necessary assurance that none of those who benefit from this legislation would ever become public charges." Senator Kennedy was similarly confident "that the people of Portuguese descent now in the United States will welcome them."[81] Importantly, after so many years of migratory stagnation, many of the Portuguese American families who sponsored these immigrants were not even related; some were not even born in Portugal.[82] The success of the Azorean Refugee Acts emerged from the organized strength—and transatlantic social connections—of the American Portuguese community. Following the passage of the Hart-Celler Act in 1965, these social connections, as well as the enduring sense of Portuguese identity and heritage in these communities, were integral to making free migration a political reality in the 1960s and 1970s.[83]

Before long, Portuguese Americans began pushing for longer-term alterations to the barriers to Portuguese immigration. In a well-timed publicity event coinciding with renewed debate over America's immigration quotas, a delegation of New England Portuguese visited the White House in May of 1963 to present President John F. Kennedy with a commemorative plaque honoring his efforts in the passage of the Azorean Refugee Acts.[84] By that July, Kennedy was publicly calling on Congress to abolish the national quotas in favor of an immigration regime that would privilege economic skills and "the family relationship between immigrants and persons already here" in allocating immigration quotas, thus ending the severe restrictions placed on "immigration from southern and eastern Europe and from other parts of the world."[85] Salazar confidante João Rocha also worked in the background, lobbying for the immigration overhaul. As a reward, he was invited to the eventual signing of the 1965 immigration reform bill, co-sponsored by Kennedy's brother, Massachusetts senator Edward Kennedy, and even received one of the signing pens as a gift.[86] The 1965 reform would enable hundreds of thousands of Portuguese immigrants to make their way to Massachusetts.

This was certainly not the end to which the Portuguese state had originally aspired when it began its project of emigrant community building. Nonetheless, the ways in which Portugal worked to strengthen emigrant pride and cohesion in the midcentury era gave Portuguese Americans the sense that they had a powerful ally in Lisbon. Rather than "Americanizing" in an era of migratory stagnation, they instead cited their equal status as "apostles of civilization," part of a grand Portuguese global empire, in their struggles for respectability.[87] Continued traditions of feasting, religious parades, Portuguese language classes, and ethnic media and newspapers—some of which were directly supported by the Portuguese state—functioned as a sort of life support for Portuguese nationalism in an era of immigration restriction.[88] As a result, the Portuguese were one of the few European immigrant groups with significant bursts of immigration to the United States both before and after the reign of America's quota regime.[89] Although a new legal framework may have made this migration possible, Portuguese social connections helped make it a reality.

Labor on the Move

Midcentury Portugal may seem a strange place to begin to understand the contours of the economic transformation that would upend the Massachusetts economy in the 1960s and 1970s, but it played a crucial role in that revolution. After all, it was in remote villages all over the Azores that Massachusetts manufacturers found a source of migrant peasant labor with deep connections to existing Massachusetts communities, increasingly eager to emigrate almost anywhere in search of a better life. Following a series of new immigration reforms—lobbied by the Massachusetts Azorean community—this is exactly what they did. Capitalizing on their transatlantic familial connections, Azorean farmers left for Massachusetts in droves. A sudden second wave of Portuguese immigrants flooded America's shores. From 1960 to 1979, some 175,000 Portuguese, mostly Azorean migrants, made their way across the ocean.[90] The Azores virtually emptied out, as half of the island's population left in the two decades after 1957.[91] Precisely because it was more than just "poverty" that made these migrations possible, these migrants would come with distinct ideologies that were not always conducive to their transformation into industrial proletariats.

In its efforts to more firmly connect the emigrant communities of Massachusetts to their Portuguese brethren, the Portuguese empire had inadvertently created some unintended consequences back at home. Even though restrictive quotas closed off the United States to most Azoreans from 1924 to 1965, the dream of American immigration was never quite dislodged from the Azorean mindset.[92] In villages across the archipelago, Azorean Cristóvão de Aguiar observed, midcentury peasants were the recipients of "letters stuffed with pretty things and dollars, speaking of a life of abundance, without problems . . . bags with clothing sent from relatives, with that special smell that makes people say: 'Smell the clothing of America!' America, America! A word that is pronounced with a mix of religiosity and aspiration."[93] Azorean American poet Álamo Oliveira recorded what it was like to live on the other side of that divide. His poem "Letter from João Valente" chronicled the melancholy yearnings of his brother back home in the Azores: "I was happy to hear that you have/ A freezer and a new car/ Sofas, closets, frying pans/ And dungaree overalls. . . . And with a fistful of dollars / You outfitted yourself in a store/ Not even a gentleman from Lisbon/ Can spend money that way! . . . It all sounds like a dream!/ I weep with happiness!/ What kind of land, brother/ Gives so much so fast?"[94] When Dr. Henrique Martins de Carvalho reflected on "the problem of the Azores" for a 1973 report on emigration, he found that the difficulty was that Azoreans were, on the whole, just too American. "Few [Azorean] families lack in the United States or Canada one or more relatives"; they speak "in American terms," and, most troubling to Carvalho, they "fix their aspirations" in America.[95]

As stories like these attest, while poverty alone did not push these Azoreans to "fix their aspirations" in America, it was undeniably a potent factor in causing Azoreans to look there with both wistful hope and stinging envy. The twentieth-century Azorean economy was ruled by meat production, dairy export, and a small group of rural elites who monopolized most of the islands' available land.[96] The system of "arrendamento"—the vicious institution of rural land tenancy in which poor farmers had to rent land, cattle, and equipment from local elites—had remained virtually unchanged since the nineteenth century.[97] In fact, it was not unknown for some impoverished Azorean farmers to find themselves forced into contracts in which they rented single cows in exchange for a certain recurring payment in milk.[98] As Azorean intellectual Luís Ribeiro described it in 1940, "the prosperity of the territory is in the hands of a very small number of individuals, and the bulk of the population lives [on] starvation wages . . . overburdened by sometimes excessive rents and subject to all the risks and vicissitudes of farming."[99] Little changed in the ensuing thirty years.[100] The economic power of these rural elites to control access to land—as well as their political power in obstructing state efforts to industrialize either Portugal or the Azores—kept much of the archipelago locked in stagnant poverty.[101]

In the late 1950s, the Portuguese state sought to remedy this situation through an ambitious, short-lived project of colonial re-settlement in Africa. The plan responded to Azoreans' very real demands for emigration. Until the

mid-1960s, however, this was politically impossible. The United States restricted immigration, and Portugal restricted emigration, wary of letting population flight further sap its already declining economic and imperial power.[102]
African re-settlement thus served the dual purpose of fulfilling Portugal's imperial ambitions while ostensibly easing domestic poverty.[103] As a result, the
state explicitly sought out poor, landless families for re-settlement, offering
potential migrants free transportation, agricultural implements, a three-
bedroom house, five acres of irrigated land, twelve acres of "dryland," and
forty acres of common grazing land in Angola. In exchange, migrants would
be expected to slowly pay the state back. They were unambiguously informed
they would lose their land if they "displayed maladjustment to the life centered on colonization to which they belong, disinterest, or bad moral, family,
or social behavior."[104] Nonetheless, for farmers locked in a brutal system of
rural tenancy, the offer of free land, a free house, and a free farm was hard to
pass up.

The reports the Azorean government produced in categorizing and
characterizing those eligible for re-settlement painted a dismal picture of
Azorean rural life.[105] Farmers targeted for re-settlement included Jose Vieira
Jr., a father of nine children, who, as one state report described him, "neither possessed nor possesses anything"; Antonio da Camara, with eight children, living off two-and-a-half alqueires (no more than .86 acres) of mostly
rented land and intermittent agricultural wages earned by himself and two
of his daughters; and Jose Salvador Correia, with ten children, "living in extreme poverty, always living on the product of his and his children's daily
labor . . . the home environment is the poorest I have ever encountered, but it
has always been so." "Living on the product of their labor, on land that must
be rented" became a constant refrain in official reports.[106]

Some Azoreans wrote directly to the state to plead for colonial re-
settlement on the grounds of their crushing poverty. Saul Tavares de Chaves
told the civil governor of the "general contentment witnessed upon the news
of emigration for colonists that wanted to move to the overseas Portuguese
provinces—Angola and Mozambique. . . . I, and others, are very anxious to
emigrate."[107] Antonio da Costa, too, wrote the governor begging for consid-
eration: "The life of a farmer, gaining 15 escudos [a day] is not sufficient to
live."[108] Manuel Medeiros Cabral, originally turned down for colonization,
reached out in desperation to explain "his great desire to emigrate to our colonies. . . . I am poor and a worker and as such I cannot afford tickets."[109]

African re-settlement did not become the panacea the state hoped it would
be. Within a year, government officials were receiving letters from resettled

Azorean African colonists, complaining of the awful conditions of African agricultural life.[110] The state responded by trying to make potential migrants swear a "loyalty oath" promising they would not return.[111] The whole program would be canceled—and these colonists apparently returned—by 1959.[112]

What happened to these transplanted farmers in Africa again testifies to the importance of something not mentioned in the letters of impoverished Azoreans. Although poverty was a daily reality for most Azorean farmers, it was not the result of an unforgiving ecological landscape. The Azores was ideally situated for agriculture. Instead, Azorean poverty was born of distinctly social origins: an unequal distribution of land, political power, and access to agricultural resources. Of the 40,710 farm plots in the Azores in 1965, about 82 percent were less than 7.5 acres in size; yet such small plots made up a mere third of agricultural land in the Azores. Conversely, about 2 percent of farms dominated nearly one-third of the Azores's available land.[113] The Portuguese state, too terrified to take on the power of its rural oligarchs, instead attempted to uproot poor farmers and move them thousands of miles away to less fertile land in Africa.

The distinctly social roots of Azorean poverty would shape their eventual collective voyage to Massachusetts in important ways. Those who responded to the immigration reforms of 1965 came to America with a faith that they would one day return to their homeland with enough money to buy their own land, finally capitalize on the archipelago's agricultural abundance, and escape rural tenancy. "Some people get upset when [Portuguese] come to this country," Fall River immigrant Raymond Canto e Castro recalled in 1989, precisely because their aspirations were actually not fixed in America. Instead, the plan was to "save money, then go back to Portugal."[114] As Miguel de Figueiredo Côrte-Real put it in the 1990s, "in the old days, a man would come to America but not with his wife. He would make some money and go back to his country and buy a piece of land, so he could organize his life, work for himself, have his own house, have his own piece of land."[115] These migrant Azoreans sought less an American than a Portuguese dream.

Not surprisingly, then, neither industrial work nor urban living was greeted fondly by these Azorean migrants.[116] This second wave of Azorean immigrants to the South Coast in the latter half of the twentieth century often reacted to industrial Massachusetts with a mix of revulsion and bitterness. One migrant who left the Azores in the late 1950s remembered finding New Bedford to be an ugly disappointment. The city was "so dark," and the houses were "all grey."[117] For Dineia Sylvia, "everything in America seemed very dark and gray, cold and stony."[118] Elizabeth Figueiredo recalled that when she arrived in New Bedford in 1974, she "didn't like it too much": "I found it too dark and the houses were too dark and I was expecting skyscrapers."[119] For Maria Tomasia, arriving in 1960, coming to America was nothing short of a "nightmare." "We left this very lush green place, blue skies, green ocean. . . . And then I get off the plane in Boston and all I see is gray! Gray smog, gray buildings, everything was gray! And I'm like, What is this? Limbo? Then I'd think, well, maybe this is just the airport—things are going to get better. Little did I know. Things got worse!"[120]

FIGURE 6.2 1960s New Bedford. Courtesy of Spinner Publications, New Bedford, MA.

Moreover, these newcomers' working lives were anything but contented. Fernanda DeSousa, whose family immigrated to Fall River in 1974, recalled that her mother's work at the Shelburne Shirt Company left much to be desired. "My mother wasn't used to working in a factory. In Portugal, she stayed at home and took care of us. Soon after, my sister went to work with my mother. Mom cried almost every night because she didn't like working all day in the factory, then coming home and having to put dinner on the table."[121] Dineia Sylvia similarly remembered that her mother "always said she should have gone to school when she came here." She too "used to cry at night because she found things to be quite difficult."[122] Azorean Americans frequently drew on the Portuguese cultural construct of "saudade"—a centuries-old concept denoting a powerful and inescapable longing for what has passed, often flaunted as a sort of unique emotional marker of the

Portuguese people—to describe these immense feelings of grief.[123] Although migrant Azoreans generally celebrated the material splendor they found in America, they often nonetheless missed the closely knit social life of the villages they left behind.[124] It is not surprising that most Azorean American art and cultural output, in everything from songs and books to poems and plays, has been defined by this "saudade de terra": a profound longing for the land and life they left behind.[125]

Consequently, in contrast to the wave of Portuguese migration in the early twentieth century, most hoped their children would one day escape the factory floor. Education emerged as a newfound priority for these Azorean immigrants, a desire reinforced by the systematic denial of education under Portuguese fascism. For Maria de Jesus, "we came to America in search of a better way of life. Not so much for me and my husband but to be able to give my kids an education that we were never able to have."[126] For another Azorean migrant, "coming to America was very good. . . . I wanted to be a teacher, but I didn't have the opportunities. Now I would like my daughter to be the teacher I couldn't be." "We came for economic and educational reasons," another migrant remembered: "At this time, high school in Portugal was not free. It was an expensive proposition for a large family."[127] This orientation toward education and away from the factory (or the farm) was rather novel in the Portuguese American community, sometimes causing considerable consternation among entrenched Portuguese populations who did not see these new aspirations as common sense.

Nowhere was this disjuncture between "old" and "new" Azorean immigrants more apparent than in a series of "reading" group meetings run for garment workers by labor historian Susan Porter Benson in 1979. During one session, she noted, "the divisions within the locals soon became clear: the older members (those present) scorn the younger ('they don't have any values'; 'they don't know what real work is'; 'things are too easy for them')." One member, in particular, stood up and declared, "I'm Portuguese myself, but those greenhorns are different." One of the younger people in the group, "a Portuguese immigrant woman about 25 years old," spoke up to defend her compatriots, pointing out that "not all immigrants were just interested in earning money and nothing else, that she and other immigrants were interested in getting out of the shops and in the meantime taking advantage of educational programs."[128] As Azorean immigrant Jorge Pereira similarly reflected in a 1990 interview, "the earlier immigrants" had "become very selfish and do not treat the new people well," musing over whether they resented the newcomers precisely because they were "people with more

education . . . people who wanted to do different things"—people who ultimately wished to abandon the hardscrabble life of the factory floor.[129]

Coming to serve as factory workers, these Portuguese migrants would revitalize the Massachusetts economy. Nevertheless, their desire for education,
their nostalgia for the bucolic life they left behind, and their disdain for factory labor made them a poor match for lives of mass industrial production.

The burst of Portuguese immigration to cities like New Bedford and Fall
River in the 1960s appeared a perplexing turn of events. After all, why were
so many immigrants suddenly flooding an area most observers thought was
in the midst of wrenching industrial decline? As early Portuguese American
scholar M. Estellie Smith put it in 1975, having endured some "50 years of
[economic] decline" with an end "not yet in sight," the Portuguese "had worn
out their welcome and not only didn't know enough to leave but were inviting others to come and stay."[130] For many, such as Smith herself, the answer
became a sort of clinging ideological incapacity for self-improvement paired
with the stubborn inertia of chain migration. "Other immigrant groups came
to New England, worked at jobs of drudgery for a time, and then . . . remove[d]
themselves from the ranks of the disadvantaged immigrant. The Portuguese
remained in menial positions, paying little attention to labor agitators and
social reformers alike . . . willing to work extremely long hours at dangerous
work for starvation wages, often with a good-natured smile."[131] Thoroughly
convinced that Massachusetts was trapped in the grinding gears of economic
deterioration, scholars had few other explanations for the behavior of these
immigrants.

Smith was just one of many who, even into the 1980s, relied on often gross
generalizations concerning the immutable "character" of the Portuguese
people and offered sometimes bizarre justifications for their apparently sub-
missive character in a place and time of apparent economic collapse.[132] Yet
Portuguese immigrants were neither uniformly politically acquiescent, rapidly Americanizing, nor settling in deindustrial ghost towns. They were putting down roots in fast reconstructing mixed manufacturing economies.

Much had to change to make these late-century Portuguese migrations
possible. Whereas Massachusetts in the 1920s was a highly protected
economy—walled in by significant barriers to both migration and trade—
fifty years later, things could not have been any more different.

Free migration, at least from the perspective of Portugal, reigned essentially supreme, in large part due to the efforts of Portuguese emigrants in Massachusetts. Their abiding sense of Portuguese identity—carefully nurtured by the Portuguese state—ensured the continuation of an intimate transatlantic community of Portuguese migrants ready to capitalize on the new migratory regime that arose following the 1965 Hart-Celler Act.

Through their involvement in their local unions, the Portuguese of Massachusetts also helped fight to make free trade a reality in the postwar era—with equally unexpected results.

PART III

From the Needle to High Tech, from Massachusetts to the World

Toward Free Trade

GLOBALIZATION FROM THE GROUND UP

IT MIGHT SEEM only natural that by the mid-1960s, expanding Massachusetts garment firms—flush with recently arrived immigrant workers from the Azorean islands—would be peddling their goods abroad in a frantically expanding global economy. It may even seem natural that they would soon be relocating those same factories to foreign countries in search of even cheaper labor and friendlier governments. But much had to change to make this possible. Textile deindustrialization in the 1920s was a purely domestic phenomenon in part because the United States maintained a fiercely protected economy characterized by staunch barriers to the global movement of both products and people. Mills could transfer production to East Asia or Latin America only if the pathway for commodity transfer to the world's most robust consumer economy remained sufficiently unobstructed.

Over the next half century, however, the United States would again find itself drawn into free trade, immigration reform, and the orbit of global capitalism.[1] This chapter reconstructs that critical transition by excavating the roots of the political economy of free trade in Massachusetts.

It was American business owners, the story so often goes, alongside their well-funded right-wing intellectual lackeys, who spent much of the postwar era working in the background to revive a "laissez-faire," free-trade ideology many thought moribund in the wake of the economic crises of the 1930s.[2] Workers were powerless to stop them. American unions' stalwart commitment to economic nationalism, non-radical politics, and Cold War paranoia had turned them into insular, out-of-touch, and feckless institutions.[3] In the hothouse environment of late century economic growth and transformation, the isolationist American trade union establishment was ill equipped to measure up to the sudden onslaught of globalized capitalism.

From the perspective of midcentury Massachusetts, a very different narrative emerges. Free migration and free trade, at least until the 1960s, emerged as a distinctly working-class project. As manufacturers continued to fight for higher tariffs and nationalist economic policies, it was the industrial unions of Massachusetts (and their affiliates) that embraced free trade and global development as linchpins of peace and prosperity. Midcentury unions are typically characterized as insular and provincial, but the opposite was true. Workers were not "shocked" by the globalization of American capitalism. Workers forged globalization from the ground up.[4]

Making a Global New Deal

Following the conclusion of the Second World War, the American union movement redoubled its commitment to the concept of labor internationalism. Although labor internationalism itself was hardly novel, this chapter of labor activism—with its focus on creating a more equitable and prosperous global capitalist system—absolutely was. Nineteenth-century antecedents, such as the 1864 International Workingmen's Association (more commonly known as the "First International") were not only oriented more toward abstract notions of international proletarianism, but they were also of an explicitly anti-capitalist hue.[5] In light of their theoretical commitments to Marxism, organizations such as the "First International" or the anarcho-syndicalist Industrial Workers of the World would have found the idea of "humanizing" the global capitalist order incoherent at best and counter-revolutionary at worst.[6]

In contrast, postwar labor internationalism sought to gain a voice for labor from within the global capitalist system. For instance, when the International Ladies' Garment Workers' Union (ILGWU) first called upon the American Federation of Labor (AFL) to convene a body of international trade unions in 1947, its explicit aim was to create a trade union body to coordinate labor's role in the reconstruction of the postwar capitalist system.[7] Similarly, when Sidney Hillman, president of the Amalgamated Clothing Workers of America (ACWA), was put in charge of drafting a report on how the Congress of Industrial Organizations (CIO) could create a "single, powerful and effective world trade union federation," the organization that resulted, the World Federation of Trade Unions, was intended to cultivate popular prosperity amid the dynamics of global capitalist development.[8] Its objective, as Hillman explained to a French reporter in 1945, was to "[assist] in the organization of the workers in economically backward countries" in order to "increase their purchasing power and living standards . . . hoping in this way to increase world trade, create more employment and generally to promote world prosperity."[9] Although Hillman would not live to see how his dreams of labor internationalism would play out, he was one of labor internationalism's most well-regarded early advocates precisely because he dreamed of the creation of a truly "global version of the New Deal."[10]

Cold War political objectives would also help legitimize labor internationalism. Communist containment was central to the founding goals of perhaps the most important international union of the era, the International Confederation of Free Trade Unions (ICFTU). At its 1949 founding, it brought together some 48 million workers representing fifty-one different countries from around the world, including all the major American unions.[11] The Cold War context was clear in the AFL Committee on International Relations' justification for joining the international union: "These are days of tension and travail. A powerful dictatorial government with a world-wide network of [fifth] columnists and dupes, is working tirelessly to pit people against people, race against race . . . to plunge mankind into another devastating conflagration."[12] For David Dubinsky, head of the ILGWU, such concerns were clearly paramount.[13] In his article for *Foreign Affairs* celebrating the formation of the ICFTU—"World Labor's New Weapon"—Dubinsky trumpeted that "50,000,000 workers in more than 50 countries have now branded Bolshevism the arch-enemy of labor," and, in offering a new pathway to global prosperity, the international free trade union movement "may well turn out to be the blow that destroys the pretense under which Bolshevism has for several decades made most of its gains."[14] By offering an alternative to the "red menace," the international union movement was central to how American labor envisioned achieving victory in the struggle for the hearts and minds of the world's working class. Moreover, for a movement so frequently stung by the waves of repression unleashed by the anti-left hysterias of recurrent "Red Scares," the concept of internationalist "free" trade unionism gave American labor an opportunity to further flaunt its anti-communist evangelism.[15]

Cold War imperatives did not necessarily destroy the political aspirations of these labor leaders. In the labor movement, as in other arenas, Cold War–flavored arguments could make for very radical politics, pushing union leaders to embrace a broad range of internationalist projects.[16] As ACWA president Jacob Potofsky, leader of the most powerful men's garment workers' union operating in southeastern Massachusetts at the time, told the 1951 ICFTU Milan Convention, "Improving the standard of living" of workers abroad would be "the only sure weapon for fighting off communist and fascist aggression."[17] Following this same line of thought, the AFL Executive Council decided in early 1952 that, precisely because the Soviet Union would seek out "underdeveloped" nations as targets of communist expansion, workers in Africa and Asia must become "equal partners in the struggle for freedom, peace, and social economic improvement." They thus dedicated the AFL to anti-colonial causes and "economic aid to underdeveloped areas."[18] Sol Stetin, vice president of the industrial Textile Workers Union of America (TWUA), which represented ten of New Bedford's eleven remaining textile mills, recalled his experience at the Milan convention as nothing less than a political awakening.[19] It was, he told the 1951 CIO convention, "one of the most stirring experiences of my life. . . . What the CIO has done for America, the ICFTU is preparing itself to do for the entire world," adding, "I say that if we truly believe in a democratic destiny, we might well consider the idea of taking some of the billions of dollars now being spent for armaments and set up a team of 300 organizers, putting them at the disposal of the ICFTU to work in the depressed and disheartened and confused areas of the world."[20] The Cold War, in other words, helped incubate an entirely new set of radical labor internationalist objectives that became central to the ICFTU mission.

Seeking a sort of utopia of mutually reinforcing international development, global unionism, and world peace, the ICFTU made trade liberalization one of its most immediate goals.[21] Its first Manifesto in 1949 offered both an affirmation of "the duty" of "industrially advanced nations" to "[help] forward those great areas of the world . . . which have not been materially affected by the industrial revolution," while also condemning "the narrow nationalism which leads to the protection of national markets by high tariff walls and other trade restrictions."[22] American unions followed this free trade line, working in partnership with President Truman's "Point Four" program for international development and supporting the General Agreement on Tariffs and Trade (GATT), signed in 1947.[23] Free trade had long been a key goal for New Deal leaders. The famed Atlantic Charter of August 1941, in which Winston Churchill and Franklin Roosevelt spelled out their joint vision for the postwar world, called for free trade and state welfare provision as constitutive parts of their plan to secure "freedom from fear and want" for "all the men in all the lands."[24] Global investment and trade liberalization were similarly key features of Vice President Henry Wallace's vision of the Century of the Common Man.[25]

Even when faced with mounting import competition in the 1950s, American unionists continued to hold the free trade line. When the AFL-CIO's director of research submitted a report on foreign trade to the US Congress in 1957, for example, he continued to argue for freer trade in the strongest possible terms. Even the restriction of trade from nations with low labor standards would be self-defeating, he argued, as it would only further retard their development and exacerbate the gap between industrial and industrializing nations.[26] Moreover, he declared it better to continue to liberalize trade with a better social safety net for affected American workers than to erect trade barriers: "We should not be forced to keep out foreign goods simply to permit American industries, long past the peak of their efficiency, to stay in business."[27] Although never quite so extreme, leading textile unionist Solomon Barkin pushed for a similar policy of free trade paired with re-training programs for displaced workers.[28]

Harmonious free trade expansion, these workers argued, also required international unionism as ballast. This was certainly the rallying cry of one of labor internationalism's most stubborn defenders: Walter Reuther of the United Automobile Workers (UAW). While acknowledging that "a very large segment of the American [labor] movement" had historically maintained "a narrow, protectionist point of view," during a 1961 speech to the International Metalworkers' Federation, Reuther triumphantly announced that the modern union establishment had "succeeded in overcoming that backward concept," winning "over almost the entire American [labor] movement to the concept of free trade and reciprocal trade agreements."[29] Reuther also made clear that prosperous free-trade economic expansion would require labor internationalism to succeed. Indeed, the challenge, he insisted, was to not "be [victimized] by an economic rat-race, in which international capital makes one group of workers compete with the other . . . on the basis of who can live on the lowest standard of living."[30] Reuther would spend much of the 1950s and 1960s fighting to build a powerful international union, capable of "[reversing] the process . . . so that the strong can help the weak, so that the high-wage areas can help raise the wages of the low-wage areas."[31] Like many other labor leaders, he ultimately dreamed that free trade—if backed by an aggressive international union movement—could promise real global prosperity and check the seemingly untrammeled power of globally mobile capital.[32]

As a result, there always remained an edge of calculated self-interest in American unionists' attitudes on foreign development. It is no surprise that many of the unions most active in the international arena were garment and textile unions, as these industries had historically suffered the most from capital mobility and, not coincidentally, had long intellectual traditions of support for more geographically expansive visions of labor activism. Even in Reuther's case, most commentators instinctively understood that his unwaveringly internationalist position stemmed from his long-term plan for the auto workers' union to, as one journalist put it, "follow the big motorcar firms abroad, on the ground that international labour solidarity is needed to deal with great international corporations."[33] When Jacob Potofsky of the clothing workers' union attempted to shore up support for labor internationalism in the mid-1950s, he appealed to this same sort of enlightened self-interest. The CIO, he wrote, "is developing close ties with the international free trade union movement.... There are any number of industries where what happens in one country has an effect on workers in that industry in other countries. There are even several industries where that effect is made more direct by the fact that the same company or an affiliate operates both in the U.S. and abroad."[34] Even as early as the 1940s, the AFL's original committee on participation in a world trade federation reported that "our common experience in trade unionism has taught us that where there are unorganized shops alongside of union shops in any area[,] the union standards are under constant threat. This holds true on a world-wide scale."[35] These trade unionists understood, with surprising prescience, the threat international capital mobility might pose to America's economic future. Labor internationalism emerged as their weapon of choice.

Capital mobility was, by itself, not necessarily viewed with contempt by union leaders, however. Their commitments to international development often entailed outright support for increased foreign investment. Hard-nosed AFL-CIO president George Meany called in 1957 for increased foreign investment by American business as well as "a sort of international investment code which would protect the foreign investor," so that the "risks and difficulties surrounding private investments abroad could thus be reduced, if not entirely eliminated."[36] Continually pushed by the vocal demands of its Asian constituents, the ICFTU tirelessly prodded member unions toward further trade liberalization and increased foreign investment.[37] As ICFTU president Arne Geijer reminded delegates in 1959, "Only a very great plan to channel billions of dollars to the developing countries can be regarded as a solution" to global economic instability.[38] In the postwar era, most American unions followed suit, pushing for increased foreign aid, capital mobility, and protections for American capitalists investing abroad.[39] Their enemy was low labor standards, not global development.

Pleas for increased capital mobility to the "underdeveloped" world can thus be understood only within the context of the massive organizational offensive American unions and the ICFTU launched in the 1950s and early 1960s. The ICFTU, for instance, worked to set up trade union colleges and seminars all over Asia and Africa.[40] A series of seminar courses for training women trade unionists was established in La Brévière, France, in 1953, Calcutta in 1954, and Accra in the future Republic of Ghana in 1955. A permanent Asian Regional Organisation College was also founded in Calcutta in 1952.[41] In 1954, the first international trade union course took place with participants from twenty-one countries. African American garment worker Maida Springer was invited to speak on conditions in the United States; she went on to establish her own garment trade school in Kenya and serve as an advisor to trade unions in Tanzania and Ghana.[42] In its first eight years of existence, the ICFTU college program would hold some fifteen courses all over the world, including in Finland, West Bengal, Khandala, Hong Kong, Tokyo, Alipurduar, Manila, Kandy (Ceylon), Dacca (East Pakistan), Seoul, and Hitachi (Japan). Early graduating students set up their own colleges in Jamshedpur, Badampahar, and Domohani, India.[43] Others founded trade union credit cooperatives in Pakistan as well as a workers' library and savings and loan institute in the Philippines.[44]

In addition, organizations like the ICFTU lent various forms of support to unionization efforts abroad. The voluntary International Solidarity Fund, created by the ICFTU in 1957 with an annual income ranging from about $2 million to $3 million until the mid-1960s (more than double the ICFTU's entire general operating fund), allowed the organization to underwrite a variety of international organizing projects.[45] The American AFL-CIO was a major early contributor, donating some $1 million in its first year alone.[46] Throughout 1956 and 1957, ICFTU activities in Asia included sending the international union's plantation representative to assist and provide funds for a Ceylon (present-day Sri Lanka) plantation union that eventually encompassed 90 percent of the dominion's plantation workers, sending Michael Ross of the AFL-CIO to provide financial and organization assistance to Malayan rubber farmers, and sending ICFTU representatives to successfully pressure the Thai government to release jailed railway strikers (and enact a new legal code giving workers the right to strike). The ICFTU also financially supported striking dock workers in Pakistan, led organization drives in the Philippines and Indonesia, and orchestrated a successful mission to pressure the US government to improve labor conditions in US-occupied Okinawa.[47] The international union worked with the International Labor

Organisation to get a series of minimum wage laws passed in Asia, including minimum wages for sixteen trades in Ceylon as well as Burma's cigar, cheroot, and rice workers.[48] By June of 1958, the ICFTU had come to incorporate thirty Asian constituent organizations representing twelve countries and nearly 6 million workers.[49]

Similarly, the formation of the International Textile and Garment Workers' Federation in 1960 was driven by the perceived need for a special international organizing effort for clothing and textile workers. In its first two years it pushed around $12,000 into its own Asian Regional Organization.[50] A special fund was created to focus on organizing "weaker affiliates" in "developing countries," particularly in Hong Kong. In its first year alone the ILGWU donated $5,000 and the TWUA and the ACWA donated $2,000 each.[51]

Although such efforts may seem remote from the concerns of the average New Bedford or Fall River trade unionist, this was exactly how labor internationalism was supposed to work. After all, the whole reason local unions affiliated with larger unions like the ILGWU and ACWA, which in turn teamed up with powerful international bodies like the ICFTU or the International Garment and Textile Workers' movement, was to pool resources in the hope of wielding power and financial resources far beyond what a single city, state, or even national union could muster. Thus, when members Mary Roderick and Alice Buraczynski of the Fall River ACWA Local 377 made the motion in January of 1962 to "pay our Local's share of the pledge made by the National Office to the following institutions: the Eleanor Roosevelt Cancer Foundations, Afro-Asian Institute, and the Sloan Kettering Cancer Center," totaling $173.30, their actions aligned with the larger constellation of forces and sources of support that undergirded their parent union's larger, internationalist projects.[52]

Available evidence suggests that local workers were more than happy to see their union dollars go to international reconstruction efforts. In the postwar era, New Bedford's TWUA local union was pushing a sizable percentage of its incoming funds into donations, other locals, and the national TWUA body.[53] The three-month period ending September 30, 1948, for instance, saw $50,230 of New Bedford money disbursed as donations, $44,810 submitted to the national TWUA, and $7,154 given to other labor bodies, more than maxing out the $83,564 taken in through union dues.[54] Just as Portuguese operative Manuel C. Simas of the Wamsutta Mill pushed for donations to the International Solidarity Committee in 1947, others pushed for New Bedford union money to go to the YWCA World Reconstruction Fund, the Greek War Relief Association, the Red Cross, Catholic Charities, the United

Nation's Crusade for Children, and textile strikers in Rome, Georgia, as well as $42,000 to aid the CIO's southern organizing drive.[55] Those workers who had pushed for more expansive union organizing strategies during the Strike of 1928 may have lost the battle, but, ideologically, they eventually won the war. Even local unions shared in the postwar consensus backing labor internationalism.

A Fraying Consensus

By the 1960s, the acids of personal and ideological discord had begun to corrode the bases of ICFTU power and cohesion. Most salient was the issue of anti-communism. While some, like Potofsky of the ACWA, Reuther of the UAW, and most European union leaders began to adopt a far less hostile stance toward Soviet communism, others, primarily the so-called Meany-[Jay] Lovestone-Dubinsky group of the AFL-CIO, continued to pursue a doggedly anti-communist line.[56] AFL-CIO president George Meany repeatedly and publicly denounced the ICFTU for its apparent "failure . . . to carry on an effective fight against Communist domination of workers." It was not coincidental that such angry excoriations generally came alongside demands for more American power within the labor international.[57]

Animosities reached a boiling point in the mid-1960s. In 1965, Meany denounced the ICFTU as an "ineffective bureaucracy, right down to the fairies," which was widely reported by world newspapers as a not-so-veiled accusation of some sort of organizational homosexuality.[58] Simultaneously, Meany began directing the AFL-CIO to drastically cut its funding of ICFTU international organizing efforts.[59] As the AFL-CIO withdrew from international unionism, it instead leaned inward on its surreptitious relationship with the American Central Intelligence Agency (CIA) to push anti-communist union organizing abroad, especially in Latin America—almost always with devastating results.[60]

Substantive issues were at play. As one commentator put it in 1957, while Meany wanted the ICFTU to push unadulterated anti-communism in all its international dealings, most other ICFTU unionists "thought Communism could best be countered by constructive work in helping to build up the trade union movements all over the world."[61] Most European unionists despised Meany's single-minded devotion to thwarting communism over building global solidarity, but Meany faced plenty of detractors at home, too. Sol Stetin of the textile workers, describing in 1951 why "America's message heretofore [has] not succeeded in penetrating into the hearts of men," pointed to the "utter nonsense" of regaling the world with "the glories of free enterprise, and the indispensable advantages of television sets, radios, washing machines, and freezers. First they need something to put into the freezer. They need food and also freedom."[62]

Reuther, in particular, publicly lambasted Meany's "drag-foot relation" to the ICFTU, his de-funding of international organization efforts, and his often asinine anti-communism as causing "U.S. labor to become alienated from its 'natural' labor allies in the free world."[63] He received significant press for his cause when he (joined by Jacob Potofsky) condemned the AFL-CIO's boycott of a 1966 International Labour Organisation meeting simply because Meany's preferred candidate to preside over the proceedings had failed to garner enough votes.[64] Adding to the tension was the fact that Walter's brother Victor Reuther—finding himself "with a sense of revulsion" and "horrified" after learning of the AFL-CIO's role in enabling the 1964 CIA-backed coup in Brazil—ultimately leaked information on the connections between the AFL-CIO and the CIA to the press.[65] The publicity and recriminations that followed made all too clear the growing divides within the American labor movement.[66]

By the late 1960s, mutual animosity had irreparably damaged American workers' relationship with the international union movement. Already, the intransigence and relentless anti-communism of the Meany contingent of the AFL-CIO had evaporated whatever goodwill once existed for the American labor movement in international labor circles. Tired of Meany's often self-serving demands, many labor internationalists were already seeing a silver lining to the seemingly inevitable fate of AFL-CIO withdrawal from the ICFTU. At least, the argument went, the ICFTU would no longer need to pay lip service to Meany's increasingly paranoid style of anti-communist labor organizing.[67] Dashing all hopes of succeeding Meany as head of the AFL-CIO, Reuther continued his public attacks on the union's increasingly obstructionist international policies; he would ultimately cease paying UAW dues to the AFL-CIO on May 16, 1968.[68] A week later, Reuther sent a check for $18,750 to ICFTU headquarters to formally affiliate on an independent basis.[69] Meany, incensed that Reuther was even in contention for ICFTU membership, withdrew the AFL-CIO soon thereafter.[70] The move merely formalized a long-standing de facto reality. By 1966, national infighting and the subsequent withdrawal of money from the International Solidarity Fund had already spelled the end of any meaningful international organizing work on the part of the ICFTU.[71] The postwar consensus on labor internationalism unraveled.

Although such personal, Cold War–era squabbles often stole the
headlines, equally important was the increasing tendency of local unions
to balk at labor internationalism amid the mounting threat of capital mobility. As the new political economy of free trade, concretized by the labor-
supported Reciprocal Tariff Act and the GATT, began to foment increased
industrialization abroad, many American unions shifted course.[72] By 1960,
Jacob Potofsky of the clothing workers, facing increasing import competition,
was blazing a very different ideological path for his union. During a 1960 convention speech, while nominally re-affirming that "we in the Amalgamated
have long supported the reciprocal trade policy," Potofsky began calling on
new forms of import control, adding that "reciprocal trade was never intended
to become an instrument for destroying American industries by unfair competition from sweated labor abroad."[73] As one 1961 editorial in the union's
newspaper put it, "in the face of a potentially murderous threat from low-
wage clothing imports, we have recently been forced to take measures to safeguard our industry from destruction." Nevertheless, the editorialist assured
readers that the union remained committed to free trade. "Does [this] mean
we've turned protectionist?" the writer rhetorically asked, concluding that
"nothing could be further from the truth," even going so far as to say that "it
doesn't make much sense to . . . wave the 'Buy American' flag."[74] Nevertheless,
a groundswell of anti-internationalism was rapidly transforming the foreign
commitments of these unions.

Local workers may have been in part following the lead of business
owners, who had remained stalwartly suspicious of foreign development and
competition. As the owner of Auerbach Bathrobe Co. of Fall River noted
with trepidation to a local ACWA leader in 1970, "I have just returned from
a selling trip, it was a very difficult one. I was bombarded with imports, robes
from Taiwan, Hong Kong, Korea, Brazil, [Belgium], [Romania], Germany,
Portugal, Austria and England. All at considerably lower prices." While his
competitors were paying $20 a month, he complained, he was paying $2
an hour.[75] In one particularly revealing incident, Auerbach was allegedly
ordered by Sears Roebuck in 1969 to cut costs to "[meet] competition" or
face the consequences. "Time has run out," the Sears buyer (apparently) told
him: "Either you set up a new robe operation . . . or admit your incapability so
that we can look elsewhere."[76]

Auerbach may have been exaggerating. He was, after all, trying to persuade
the union to accept wage cuts. Nevertheless, for workers, stories like these
would frame a new protest ideology, one suffused with increasingly alarmist
economic nationalism. In a historic reversal of policy, many local unions

began taking to the streets, protesting in the name of import restriction, and firing off letters hoping to receive redress from the federal government under the Trade Adjustment Act for factories closed due to foreign competition.[77] When Anita Raposa, president of the local ILGWU, got the opportunity to speak at a congressional hearing on Fall River's economic condition in 1976, she spoke of only one issue: imports. She demanded "government action to stem the unprecedented flow of imports from low-wage nations that undermine U.S. jobs in the apparel industry."[78]

Much of union activism in the 1970s would center solely on the rising tide of foreign competition. When Fall River ILGWU organizer Sol "Chick" Chaikin entered ILGWU leadership beginning in 1965, he made "import restriction," not free trade, the major issue of his tenure.[79] Bucking nearly two decades of American labor activism, Chaikin put increased tariff protections, cuts to foreign development programs, and the restriction of "illegal" immigration at the center of the ILGWU political program in an endless cavalcade of pamphlets, television appearances, news magazine articles, books, protests, and congressional appearances.[80] "Import restriction" quickly emerged as organized labor's new preferred method of ameliorating the social and economic ravages of deindustrialization. Yet such tactics only further divided American workers from the international labor movement. Jacob Potofsky's decision for the ACWA to refuse to cut Japanese cloth in 1961, for instance, generated ire from internationalist allies within and outside the American labor movement, especially among ACWA partners in Japan.[81]

These unionists did not necessarily see themselves as departing from their former ideological commitments. After all, their erstwhile dedication to trade liberalization had emerged alongside and was always justified by an internationalist union project that had largely failed to materialize. As Potofsky noted in 1959, though he "favored improved trade relations among countries of the world," his fear was not capital mobility per se, but the sweatshop: "I have lived through those sweatshop days—in fact, in some of our industries, those days were not very long ago."[82] Free trade was palatable in the postwar era only because it was to unfold alongside expanding international unionism. Failing that, most unions retreated back to protectionism.

Ironically, it was arguably the success of these workers' projects of international development and free trade that drove their later withdrawal into import restriction. To compound the irony, at the very moment that international trade unionism could have potentially pushed back against the power of mobile industry seeking easy returns on crisis abroad, American unionists took on a far more insular, nationalist stance. As mobile capitalists were ramping up their efforts to expand abroad, workers were doing the exact opposite, disengaging from their international allies.

What followed was not simply a matter of workers' inability to cope with the enigma of rapidly globalizing capital. Not only were these trade unionists themselves active agents in the making of globalization, but they also fought for it precisely because they saw it as a critical step toward worldwide prosperity through an expansive international labor movement. Their successes would reshape the Massachusetts, American, and global economies.

This vision of labor internationalism, however, did not last long. A grassroots revival of more insular, isolationist unionism would reshape the ideology of the American labor movement. Partly, the decision may have been strategic. When unions pushed to open opportunities for foreign investment, the business community seethed; when unionists decried foreign competition, they often did so to the cheers of local business leaders.[83] Combating the specter of foreign competition turned trade unions and the American business community into allies. But, by blaming foreigners, unions lost what could have been a powerful weapon in their arsenal: namely, international union cooperation.

The rise of the political economy that made the economic transformation of industrial Massachusetts possible in the 1960s and 1970s—a world of relative free trade and free migration—was not simply a capitalist ploy to dismantle American industry or upend American unions. Instead, free trade, free migration, and international development were constitutive pieces of the working-class vision of international prosperity in the postwar era.[84] Together, these workers and their political projects laid the groundwork for the transformation of the Massachusetts economy in the late twentieth century. Unfortunately for workers, they had imagined such developments alongside a concomitant expansion of a global labor movement that never quite lived up to expectations. Free trade globalization became something of a Pandora's Box. Once opened, workers could not contain the forces it unleashed. The dream of labor internationalism as a viable solution to the excesses of global capital flow soon seemed quixotic and naïve.

Not all workers lost the faith. One retired garment unionist, Max Klonsky, who had cut his teeth as a New York operative before traveling to Spain to fight fascism in the 1930s, wrote an angry letter to union president

Sol Chaikin after finding himself disappointed by an ILGWU Roll Back the Imports rally in 1983.

> Our Union International is an affiliate of the International Confederation of Free Trade Unions. Why doesn't our Union secure from the I.C.F.T.U the cooperation to organize a campaign for the organization of garment workers in the countries mentioned[?] ... I have been working in the garment industry for over 50 years and a member of the union since 1934, so I remember what the conditions and wages were then and now. . . . The gains that are won through this [international] effort, small at first, will ultimately stop the super-exploitation of those workers and make it [less] and less profitable for the exploiters in this country and those abroad to continue to pit workers against workers for super profits.[85]

The reality, however, was that the AFL-CIO had only recently re-affiliated with the ICFTU after its 1969 break. As Chaikin's lame response to Klonsky might attest—voicing support for international unionism but dismissing it as a viable option, since "efforts to organize" abroad "are constrained by restrictive governments"—the sun had already set on this moment of labor internationalism.[86] Massachusetts workers would face this new era of global capitalism with few allies outside of the United States.

8

Reconstructing Industrial Ascendance

MASSACHUSETTS AND THE REORDERING OF
AMERICAN CAPITALISM

THE PEOPLE OF Calhetas, a village on the north shore of the Azorean island of São Miguel, gathered for an unusual summertime celebration. "The
anticipation was enormous," an island journalist reported, as a procession of
townsfolk, led by the district governor, marched through the village on the
traditional Azorean "carpet of flowers." Fireworks and rockets lit up the sky,
and a local marching band paraded through the streets performing a rousing
chorus of "Maria da Fonte." Calhetas's citizenry had assembled to celebrate
the long-awaited introduction of electricity to their humble community.
"And, when the Governor flipped the switch," the newspaper recorded, "the
whole parish was lit. . . . There was ebullient joy and many faces glowed with
tears of satisfaction and contentment."[1] Services like electricity and television
were finally beginning to arrive in the Azores. The year was 1973.

The celebratory parade and festival ultimately gave both the community and the representatives of the Portuguese state a chance to vent their
demands and frustrations. A young student speaker, for instance, praised the
"benefits of lighting" but also "alluded" to the other "pressing needs of the
parish, especially water distribution, street paving, etc." ("which was much
applauded"). Later, the civil (military) governor, Colonel Basílio Pina de
Oliveira Seguro, put in place by Portugal's fascist state apparatus, reassured
the villagers of Portugal's abiding interest in the "progress of all the regions
of the country," while also thanking the people for the "spontaneous" demonstration they had put on a few weeks earlier in support of their dictator,
Marcello Caetano, following a disastrous diplomatic trip to London. Indeed,
Caetano's trip to England—intended to celebrate the 600th anniversary of

the Anglo-Portuguese alliance—did not deliver the renewed international legitimacy and good feeling for which its planners had hoped. Instead, it devolved into a media nightmare, inspiring headline-stealing protests all over Britain and drawing more attention to the ongoing genocide in Portugal's African colonies. Battered by African liberation movements, its long declining international legitimacy, and the increasingly vocal demands of angry citizens at home, the Portuguese fascist state folded within the year, falling in a bloodless coup on April 25, 1974.[2]

Although a seemingly remote event of fascist pomp and local color, the 1973 Calhetas celebration encapsulated much of what drove thousands of Azoreans into the open arms of Massachusetts employers in the 1960s and 1970s. Underdevelopment, poverty, political repression, and an unavoidable military draft for what was widely regarded as a doomed effort to save a fading imperial power would become core catalysts of mass human migration— facilitated by the tight kin connections that bound Massachusetts and the Azores together. Jorge Manuel Pereira, whose family immigrated to New Bedford in 1980, vividly recalled growing up with two uncles fighting in Angola and Mozambique, a cousin fighting in Guinea-Bissau, and the constant knowledge that "unless you were smart enough or had some godfather help you get out of it," all young Portuguese men were bound for Africa's shores in the fight against independence. "I thought I would probably be killed by a land mine or something," he confessed during a 1990 interview.[3]

Such discontent was not tolerated in public discourse. Pereira recalled a pointed moment in which he was chastised by his mother for criticizing the government. "My mother looked at me and said, 'Well, there are certain things you cannot talk about and blaming the government is one,'" adding, "you see, there were secret police who would arrest, torture and kill people." It was always more than mere poverty that pushed these emigrants to Massachusetts's shores.

As thousands and thousands of Portuguese migrants fled indigent villages like Calhetas for the factories of Massachusetts in the 1960s and 1970s, they spurred something rather unexpected: rapid economic growth. Manufacturing expanded, profits rose, and unemployment plummeted. In fact, local firms were expanding so rapidly that many local manufacturing plants were encountering labor shortages by the end of the decade. The 1960s became an era of unanticipated prosperity.

This prosperity came with ironic consequences. As manufacturing thrived on new sources of cheap, immigrant labor, Massachusetts industry re-emerged as a profitable site of capital investment. Local manufacturing firms were hungrily brought into the fold of burgeoning corporate behemoths. Proprietary garment and electronics factories transformed into mere subsidiaries of massive conglomerates, many of which were, at the same moment, picking up firms in Latin America and East Asia. In an unexpected turn, immigration fueled prosperity, and prosperity fueled an unprecedented multinationalization of American capital. Through the peculiar entanglements of global capitalism, emigrant peasants from tiny villages like Calhetas would lay the groundwork for both the resurgence and collapse of Massachusetts's mixed manufacturing economy.

Industrial Triumph

The reopening of Massachusetts's borders to new migrants in 1965 became a turning point in the state's economic history. The early 1960s had been a time of relative stagnation in Massachusetts, with yearly capital expenditures in manufacturing remaining essentially unchanged from 1958 to 1964.[4] In the mid-1960s, capital expenditures in manufacturing suddenly skyrocketed.[5] Expenditures in 1966, at $480 million, surpassed Massachusetts's 1957 record year by almost 50 percent.[6] The year 1966 alone saw 248 firms added to the state, durable goods spending shoot up 244 percent, electrical machinery investment rise a staggering 444 percent, and even the capitalization of textiles and apparel increase 165 and 71 percent, respectively.[7] By 1967, Massachusetts manufacturing was growing at nearly three times the national pace.[8] In fact, the state's manufacturing investment growth outpaced the national average from 1966 to 1973 in all but two years, sometimes by tremendous margins.[9]

In part, the expansion of Massachusetts industry in the late 1960s was a product of increased wartime expenditures. As one New Bedford journalist put it in 1966, "The Viet-Nam war has had many effects on the world. One, in New Bedford, has been to boost business."[10] Almost all areas of the United States absorbed wartime spending, but the growth of Massachusetts manufacturing was explosive. In 1970, Massachusetts manufacturing investment grew almost 25 percent while, nationally, manufacturing investment increased less than 1 percent.[11]

It is no coincidence that this marked buildup of industry ran concomitantly with a spectacular burst of immigration to the area. Manufacturers, after all, had a seemingly endless stream of cheap labor at their disposal. Portuguese immigrants were entering New Bedford at the steady pace of about twenty a day.[12] Although municipal leaders struggled to manage the city's ballooning public school rolls—conservative, Catholic Azorean families often came with many children in tow—finding jobs for these workers was surprisingly easy.[13]

The social and kin connections these Azoreans had maintained in Massachusetts proved crucial in this regard. Most Portuguese immigrants to the United States came under the aegis of a familial connection to either a resident alien or a brother or sister with American citizenship.[14] Azoreans got "pretty readily into employment," reported the head of the New Bedford Division of Employment Security in 1966, precisely because "they have relatives working, mostly in the garment shops, who get jobs for them."[15]

In fact, New Bedford's municipal authorities flaunted the ease with which Azoreans found a place in the city's reconstructed "mixed" economy. When Leo S. Harrington of New Bedford's welfare department was asked about what problems his office was experiencing in helping new immigrants apply for aid, his answer was telling: "No problem at all ... There just aren't any [immigrants applying]."[16] Azoreans were "quickly absorbed into the labor force," another city official noted in 1966.[17] Optimism continued untrammeled through the close of the decade. An exultant New Bedford mayor declared in 1969 that "we find these people to be industrious, capable, and they fit in rather quickly to the pattern of industrial life as it exists here in New Bedford. . . . We have a continuing pool of workers who are assets to the industrial economy of our city."[18] The Portuguese, after all, were not migrating to an area in decline; they were migrating to a reconstructed garment and small-electronics economy that welcomed them.

Local manufacturers, for their part, were vocally enthusiastic about these new migrants. "They're willing to learn and they're willing to work. . . . They're very well mannered and well-disciplined—unlike some of our own boys and girls," one local garment employer told reporters in 1966.[19] By then, local companies were placing calls to the Portuguese consul in order to recruit workers directly from the Azores.[20] Three years later, with factories facing persistent labor shortages, local Republican congresswoman Margaret Heckler was publicly encouraging more Azoreans to immigrate to the area.[21] Al Markson, a local garment manufacturer, complained that although "we'd like to expand our operations in New Bedford . . . we can't because of the labor shortage. Several manufacturers in the city have found that they must expand elsewhere [because they are] facing labor shortages [here]." Samuel Ades, owner of States Niteware in New Bedford, made much the same observation: "I employ 300 people now, but I could easily employ 350 to 400 if I could get them." When asked about these shortages, his son cited prevailing "affluence" as the problem: "As society becomes more affluent, women prefer to stay at home rather than go to work." Samson Segall, who founded Eastern Sportswear in 1946, offered a similar diagnosis. New Bedford's problem was "overemployment," he contended, as it created "complacency in the worker, who if not satisfied with his present job, can move across the street to another employer."[22] The fact that New Bedford was not a "rust belt" dystopia, it seems, was not good news for these garment industrialists.

Many industrialists would later confess that they likely could not have stayed open in the area if not for the sudden influx of Portuguese migrants. In the words of one late 1970s New England mill owner, "Nobody wants to do weaving except the Portuguese."[23] For local business operators in the late 1960s, affluence was the problem, not long-term decline or mass migration.

Renewed prosperity came to fundamentally upend the structure of industrial Massachusetts. Most obviously, this new profitability of Massachusetts manufacturing spurred a wave of mergers, incorporations, and acquisitions that quickly displaced proprietary firms and routed out family companies.[24] The "Massachusetts Merger Merry-Go-Round," as it came to be known by the state's largest organization of manufacturing capitalists, the Associated Industries of Massachusetts, became a frequent topic of interest amongst local businesspeople.[25] In 1967, fifty-seven Massachusetts firms were acquired by out-of-state corporations, and another fifty-nine were bought by in-state companies. In 1968, 106 were acquired by out-of-state and seventy-six by in-state corporations, giving Massachusetts the highest merger rate in the nation. In that year alone, some 34,000 Massachusetts workers came under new corporate ownership, leaving about 21,500 newly employed by out-of-state corporations. Overall, from 1967 to 1974, 770 Massachusetts firms were brought into the fold of larger national and multinational corporations.[26]

Conglomeration and multinationalization fundamentally transformed the relationship between community and capital. In former eras of capital migration, there had always been certain capitalists left behind, fixed to Massachusetts as a particular locale and thus willing to put forth their own time and resources toward economic revival. By turning proprietary firms into tiny nodes in vast conglomerate empires, capital owners were no longer emotionally or financially invested in local communities. The whole theory of conglomeration seemed to suggest that the best use of these factories would be to drive them into the ground, using their profits to fund expansion into new fields and new areas. Prosperity ultimately made Massachusetts shops a favorite target of expanding conglomerate empires looking for a solid economic foundation on which to push further expansion abroad. In so doing, it laid the groundwork for 1970s collapse.

The Conglomerate Ethos

America's first great conglomerateur, Royal Little, was, above all else, an exquisite manipulator of the tax code. Born in 1896 to a prosperous family in Wakefield, Massachusetts, Royal benefited from a well-connected uncle, Arthur D. Little—whose name would become synonymous with the rise of modern business consulting—who ensured his placement at some of the best preparatory schools, universities, and firms, despite his poor record of academic and business achievement. With his uncle's assistance, he was put, quite early in his career, at the helm of a Rhode Island rayon mill. The mill, however, struggled mightily amid the depression days of the early 1930s. Little—with a $200,000 inheritance—thus decided to change tack. He instead took up a partnership at a prestigious Wall Street investment firm. The timing could not have been worse. Little watched in horror as his inheritance evaporated amid the Great Depression's "double-dip recession" of 1937. Adding insult to injury, Little felt himself "burned" by an imposed higher tax burden because the IRS categorized the blunder as a "short-term capital loss" rather than a "business expense," as Little had hoped.[27]

The fiasco became a turning point in his life. As Little recounted in his book, *How to Lose $100,000,000 and Other Valuable Advice*, "If the government could take advantage of a technicality in the law[,] perhaps I could do the same to them in return. . . . What the IRS gained by treating me unfairly in 1937 has cost them many, many millions of dollars since."[28] Little was determined to beat the IRS at its own game.

Ultimately, there was no single event or cause of the conglomerate craze. If there was any guiding philosophy or logic at the foundation of this sudden burst of mass corporate diversification, it was the simple desire to use the profits of acquisition to drive further acquisition and, in the process, hopefully avoid the sting of potential anti-monopoly enforcement. In Little's case, his interest in the concept seems to have sprung from little more than his furor over an inconvenient tax ruling.

Little's key insight was simple but its effects were profound. While profits over a certain threshold were subject to almost confiscatory tax rates, a (profitable) company could simply buy up another (unprofitable) one, liquidate it if necessary, and, in the process, manufacture enough red ink to cook up substantial tax savings. That discovery would fuel all of Little's subsequent schemes. In 1943, he changed the name of his company to Textron Inc. and began to put his idea into practice. In 1944, he bought out a Rhode Island producer of unfinished cloth—Manville-Jenckes—for $5.5 million, only to turn around and liquidate enough assets to net a cool $2.2 million, which, combined with its tax loss carry-forwards, more than paid for the factory. As an added bonus, he was then able to run what remained of the plant for whatever extra profit it could generate. Over the course of the 1940s, Little orchestrated a wave of buyouts just like this one, acquiring seventeen textile mills and twelve garment factories all over New England. Armed with his newfound tax-code tycoonery, Little transformed his struggling Rhode Island textile firm into the world's first conglomerate.[29]

He soon realized that conglomeration could also bring in much-needed infusions of liquid cash—knowledge he exploited to literally save his company from the brink. When Little first began the long, complicated process of seeking to buy out the American Woolen Company, which was three times the size of Textron, he sold it to stockholders in the company's 1953 Annual Report with the promise that "if we obtain control of the board of directors of American Woolen Company, we are confident that the experience, the 'know-how' and the enthusiasm of our organization assures eventual rehabilitation and success for this fine old company." Reflecting on that annual report almost three decades later, Little admitted this was not an entirely accurate statement: "You will notice that at no point [in our 1953 Annual Report] have we stated the real purpose of our proposed merger of the American Woolen," namely, "they were loaded with cash and had a $30 million loss carry-forward." Textron, for its part, was completely out of money. So American Woolen Company's cash on hand, extant assets, and associated tax privileges made it an attractive source of quick cash. "As a result of this merger and the use of their surplus cash, loss carry-forward, and losses of millions of dollars on the sale of fixed assets that were later liquidated, Textron was able to continue its unrelated diversification program." As Little would later confess, "Without the American Woolen merger, Textron would have never amounted to anything." Corporate acquisition effectively saved Textron from bankruptcy.[30]

Little's strategies came at a high price for companies he targeted. After all, his whole point was to strip factories of their capital assets and cash on hand, exploit their tax privileges, and then run them into the ground for whatever leftover profit might be generated. Factories did not last long under Textron's tutelage. So flagrant was Royal Little in his pell-mell strategy of conglomerate expansion that he was eventually subjected to a full congressional probe in 1948. Solomon Barkin of the Textile Workers' Union of America prepared a series of exhibits to prove Textron's strategies of exploiting and ultimately dismantling local mills, including "The Milking and Closing of Manville

Jenckes Corp." and "The Mining and Stripping of the Nashua Manufacturing Co.," which Textron had shut down only three years after acquiring it.[31]

Little soon began buying out firms well beyond Textron's foundation in the textile and garment industries. In 1953 it was Burkhart (batts and pads for cars, trains, and airplane seats); in 1954 it was Dalmo Victor (radar antennae) and MB Manufacturing (aircraft parts); in 1955 it was Homelite (electrical generators), Camcar (small metal parts), Coquille Plywood, and Kordite (plastic clotheslines); in 1956 it was the General Cement Manufacturing Company; and in 1957 it was Fanner Manufacturing (iron foundry parts) and the American Screw Company ("TEXTRON, INC. MAKES OFFER TO SCREW COMPANY SHAREHOLDERS," read the headline of one local newspaper, much to Little's amusement).[32] The process continued right up to Royal Little's 1961 retirement.

Little seemed a virtuoso. He had transformed a small textile mill into a multi-million-dollar company that paid almost nothing in taxes. From 1952 to 1959, Textron netted $55 million in income, while paying out only $634,000 in taxes, an effective tax rate of about 1 percent.[33] "It has now been shown," Little exulted in 1968, "that through the combination of normal internal growth, plus growth through unrelated business acquisitions, you can get a better cumulative growth rate on capital than can be obtained in any normal, single industry operation. . . . You just can't beat it unless you're the one in a hundred thousand that comes up with a Xerox or Polaroid."[34] Not surprisingly, many businesses would soon seek to follow in Little's footsteps.

Little became a prophet of "unrelated diversification." His philosophy of (and justification for) conglomeration, however, was not always entirely consistent. The five objectives of conglomeration, as Little spelled them out, became oft-repeated mantras for future would-be conglomerateurs.[35] "1. Eliminate the effect of business cycles on the parent company by having many divisions in unrelated fields. 2. Eliminate any Justice Department monopoly problems by avoiding acquisitions in related businesses."[36] The expectation was that conglomerates would outfox federal anti-trust regulators with the added benefit that, within the corporation, losses in one industry could be offset by the gains of another. A bad year in metal fabrication could be offset by a good year in sugar cultivation, for instance.

Those who followed Little's next two "objectives" would have seen much to admire in the factories of southeastern Massachusetts. "3. Eliminate single industry's temptation to overexpand at the wrong time. . . . Rather than overexpand any division, use surplus funds to buy another business. 4. Confine acquisitions to leading companies in relatively small industries."[37] Little reasoned that there were plenty of small, profitable producers in otherwise sluggish industrial fields. While these were terrible candidates for internal expansion or investment, they were, nonetheless, fantastic sources of profit that could be tapped to fuel expansion into newer fields with higher returns. This tactic became colloquially known as "milking the cash cow": buying out and tapping the profits of profitable but stagnant firms (such as textile or apparel shops) to help fuel expansion into higher growth-potential fields.[38]

Nothing lasts forever; so it was with the targets of conglomerate expansion. The problem, frankly, was that Little's first objective (relying on diversification to weather the tempests of economic calamity) stood in contradiction to almost all the others and, in particular, to his final "objective." "5. Having made a complete analysis of all major manufacturing companies' return on net worth and found that only about twenty-five in 1952 earned over 20 percent on common stock equity, I set that rate of return in 1953 as Textron's goal for the future."[39] While, in theory, conglomerates operated under the notion that the strong could protect the weak (hence Little's "first" objective), in reality, most conglomerates set profitability targets for their various divisions and subdivisions. Stable, acquired firms were left in a double bind. Their earnings, rather than being reinvested, were funneled away to outside ventures. Starved of reinvestment, they decayed. When their decrepit remains finally failed to hit profit targets, funds were not diverted from the "strong" to protect them; they were instead shut down. Established factories would nourish others while they themselves were starved.

By the 1960s, Little's slash-and-burn corporate conglomeration practices had been elevated to management orthodoxy. Bruce Henderson, who founded the Boston Consulting Group in 1962, became the outspoken champion of the emerging "portfolio" view of the corporation, in which each management head was to act "as an investor, not as an operator."[40] The point was to deemphasize what exactly a corporation made or did and instead to focus on the capital returns it produced. As historian Louis Hyman explains, Henderson imagined a "2 by 2 matrix, with growth on the vertical axis from low to high, and cash generation on the horizontal axis, from high to low," and ultimately argued that corporate strategy should revolve around taking from the "cash cows"—mature industries "where the growth is low and the cash flow is high"—to fund both "high-growth, high-cash creating companies" and the "problem children," those with low cash flow but high growth potential.[41] Henderson simply formalized what Little had long practiced.

Conglomeration became an opening salvo in a longer campaign to free American business from any meaningful sense of local commitment. Since essentially the dawn of American business education in the early-twentieth century, the typical business student would have learned that publicly traded businesses existed to serve their stakeholders, including their consumers, workers, suppliers, and local communities.[42] Management was a science of efficiency and public service. As Wallace B. Donham, the second dean of Harvard Business School, summarized his vision of the school's mission in 1926, "the development . . . of socially minded business men is the central problem of business. . . . Our objective, therefore, should be the multiplication of men who will handle their current business problems in socially constructive ways."[43] Such thinking was never intended to seep into the more rough-and-tumble world of small- and medium-sized, privately owned businesses—just the sorts of firms that tended to dominate the economic landscape of industrial Massachusetts.[44] But publicly owned "big business" was supposed to play by a different, more rarefied, set of rules.

A new generation of capitalists—like Henderson and Little—argued that big business should not be socially minded and should not seek to serve stakeholders or solve problems in "socially constructive" ways. Conglomerate acquisitions and divestitures were to be judged not by whether they fit into existing core competencies or would have socially baleful or productive consequences. They would be measured by the simple yardstick of return on capital. This was the essence of the famed "Shareholder Revolution" of the latter decades of the twentieth century.[45] The shift was not instantaneous, but it was tectonic. The Business Roundtable—the United States' preeminent association of business executives—as late as 1981 issued a *Statement on Corporate Responsibility* espousing the older, stakeholder view of American business. Business, it argued, existed to serve "customers," "employees," "communities," "society at large," "suppliers," and, coming last, "shareholders." As such, the statement concluded, business "must be a thoughtful institution which rises above the bottom line to consider the impact of its actions on all, from shareholders to the society at large."[46] By 1997, its revised *Statement on Corporate Governance* struck a very different chord. It began by declaring that "the principal objective of a business enterprise is to generate economic returns to its owners," with the addendum that "the interests of other stakeholders" were merely "relevant as a derivative of the duty to stockholders." "The paramount duty of management" was, simply put, to enrich "the corporation's stockholders."[47] Business's social responsibility began and ended with the pockets of shareholders.

While conglomerate diversification itself may have not lingered long as a popular business strategy, this view of the corporation—the evaluation of all transactions and acquisitions in terms of investment return, pure and simple—became the new norm. If an established auto manufacturer could make 4 percent annually producing cars but 7 percent each year buying up financial derivatives, the only rational thing to do—these theorists held—was to shut down the assembly lines. The conglomerate, in other words, was the first step in the breakdown of the "stakeholder," more community-centered theory of corporate governance.

In Massachusetts, the effect was transformative. These emerging management strategies viewed "mature" industries as simply a source to tap for investment capital to fund new ventures in emerging sectors. Successful small manufacturers all over the state would be swept up in the process. Profits were siphoned off to fuel further conglomerate expansion; abandoned husks were left behind once revenues dried up.

Fracturing Community and Capital

Conglomerate theory called for capital owners to view acquisitions in a much more straightforwardly instrumental way: as sources of cash flow and nothing more. As former local owners and executives were transformed into mere "middle managers" in a vast sea of diversified conglomerate enterprise, their politics shifted to match. Their local commitments narrowed; they embraced a much more radical, laissez-faire agenda. Unlike previous generations of local capitalists—embedded in the local community—these subsidiary heads and presidents showed little interest in building a long-term future for industry in Massachusetts.

Racial equality formed one core issue that corporate absorption tended to displace from business operators' concern. In the mid-1960s, Massachusetts's business leaders had taken a surprising level of interest, and a surprisingly progressive orientation, toward racial matters. Walter H. Palmer, an executive of Raytheon, headquartered in Lexington, made a name for himself assisting local civil rights and public transit activists in the struggle to increase job prospects for Boston-area African Americans.[48] Palmer even used a series of articles published by the Associated Industries of Massachusetts (AIM) to encourage fellow business leaders to embrace a more racially inclusive agenda. He asked business representatives to join him in pushing for increased "government spending," the "massive rehabilitation of our slums," and the redemption of "American individualism" from "selfishness" and "material prosperity" in the fight to bring equality to Black workers.[49] By 1968, even the president of AIM was prevailing on Massachusetts industrialists to back the "black power" movement, declaring that "organized black power is the best hope we have that the deprived black man will acquire enough strength and capability to pull himself up by his own proverbial bootstraps."[50]

In fact, by the late 1960s, many Massachusetts capitalists saw their struggle to lower corporate taxes as making them allies with contemporary urban reformers, since they shared in the struggle to spur industry in Massachusetts's urban core.[51] AIM never missed a chance to emphasize its alliances with pro-labor, Democratic factions with whom it worked in the struggle to lower taxes for urban manufacturers. In 1970, Michael Paul Feeney, a former factory worker turned pro-labor Massachusetts representative, complained that he "never thought [he'd] see the day . . . when Democrats would be fighting Republican governors to give industry in Massachusetts a break that it sorely needs."[52] In promoting urban rejuvenation and racial equality, AIM was happy to extol its support for (and support of) folks like Feeney.

As the scope of Massachusetts manufacturing nationalized and, in many cases, multinationalized, AIM began to drop its emphasis on the particular interests of Massachusetts industry. Instead, it slowly began to pursue a more geographically unhinged, laissez-faire agenda. In 1971, its monthly publication featured a long-form editorial on the virtues of free trade, a tremendous departure for an organization long defined by its staunch protectionism.[53] The Association also began to embrace a more conspiratorial mindset when it came to the seeming "war" on the free enterprise system. It began to urge members to check in on how "the basics of our economic system" were taught in local schools.[54] One member even started a ten-week program at Walpole High School that provided both vocational training and an education in the virtues of free enterprise ("freedom" after all, "can only be preserved if more people are aware of the tremendous advantages of the Free Enterprise System and become convinced of the need for their support").[55] Local business operators were increasingly urged to fight for the interest of "free enterprise" as a sort of disembodied ideal.[56] As the president of the association fretted in 1978, "There are plenty of spokesmen for the poor, the unemployed, the socially or physically disadvantaged, and for every variety of narrow special interest or identifiable ethnic or racial group. . . . But how about the people picking up the tab: who speaks for them?"[57] Although "free enterprise" sentiments had survived among a select few business radicals throughout the twentieth century, it did not become the mainstream ideology of the Associated Industries of Massachusetts until its membership began to shift from owners and capitalists to executives and middle managers.[58]

This was no coincidence. The increasing disassociation between Massachusetts industrialists and local politics was driven by the transformation of firm owners into middle managers—or, alternatively, the increasing isolation and impotence of corporate heads buried deeper and deeper in the labyrinths of conglomerate expansion. After all, as newly minted middle managers struggled to adjust to their relative powerlessness in ballooning corporate hierarchies—facing seemingly ceaseless corporate restructuring and conglomeration plans—they often bolted toward new forms of political radicalism.

The story of Leo F. St. Aubin and the New Bedford Rayon manufacturing company is a case in point. Set up in 1928 by a Delaware company—likely placed in New Bedford due to the prevailing rock-bottom wages in the city—New Bedford Rayon provided respectable returns throughout most of its early life.[59] As a result, in 1951, it was bought out by Mohawk Carpet Manufacturers, which, by the mid-1950s, had acquired a manufacturing base spread over Amsterdam (New York), Brockton (Massachusetts), Dillon (South Carolina), Mexico City (Mexico), New Castle (Delaware), and Phoenixville (Pennsylvania).[60] In 1956, Mohawk merged with Alexander Smith, creating the multi-divisional Mohasco corporation, the world's largest carpet manufacturer.[61] By 1959, Mohasco had shut down every northern plant except its New Bedford factory, moving plant machinery southward. Amsterdam equipment went to Mexico; Phoenixville equipment went to Greenville, Mississippi.[62] Rather than shutting down the New Bedford plant, Mohasco decided to sell it off in 1969. It received offers from four corporations and sold to Empire Synthetics.[63] The plant stayed open until an unfortunate combination of price increases and an ill-timed factory fire forced its liquidation in September 1970.[64]

The president of New Bedford Rayon, Leo F. St. Aubin, was arguably more a victim than engineer of these machinations. St. Aubin could only stand by powerlessly as Mohasco considered a merger with the American Standard toilet and plumbing manufacturing company (a "fast moving conglomerate" with a "young president who is really on the make," as St. Aubin wrote in a personal letter). The veteran rayon manufacturer had "many reservations." St. Aubin surely suspected that ownership by a plumbing company would not bode well for New Bedford's long-term rayon production future—but he had little choice in the matter.[65] The sale of the plant to Empire did not make his life any easier. "For the first time since the first of July [when New Bedford Rayon was sold], I have had a few minutes to sit down and catch my breath," he wrote a friend in late October.[66] "[My wife] and I had a very rough summer. . . . For no good reason at all the retina of my left eye split and this had to be corrected. . . . We got through the selling of New Bedford Rayon Division to Empire Synthetics. . . . This has been a complete change of pace and [they are practically] changing the complete operation. . . . Business has been completely chaotic."[67] St. Aubin's papers certainly do not jibe with the image of the assertive and increasingly savvy late twentieth-century executive. He often instead comes off as a manager harried by the tempestuous corporate restructuring of his plant, with relatively little control over his future.

In addition to taking a personal toll on St. Aubin, the process forced him to cut back on his local commitments. As he spent most of his time at corporate headquarters in New York City or chasing new markets in Canada, he withdrew from many of the community programs with which he had been previously involved, such as his role in the "Onboard" Concentrated Employment Program, simply because he was constantly getting pulled out of southeastern Massachusetts.[68] Similarly, he cut his payments to the New Bedford Chamber of Commerce—the board long known for sponsoring industrial development in the region—under pressure from the plant's new ownership.[69] Most strikingly, St. Aubin began firing off numerous angry letters to politicians and policymakers, pushing for a more business-friendly posture.[70] To cap it off, he was convinced that the 1970 fire that finally destroyed New Bedford Rayon—only a month after the New Bedford race "rebellion" in July—was intentionally set as a reaction to the company's past support for creating more jobs for African Americans. Although St. Aubin had—in his mind—invested considerable time, money, and energy toward the cause of racial equality, the experience left him bitter and dejected. He summed up his state of mind in a letter to representative Hastings Keith:

> We at New Bedford Rayon have served on all kinds of committees— CEP, Onboard, etc., Give-away programs and feeding professional parasites. New Bedford Rayon itself has spent over $70,000 in the past few years trying to train the so-called 'underprivileged' groups to be rayon spinners (males), cone winders (females) which have minimal training periods of ten to twelve weeks that eventually pay $2.63 ½ per hour in base wages. . . . And after 60 or 70 trainees, we end up with possibly two that are still working; and we have been bombed out probably as a result of our training programs in disagreements with some of the minority groups. . . . [Go into] any of the bargain marts where the masses trade and see how much of the day to day wearing apparel is made in Hong Kong, Taiwan, Japan, etc. . . . Stop taxing the public

and industry to death—City, State, and Federal. . . . Stop all of these so-called 'do good' programs. We will soon have the whites setting up Vigilante groups. . . . Why did not Governor Sargent send the National Guard to New Bedford?" . . . [Labor and minority groups] have become part of little groups that disregard the rights of common decency in the ordinary citizen.[71]

St. Aubin saw himself more as a tragic figure than a capitalist puppet master. Although it is impossible to determine the exact trajectory of his politics, it is clear that the Empire Synthetics buyout and the subsequent fate of New Bedford Rayon left St. Aubin's local commitments slashed and his politics strongly pro-business and anti-minority—a noticeable turnaround for a man who had, just a couple years earlier, personally pledged thousands of dollars to the local United Fund.[72]

In a very real sense, then, the morphing of local industrialists into middle managers of vast multinational conglomerates weakened the connection between capital and community that, although never powerful enough to thwart capital mobility entirely, had at least ensured that some local elites identified their political interests and aspirations with the state of Massachusetts. When Massachusetts voters turned down a string of what was decried as "anti-business" legislation in the late 1970s, AIM's chairman credited the victory not to an organized phalanx of manufacturing capitalists, but to the "strong grass-roots effort of 'middle management' people in industry itself. . . . They wrote letters, distributed pamphlets, and even manned the polls," showing that industry could "beat the 'activists' at their own game."[73] Although the wave of major "race riots" that swept the country in the closing years of the 1960s—including the bloody New Bedford "rebellion" of 1970—has often been blamed for declining business investment in the urban core, the erosion of proprietary capitalism played a critical role in severing American business from America's inner cities.

Global Capitalism Unbound

Boding equally poorly for the future of industrial Massachusetts, its massive economic growth in the 1960s was also inextricably bound to the special incentives local governments and the state offered to mobile industry. The problem was not so much the incentives themselves as the global chain reaction they had spurred. States all over the nation and world began to copy the strategies Massachusetts had been honing since the nineteenth century.

Increasingly, "global capitalism" became a vicious contest of countless local economies seeking to outrun one another in the mad dash for mobile capital. Massachusetts was unique enough in this endeavor that it easily reaped the benefits of industrial seduction in the 1930s; by the 1960s, its enticements were increasingly drowned out by a worldwide chorus of advertised incentives and inducements for mobile capital.

"Industrial relocation" had itself become something of an industry within industry by the mid-1950s. Companies like Fantus Factory Locating Service and Conway Data assisted businesses in moving into other states and nations in search of the cheapest labor and best incentives.[74] In October 1956, Conway even began to publish a nationally circulated magazine, *Industrial Development*, that gave mobile capitalists a one-stop source on all the myriad incentives offered to them in different areas of the United States. Local boosters and business interests—from the Erie Railroad ("Ideal plant site in the heart of industrial America") to the Baltimore Industrial Area ("You'll find a site that's right!") to the Rhode Island Development Council ("world's most skillful people . . . competitive tax structure + excellent deep water ports")—had a central venue in which to advertise their special appeal to mobile capital.[75] The very first issue of *Industrial Development* in 1956 contained an index of the more than 5,000 state, local, and regional "development" organizations in the United States, all "seeking in various ways to lure you to specific localities. . . . On the average, two new groups come into existence every week."[76] Thus, even when the New Bedford Industrial Development Commission did advertise in *Industrial Development* ("LABOR—large resident pool, all skills . . . HOUSING—Suburban living for key personnel"), it faced staggering competition.[77]

Moreover, a trickle of local- and state-funded "industrial development" programs in the early 1950s had become a veritable flood of public spending and manpower by the 1970s. In 1976, *Business Week* declared it a "Second War Between the States."[78] By then, there were well over 50,000 industrial development organizations all over the country, and Massachusetts's sizable $2.36 million investment in luring mobile industry to its shores in 1974 was not far over Washington State's $2.3-million investment or Alabama's $1.9-million contribution.[79] Its industrial development staff of 96 public workers paled in comparison to the 358 in Ohio, 200 in Pennsylvania, and 183 in Tennessee.[80] Its advertising budget of $270,000 was a far cry from Michigan's $1.5 million or New Jersey's $600,000 expenditure.[81]

Direct industrial financing was also on the rise nationwide. The various American states had issued about $20 million in industrial development bonds in 1957; ten years later, it was $1.8 billion. By the late 1960s, that number was over $3.5 billion. Tax-free financing for industry went from less than a half billion dollars in 1969 to $3.5 billion in 1977.[82] A 1977 study by the Associated Industries of Massachusetts discovered that nearly half of all of New Hampshire's current employment could be traced to factories that had moved from Massachusetts, likely having left in order to take advantage of any of the numerous inducements New Hampshire industrial boosters could offer.[83]

When the state of Massachusetts and cities like New Bedford and Fall River had begun engaging in the use of public money to lure industry in the 1930s and 1940s, they were pioneers of sorts. By the 1960s and 1970s, industries could play states and cities against one another to get the most state financing, tax abatements, and free land possible.[84] New Bedford's 1971 industrial park was not quite as effective when twenty-three other Massachusetts cities had parks too. Collectively, the state had 5,769 acres of industrial park space.[85]

Massachusetts faced industrial development competition from other nations as well, all copying the tactics pioneered by the various American states. South Korea, for instance, took a large portion of the $2.6 billion in aid it received from the United States between 1945 and 1958 and funneled it to foreign industrial developers.[86] By 1975, US aid to South Korea totaled $11.6 billion.[87] Under the leadership of Park Chung-hee in the 1960s, South Korea continued to induce export industry development through inexpensive credit, tax abatements, tariff protection, and a devalued currency, all of which paid huge dividends when, over the course of the 1970s, the value of South Korea's exports ballooned 4,000 percent.[88] Taiwan too began offering textile and apparel exporters tax rebates and duty-free "export processing zones" to catalyze industrial development.[89] The 1949 creation of the Ministry of International Trade and Industry in Japan began decades of strict import control, the injection of public funds into industrial research and development, and cheap and easy credit through the Development Bank of Japan and the Industrial Bank of Japan.[90] Although the rise of the "developmental state" and state-led industrial development is often heralded as a novel phenomenon that took over the nations of East Asia and Latin America in the late twentieth century, the US states were crucial forerunners.[91] Federal officials may continue to wring their hands over "unfair" inducements to industrial development abroad, but the progenitor of state-led industrial development was more Alabama or Massachusetts than South Korea.

Not surprisingly, East Asian industrial development was about as successful as its American antecedents. A potent combination of state money and low wages—itself partly rooted in the failures of mid-century global union activism—helped incentivize rising conglomerates to seek new opportunities outside the United States.[92] From 1950 to 1980, United States foreign direct investment increased by a factor of sixteen; American domestic investment grew about half as quickly.[93] Such huge investment abroad often devastated local industries. The $1.2 million pushed into foreign textile firms in Indonesia from 1969 to 1974, for example, slashed handloom employment in that country by 80 percent while creating new employment opportunities for only about one-quarter of the 250,000 left jobless.[94] Thus, not only did East Asian states fashion themselves into magnets for mobile capital, but as factories opened in places like Taiwan, South Korea, and Japan, East Asia's "lure" became a self-fulfilling prophecy. The devastation of local industries—besieged by machine-made goods—left workers desperate, poor, and willing to work for abysmal wages. Meanwhile, non-migrating garment and electronics firms in cities like New Bedford and Fall River were forced to compete with their new, low-overhead East Asian counterparts.[95] Import competition exploded.

The first glimmerings of the so-called import menace emerged with these industrial development schemes in the 1950s and 1960s. The years spanning 1953 to 1956 saw Japanese cotton apparel exports to the United States grow 3,250 percent.[96] American cotton imports from all nations almost tripled from 1966 to 1972.[97] By 1971, foreign imports of dress and sport shirts totaled about half of domestic production figures.[98] Because the trade agreements codified by the 1974 Multi-Fibre Agreement regulated import quantity rather than value, high-priced apparel like suits and trousers became especially susceptible to import competition.[99] The decade after 1966 saw American suit imports increase by a factor of nearly fourteen and sport coat imports increase by a factor of twelve.[100] By the 1970s, then, state-led industrial development was amplifying competition between places scrambling for capital investment and manufacturers scrambling to cut costs. Pressure emanated from all sides, from New Hampshire to Taiwan.

———

The second half of the 1960s was a somewhat surprising moment in the economic history of Massachusetts. New immigrants flooded into factories, industry expanded, and unemployment declined. In light of what was to come, this moment of industrial renaissance has generally been neglected or forgotten, both by locals and historians. Yet the crisis that followed is incomprehensible without first looking to its recurrent co-conspirator: prosperity. By spurring a merger wave that turned proprietary garment and electronics firms into mere subsidiaries of national and multinational conglomerates, the prosperous 1960s would ensure that the crisis of the 1970s would be somewhat exceptional in the state's history. Business owners' political concerns had become more insular, more unmoored from the community; Massachusetts was grappling with increasing competition from other states and nations in its endless push for industrial expansion. All told, such developments did not portend sustainable prosperity for the South Coast.

9

Industrial Twilight?

MASSACHUSETTS AND THE REORDERING
OF GLOBAL CAPITALISM

IN 2013, THE *Wall Street Journal* featured an article on an unlikely subject: an abandoned textile mill in New Bedford slated to be transformed into
a giant grow house for medical marijuana.[1] The story of that factory—the
Hathaway Mills—is, in many ways, the story of the Massachusetts South
Coast writ small.

The first Hathaway immigrated to the United States in 1630, and, by the
eighteenth century, the Hathaways had entrenched themselves as major local
landowners and sea captains. Humphrey Hathaway built ships and ran a
whale oil refinery. His sons Thomas Schuyler and Francis grew his business
into a major whaling and merchant trade operation. The two bachelors also
raised their orphaned nephews, Francis and Horatio, who eventually entered
and expanded the Hathaway firm.[2] New Bedford whaling and, with it, the
Hathaways thrived.

As whaling foundered on the shoals of technological change and
tightening environmental constraints, capitalists as smart as the Hathaways
were quick to read the tea leaves. Horatio Hathaway largely abandoned maritime pursuits in the 1870s; he instead spearheaded the effort to organize
the city's fourth textile operation in 1881, the Acushnet Mills. The Hathaway
Mills, also founded by Horatio, was built just seven years later.[3]

There is, however, one way in which the Hathaway Mills' story diverges
from so many of its peers. In 1934, a local booster, Seabury Stanton, took
the helm. Even though, in his words, "many New England mills were closing
their doors and liquidating," he decided that there was still "a place in New
England for a textile company that had the latest machinery and capable

management."[4] While other operators were shuttering factories, Stanton successfully piloted the Hathaway Mills through the Great Depression. The Hathaway was then able to reap the profits of a massive upsurge in cloth demand during the Second World War and the Korean War.

Success, however, came with unexpected consequences. By the postwar period, these prosperous mills attracted the interest of the rising corporate conglomerates of the era. The Hathaway was absorbed into the Berkshire Fine Spinning Associates of Adams, Massachusetts, in 1955. The Berkshire Hathaway corporation now boasted some seven plants, 500,000 spindles, 12,000 looms, 5,800 employees, and a yearly production of 225 million yards of fabric—enough to wrap the earth's equator in cloth five times over.[5]

The mill welcomed the attention of a young, upstart investor from Nebraska, Warren Buffett, who saw potential in the undervalued firm. In 1962, Buffett began buying into Berkshire Hathaway at $7.50 a share. By 1965, he had achieved a majority stake in the company. He summarily booted Stanton— who had long made clear his personal commitment to keeping the plant open in New Bedford—and began using the factory's earnings to help diversify his own business ventures, quickly buying up the National Indemnity Co., the Illinois National Bank, Sun Newspapers, and Blacker Printer Incorporated. Arguably, Buffett ran the Berkshire Hathaway mill into the ground to make the Berkshire Hathaway conglomerate a rousing success.[6] Indeed, since 1965, Berkshire Hathaway's per-share book value has grown 3,787,464 percent.[7]

After two decades, Buffett abruptly ended Berkshire Hathaway textile production, simply telling stockholders that "in the end nothing worked and I should be faulted for not quitting sooner." As the mill stared down a future as a potential marijuana grow house, the mayor of New Bedford personally appealed to Buffett in December of 2013 to "rescue" the building that served as the basis of his multibillion-dollar conglomerate. Buffett was unpersuaded: "I don't know what you'd do with that place."[8] The mill was demolished in January of 2014.[9]

The stories of factories like the Berkshire Hathaway are often framed within the context of the tumultuous period of creeping globalization and industrial upheaval that began in the mid-1970s. This era has been largely understood as following one of three plot lines: a story of sudden "shock," inevitable "creative destruction," or long-term "disinvestment." Adherents of the "shock" narrative focus on the unique, macro-economic conjunctures of the moment: the rise of the Organization of Petroleum Exporting Countries (OPEC), the 1973 and 1979 oil crises, the fracturing of the liberal social coalition of the postwar era, and the ways in which the industrialization of the "global south" hastened the collapse of American and European manufacturing hegemony amid a new, "globalized" economic order.[10] For practitioners of "creative destruction," history and agency are mere window dressings on the long-term ineluctable historical processes at work: the inevitable stages of economic development all nations traverse on the upward ascent toward "post-industrial" status.[11] In their eyes, the disintegration of American manufacturing, besieged by a rising "knowledge economy," was an essential, unavoidable concomitant of continuing American affluence and economic development.

Many American social and political historians instead tend to see the crisis of the 1970s as a story of grinding "disinvestment." They portray late century deindustrialization as an outgrowth of long-term policy failures at all levels of government—a product of postwar suburbanization, racial segregation, and urban neglect. The crisis of the 1970s, by this reading, was rooted in a longer crisis of American industrial development going back to the end of the Second World War.[12] It is in this sense that Bennett Harrison and Jean Kluver, among the first to popularize the very term "deindustrialization," would come to describe the entire era from the 1930s to the 1970s as, at least in New England, "a sustained period of economic decline" containing "two generations of 'deindustrialization' and 'hollowing.' "[13]

By re-centering Massachusetts within a broader, global web of labor and capital in constant motion, an alternative narrative of late century industrial transformation emerges. From the perspective of Massachusetts, the long crisis of the 1970s was hardly the moment of industrial twilight it has so often been made out to be. It was neither the beginning of an irreversible decline in Massachusetts industry nor the climax of a longer economic crisis that began in the early twentieth century.

It was an unexpected result of 1960s prosperity. As local manufacturing firms like the Hathaway Mills were hungrily brought into the fold of emerging corporate conglomerates, their profits were summarily drawn off and pushed into expansion into other industries and other areas around the world. In what might be described as a sort of parasitic industrialism, these local plants were rapidly devoured by the era's rising conglomerate powerhouses, their earnings redirected into further corporate expansion outside the state, and their fixed capital assets run into the ground and liquidated at the point of exhaustion.

It was not economic crisis at home that pushed American capital to seek greener pastures elsewhere. In fact, it was profitable Massachusetts mills that helped build these gargantuan conglomerates in the first place. Run hard, starved of reinvestment, and having ultimately served their purpose, these factories would be shuttered by the conglomerates they themselves helped create.

In other words, Berkshire Hathaway's story was not unique. Although not every piece came together at the same time for every New Bedford or Fall River firm, the stories behind many of these old mill buildings make for a common narrative. Textile mills, built with whaling money amid catastrophe in that industry, were transformed into garment or electronics firms amid crisis in the textile industry, bought out by some corporate conglomerate in the 1960s, and then, over and over again, run into the ground to buy up new firms and new enterprises in other states and abroad. In so doing, these old mill buildings became the foundation for the coming explosion of apparel and electronics imports to America—the opening act in the slow deterioration of the Massachusetts "mixed economy."

"Milking the Cash Cow" at the Morse Drill Company

New Bedford's Morse Drill was well known to local workers for its pioneering history and, more important, its excellent pay and benefits. Stephen Ambrose Morse, inventor of the modern twist drill, founded Morse Drill in 1864.[14] It remained a fixture of the community as one of the handful of ancillary machine shops that supplemented the city's other industries, weathering the many ups and downs of the local economy. Morse jobs were especially prized in the context of the city's enduring dearth of well-paid, "masculine" work. By the mid-1970s, most Morse employees enjoyed employer-provided health insurance coverage, pensions, life insurance, and twelve holidays and four to five weeks of vacation each year.[15] Morse's wages were exceptional; by the early 1980s, the average Morse worker took home $8.32 an hour, some 66 percent more than the average textile operative.[16] As Morse's president joked in 1969, "The typical Morse Cutting Tools employee tends to characterize New Bedford's blue-collar society in two types: those who work at Morse and those who wish they did."[17]

In 1968, Morse was bought out by the Gulf+Western (G+W) corporation in an orgy of conglomeration. Established in 1958 on the foundation of a run-down Michigan bumper manufacturer, G+W was the brainchild of CEO Charles Bluhdorn, nicknamed the "Mad Austrian."[18] A blustering, fiery eccentric with a penchant for "creative accounting," he was known to leaf through the Standard & Poors "tear sheets" (page-length summaries of various American companies), scouring them for bargain buys.[19] From 1958 to 1967, Bluhdorn's Gulf+Western averaged a new corporate acquisition every six weeks. In one particularly frenetic period of buyout activity in January of 1968, he essentially doubled the size of G+W in a mere forty-eight hours.[20] Bluhdorn then followed that up by buying an additional nineteen other companies over the rest of that year.[21]

The conglomerate tendrils of G+W reached into auto parts, musical instruments, cigar making, metal plating, foundries, wire companies, zinc mining, electrical parts, horse breeding, record labels, machine tool production, pantyhose manufacturing, Beauty-Rest mattresses, Dominican sugar fields, Madison Square Garden, Paramount Pictures, and Desilu Productions, to name just a few of the 150 or so industries and companies Bluhdorn collected over his lifetime.[22] Nobody missed the parody in Mel Brooks' 1976 comedy, *Silent Movie*, when the (literally) rabid executives of the "Engulf & Devour" Corporation (its slogan: "OUR FINGERS ARE IN EVERYTHING") concocted plans to consume an endangered movie studio.[23]

On the face of it, G+W could be seen as driven by little more than Bluhdorn's self-aggrandizing fantasies.[24] But there was a certain sort of circular logic to G+W's rambling spread. Companies could be purchased, squeezed for both profits and the expanded access to credit they offered, and then used to fuel further expansion. If Royal Little's turning point was his 1937 tax troubles, Bluhdorn's was his realization that his ownership stake in a factory (even a crumbling bumper factory) could vastly improve his ability to access credit. Approaching banks for money as a standalone commodities trader—a sort of wheeler and dealer, as Bluhdorn once was—he seemed a risky bet with few underlying assets.[25] But, as a factory owner, Bluhdorn's status appeared qualitatively different. In the words of Michael Korda, the former editor-in-chief of Simon & Schuster, which was itself folded into G+W in 1975, banks knew that "somewhere in the wasteland of the industrial Midwest, there was a real Dickensian factory, belching smoke and turning out rear bumpers for Studebaker. . . . Bankers, Bluhdorn discovered, loved bricks and mortar."[26] More precisely, banks loved collateral and cash flow; factories seemed to promise both in tangible form.

If Little saw new acquisitions as a means to tax savings, Bluhdorn saw them as means to expanded credit access, which could be leveraged into further corporate acquisition. "Each acquisition financed the next," Korda observed; "it was a recipe for rapid growth not unlike a giant Ponzi Scheme."[27] Ultimately, G+W's ballooning need for credit, combined with the allure of

Vietnam War–era profits, wrenched Morse Drill into the Gulf+Western orbit in 1968.[28]

Not surprisingly, G+W treated its heavy manufacturing holdings as not much more than a means toward funding its other "growth potential" ventures. It invested little in Morse. Before its takeover, the New Bedford plant was in talks to move out of its antiquated multi-story facility (in which products would literally have to be hauled from floor to floor anywhere from eight to thirteen times) to a newer facility in the city's industrial park; but these ideas were scrapped after G+W acquired the plant.[29] In the machine tools accessories industry, a typical firm of Morse's size soaked up an average of $1.4 million in investment every year in this era.[30] By contrast, Gulf+Western invested less than $800,000 into Morse during the entire five-year period spanning 1977 to 1982.[31]

Gulf+Western, for its part, was fairly open about its "cash cow" philosophy. As the company detailed its "asset redeployment" strategy in 1981, the plan was to continue to "[shift] assets from operations in which substantial capital investments would be required to bring their facilities to competitive standards" toward more profitable stock and bond options. That same year, manufacturing accounted for 23 percent of G+W profits, furnishing an income of $107 million; the conglomerate, however, invested only $6 million into cost-saving improvements across its entire manufacturing division. Simultaneously, Gulf+Western pushed $386 million into stock purchases.[32] In effect, neglected manufacturing plants were run into the ground to fuel a spree of equity and security purchases. "It's like running a car without oil," one angry New Bedford worker fumed.[33]

Morse workers, for their part, did not stand idly by while, in their minds, the factory was recklessly exploited for profits. In 1982, they went on strike with a somewhat novel demand: increased corporate investment. Posters with "STOP MILKING MORSE!" (alongside a cartoon of a man with a "G&W" suit milking dollars out of a cow, drawn up by famed labor cartoonist Fred Wright) littered New Bedford.[34] As Gulf+Western sought to compensate for declining profits by demanding major union concessions, workers sought to show that the real issue was continuing under-investment in the plant.[35]

The United Electrical Workers ultimately hired an industrial consultancy firm to investigate (and demonstrate) G+W's systematic "milking" of Morse for profits, launching a massive press and community campaign in the process.[36] As one 1982 union press release put it, "We call on Gulf & Western to make the investment to bring Morse up to competitive standards after years of neglect—or else to sell this plant to a company with a long term interest in

FIGURE 9.1 United Electrical Workers Poster, "Stop Milking Morse." Reprinted from Harrison, "Gulf + Western," 21. Courtesy of Dan Swinney, *Labor Research Review*, 1982, and the Kheel Center for Labor-Management Documentation and Archives, Cornell University.

the cutting tool business. . . . Gulf & Western has no right to milk Morse, run it into the ground, and then liquidate it."[37] In response, the New Bedford city council would demand that G+W explain their plans for Morse, in light of the fact that, as the council resolved, "during the last two decades, Morse and almost all the major plants in New Bedford were bought by conglomerates and now are run by people outside our city. . . . No community can ever achieve economic security when these conglomerates are able to buy up plants, drain them and then close down without regard to the local area."[38] Such strategies left Morse's management nonplussed. Union organizer Ron Carver later remembered that he knew the union was winning when an exasperated company executive asked him, "What's the matter with you guys? Can't you run a normal strike?"[39]

Although the 1982 strike was settled with new commitments to corporate investment, about a year later, Gulf+Western did in fact announce plans to liquidate the plant.[40] Betrayed workers responded by successfully convincing city leaders to threaten an eminent domain seizure of the plant if G+W tried to follow through on its shutdown plans rather than selling it to an owner interested in keeping it running in the city.[41] Ironically, when New Bedford contracted with Georgetown University's Institute for Public Relations to explore whether the city actually had legal standing to use eminent domain proceedings to ensnare a runaway factory, the legal go-ahead it received was predicated, in part, on a 1966 amendment to the Massachusetts constitution declaring that "the industrial development of cities and towns is a public function and the commonwealth and the cities and towns therein may provide for the same in such manner as the general court may determine."[42] In other words, the Georgetown analysts found that a constitutional amendment originally adopted to ease the flow of public money into the pockets of industrial developers might also allow public power to be used for purposes other than filling corporate coffers.

Nevertheless, New Bedford's threat to essentially municipalize local drill production worked. Gulf+Western instead sold the plant off in May 1984 to a Michigan capitalist, James Lambert, with workers agreeing to cuts in wages and benefits.[43] The victory was widely celebrated by city and state leaders as a major win for the Massachusetts economy. Governor Michael Dukakis proclaimed it "a Massachusetts success story."[44] The union, too, thanked the community for its support in an open letter in the local newspaper. "To Our Community: Thank You. . . . Across the country[,] giant multinational corporations that gobbled up local plants in the 1960s have begun to liquidate many of those plants after milking them for profits. Our community cried 'foul' and demanded better treatment. We got it."[45]

The long crisis of the 1970s would eventually take Morse Drill, too. Already, the Gulf+Western debacle had seen a workforce that once amounted to 1,800 slowly pared down to 375.[46] The plant lived on for a few years under Lambert Consolidated Industries Inc., but, following the diversion of some $1.5 million in Morse capital into two new (failed) divisions, Lambert slashed production at Morse, losing $400,000 in sales and leaving the company to file for bankruptcy in January of 1987.[47] Workers again rejoiced when a federal judge determined that the plant could not be sold to a competitor planning to simply shut it down.[48] Instead, the plant was sold to a Scottish manufacturer who operated Morse for another three years before closing it down for good in January of 1990.[49] By then, Morse employed only sixty-seven workers.[50]

The Morse plant has since been demolished, leaving two empty fields in the middle of New Bedford. Part of one field was turned, in 2009, into a "serenity garden," but, instead of achieving its original goal of giving "the community [a place] to grow its own vegetables and flowers and bring the property to some type of substance within the neighborhood," as one city councilor hoped, it instead devolved into "a hangout for drinking, criminal activity, drug dealing [and] late night nuisances that the neighbors just can't handle."[51] After a man was found dead there in 2014, the unofficial "park" was closed.[52] There has been some talk of turning the other half of the property into a dog park, but even that notion faces major obstacles.[53] After years of pollution from the so-called Morse "weeping wall"—the east wall of the factory that infamously leached a continual flow of mysterious oil into the adjacent street—the prospects are dim for re-developing the toxic remnants of Morse Drill.[54] Nearby residents still complain, decades later, of the noxious smells that emanate from the poisoned earth.[55]

Monopolization and Conglomeration at J.C. Rhodes

The corporate mergers of the 1950s and 1960s, to be sure, were not an entirely new phenomenon. But the rabid conglomeration of this era was quite different from the waves of takeovers and acquisitions that had preceded it. The story of New Bedford's J.C. Rhodes plant is a case in point. It experienced countless acquisitions, sales, and re-acquisitions over its existence, functioning under the umbrella of monopoly, conglomerate, and private equity control. For J.C. Rhodes, the road to liquidation was punctuated by the various demands and stresses these various corporate regimes placed on it.

A manufacturer of shoe eyelets that moved to New Bedford in 1891, J.C. Rhodes was first folded—along with thirty other shoe production firms—into the newly dominant United Shoe Machinery Co. in 1905.[56] A monopoly in every sense of the word, United Shoe controlled 98 percent of American shoe machinery output.[57]

Monopolies of the late nineteenth and early twentieth centuries were quite different from the conglomerates that came nearly a century later. They functioned on the dispassionate logic of vertical and horizontal integration. It was this era that saw, as business historian Alfred Chandler Jr. famously put it, "the visible hand of management" supplant "the invisible hand of market forces."[58] In other words, monopolists sought to replace the anarchy of market-driven resource allocation with the rationalizing power of managerial dominion, buying out and assimilating potential competitors (horizontal integration) while attempting to subsume all parts of the productive process—from raw material to finished product—into a single, coordinating, corporate entity (vertical integration).[59]

This was precisely how United Shoe justified its existence. As its own 1911 corporate history, *The Story of Three Partners*, recorded, "There was a time, in the early, chaotic days of shoe machinery manufacture, when the shoe manufacturer was forced to depend upon many makers of shoe machinery for the proper equipment of his factory. To-day all that is changed. All the machines required . . . may now be obtained from this one concern—United Shoe Machinery Company."[60] Monopolies, by their nature, focused on narrow market niches. Acquisition and assimilation were the strategic manifestations of the desire for coordination and freedom from competition.

The whole point of conglomeration, as it emerged in the 1950s and 1960s, was to target unrelated businesses far outside a firm's core competencies and—following the prescriptions of conglomerate orthodoxy as promulgated by pioneers like Royal Little and firms like the Boston Consulting Group—exploit "low-growth" but cash-rich producers in order to expand into "high-growth" sectors. Monopolism was a strategy of focus and fortification; conglomeration was a policy of dilettantism and diversification. United Shoe, focused as it was solely on shoe machinery, was surely a corporate monopoly, but it was no corporate conglomerate.

Beginning in the 1950s, J.C. Rhodes found itself thrown into the chaos of the conglomerate craze. It began in 1956 when federal anti-trust proceedings forced United Shoe to offload two of its divisions: W.W. Cross & Co. and New Bedford's J.C. Rhodes.[61] The two plants were quickly bought out by the Plymouth Cordage Company—a rope and twine manufacturer—and re-organized as Plymouth Cordage Industries, or the PCI Group, in 1956.[62] Then, beginning in 1959, an enterprising conglomerateur, Victor Muscat, began a campaign to transform his father's toothpaste tube manufacturer into something much more imposing.[63] He quickly reconfigured his father's enterprise as the Defiance holding company and began pushing outward into aluminum fabrication, real estate, insurance, radio electronics, electronic dyers, and paint making. In addition, he bought out another New

York holding company, BSF, with interests in finance, art supplies, mining, Central American railways, and the American Hardware Co.—which itself had already acquired a 33 percent stake in Plymouth Cordage.[64] Upon discovering that one of the concerns under the BSF umbrella held mostly toxic assets (in the form of a struggling body-building company and a moribund textile concern), Muscat engineered a hostile bid to take complete control of American Hardware Co., presumably in the hope that its firmer financial position would help anchor the newly acquired BSF's ballooning debt load.[65] American Hardware successfully fended off BSF by launching its own takeover of Plymouth Cordage. By taking majority control of Plymouth Cordage, American Hardware was able to issue more shares, thus diluting BSF's power and quashing its takeover bid.[66] By February 1963, BSF's hostile takeover attempt had been rebuffed (via a totally unrelated takeover) and J.C. Rhodes instead became a factory within the PCI Group of the Plymouth Division of the American Hardware Corporation.[67]

In essence, a toothpaste tube factory took over a holding company with an ownership stake in a hardware manufacturer that had shares in a rope company that owned a New Bedford shoe eyelet producer. Upon discovering the weak financial position of the holding company, the toothpaste tube factory tried to take over the hardware company directly. The hardware company successfully stopped them by taking majority control of the rope company. Conglomeration was often a complicated and confusing business.

The grinding wheels of conglomeration kept spinning. Just a year after American Hardware had evaded BSF, the Emhart Company—originally founded as a Connecticut glass machinery manufacturer—began buying up shares of American Hardware.[68] By 1966, Emhart seized majority control, and J.C. Rhodes found itself again in new hands. It was part of a newly sprawling multinational with seven divisions and nine subsidiaries from the Far East to Europe, producing guns, refrigeration equipment, fertilizers, pesticides, architectural machinery, and, now, shoe eyelets.[69] A wave of layoffs at J.C. Rhodes followed in 1974, and Emhart decided to shore up its position through further conglomeration. It launched a hostile takeover bid, targeting the remnants of United Shoe Machinery—the same erstwhile monopoly that had once controlled J.C. Rhodes.[70] But, to shield itself from potential anti-trust proceedings, Emhart first spun the PCI Group off as its own enterprise in 1975.[71] Seven years later, with Ronald Reagan in the White House and anti-trust sentiment having effectively evaporated from the halls of the Justice Department, an emboldened United Shoe (rebranded as USM, a division of

Emhart) fearlessly re-purchased the PCI Group for $9 million. Emhart and United Shoe had bought J.C. Rhodes twice over.[72]

When the dust settled, the New Bedford plant had changed hands six times over the course of two decades, repeatedly scooped up and offloaded by various conglomerate enterprises that had no particular interest in eyelet production but simply saw the factory as a source of cash to help push forward the long-term goal of further conglomerate expansion.

As with so many factories before it, once the cash flow began to subside, these smaller manufacturers were of little use to their conglomerate heads. In 1986, US Attorney Robert Mueller slapped the USM division of Emhart with the largest fine ever levied under federal pollution statutes. The $1,025,000 fine, stemming from a forty-one-count criminal indictment, was the result of J.C. Rhodes dumping 44,000 gallons of "untreated industrial wastewater" into the New Bedford sewer—on a daily basis.[73] It was probably not unrelated that, one year later, the PCI Group was again spun off as its own corporation.[74] Emhart and USM had both twice bought and twice sold J.C. Rhodes.

Much like Morse Drill, J.C. Rhodes experienced the crisis of the 1970s not as a sudden "shutdown" but as a slow withering away of production as it was tossed back and forth between various corporate heads. In 1996, one anonymous employee of twenty-three years described how Rhodes's torturous corporate history had engendered its decline: "I have been intimately involved with this business for much of my life. . . . The company has gone through many ownerships . . . [and] I have seen PCI's sales cut in half over the past 23 years." The long road to J.C. Rhodes's eventual closure, he argued, was paved with decades of "deterioration . . . caused by imports, in terms of closed divisions, less sales volume, and lower profitability" as it was swapped between various corporate heads over and over again.[75]

From the perspective of industrial Massachusetts, the essentially inevitable end of incorporation was indeed the shutdown. This could take one of two paths. One was unique to corporate conglomeration. A plant, like Morse, could be effectively "milked" for profits until its infrastructure was so outdated or worn down that liquidation seemed the only rational option. The second path harkened back to past eras of industrial downsizing. A corporate entity with production facilities somewhere cheaper (in terms of wages, taxes, or regulatory costs) would buy out a manufacturer simply to move its fixed capital assets. The latter would be the fate of J.C. Rhodes. But, coming as it did in the 1990s, the story involved a somewhat novel twist.

Private Equity and the Final Chapter
of J.C. Rhodes

By the last two decades of the twentieth century, the conglomerate had begun to give way to its almost natural apotheosis: the "private equity" firm. J.C. Rhodes would find itself swept into the "private equity" fold by no less than the original progenitor of the concept.

At the most basic level, private equity firms are investment management companies that use massive amounts of debt to buy up unrelated companies in the hope that—within a three- to five-year window—they can either liquidate or rehabilitate them to sell at a profit.[76] Like conglomerates, private equity firms are managed with a strictly "portfolio" view of the corporation: they seek to maximize return on investment through the acquisition of unrelated, undervalued firms with solid cash-flow potential.[77] But, unlike conglomerates, private equity firms keep their unrelated acquisitions firewalled. They pay no lip service to seeking synergies or hedging risk between distinct industrial fields, as had been originally spelled out by conglomerate pioneers like Royal Little. Their goal is not to create massive corporations that can skirt anti-monopoly law; their aim is to generate maximal returns for corporate shareholders. Conglomerates feasted on firms in the name of profit for the sake of bigness—using the profits of one firm to buy up the next, as G+W had done.[78] Private equity feasts in the name of profit for the sake of shareholder return—feasting, dispersing the goods, and moving on to the next target, fueled by credit.[79] From the perspective of industrial Massachusetts, both viewed local manufacturing plants as sources of short-term gain, not as sites of long-term commitment.

Private equity's growth in the 1980s was actuated in part by the faltering financial returns of American conglomerates themselves. Inherent in the conglomerate form was a structural flaw vis-à-vis their relationship to financial markets. The conglomerate's whole mission centered on using retained earnings to shore up their size and grip on unrelated industries.[80] But, as profits were diverted into further expansion—rather than to shareholders—conglomerates developed a chronically worsening gap between their share price and their accumulated assets. They grew into imposing multinationals with minuscule share values.[81] As a result, increasingly skeptical shareholders—seemingly deprived their due in the name of further corporate expansion—began to wonder whether the conglomerate form was, at best, idle overhead, and at worst, unnecessary bureaucracy and red tape crushing what would otherwise be successful independent firms.[82] As conglomerates flailed in the

1970s, rocked by the oil crisis and declining profits, investors largely lost interest in these corporate behemoths.[83]

As conglomerates faltered, the leveraged buyout (LBO)—and the prospect of using debt rather than retained earnings as the fuel for corporate conquest—emerged as the preferred means of corporate acquisition. The LBO was the brainchild of Jerome Kohlberg Jr., who joined the investment firm Bear Stearns in 1955.[84] Stuck in the unexciting corporate finance department in the late 1960s and 1970s, Kohlberg crafted a novel "service" intended to help conglomerates unload struggling divisions (or struggling divisions free themselves from conglomerates): the leveraged buyout.[85] He would use the assets of a target acquisition as collateral to take on a massive loan from some outside source (covering anywhere from 70 to 100 percent of the acquisition cost), buy the firm out, and then foist the debt onto the newly acquired firm.[86] Because the buyout was facilitated through debt, Kohlberg could acquire truly colossal corporate empires at almost no cost to himself. And because the acquired firm was ultimately the one saddled with the debt liability—despite the fact that the debt was used by Kohlberg to buy the company in the first place—he had little to lose if the firm failed (since the debt was not technically his), and much to gain if it succeeded (since he could sell off his ownership stake in the firm at a profit).

Kohlberg ultimately left Bear Stearns in 1976 to create a new financial firm dedicated to leveraged buyouts—Kohlberg Kravis Roberts (KKR)—and launched a spree of "private equity" acquisitions.[87] The first leveraged buyout of a large, publicly traded company was KKR's takeover of Houdaille Industries in 1979. KKR itself contributed a mere $1 million of its own money to the purchase of the $335 million company.[88] The rest was Houdaille's to pay. Beset with the enormous debt leftover from its own purchase, Houdaille was forced to repeatedly slash its workforce in an attempt to stay afloat; it had essentially collapsed by the end of the 1980s. KKR investors still made a 22 percent yearly return on the deal.[89] The "private equity" concept seemed to offer all the advantages of conglomeration with none of the risk.[90]

The 1980s would thus become another era of buyout mania. Over the course of the decade, 2,597 leveraged buyouts occurred; nearly half of American public companies experienced at least one takeover attempt.[91] Textile and apparel plants were some of the most common targets.[92] By the end of the decade, KKR was holding on to thirty-five companies with $59 billion in assets, making it the nation's fifth largest corporation.[93] Jerome Kohlberg Jr. ultimately left KKR in 1987 to form a new private equity business with his son—Kohlberg & Co.—raising $300 million in initial investment capital.[94] About a decade later, Kohlberg and J.C. Rhodes collided.

Kohlberg's initial target was a Connecticut manufacturer—Scovill Fasteners, Inc., with roots going back to 1802—which was itself caught up in the gyrations of a relentless series of corporate takeovers.[95] It had initially grown into a conglomerate with six divisions of its own, including the Shrader Automotive Group, Hamilton Beach Housewares Group, Yale Security, NuTone Housing Group, and the original Scovill Fasteners Group.[96] In 1985, it was purchased by First City Properties, Inc. for $523 million; all of its external divisions were then stripped out and sold for more than First City had paid for the conglomerate in the first place.[97] Only the original Scovill Fastener Group was left behind. First City ultimately filed for bankruptcy, and Scovill was folded into Alper Holdings in 1992 and then acquired, via leveraged buyout, by Kohlberg & Co.'s private equity firm in 1995 for the price of $41.5 million.[98]

The "discipline of debt" and, presumably, Kohlberg advisors, would push Scovill down a path of radical restructuring. In its two years as a Kohlberg portfolio company, Scovill paid about $1 million to Kohlberg in management fees. In turn, Scovill quickly liquidated one of its manufacturing lines, opened a new shop in Mexico, and established a new "distribution network" in Asia.[99] Three months after acquisition, Scovill also started buying up some of its competitors, including the Rau Fastener Company of Rhode Island and New Bedford's PCI Group. The J.C. Rhodes plant thus became the property of the Kohlberg & Co. private equity firm.

J.C. Rhodes's workers appeared to initially treat the Scovill purchase as just another chapter in a long history of corporate annexation. As such, they were clearly befuddled when, only eight weeks later, Scovill announced the plant would be shuttered, its machinery moved, and its workers laid off.[100] J.C. Rhodes was still a profitable company, after all. As machinist Phil Mello told a local reporter, "We still can't figure out why this company, if they're making a profit at two plants, wants to destroy our jobs."[101] Workers were used to seeing plants tapped for profits and run into the ground, as had happened at Morse. But why buy a perfectly profitable company simply to shut it down?

Likely adding to the confusion was the fact that all the tried and true tactics of industrial persuasion seemed of no use. When union leaders sat down with Scovill management, they floated the idea of contract changes or state incentives, hoping to save the plant. It was of no use; Scovill only wanted to discuss severance.[102] When the union lined up multiple investors willing to purchase the plant, the workers were rebuffed.[103] When the union leaders conscripted Senator Edward Kennedy, Senator John Kerry, and Representative Barney Frank to join them in lobbying Scovill to sell the factory to someone who might keep it open in Massachusetts—using letters, petitions, and even mass action rallies—Scovill was unmoved.[104] Massachusetts governor Bill Weld similarly tried to ply Scovill with the oft-employed weapons of industrial seduction—offering slashed taxes, increased business incentives, and his personal pride in the fact that "we have significantly cut workers' compensation rates" in the state—but it was to no avail.[105] As Barney Frank described one of his negotiation sessions with the intractable Scovill representatives, "I [got] the distinct impression the people we negotiated with wished we were all on another continent."[106] Why would a corporate head be so eager to close a profitable factory they had just bought two months earlier? Even G+W had bothered to run Morse into the ground before it attempted to shut it down. What was motivating Scovill and its private equity parent, Kohlberg?

Scovill offered a series of curious explanations for its behavior. Undoubtedly the go-to claim made by Scovill representatives was that the factory was failing. "I don't believe the people know or believe the other side, that is the business is not profitable," Scovill president David Barrett repeatedly told reporters.[107] Objectively, it is hard to see this as something other than corporate gaslighting. The plant was not only profitable, but it was also quite a bit bigger than Scovill, with literally three times the sales volume.[108] J.C. Rhodes was still the nation's largest producer of shoe eyelets and still the sole producer of eyelets for major manufacturers like Tommy Hilfiger, Rockport, and Converse—the last of which alone ordered 450 million parts from the New Bedford plant each year.[109] At other times, Scovill representatives offered the even more unusual argument that a factory shutdown would actually be better for workers: "I think acting irresponsibly would be to completely ignore the business climate" and let the plant "go bankrupt and not have the ability to at least provide benefits to the workers."[110] All of these arguments—stressing the apparently dreadful state of the factory and its market—did not seem to square with the fact that Scovill had just purchased the factory a couple months earlier. Again, if the factory was so unprofitable and so far beyond saving—why buy it?

What few realized was that Scovill was acting as neither business operator nor conglomerateur. Its interest was not in exploiting the plant's profits to fuel expansion, and it certainly was not in serving the plant's local stakeholders. Instead, what made J.C. Rhodes attractive to Scovill (or, more likely, what made J.C. Rhodes attractive to Kohlberg & Co. advisors, who would ultimately charge Scovill an additional $1 million in management fees for their role in organizing this single, particular acquisition) was its existing sales contracts, its machinery, and the prospect of transporting both to Scovill's plant in tiny Clarkesville, Georgia, with a population of 1,151.[111] As the hand-written notes of one desperate union meeting with Scovill representatives record, union leaders repeatedly pushed ("NOTHING WE CAN DO?") to see what they could possibly offer to keep the factory in New Bedford, but Scovill's representatives remained unfazed, insisting the unionists were missing the whole point: "COST … WAGE SAVINGS … MANAGEMENT DISISION [*sic*]." The union's notes recall Scovill's lawyer lecturing them: "2 PLANTS AND ONLY NEED ONE … NOT IN THE PICTURE TO SELL THE BUSINESS. THE CO IS EXTENT [*sic*]"—that is, the New Bedford factory was not coming back—"MONEY WOULD BE SET ASIDE FOR THE EFFECTS … BARGAIN THE EFFECT."[112] This was to be a discussion about severance and severance only. As state senator Mark C. Montigny realized after his discussion with Scovill, even in purchasing the factory "they were basing the value of the company on running the plant down South … They wanted to move it all along."[113] J.C. Rhodes was worth a lot more to Scovill dead than alive; selling the factory to some other operator would leave them bereft of machinery and stuck with an unwanted competitor.

For workers, the closure was devastating. As Richard Andrade glumly remarked to a local reporter, "Where are you going to go? Who's going to hire a 44-year-old man? … There ain't nothing in New Bedford."[114] Joseph Pacheco, who worked at the factory for thirteen years, echoed the senti-ment: "I'll probably lose my house. … I asked if I can make out an applica-tion [at other plants] and their answer is always, 'We're not hiring.'" "Before [working at J.C. Rhodes] everywhere else I had worked I had gotten laid off from," toolmaker Ed Voisine reflected.[115] As twenty-eight-year-old Antone Teixeira bluntly put it, "My wife don't work. I'm not that well educated. I don't know where I'll find work, unless they're hiring at Burger King." Stable, union jobs were on the decline in the city. Kevin Richard, father of two, expressed the dim hope that "I probably could find a job in Providence or Boston." "I know [my next job] probably won't be in Massachusetts," Robert O'Brien mused.[116]

Despite these hardships, the political and intellectual climate had changed to the point that J.C. Rhodes's workers did not benefit from the goodwill and community support the Morse workers had garnered a decade previously. As in the Morse case, the city of New Bedford initially moved forward with em-inent domain proceedings against Scovill. But, even as workers volunteered to cover the purchase price, the idea collapsed under the combined weight of corporate legal challenges, local opposition, and the veto of the city's Democratic mayor.[117] Local business leaders fumed that all the attention the Scovill shutdown was generating was just further compounding the problem of making the city look "attractive" to mobile capital. "What we are most concerned about is the very real potential that New Bedford will be perceived as being anti-business. We cannot afford for that to happen," the president of the local Chamber of Commerce warned the New Bedford City Council.[118]

Importantly, the Shareholder Revolution gave the opponents of potential eminent domain proceedings a shared language and ideology through which to decry the whole concept. "That's the kind of thing that drives businesses crazy," said a furious Kev Kevelson—the owner of Ideal Bias Binding Corp. of Fall River, a business founded by his grandfather in the 1930s—describing Congressman Barney Frank's efforts to save the factory.[119] "[He's] taking a position that companies exist to provide jobs, not profit for the owners. Why would anyone want to locate in Fall River or New Bedford if this congressman doesn't want you to maximize our profit?" Kevelson certainly did not see himself as owing anything in particular to the community: "If I can make more money somewhere else, I'll go."[120] As Russell Sinclair, whose family owned a local candy factory, remarked, "In a capitalist society it is a moral imperative that a business lawfully try to maximize its owners' return on investment. . . . I get very frightened when I hear the mayor of New Bedford threaten to seize private property by force with the justification that the needs of some citizens outweigh the constitutional rights of others."[121]

Councilman David Gerwatowski, who cast the deciding vote in denying eminent domain and sealing J.C. Rhodes's fate, justified his own decision in similar terms: "My feeling is that to seize someone's private property to keep some jobs here is not in the realm of public purpose."[122] There is probably no stronger testament to the overwhelming triumph of shareholder rights ideology over the erstwhile recognition of a corporation's responsibility to its stakeholders than Gerwatowski's. After all, two of those lost jobs belonged to his father, Fred, and his brother-in-law, Paul Sylvia.[123] Scovill and Kohlberg were not out to serve communities or customers, or even to fill corporate coffers. Their sole motivation was shareholder return. By the 1990s, many policymakers in Massachusetts found that perfectly acceptable.

J.C. Rhodes machinery was packed up and sent southward. The factory closed in August 1996.[124] But, as always, the factory closure seemed to create new opportunities. Barry Chouinard, a Vermont textile operator, toured the city soon thereafter: "There's a lot of highly-skilled displaced textile workers in New Bedford, and a lot of good commercial real estate at a good price," he told reporters.[125] The director of the local development agency also pointed out that all the publicity surrounding the J.C. Rhodes fiasco might have been good for the city, as it shined a spotlight on New Bedford's enduring attractions: "the incentives the state of Massachusetts has to offer. The [low] cost of living," and the "available workforce."[126] It was a familiar story. Desperate workers, desperate governments, and empty factories would help generate economic renaissance in the city of New Bedford.

Faceless Factories

In some ways, Morse and J.C. Rhodes are exceptional cases. They were factories outside of the cloth, clothing, and small electronics mainstream that defined the South Coast of Massachusetts in the midcentury era. They also tended to hire more men—and paid better wages—than their industrial peers. As such, they generated much more local consternation and controversy when their corporate heads sought to shut them down. The area's numerous small electronics and garment factories were also swept up in the conglomerate fervor, but they disappeared with much less fanfare. Consequently, their stories are more difficult to trace. These other factories employed mostly women, paid less, and garnered less attention—both at the point of acquisition and of liquidation. Their fate, however, was the same.

Take the Aerovox complex on New Bedford's Belleville Avenue. Originally started in New York in 1922, the Aerovox capacitor company was lured to the empty Nonquitt Mill on the banks of the Acushnet River with a massive funding package from city leaders.[127] By the 1960s, it had expanded to California, Canada, New York, and South Carolina. By 1972, it had even spun off its own multinational subsidiary, AVX, only to have this—its own subsidiary—buy up and subsequently sell off what remained of the parent company following the 1973 crash. What was left of the original Aerovox firm was bought up by local capitalists, and employment was slashed. It was then bought by the RTE Corporation in 1978, which was in turn bought out by Cooper Industries, which in turn consolidated the plant into the Delaware-based Aerovox Holding Corporation. The company then bought out Capacitores Unidos, creating Aerovox of Mexico. Today, all manufacturing in New Bedford is automated: Aerovox manufacturing jobs are found only in Ningbo and Shanghai, China, India, and Juarez, Mexico. AVX, for its part, was acquired by the Japanese multinational Kyocera. Still headquartered in

Aerovox's old South Carolina plant, AVX, as of 2023, operates thirty-five plants in sixteen countries.[128]

The original Aerovox building was demolished by the EPA as an environmental hazard in 2010. The AVX multinational, in what was likely a calculated public relations move, agreed to pay the EPA about $3 million for the massive environmental damage Aerovox had caused in New Bedford over the years, despite the fact that AVX itself had never technically operated in Massachusetts. When AVX spokesperson Donna Lees was asked why her company was paying to fix environmental degradation in New Bedford, her response—"I really don't know"—spoke volumes about the circuitous genealogies of conglomerate capital.[129]

Garment production—historically built on a business model of small, flexible contract production that forestalled mass, multi-divisional production—was not immune to the forces of conglomeration.[130] New Bedford's Calvin Clothing, with roots dating to the 1920s, was acquired by Palm Beach Co. in 1968, which was later acquired (via leveraged buyout) by Merrill Lynch in 1985, then sold off to Crystal Brands in 1988, which was later acquired by Plaid Clothing Group in 1992, which shuttered the plant two years later.[131] Just as Bedford Shirtmakers of New York acquired New Bedford's Massachusetts Shirt Mfg. Co. in 1968, Fall River's Shepard Clothing was acquired by US Industries in 1969, and Jonathan Logan Inc. acquired Davis Sportswear Company in 1966, whose Fall River Clothing Mfg. facility would bring Pine Inc. into the Davis-Jonathan Logan fold in 1967, filling government contracts for military coats.[132]

Although garment factories often held out longer after acquisition than their textile- or electronics-producing counterparts, their eventual fate was often the same. Anderson-Little, the national pioneer of "factory direct" suit production that originally opened in Fall River in 1936, emerged as a conglomeration target in the 1960s. Huge consumer demand for men's suits in the postwar period helped grow the family firm to eleven outlets in 1960—all fed by Anderson-Little's main manufacturing plant in Fall River. The next six years saw Anderson-Little amass twenty-nine new stores, leading to its subsequent buyout by the Richman Brothers national chain in 1966. Three years later, Richman Brothers was bought out by the even more massive Woolworth Corporation. Although Woolworth continued to operate Anderson-Little for about two decades, declining profits led to the closure of all three South Coast manufacturing plants and all but seven stores in 1992. The remaining stores were picked up by the Gentlemen's Wearhouse subsidiary of the Cliftex

Corporation—a garment manufacturer started in New Bedford in 1941 that, facing declining demand for suits, was attempting to make a new start in retail. Six years later, Cliftex closed all remaining Anderson-Little outlets; three years later, Cliftex was bankrupt.[133]

About $7 million in state subsidies and federal tax credits later, the Cliftex Mill was renovated as a senior living facility. Barbara Baliko, a long-time Cliftex stitcher, had the honor of cutting the ribbon at the opening of Cliftex Lofts and becoming the converted mill's first resident in May of 2013.[134] Cliftex joins a variety of other mills in having its main asset to the city be in housing those it formerly employed—namely, the elderly.

By the late 1970s, the vice president of the New Bedford Chamber of Commerce was happy to flaunt the string of "nationally-recognized names" one could find in the city: Goodyear, American Brands, Continental Screw, Johnson & Johnson, Berkshire Hathaway, Teledyne, Polaroid, Borg-Warner, Augat, and Clipper Craft, to name a few. But the "incorporation" of New Bedford's local factories came with a hefty price tag.[135] When these proprietary firms were transformed into subsidiaries of giant conglomerates, the shift also ensured that Massachusetts's prosperity would be tapped to expand operations all over the nation and the world.[136] A new generation of management executives found themselves overseeing local factories—but they lacked any local connections, local concerns, or local accountability.

Massachusetts, of course, was not alone. By the end of the 1970s, the foreign output of American multinationals exceeded the combined gross domestic product of every country in the world apart from the United States and the USSR.[137] As these conglomerate multinationals continued to invest in both the American South and the global periphery—attracted by lower wages and greater offers of state assistance—machinery and fixed capital remained un updated back home. As machines degraded in Massachusetts, profits waned. The long crisis of the 1970s became the drawn-out, torturous offloading of these firms once their profits had been exhausted.

All told, the story of industrial Massachusetts is a poor fit with existing narratives of late century industrial decline. The 1973 crisis was hardly the result of long-term "disinvestment." It was in fact Massachusetts's prosperity in the 1960s—itself driven by the mass migrations of the era—which, in generating the profits that made multinational manufacturing possible, undergirded the long economic crisis that followed. But Massachusetts's trajectory was also not a story of "shock." Unlike 1920s textile deindustrialization, in which capital and machinery fled southward amid economic turmoil, it was not the 1970s crisis that spurred economic globalization. Conglomerates were not buying up firms abroad because they were in the throes of turmoil at home; they were buying up firms abroad because they were making so much money in Massachusetts. In this complicated milieu, migration drove prosperity, prosperity drove conglomeration, and conglomeration ultimately catalyzed the collapse of the "mixed manufacturing" economy.

10

The "New" Economy

MAKING HIGH-TECH MASSACHUSETTS

THE 1970S ARE commonly remembered as a grueling era of crisis and decline. Starved for one of the most critical energy inputs of the era—namely, oil— worldwide industrial production fell 10 percent after 1973.[1] In Massachusetts, as in much of America, cutbacks in defense spending, skyrocketing inflation and energy costs, and mounting competition from emerging manufacturers abroad made this worldwide slump seem like a never-ending economic nightmare.[2] By 1975, the unemployment rate in Massachusetts was 11.2 percent, the highest in the country.[3] Angry, jobless protesters marched on Boston Common; the *Boston Globe* found the whole thing "reminiscent of the Great Depression."[4] Economic turmoil came to fuel a sort of social malaise—"a crisis of confidence," as President Jimmy Carter famously put it in 1979—a sense that something was deeply flawed at the "very heart and soul and spirit of our national will."[5] Rust-belt tableaus of shuttered factories and snaking unemployment lines dominate popular memory of the 1970s and 1980s.

And yet, for industrial Massachusetts, the experience was less a climactic finale than a familiar refrain. After all, capitalists who weathered the 1970s crisis had a century of history to inspire them. Like their predecessors, they were quick to find ways to transform crisis into renewed industrial ascendance. The chairman of the Associated Industries of Massachusetts (AIM) argued in 1974 that there was actually a "'plus' side" to "crisis": a "reaffirmation of some of the qualities that made us a great nation . . . qualities which many said were forever lost to apathy, indolence and self-indulgence."[6] A year later, confidence reigned only more supreme. "Politically, industry's hour has come. It is an opportunity born of adversity, of course—of 'crisis,' in fact," but he nevertheless declared it industry's moment to fight "the heavy taxes, high fixed costs, entrenched bureaucracy, the outflow of talent, the in-migration of the dependent and unskilled, the extravagant promises, the chaos of social programs."[7]

Massachusetts capitalists would use the 1970s to turn economic disarray and social discontent into an unprecedented expansion of direct state aid to business. It was not all that different from New Bedford's plans a century earlier. These programs boiled down to massive cuts in social spending in order to channel more public money toward private business. Not unlike the 1870s, in the 1970s, a pervading, intangible sense of collective decline gave Massachusetts industrialists the political capital necessary to fundamentally transform the political economy of Massachusetts manufacturing. They leveraged this power into the creation of a new, "high-tech" economy.

Local workers also seized the moment. They, however, were left much more disappointed—but their disappointments had little to do with any unsatisfied, yearning desperation for the halcyon days of industrial supremacy. Instead, their frustrations centered more on the overabundance of factory jobs they faced.

As policy leaders attempted to reorient the educational and physical infrastructure of Massachusetts to adapt to the needs of the "new economy," workers followed suit. They trained up for the coming onslaught of high-tech jobs. But in New Bedford and Fall River, it was an onslaught that never came. And as reality crushed idealism, workers' creeping realization that they had been trained for jobs that were never going to arrive set off a crashing wave of discontent. Disillusioned workers proved loath to slink back through the factory gates, much to the dismay of local policymakers and capitalists.

"Rust Belt" Massachusetts hardly turned out to be the stuff of Bruce Springsteen balladry. Massachusetts business was actually booming. Desperate policymakers shoveled public money into private development, engendering a surge of "high-tech" research and manufacturing in the Boston area. Unemployment certainly climbed—but garment and textile factories ultimately proved much more resilient than their male-dominated machinery and heavy manufacturing peers. By the end of the 1970s and into the 1980s, many factories were again complaining of labor shortages. Workers were certainly angry and disenchanted—but not because they were desperate to return to the tedium of the factory floor. Instead, many seemed convinced they had been sold a false bill of goods. Their training was supposed to prepare them for the "new economy," not for a life sewing zippers.

For many industrialists, the problem was not that industry was abandoning local communities. To the contrary, it seemed as though local communities were abandoning industry. The factories were not all suddenly gone. But with most of the high-paying, male-hiring firms like Morse and J.C. Rhodes gone, the city had little else to offer but low-paying, industrial monotony targeted at women and immigrants. Workers balked.

The twin forces of conglomerate disinvestment and global competition may have begun the process of hollowing out these factory cities, but it was— somewhat unexpectedly—workers' disinterest in factory labor that delivered the mortal wound.

High-Tech Massachusetts

When the industrial economy began to sputter in the early 1970s, the state government leaped into action. Policymakers launched a series of business handouts and social welfare cuts. First came a series of "pro-growth" bills (dubbed "Mass Incentives") in 1973, intended to attract manufacturing and research and development firms to the state. The investment tax credit was tripled, tax credits were added for new hires, and the state instituted a loss carry-forward tax provision.[8] By 1977 the state was offering new businesses free vocational training, tax-exempt revenue bonds of up to $4 million, sales tax exemptions for machinery, and specific incentives to multi-state corporations if they at least concentrated most of their employment in Massachusetts.[9] Additionally, a sort of "alphabet soup" of state-supported development institutions were created over the course of the 1970s: the Massachusetts Industrial Finance Agency (MIFA), the Massachusetts Technology Development Corporation (MTDC), the Massachusetts Capital Resource Company (MCRC), and the Bay State Skills Corporation (BSSC), to name a few.[10] While handouts to business were on the rise, social welfare spending was on the decline. Massachusetts passed a number of historic cuts to its welfare programs in the mid-1970s. The most dramatic entailed removing all employable persons younger than forty from the state's relief fund.[11]

The Massachusetts High Technology Council (MHTC)—a lobbying group of high-technology capitalists formed in 1977—worked tirelessly to ensure that technology entrepreneurs would be the primary beneficiaries of government largesse. For the MHTC, tax cuts became a particular priority. Curiously, despite the group's relentlessly pro-business rhetoric, their politics centered less on corporate taxes and more on individual taxation. In particular, the MHTC consistently decried income and property taxes as a major roadblock to future tech expansion in the state.[12] "The principal cause" of the "deterioration" of the Massachusetts "business climate," the

MHTC held, was "the rapidly rising tax burden in the Commonwealth, particularly as it impacts individual taxpayers," who were apparently "being drawn to other parts of the country," pushed out by the ballooning weight of the state's tax load.[13] In turn, the group successfully pushed Massachusetts's governor into signing, in 1979, a "New Social Contract for Massachusetts"— which promised a quid pro quo exchange of 150,000 new jobs for broad commitments to tax reduction.[14] In addition, the MHTC funneled hundreds of thousands of dollars toward the campaign to enact Proposition 2½, placing a 2.5 percent limit on both annual property taxes and future tax increases.[15]

Objectively, much of this activism was more opportunistic than rooted in genuine worry over the fate of the high-tech economy. The highly touted 150,000-job "social contract," for instance, failed to note that these 150,000 jobs were already slated to arrive in the state regardless of whether policymakers agreed to the tax cuts.[16] Similarly, no real evidence was ever given showing that labor recruitment efforts were actually being stymied by competition with lower-tax states. Edson de Castro, who founded Data General in 1968, would later recall that "the number one problem was attracting talented people to the state of Massachusetts," because "Massachusetts was way off the deep end in terms of personal taxation."[17] Ironically, when de Castro's own company decided to relocate a major project to North Carolina in 1979, the whole process seemed to belie his confidence that employees were itching to move to lower-tax locales. As one engineer bluntly put it, "I thought North Carolina sucked." It was, he thought, "not a place where I wanted to bring up my wife and family."[18] Similarly, although the MHTC complained endlessly that "professional engineers and managers" required "pay differentials as much as 20 to 30 percent to work in Massachusetts to offset the higher cost of living and the higher state and local tax burdens," in reality, tech wages in Massachusetts were lower than national averages.[19] None of this mattered. As other industries floundered, high tech seemed poised to leap into the future. Precisely because other industries were floundering, the state government largely capitulated to MHTC demands.

As in eras past, these policy changes were, on paper, remarkably successful. The decade after 1979 saw the advent of the so-called Massachusetts Miracle. The high-tech sector boomed as 440,000 new jobs were created—mostly in microcomputer production—and high-tech industry soon provided one out of every three jobs in Massachusetts.[20] Tech giants like Raytheon, Lotus, and Digital Equipment Corporation (DEC) proliferated within the Boston suburbs along Route 128.[21] The politics of crisis had seemingly carried the day.

The ideological victory of "high technology" was no more apparent than in the state government's radical shift in the tactics it employed to attract mobile capital. No longer did the state-run Department of Commerce and Industrial Development extol the low wages of cities like New Bedford in its overtures to mobile capital.[22] Instead, industrial development propaganda acclaimed the unique "environment" of Massachusetts, "conducive to the creation and growth of great ideas and great people."[23] Development publications increasingly took the high cost of manufacturing in Massachusetts as a given, instead trying to re-direct attention to the other intangibles the state offered industry, in particular the educational attainment of its workforce and the state's technical and educational infrastructure.[24] As Evelyn Murphy, the state's secretary of economic affairs put it in a 1983 preface to an industrial development pamphlet entitled *Massachusetts . . . Creating the Future*, "Massachusetts is an economic paradox. Its handicaps—minimal natural resources, distance from America's industrial heartland, heavy dependence on imported oil—could make it a place of the past," but "much of what will make the future is made here. The ideas for a new age stream from our universities, laboratories and institutions."[25] Increasingly, the state government—so key to industrial development in an age in which mobile capital could play governments against one another in the search for the ideal location—began to explicitly privilege the creation of a high-tech economy and, as a result, certain regions of the state.

The rise of the high-tech economy ultimately shifted the center of industrial Massachusetts out of areas like New Bedford and Fall River and toward the state capital. Most high-tech research, after all, occurred in the suburbs of Boston.[26] Some mill towns benefited from the "high-tech" boom, but only those near enough to the Boston area to serve as low-priced alternative locations for mass manufacturing.[27] As such, about 90 percent of high-tech manufacturing jobs created in the four years following 1979 were in the four cities of Boston, Lawrence, Haverhill, and Lowell.[28] In the 1970s, unlike the 1870s, Lowell and Lawrence were racking up industrial jobs while Fall River and New Bedford declined.

Even so, manufacturing jobs were rarely created at the same rate as service sector work, and manufacturing jobs were always more prone to relocation.[29] There was great fanfare, for instance, when DEC opened up a Roxbury manufacturing plant in the late 1970s; a little over a decade and $7 million in public subsidies later, DEC shut the facility down, deciding it could obtain the same parts on the open market more affordably.[30] Nevertheless, it was a source of endless frustration to South Coast leaders that in the decade following 1975, about three-quarters of new job creation in Massachusetts occurred solely in the Boston area.[31]

In response, New Bedford and Fall River workers and city leaders desperately pushed money into new vocational and educational programs and schools, hoping to attract higher-paying high-technology firms to the area.[32] State and local leaders, after all, did not necessarily intend to leave the South Coast entirely out in the cold. Many, like Governor Michael Dukakis, hoped a mix of educational reform and local cheerleading would help make the South Coast into a high-technology magnet to rival Boston.[33] George Kariotis, founder of the Woburn technology firm Alpha Industries, was put in charge of a sprawling project to transform Massachusetts's educational infrastructure to fit the needs of the blossoming high-tech sector.[34] Kariotis was confident that such an overhaul would have to entail a mass movement of high-tech firms to cities like Fall River and New Bedford. "They'll have to do it," he told one reporter, "not only because the untapped labor pool is in [these] cities, but because of the energy crisis."[35] The most concrete achievement in this regard was the unification and consolidation of the old New Bedford and Fall River Textile Institutes into a full, public university in Dartmouth—perched between the two cities—finished in 1971.[36]

But Boston-area technology firms never took the bait. Exasperated regional and state leaders, in a last-ditch effort to bring "high tech" to the area, pushed $150,000 into the creation of a Southeastern Massachusetts Economic Development Committee to pay for travel expenses, mass mailings, and a two-day conference in Palo Alto, all in a desperate ploy to lure California technology firms to the South Coast.[37] Advertisements targeting mobile capitalists—"High Tech: Go East and Grow"—were printed in 1982.[38] Fall River's Office of Economic Development (FROED) similarly made attracting high-tech industry and encouraging "high tech education" central to its economic development strategies, with discouraging results.[39] "We have a feeling of frustration," Robert Karam, head of FROED, told reporters, "because we have not been discovered by the Rte. 128 [Boston-area] companies."[40]

In contrast to what was happening at the state level, the booster materials South Coast leaders produced continued to highlight many of the same appeals that had undergirded exhortations to mobile capital since the 1920s. A 1982 pamphlet generated for circulation to California high-tech firms reaffirmed a familiar set of advantages: the friendly posture of the city and state governments, tax and financial incentives, "significantly lower" housing and rent costs, and the availability of cheap mill space.[41] As one local leader recalled of his trip in 1982 to California to bring "the next Apple, Microsoft or Dysan Corp. to our shores," the "pitch" was as it always was: "Come to our region because we have empty mills, loyal labor, lower costs and great beaches."[42] Local leaders remained steadfastly convinced that once they developed an appropriately educated workforce, Boston-area high-tech firms would have to submit to the will of economic rationality and chase lower costs and higher state handouts on the South Coast.[43]

But high tech proved remarkably unbending. Ironically, the problem was that high-tech capital was actually much more geographically "sticky" than manufacturing capital, despite the fact that manufacturing was, in theory, reliant on a much more "fixed" set of capital assets. There were many reasons high tech was trapped in the Boston orbit, but paramount among them was that so much of high-tech development was based on federally funded research conducted at local universities.[44] The personal influence of Massachusetts Institute of Technology (MIT) professor Vannevar Bush, who convinced Franklin Delano Roosevelt to create the National Defense Research Committee (NDRC) and the Office of Scientific Research and Development (OSRD)—both of which were put under Bush's command—loomed large.[45] Bush ensured that a steady flow of federal dollars made their way to the state. Amid World War II, the OSRD channeled $425 million into Massachusetts research projects, with MIT standing as the largest beneficiary.[46] During the 1950s, the state would garner $6 billion in defense contracts, and $1 billion each year during the 1960s.[47] By then, federal dollars drove 65 percent of all high-tech spending in Massachusetts.[48]

As the federal government pumped money into Massachusetts research universities, they quickly spun off new firms to commercialize their innovations. One 1986 study determined that some 400 local firms— employing 175,000 and generating $29 billion annually—had their origins in research programs conducted at MIT.[49] When the executive director of Boston's Council for Economic Action paired with the Bank of Boston's chief economist to explain the area's recent revitalization in 1985, their conclusions highlighted the "long history of federal government-sponsored technical research" and "the availability of large pools of nonunionized and relatively low-wage labor."[50] "High-tech" Massachusetts, in other words, flowered out of low wages, business subsidies, and the generous federal funding of Boston-area universities.

Similarly, the structure of American finance ensured that high-tech firms, once they flew the university coop, were reticent to leave the comfort of the Boston area. High-tech firms were heavily dependent on venture capital funding, which by its very nature tended to privilege existing financial centers.[51] Risk-averse venture capitalists, in turn, were much more comfortable investing in enterprises nearby, where they could easily check in to see how things were progressing.[52] Jack Bush—son of Vannevar—recalled this tendency during a 1985 interview, describing his own experience seeking venture funding: "The venture capital company in general is ultra conservative. They've got to defend their decision if something goes sour."[53] Venture capitalists often responded to such uncertainty by wanting to cultivate a personal, "mentoring" relationship with the entrepreneurs they sponsored. George Doriot—who effectively founded modern venture capitalism in 1946 with his Boston-based American Research and Development Corporation— maintained a surprisingly close relationship with the companies in which he invested, literally referring to them as his "children."[54]

Finally, as ancillary high-tech service industries thronged around Boston, the process of high-tech development became something of a self-perpetuating cycle. Bill Foster, who started Stratus Computer in Natick, told an interviewer in 1985 that "people that do our sheet metal for us, people that produce our PC boards, or who stuff components on the PC boards, that's all done by local companies. . . . Having them local is very important, because if you have a quality problem, you want to be able to drive over quickly and see what's going on."[55] "There's kind of a cycle you see here," he explained, since it was critical to be "in an area where there are a lot of big computer companies so you can draw experienced people away from them. And the big companies need to locate in an area where there are a lot of schools so that as they lose people to the start-ups, they can replace them with people fresh out of school."[56] Boston's high-tech dominance, once set in motion, became self-sustaining. Ken Fisher, who founded Encore Computer in Marlborough, could hardly imagine having started anywhere else. "I grew up in Omaha, Nebraska, and I go out there and think, I could have never started Encore in a place like this. I couldn't even find a lawyer who would know how to incorporate the company properly."[57]

It was in this context that South Coast leaders would attempt to weather the economic changes of the 1970s. Local leaders schemed to ensnare high-tech business, but their endeavors proved doubly ineffective. On the one hand, they were unable to surmount Boston's educational, financial, and government-subsidized advantages.[58] "High tech" simply never took the South Coast's bait. More problematically, the South Coast's "build it and they will come" strategy—undergirded by policymakers' undimming conviction that a more educated workforce, more industrial parks, and more universities would inevitably attract strained high-tech companies—laid the foundation for a period of unprecedented discontent in the South Coast. A bewildering mix of high unemployment, labor shortages, angry workers, and equally angry businessowners would mark much of this period.

Low-Tech Massachusetts

In the latter decades of the twentieth century, South Coast workers wrestled with a familiar paradox: surging unemployment rates were paired with long lists of unfilled jobs. Advertisements for open, low-wage positions in mind-numbing industrial work proliferated alongside a pointed scarcity of these much flaunted "new economy" jobs. When local workers protested, city leaders were quick to see it all through the prism of deindustrialization and rust-belt decline. They assumed that workers simply wanted more jobs—or that these workers must be somehow ignorant of all the great industrial jobs the city still had. But these protests—such as the New Bedford "race riots" or "rebellion" of 1970—often reflected a much more complicated critique of an economy based on low pay, crummy jobs, and the constant lure of desperation. Critically, as local workers felt themselves denied their rightful place in the "new economy," they generally refused to peaceably return to the "old" one. Voting with their feet, these unhappy workers played their own role in the unfolding drama of industrial decline on the Massachusetts South Coast.

In many ways, this era played out much like previous periods that paired high unemployment with unfilled positions in decidedly unattractive lines of work, but one factor made this era in the South Coast's history somewhat unique. The social upheavals that marked this time were largely driven by three minority groups that had long been in the area but were becoming increasingly pushed together and politically activated, namely, the area's African Americans, Cape Verdeans, and Puerto Ricans.

For New Bedford's African Americans, clustered primarily in the city's West End neighborhood—3,588 called the city home in 1970—their long-standing ties to the community only sharpened their sense of discontent over their lack of access to decent housing, jobs, or equitable treatment at the hands of the justice system.[59] Unlike in many other northern cities, New Bedford's African American families could often trace their heritage to the antebellum era, when New Bedford first emerged as a celebrated destination for fugitive slaves.[60] In fact, there had probably been more African American out-migration than in-migration in the years since the Civil War.[61] The West End became a neighborhood in the throes of decline. Following the Great Depression, its housing stock was largely swallowed up by a small number of wealthy landlords. Decades of neglect, racial discrimination, and residential destruction under the banner of urban renewal conspired to transform much of the neighborhood into an overcrowded slum.[62] One local reporter was clearly shaken by what he saw after a group of Black activists took him on a tour of the fifteen-block "hard-core slum" at the heart of the West End in 1967. "There are houses with no bathroom sinks, with useless bathtubs, disconnected toilets and smells of staggering potency."[63] No longer a celebrated beacon of freedom, the "Negroes' New Bedford" had become a "city of rat-infested, drafty tenements."[64]

Another long-standing community of color, the Cape Verdeans, historically clustered in the South End of the city, existed in a somewhat tense relationship with the city's other "Black" community in the West End. Numbering about 16,000 in 1977, the Cape Verdeans also had a long history in the city, stretching back to the very same whaling ships that brought Azoreans to New Bedford.[65] After whaling's decline, former Cape Verdean whalers quickly snatched up decommissioned vessels and developed a thriving trade in both people and goods between the islands and Massachusetts.[66] From 1860 to 1940, 23,168 Cape Verdeans arrived in New Bedford, representing around 85 to 90 percent of all Cape Verdeans arriving in America.[67]

As Portuguese colonials of generally mixed-race heritage from an archipelago some 350 miles off the coast of Africa, Cape Verdeans struggled to find a settled place in the American racial hierarchy. On the one hand, learning early, as one immigrant put it, "that black people sit at the bottom of the American totem pole," Cape Verdeans often looked down on and desperately tried to distance themselves from those they called "American colored people."[68] Since they were themselves of variable skin tone (one Cape Verdean mother recalled that each of her three children was assigned a different race by New Bedford's public schools: one was white, one Black, and another "Mulatto") Cape Verdeans often proudly proclaimed a "caucasian" Portuguese identity, regardless of the vagaries of their skin pigmentation.[69] One incensed Cape Verdean lectured the local newspaper in 1965 after the mayor had lumped Blacks and Cape Verdeans together as "negroes" during a recent speech: "The Negro population in the city is negligible. . . . The races of man are divided into three classifications, namely: Caucasian, Mongolian, and Negroid. Therefore, Mayor Harrington has mislabeled the Portuguese-Americans of Cape Verdean extraction as Negroes."[70] As Cape Verdean Jack Custodio recalled in a July 1988 interview, despite his own dark skin, "I grew up and my mother taught me to say, 'Those damn niggers in the West End.' I said it like any other little white boy."[71]

Puerto Rican migrants were much more recent arrivals compared to Cape Verdeans and African Americans. Following the Second World War, a slow trickle of Puerto Rican families (many of whom had already resettled in New York City) began departing for New Bedford. Although it is difficult to track down the exact cause of this migration, it is possible that they arrived chasing farm work in local orchards and cranberry bogs, and they simply settled in New Bedford at the end of the growing season.[72] It is also possible that, considering how quickly Puerto Rican men enmeshed themselves in the local garment trade, they were simply following the runaway garment firms that made the very same journey from New York to New Bedford.[73] Other Puerto Rican migrants would later cite the lack of local racial discrimination and availability of affordable housing as their reason for making their way to the city.[74] Regardless, by the late 1960s, New Bedford was home to somewhere around 800 Puerto Rican families, mostly living in the city's South End.[75]

These three seemingly disparate groups would find themselves increasingly pushed together by the centripetal forces of the social and ideological changes of the 1960s. New Bedford's sprawling urban renewal programs of the era, in particular the mass demolition of South End residences to make way for more lucrative waterfront industrial development, forced many Puerto Ricans and Cape Verdeans out of the South End and into the largely African American neighborhoods of the West End—simultaneously compounding the housing issues that fueled so much anger.[76] At the same time, surging interest and activism back in Africa in the name of decolonization and pan-Africanism began to soften some of the antipathies that had formerly divided these groups.[77] Black Power ideology, blossoming in America, had much the same effect.[78]

Finally, the Vietnam War—pulling so many poor people of color into the orbit of the armed services—seemed to have an especially jarring impact on the racial views of Cape Verdeans. As local Black Panther Gordon Ribeiro would later recall in his autobiography, after being sent to the American South for military training, his feelings of Cape Verdean superiority came crashing down. "Down South, I clearly saw that I was a Black man. In Columbia, South Carolina, I could see how people looked at me, how they stared at me, how they talked to me." In the South, there was only Black and white, and Ribeiro was Black: "That's when I knew there was no difference between Cape Verdeans and African Americans."[79] For so many young Cape Verdean men, the twin forces of Black Power ideology and a sweeping military draft tended to erode inherited notions of Cape Verdean distinction and difference.

It is for this reason that even naming the weeks of protest, vandalism, rock throwing, car burning, barricades, sniper fire, tear gas, and arson that rocked New Bedford in the summer of 1970 is such a difficult matter.[80] To this day, white residents largely refer to the episode as the "race riots." Most participants, however, rejected (and still vehemently reject) the term. As local community leader Dr. Herbert Water Jr. remembered it, "it was never a race riot; it was a social movement."[81] For "Parky" Grace, former leader of the local chapter of the Black Panthers, "it wasn't a race riot. There were blacks, Puerto Ricans, and whites in the crowd.... It was just the people coming together."[82] For people like Grace, it was "the rebellion," and they celebrated its multiracial character.[83]

The most immediate cause of "the rebellion" was anger over racial discrimination and recurrent police harassment. The upheaval started on July 8, 1970, when a local Black leader, Warren Houtman, was handcuffed by police—apparently over a "defective taillight"—and detained with no formal citation or explanation. A crowd of Black residents responded by gathering at the police station, chanting and singing.[84] Soon thereafter, local Blacks began encircling the West End neighborhood with roadway "barricades"—made of overturned vehicles and other rubble—attempting to effectively reclaim control over a neighborhood so long scarred by police brutality and a court system that seemed firmly tilted against Black residents. The police quickly put up barricades of their own.[85]

What began as an impromptu burst of anger over an act of wanton police overreach spiraled into weeks of protest, violence, and vandalism—punctuated by the cold-blooded murder of a Black youth named Lester Lima. After three white men (from nearby Acushnet and Fairhaven) decided to do a bit of what might be described as "riot tourism," they somehow maneuvered through the police barricades that enclosed the neighborhood (or, as many angry Black residents would later suggest, were perhaps intentionally allowed through).[86] The three men drove right into the center of New Bedford's West End. A group of Black youth apparently surrounded the vehicle and began beating it with sticks and throwing bricks.[87] Incensed over the damage to his car, the driver sped home, grabbed a shotgun, returned to the West End, and indiscriminately fired into a random crowd of Black residents.[88] Three were injured and a seventeen-year-old boy was killed.[89] Despite an admission of guilt, an all-white jury eventually acquitted the three men of all charges.[90] Anger swept through the Black community. It all seemed like proof positive that the city's institutions were beyond redemption and that Blacks needed to reclaim sovereign authority over their own neighborhood and their own welfare. Black Panther Peter Antone stated this position clearly to the mayor: "The time is now to revolt against your fascist system and pig society. . . . The pigs are not going to come into our community anymore and take us off the streets."[91] The city seemed at a breaking point.

Reeling from their inability to understand the "rebellion," flailing city leaders groped for any scapegoat available. "Mayor Rogers has spent a great deal of time searching for an easy answer," reported a frustrated Thomas Irving Atkins, a Black Boston city councilor dispatched to the city by the governor of Massachusetts.[92] The mayor quickly chalked the whole incident up to a case of "outsiders using SDS and Panther tactics."[93] Firebrand city councilor William Saltzman would call the protests a conspiracy "by blacks and ultra-liberal whites, to bring in the Black Panthers."[94] In another interview, Saltzman was even more blunt. "Someone has to collect the garbage. The blacks have to keep cleaning the streets until they get some brains. . . . The city treats the colored very well. . . . Most of the black mafia that started this strike, they like it. It makes them feel big."[95] Saltzman gloried in his own racial prejudice, but he actually understood something that many other city officials missed, namely, that much of the anger stemmed from the sort of jobs available to local residents—especially residents of color.

Finding that such claims of "outsider influence" usually elicited mockery, city leaders changed course, settling on a much more familiar political position. What was needed, they proclaimed, was more factory jobs and more public money being shoveled into private hands.[96] For weeks, it seemed the mayor could not speak in public without trumpeting vague assertions that he would soon be making a big announcement about some new factory that would be making its way to the city.[97] When the *Boston Globe* requested records relating to the education of Black students in New Bedford, an irritated superintendent shot back: "I don't see why the *Boston Globe* has the right to come here investigating this. . . . You know, there is only one thing that will really help the black people: J.O.B.S."[98] Following suit, in the wake of the unrest, the Southeastern Regional Planning and Economic Development District sent a list of demands for policy changes to the Economic Development Administration (EDA), concerned that "ghettos and minority problems are serious and growing here." The obvious answer, the development agency insisted, was more "flexibility in the use of EDA money"; in particular, it wanted to be able to use public money to build plants or buy equipment that could then be made available to industrialists.[99] It was a familiar refrain: what was needed was more public money for private development.

It may have been an old strategy, but it was also an ill-fitting one. After all, an uneasy recognition prevailed that New Bedford actually did have jobs available—of a certain variety. During the last wave of Black unrest in 1968, the mayor had found himself flummoxed over the fact that there were "enough vacancies and job possibilities" available to "absorb all employable persons now on the unemployment rolls."[100] He decided it all must have been a problem of "lack of communication, not a lack of jobs"; his solution was a "mobile trailer," advertising all the "unskilled" jobs available for the people of New Bedford, that could be towed around the "city's hard-core unemployed" neighborhoods.[101] The mayor was not delusional; even deep into the 1970s crisis, New Bedford surveys still routinely found "hard-to-fill" jobs in the city, almost always concentrated in textiles and apparel.[102]

The mayor's obsession with increasing the number of jobs stemmed from a critical and perhaps willful misunderstanding of what local men and women of color were demanding. The 1970s protests were not simply about "more jobs," as city leaders so often understood it. Instead, local minority groups made it clear that they did not want the lousy unskilled jobs that would have been displayed on the mayor's mobile jobs "trailer." They wanted decent jobs and decent wages, and they did not want to be discriminated against in accessing those jobs.

Over and over again, local workers of color found these sorts of jobs extremely difficult to pin down. Some of this was certainly driven by discrimination, emanating from both union halls and executive boardrooms. In one particularly galling incident, a local Cape Verdean plumber named John A. Senna successfully lodged a complaint with the Massachusetts Commission Against Discrimination after his attempt to join the Plumbers and Steamfitters Union was denied. Finding the state commission unsympathetic to its cause, the union simply raised its entrance fee to an exorbitant $3,000. The union's business manager offered no apologies: "If $3,000 is too much let them go to non-union work.... Senna can abide by the union rules or go back to nigger outfits [government programs], or back to the cottonfields for all I care."[103] Anger over this sort of brazen discrimination drove much of this era's "racial" discontent.

Beyond discrimination, there was also a deeper critique of the type of jobs these South Coast cities had so long sought to attract. This sentiment—that there were indeed jobs in New Bedford, just not very good ones—ran like a recurring background joke among interviewees when the Boston public access program *Say Brother!* traveled to New Bedford to get the inside scoop from local Blacks in the aftermath of the "rebellion."[104] When a group of Black men were asked "Are you trying to get a job?," one quickly responded that "there ain't no jobs at all"—until another in the group pointed out that "You can get a job in a fish house!" The interjection was met with laughter and calls of "Now who wants to work in a fish house?" and "That's what I'm trying to tell you, man!" In another group interview, a young man explained that "if [local mills] do give a Black person a job, it's something like sweeping up the floors," before another in the group added that "They'll give people jobs—they'll give people . . . like, greenhorn jobs [with] low minimum wages." The group snickered as the interviewer asked him to clarify what he meant by "green-horn" jobs: "Greenhorns that come from over . . . [laughter] . . . from over across the ocean there. People that work below minimum wages, you know?" When a Black West End woman was asked "What kind of places . . . [can you] work around here?," she simply scoffed before replying in a flat, unimpressed tone: "A factory."[105] Longtime Black residents understood the problem all too well. The issue was not a complete lack of jobs, but an overabundance of what they saw as "greenhorn" jobs: low-paying opportunities targeted at desperate immigrant workers.

This gets to the crux of what was stoking so much of New Bedford's summer of unrest: the area's approach to economic development was leaving behind a trail of disillusionment and seemingly broken promises. Local NAACP president William Carmo blamed the "rebellion" squarely on the city's job training infrastructure. In particular, he highlighted the "Learning to Learn" job skills program, which took in hundreds of applicants with not nearly enough skilled jobs to offer in turn. "This precipitated some of the violence," he explained: "The kids wanted to work. But they found out there wasn't enough room for all of them."[106] This too was a frequent refrain among area Blacks interviewed by *Say Brother!*: "I finally decided [three years ago, on leaving the military] that it was time for me to get some kind of a training where I could benefit. . . . I finally got myself a trade, and this trade hasn't accomplished me nothing because I've been running every two months looking for a job. And I'm tired of it. . . . And these other brothers they know just what I'm going [through] because they've been through it too!" As local Black Panther Jimmy Magnett described a local anti-poverty program, "They trained niggers for 12 to 16 weeks. After they completed a course, there was no job out there. Period. Nothing."[107] The placement rates of the city's local "retraining" government programs were indeed dismal; most trainees dropped out and simply took up work in the garment trade.[108]

Despondence and hopelessness would only be compounded in the coming years, extending far beyond the Black community. As new generations of New

Bedford workers were encouraged to seek education in order to adapt to the new job requirements of the Massachusetts Miracle, they found little opportunity in the South Coast. By the early 1970s, the highly touted Southeastern Massachusetts University (progenitor to the University of Massachusetts Dartmouth) found that three-quarters of graduates had to look outside of southeastern Massachusetts for employment.[109] Those who did not leave found few opportunities to ply their new college skills in the (nonexistent) local high-technology economy. Although immigrants like Emidio Raposo, a thirty-six-year veteran of Morse Drill, could declare with pride in 1987 that "all my children are college-educated," regional conditions nevertheless ensured that these college graduates were navigating a fairly cramped service economy: one of Raposo's children was a priest, another graduate-educated daughter was a nun, and his other daughter was a counselor.[110] The theory was that appropriately trained workers could attract new, high-tech business. The theory was wrong.

Training workers for jobs that never arrived deepened the sense of gloom among disaffected workers and taxpayers alike. "You name a Federal Program—and we've got it," Gerald Cusick, head of New Bedford's Industrial Development Commission, grumbled in 1970.[111] And yet, all this federal money and federal programming seemed to have made little difference. One local anti-poverty agency had trained some 1,000 residents, but, as the agency's director noted, "we'll be lucky if we can place 100 of them in jobs. Where the hell can you put them when there are no jobs here[?]"[112] This became a frequent topic of debate after the "rebellion." Over the decade preceding the 1970 unrest, the city had absorbed $44 million in state and federal money with an additional $66 million on the way.[113] Why had so little changed? As Massachusetts representative Margaret Heckler fumed during one 1976 congressional hearing, "I'm really a little tired of the make work projects. . . . We spent billions of dollars on manpower training . . . [and] very few people got jobs. . . . And I, in fact, think they are a fraud. They make people believe they are going to have an opportunity at the end of the course, and at the end of the course they are unemployed."[114]

A sudden dearth of immigrant labor—paired with a glut of unhappy, disillusioned workers—launched the South Coast back into a familiarly paradoxical mix of persistently high unemployment and frequent labor shortages. As a mix of emigrant remittances and the eventual end of fascism brought more economic growth to the Azorean islands, immigration dried up; local manufacturers were finding desperate workers harder and harder to come by. Open positions began to stack up in low-paying manufacturing work. In 1973,

94,000 in the state were drawing unemployment payments, while somewhere between 10,000 to 20,000 jobs in the state remained unfilled.[115] As the executive vice president of the New Bedford Chamber of Commerce noted as early as 1971, "We have a time of relatively high unemployment, and, at the same time, we have jobs going begging."[116] Aaron Mittleman, president of the Northeast Apparel Manufacturers Association, brought up the same issue during a 1976 congressional hearing: "It is a paradox that even when work is available, this area suffers from high unemployment."[117] Most business operators were confident they knew why this was so.

For many members of the Massachusetts business class, the argument was that welfare—and, specifically, unemployment compensation—had conspired to make garment and other types of manufacturing work unattractive. This was "the crux of the problem," one local business operator told reporters in 1971, adding that "the answer does not lie in increasing wage rates so that they are higher than welfare and unemployment compensation, and other government subsidies, for such action could make many companies noncompetitive and possibly force some out of business."[118] The mayor of nearby Attleboro saw things in similar terms: "A major contributor to the already bulging unemployment rolls is the unemployment checks doled out by the Department of Employment Security. . . . Food stamps, social security, unemployment security, low income housing, rent supplements and low cost medical care and education . . . have removed the economic motivation for working hard from our lives."[119] The leader of the Apparel Manufacturers Association conveyed this same idea in the starkest terms: "Uncle Sam is our biggest competitor for workers in the factories."[120] In this sense, "welfare" opposition became a rational political end for these business and political leaders. After all, these factories were founded on trying to get desperate workers to stitch pants for $1.80 to $2.00 an hour. This accordingly entailed a desire to foreclose other, more attractive options workers might find.

These manufacturers had a point. Workers were indeed abandoning factory labor. But their reasons had little to do with unemployment insurance or generous welfare handouts. Instead, the trend represented the culmination of decades of simmering disdain for factory labor itself. Across the board—regardless of skin color or ethnicity—an emerging generation of educated workers would show little interest in a life sewing clothes or wiring capacitors. Representative Heckler noted this problem during the 1976 congressional hearing, bemoaning the fact that no child dreams of one day stitching pants for the rest of their life: "One of the reasons people don't work is that they have lost—that the society has lost—respect for the skills that really keep our society going. Not everyone has to be a college graduate. . . . I think it is time to come back to the respect for labor."[121]

Despite the mythology, even "greenhorn" Azorean immigrants had not come to America dreaming of a life on the factory floor, and their antipathy for industrial work had certainly not dimmed in the ensuing decades. Such feelings were captured by anthropologist Louise Lamphere, who studied the largely Portuguese apparel and textile workers of nearby Central Falls in the late 1970s. "There is nothing good about working," María Pino told her.[122] "Do you know what it is to have to work eight hours there? There is nothing that I like about my job," Amelia Escóbar reported.[123] "In the factory . . . they make us feel inferior. . . . It's always a Portuguese who goes to work there (by the hot furnaces). They are the ones that always have to sacrifice," said Maria Lídia Mendes.[124] As such, despite the economic crisis, labor turnover was surprisingly high. One forelady summed up the situation for Lamphere in the following way: "About three fourths of them quit, you know. They get in here and see what it's like and then leave. . . . The good ones quit and I end up with all the rest."[125] High turnover in times of high unemployment was not a new phenomenon in industrial Massachusetts. After all, the sorts of jobs that crisis tended to attract were never the ones to which most workers aspired.

Black workers saw the factory in similar terms. As local Panther leader Parky Grace recalled of his own inauguration into industrial New Bedford in the 1960s, "I finally got a job . . . in Eastern Sportswear. . . . My mother worked there. . . . It was pretty decent, but, then, y'know, we had like these speedups." As machine speeds were increased and workers were tasked with increasingly heavy workloads, Grace soon realized he was "doin' the work of four to six people. And, it would just pile up, pile up."[126] When a 1970 congressional investigation was launched into the "extent of subversion" by the American "new left," it found that local radical groups were targeting Fall River and New Bedford's "unusually large number of females working in the garment factories" precisely because "these factories are for the most part a low-wage industry and there is much discontent voiced by the female workers."[127] The upheavals of the era cannot simply be chalked up to the "outsider influence" of radical elements; crummy factory work was a deep wellspring of 1970s radicalism.

These trends continued unabated into the 1980s. By 1989, the business agent of the ILGWU Local 178 saw the biggest problem the union faced as simply "getting people. . . . We cannot get the people."[128] Despite the persistent "industrial wasteland" mythology of the Northeast, local economic studies kept finding the exact opposite. When the five major mayors of the region established the Southeastern Massachusetts Partnership in 1986, the major report it released in 1991 found that "the problem is not that there are not enough manufacturing jobs, the problem is perhaps that there is a preponderance of lower value added, lower wage manufacturing firms in Southeastern Massachusetts."[129] As one business journalist summed up the situation in 1989, "recruiting drives in local high schools and vocational schools turn up few candidates for jobs that start at 6 [dollars] an hour for unskilled work. Students, turned off by images of dirty sweatshops and convinced that the factories have no future, prefer to put on a tie, even if it means a lower-paying job in a bank, insurance company, or real estate firm."[130] In other words, it was not merely a wage problem, nor a "welfare" problem. Workers were taking a pay cut to avoid the dead-end monotony of factory life.

The South Coast garment trade declined, in part, due to worker disinterest. As Azorean migrants, Cape Verdeans, Puerto Ricans, and Blacks took advantage of the area's expanding education infrastructure and its lofty promises of jobs in the new economy—without a concomitant expansion of local demand for highly skilled workers—they were often left jobless or forced to migrate elsewhere in search of better lives in an increasingly two-tiered, high-tech and unskilled, service economy. From 1990 to 2000, New Bedford lost an average of nearly two residents every single day, day after day.[131] Second-generation Azorean immigrants may have not necessarily made good on their parents' dreams of returning home to achieve subsistence living, but they did ultimately seek a life outside the factory. To the degree that they were successful, they too became accomplices in the un-making of the mixed manufacturing economy.

———

Mirroring the closing moments of so many other eras of productive regime collapse in Massachusetts, the "deindustrialization" of the 1970s—the global restructuring of the conglomerates forged in the 1960s—was itself made into political fodder in the drive to create a new productive regime: "High-Tech" Massachusetts. The 1973 crisis ultimately gave "high-tech" entrepreneurs crucial political legitimacy in their campaign to re-shape capital-state relations, successfully pushing the state to cut back government spending on social welfare while ramping up state investment in "high-tech" industry.

Taken at the level of the state, it would seem the 1970s was less an era of deindustrialization than one of linked inter-regional and global restructuring. It is fitting that just as the South Coast industrial core was born out of a capital crisis in the Boston area in the 1870s, the 1970s saw a burst of Boston-area industrial growth fed by the South Coast's collapse.

Even this seemingly most classic case of "deindustrialization," then, was no all-encompassing spectral menace emerging from First-World affluence.[132] It is not entirely clear that the story of late century Massachusetts is a story of deindustrialization at all. Although it is undeniable that numerous South Coast plants closed down or slashed employment in the 1970s and 1980s, complaints of labor shortages persisted. As in previous generations of economic change, low-paying factory labor remained relatively plentiful. Factory owners could be forgiven for thinking workers were abandoning them—not the other way around.

Conclusion

THE LEFTOVER, BRICK-AND-MORTAR carcasses of Massachusetts's erstwhile industrial supremacy may appear to be vacant old mills, but, as the 2007 immigration raid showed, this is not usually the case. The foreboding factory exteriors that line Rodney French Boulevard in New Bedford's South End are a case in point. Starting from the east, the distribution center for Cornell Dubilier—an electronics company Frank Leary successfully wheedled into New Bedford in 1940—is housed in the former Holmes Mill.[1] Further along is the old Booth Manufacturing Company building, which now houses an Allegheny Technologies plant (metal fabrication) and Brittany Global Technologies. Despite its lofty name, the latter appears to be a camouflage cloth producer for the military.[2] What was once the Kilburn Mill—the old home of the Bianco factory, raided in 2007—houses a furniture warehouse in one building; the other has been converted into a massive events center and boutique mall. With a half-million square feet of space available, it is stocked with around 130 tenants, running the gamut from textiles to photographers to gyms to jewelers.[3]

Overall, it is hardly a collection of burned-out factories. Large, billboard-clad corporate behemoths like the Berkshire Hathaway may be gone, but these now nameless mill buildings are still home to countless smaller firms and subsidiaries. According to one 2008 survey, 86 percent of the floorspace in New Bedford's seemingly "empty mills" is occupied in some way.[4]

Nonetheless, since the closure of many of the area's last remaining corporate garment and textile factories in the 1990s, there has been an increasing struggle to determine what the next economic regime to define these cities will be. New Bedford's lucrative fishing industry—employing over 6,000 workers—has helped to soften the blow of factory closures on the local economy, but that industry too has come under increasing stress.[5] A combination of federal regulations passed in 2010 to prevent further overfishing, a spate of foreign private equity takeovers, and mounting environmental pressure on Atlantic scallop habitats have put New Bedford fishing in an increasingly precarious position.[6] A declining number of fishermen are working more hours for dwindling pay.[7] "Tell me how I can catch 50,000 pounds of fish yet I don't know what my kids are going to have for dinner," local fisherman Jerry Leeman rhetorically asked a local journalist in 2022.[8] Moreover, unlike the garment industry, fishing is a male-dominated enterprise, so it has been of little help to women workers facing narrowing opportunities in the city. As Gail Fortes of the Southeastern Massachusetts YWCA explained to a reporter, for the single mothers working multiple part-time jobs with whom she largely works, opportunities in fishing can seem rather meaningless.[9] Compounding matters further, city leaders' dreams of turning New Bedford into a hub for "green energy" growth through offshore wind development threaten to further disrupt fishing's already tenuous fortunes, introducing towering turbines with the potential to obstruct radar systems, snag nets, and disturb ecosystems.[10]

In policymakers' hopes for local redemption, the lure of crisis still looms large. Following the relocation of the University of Massachusetts Dartmouth's College of Fine and Performing Arts to New Bedford's downtown, city planners have sought to remold the city as a "creative economy." The goal is to attract young artists and "eclectic shops and restaurants" to create a thriving arts and tourism industry—based, of course, on New Bedford's low rents, cheap mill space, and the marketability of the city's famed whaling past.[11] "The mayor does not want to see any resident or artist priced out of the New Bedford market," Matt Morrisey, executive director of the New Bedford Economic Development Council, told a reporter in 2007: "We are carefully planning to ensure there is a very clear balance."[12] While these efforts are admirable and are slowly beginning to bear some fruit, in the interim, the city's store of aging workers—and the "care" economy it now undergirds—has become one of its most important assets.[13] While 7 percent of New Bedford laborers work in manufacturing, about 60 percent work in the service sector: occupations in healthcare (15.4 percent of the city's workers), office administration (10.4 percent), food and restaurant work (10 percent), and education (7 percent) predominate. The city now has more nurses, medical assistants, and home health aides than manufacturing workers.[14]

Fall River's Office of Economic Development (FROED) is similarly still engaged in many of the same tactics that have long defined the city's struggle for economic ascendance. For these city leaders, the past is a constant reminder of the future. "Nearly 100 years ago, the City of Fall River secured its place as the textile capital of the world," FROED's website proudly declares. "Today, the City of Fall River is embarking on a second renaissance."[15] "You're seeing a city reinvent itself," Robert A. Mellion, president and chief executive of the Fall River Area Chamber of Commerce, recently told journalists.[16]

Again, the inducements available in a struggling city loom large in Fall River's pitch to investors: "FROED helps businesses evaluate the many advantages of locating in Fall River, offering aggressive incentive programs including low-interest financing, tax exemptions, employee recruitment and training services, and site selection assistance."[17] The city recently threw out nothing short of "a red carpet," as one reporter described it, to bring an Amazon.com distribution center to Fall River.[18] City agencies prepared a "shovel-ready" site in a municipal industrial zone, expedited permit approvals, and procured federal money to build a nearby highway interchange to the facility.[19] In a city council meeting lasting less than three minutes, Amazon also received a fifteen-year tax exemption valued at around $100 million. At 1.3 million square feet, the new warehouse is one of Amazon's largest and, at peak times, its highest volume fulfillment center in the country.[20] Around 1,200 employees work ten hours a day in what Amazon describes as "fast-paced, physical roles."[21] About 12 percent of them will experience "serious injury" on the job—a rate over three times the industry average.[22] Fall River's behemoth distribution center has become another tangible reminder that cities can use the lure of desperation to amass jobs—but not usually great jobs.

The city has also added a variety of new luxury apartments and condominiums, fitting with the mayor's plan to attract young, urban professionals priced out of nearby Providence, Rhode Island. Nearly $2 million in tax credits helped turn Fall River's old Quaker Fabric Corp. into Commonwealth Landing apartments, with "water views, hardwood floors, high ceilings, [and] granite kitchen counters."[23] By all appearances, Fall River's strategy continues to be defined by marketing the virtues of crisis: cheap rents, cheap labor, and plenty of local, state, and national incentives.

Although many economic planners have attempted to craft long-range plans that will (hopefully) one day bring high-wage jobs to these cities, short-term efforts still too often go toward garnering unattractive, low-wage work. No better example of this can be found than New Bedford's recent, relentless push to attract a $650-million Foxwoods Casino to the city.[24] As local pastor David Lima pointed out, "The casino companies look for cities with high unemployment to come into because those are the only places where people will vote for them."[25] While casino opponents made moral and social arguments, proponents championed the revenue and jobs it would bring to the city. Anthony R. Sapienza, chairman of the business and development committee for the Greater New Bedford Workforce Investment Board—in pointing to the estimated 2,164 construction jobs and 3,831 permanent jobs the casino was poised to create—argued that "rising tides lift all ships. . . . Economic growth gets economic growth. . . . People are just going to come out of the woodwork for those jobs—kind of like what will happen in Fall River, when Amazon opens their facility there."[26] Almost completely ignored in the casino debate was a question that has long plagued local workers faced with the various "redevelopment" ploys that have rocked these cities over the past 150 years: are these jobs worth having?

From the perspective of the long history of South Coast industrialization, it would seem the problem is not that New Bedford or Fall River lack jobs. After all, so many immigrants would not be continuing to venture to these cities if there were no jobs to be had. Even in the seemingly depressed 1990s, one Salvadoran immigrant recalled that local bosses were so desperate for low-wage workers that they "would come to your house and knock on your door and offer you work."[27] Crucially, this state of paradoxically high unemployment and labor shortage has become a bizarre but defining aspect of industrial Massachusetts. It is an enduring demonstration of both the practical advantages and recurrent vulnerability of development schemes premised on the lure of capitalist calamity. It suggests a critical insight: the issue that most plagues these cities is not a lack of jobs in the abstract but a lack of high-paying, stable jobs.

It is perhaps understandable that harried New Bedford and Fall River economic and city planners—besieged, as they are, by entrenched poverty and constant waves of economic catastrophe—have tended to prioritize short-term growth based on the appeal of crisis. Theirs is an indisputably Sisyphean task by the measure of the arguments offered here. In addition, the two cities have garnered reputations as violent, poor, and riddled with crime. "Everywhere you go, there's shooting," Fall River bartender Jen Machado told journalists investigating why so few young people are attracted to the city.[28] Local residents were understandably horrified in 2015 when a national travel blog rated New Bedford and Fall River the two "worst places to live in Massachusetts" (adding colorful observations such as "the residents here are chronically underemployed" and "between New Bedford and Fall River, there were 173 reported rapes last year. Just wow.").[29] In 2016, another media outlet labeled Fall River the fifth worst city to live in America; a 2020 report found that the two cities led Massachusetts in terms of opioid overdose deaths; in

March 2023, New Bedford and Fall River were ranked among the ten most dangerous cities in the state.[30] The news never seems to get any better.

Moreover, these city planners are hardly unique in their desperate search for jobs. Presidential State of the Union addresses and political campaigns rarely fail to mention some kind of plan to bring jobs—especially manufacturing jobs—back to America's shores. Donald Trump's entire presidency was, in some sense, founded on just these sorts of promises. "Plants and companies are coming back into our country. . . . They don't want to leave anymore because they know they're leaving a very good thing," Trump announced, somewhat prematurely, on October 6, 2017—National Manufacturing Day.[31] Although many news outlets suggested it was Trump who had proclaimed the first Friday of October a celebration of American industry, the holiday was actually codified by Barack Obama, whose own 2012 "Blueprint for an America Built to Last" similarly began with "an economy built on American manufacturing."[32] For President Biden, "U.S. manufacturing was the Arsenal of Democracy in World War II, and must be part of the Arsenal of American Prosperity today."[33] Right or left, the drive to restore some lost era of industrial supremacy is nearly ubiquitous.

Yet, just like in the 1970s or the 1930s, there is rarely discussion of whether people actually want manufacturing jobs. After all, what made these jobs attractive in the mid-twentieth century was not the monotony and relentless grind of industrial toil but the prospect of union representation, high wages, and fair working conditions. These benefits did not emerge spontaneously from the factory floor. They were the proceeds of an intense political, cultural, and ideological struggle workers and their middle-class allies waged—a struggle that achieved spectacular, albeit ephemeral, gains in the decades following the Great Depression. In other words, the contemporary nostalgia for industry is really a nostalgia for a much simpler concept: good, stable jobs.[34]

This is precisely what makes the hollow sort of "creative destruction" that has long defined Massachusetts so alluring but its benefits so evanescent. As the case of industrial Massachusetts shows, catalyzing growth through crisis—reliant as this process is on abysmally low wages and the bestowing of government largesse upon business—often promises renewed growth, but not renewed affluence. The current state of cities like New Bedford and Fall River—now some of the poorest in Massachusetts—serves as a reminder of the glaring shortcomings of this developmental strategy.

An analysis of the long history of industrial development in Massachusetts reveals surprising insights about the trajectory of capitalist expansion in the modern world. Despite the fact that Massachusetts is often portrayed as a sort of paradigmatic case of industrial revolution, its development poorly fits reigning models of industrialization and deindustrialization. The explanations given by economists and historians for the origins of industrialization and the broader concept of modern economic growth variously point to critical ideological, cultural, institutional, technological, or resource preconditions. While these accounts may differ in their appraisal of what served as the metaphorical "power plant" of industrial transformation, they all share a fundamentally linear concept of economic progress. In other words, they all hold that once a state or nation achieves the right set of institutional, technological, or resource attributes, industry is sure to follow.[35] And, in turn, once industry has matured to a particular level, the iron laws of comparative advantage demand a switch to a more knowledge-intensive, post-industrial economy.[36]

By focusing on how a particular locale—like Massachusetts—actually managed to aggregate both the migrant labor and mobile capital necessary for mass production, a much more cyclical story of the makings of economic progress emerges. Hardly rooted in the maturation of handicraft or agricultural production, the industrial era in South Coast Massachusetts was launched by desperate capitalists looking to take advantage of a prevailing labor crisis. Hardly an organic productive boom powered by new technology, cultural achievement, or liberal ideology, so much of what marked the rise of mass manufacturing in Massachusetts came from the mobility of industrial production and its factors: the ways in which state and local leaders coaxed capital and labor to their shores, and the ways in which workers, capitalists, and policymakers battled over the shape of each succeeding economic regime. Hardly a long-wave process of nineteenth-century industrialization and twentieth-century deindustrialization, these transformations were wrenching processes of constant economic creation and re-creation that came at the price of interminable economic destruction and revolution.

Looking outward from Massachusetts, the history of global capitalism has been the chaotic summation of countless local histories. It is the end product of the incessant machinations of innumerable local actors constructing and reconstructing innumerable local economies, each struggling to use crisis to outmaneuver one another in the game of capitalist seduction. The spiraling "race to the bottom" is not simply a present-day conundrum; it is a structural facet of how industrial capitalism expanded over the last two centuries.

Such a story is certainly less optimistic than conventional tales of steady, progressive economic development. But seeing crisis and globalization as critical aspects of how so many cities, states, and nations first achieved modern economic growth might help demystify these last few decades of surging capitalist expansion amid a gnawing sense of escalating impoverishment. Local economies often rely on high business subsidies and cheap labor appeal to attract industry. If industrial Massachusetts is any guide, these are time-tested tools to foster short-term growth and cannibalize long-term prosperity.

Notes

Manuscript Collections

AESL-CLMR	Arthur and Elizabeth Schlesinger Library: Consumers' League of Massachusetts Records
AFKLFR	Ambrose F. Keeley Library, Fall River, Massachusetts
ANTT-AHMNE	Arquivo Nacional Torre do Tombo: Arquivo Histórico do Ministério dos Negócios Estrangeiros, Repartição dos Negócios Políticos
ANTT-AS	Arquivo Nacional Torre do Tombo: Arquivo Salazar
ANTT-MI	Arquivo Nacional Torre do Tombo: Fundo, Ministério do Interior
BLHC-ABNB	Baker Library Historical Collections: Account Books and Other Material Relating to the Whaling Industry Chiefly from New Bedford and Nantucket, Mass.
BLHC-AMS-FRIW	Baker Library Historical Collections: Annawan Manufactory Series, Fall River Iron Works Collection
BLHC-BMC	Baker Library Historical Collections: Boston Manufacturing Company Records
BLHC-CFBR	Baker Library Historical Collections: Coolidge Family Business Records
BLHC-CMBR	Baker Library Historical Collections: Charles W. Morgan Business Records
BLHC-KPCP	Baker Library Historical Collections: Kidder, Peabody & Co. Papers
BLHC-LMC	Baker Library Historical Collections: Lawrence Manufacturing Company Records
BLHC-MMC	Baker Library Historical Collections: Merrimack Mfg. Co. Papers
BLHC-MS-FRIW	Baker Library Historical Collections: Metacomet Series, Fall River Iron Works Collection

BNPL	Biblioteca Nacional de Portugal
BPARD-AACP	Biblioteca Pública e Arquivo Regional de Ponta Delgada: Arquivo da Administração do Concelho de Povoação
BPARD-VP-AACL	Biblioteca Pública e Arquivo Regional de Ponta Delgada: Verbetes de Preço Médio dos Géneros para Determinação do Rendimento Colectável, Item 1743, Freguesia de Santa Cruz, Repartição da Fazenda Pública, Arquivo da Administração do Concelho de Lagôa
BPARPD-AGCDPD	Biblioteca Pública e Arquivo Regional de Ponta Delgada: Arquivo do Governo Civil do Distrito de Ponta Delgada
BPARPD-ASPAM	Biblioteca Pública e Arquivo Regional de Ponta Delgada: Arquivo da Sociedade Promotora da Agricultura Micaelense
BPARPD-FPEC	Biblioteca Pública e Arquivo Regional de Ponta Delgada: Fundo Particular de Eugénio do Canto
BPARPD-FPER	Biblioteca Pública e Arquivo Regional de Ponta Delgada: Fundo Particular de Ernesto Rodolfo Hintze Ribeiro
BPARD-FPTB	Biblioteca Pública e Arquivo Regional de Ponta Delgada: Fundo Particular de Teófilo Braga
FIAC-OHJP	French Institute, Emmanuel d'Alzon Library, Assumption College: Oral History Project Coordinated by Josephine Perrault, 1981–1984
HLHU-DFLC	Houghton Library, Harvard University: Daniel B. Fearing Logbook Collection
IISH	International Institute of Social History, Amsterdam, Netherlands
IISH-ICFTU	International Institute of Social History: International Confederation of Free Trade Union Archives
IISH-ITGLWF	International Institute of Social History: International Textile, Garment and Leather Workers' Federation Collection
KCLA	Kheel Center for Labor-Management Documentation and Archives, Cornell University Library
KCLA-ACTWU-FR	Kheel Center for Labor-Management Documentation and Archives: ACTWU Fall River Local Minute Books on Microfilm
KCLA-ACWA	Kheel Center for Labor-Management Documentation and Archives: Amalgamated Clothing Workers of America Records
KCLA-ILGWU-DD	Kheel Center for Labor-Management Documentation and Archives: International Ladies' Garment Workers' Union, David Dubinsky, President's Records
KCLA-ILGWU-FU	Kheel Center for Labor-Management Documentation and Archives: International Ladies' Garment Workers' Union, Frederick F. Umhey, Executive Secretary Collection

KCLA-ILGWU-PUB	Kheel Center for Labor-Management Documentation and Archives: International Ladies' Garment Workers' Union Publications
KCLA-ILGWU-SC	Kheel Center for Labor-Management Documentation and Archives: International Ladies' Garment Workers' Union, Sol Chaikin Papers
LSE-WEBB	Archives and Special Collections, London School of Economics and Political Science: [Sidney and Beatrice] Webb Trade Union [Collection], Section C
MCGILL-CC	Rare Books and Special Collections, McGill University Library: Canadien Collection
MHS	Massachusetts Historical Society, Boston, Massachusetts
NBFPL	New Bedford Free Public Library
NBFPL-MAS	New Bedford Free Public Library: Mayor Ashley Scrapbooks
NBFPL-WPS	New Bedford Free Public Library: William J. Potter Sermons
NBWMRL	New Bedford Whaling Museum Research Library
NBWMRL-BFP	New Bedford Whaling Museum Research Library: Bennett Family Papers, Subgroup 4, Thomas Bennett Jr. Papers
NBWMRL-HFBR	New Bedford Whaling Museum Research Library: Hathaway Family Business Records
NBWMRL-JBBR	New Bedford Whaling Museum Research Library: Jonathan Bourne Jr. Business Records, Series G
NBWMRL-NBRR	New Bedford Whaling Museum Research Library: New Bedford Rayon, Inc. Records, Subgroup 1
NBWMRL-NBRR-CC	New Bedford Whaling Museum Research Library: New Bedford Rayon, Inc. Records, Subgroup 2, New Bedford Area Chamber of Commerce Records
NBWMRL-PMCR	New Bedford Whaling Museum Research Library: Pierce Manufacturing Corporation Records, Subgroup 1
NBWMRL-POHC	New Bedford Whaling Museum Research Library: Purrington Oral History Collection
PEM	Peabody Essex Museum
RYLANDS-OCSL	John Rylands Library, University of Manchester: Archive of the Amalgamated Association of Operative Cotton Spinners and Twiners [of Lancashire and Adjoining Counties]
RYLANDS-OCSTB	John Rylands Library, University of Manchester: Archives of the Operative Cotton Spinners and Twiners' Provincial Association of Bolton and Surrounding Districts

UMASSA-ACTWU-NERJB	University of Massachusetts Amherst Special Collections: ACTWU, New England Regional Joint Board
UMASSA-ACWA-BJB	University of Massachusetts Amherst Special Collections: Amalgamated Clothing Workers of America, Boston Joint Board
UMASSA-ACWA-NE	University of Massachusetts Amherst Special Collections: Amalgamated Clothing Workers of America, New England Joint Board
UMASSA-FRLFA	University of Massachusetts Amherst Special Collections: [Fall River] Loom Fixers Association Records
UMASSA-FRYFU	University of Massachusetts Amherst Special Collections: [Fall River] Yarn Finishers Union
UMASSA-TWUA-NBJB	University of Massachusetts Amherst Special Collections: Textile Workers Union of America, New Bedford Joint Board Records
UMASSD-FMPAA-ABAP	University of Massachusetts Dartmouth, Ferreira-Mendes Portuguese-American Archives: Portuguese Alliance Benevolent Association (Associação Beneficente Aliança Portuguesa) Records
UMASSD-FMPAA-CVP	University of Massachusetts Dartmouth, Ferreira-Mendes Portuguese-American Archives: The Carlton M. Viveiros Papers
UMASSD-FMPAA-JRP	University of Massachusetts Dartmouth, Ferreira-Mendes Portuguese-American Archives: João Rocha Papers
UMASSD-FMPAA-OHP	University of Massachusetts Dartmouth, Ferreira-Mendes Portuguese-American Archives: Oral History Project
UMASSD-NB1928	Claire T. Carney Library Archives and Special Collections, University of Massachusetts Dartmouth: New Bedford Textile Worker's Strike of 1928 Oral History Interviews and Research Collection
UMASSD-SMREDC	Claire T. Carney Library Archives and Special Collections, University of Massachusetts Dartmouth: Southeastern Massachusetts Regional Economic Development Collection
UPASC-UE277	Archives & Special Collections, University of Pittsburgh Library System: UE [United Electrical, Radio and Machine Workers of America] Local 277 Records

UPASC-UE284   Archives & Special Collections, University of Pittsburgh Library System: Records of United Electrical, Radio and Machine Workers of America Local 284

UPASC-UEDIST2   UE Archives & Special Collections, University of Pittsburgh Library System: [United Electrical, Radio and Machine Workers of America] District 2 Records

WLHU-HBH   Widener Library, Harvard University: Henry Beetle Hough Scrapbook

WLHU-OC   Widener Library, Harvard University: Open Collections Program

Newspapers and Periodicals

AA	*A Alvorada* (New Bedford)
AIM	*AIM Industrial News* (Published by the Associated Industries of Massachusetts)
AO	*Açoriano Oriental* (Ponta Delgada, Açores)
AWCR	*American Wool and Cotton Reporter*
BDG	*Boston Daily Globe*
BDR	*Boston Daily Reporter*
BG	*Boston Globe*
BNBFW	*Barron's National Business and Financial Weekly*
DDA	*Diario dos Açores* (Ponta Delgada, Açores)
DDN	*Diário de Notícias* (New Bedford)
ES	*Evening Standard* (New Bedford)
FRHN	*Fall River Herald News* (Fall River)
HN	*Herald News* (Fall River)
ID	*Industrial Development: The National Magazine of Area Analysis and Business Site Selection*
IND	*Industry* (Published by the Associated Industries of Massachusetts)
INR	*Industrial News Reporter*
IWJ	*Industry: A Weekly Journal of Industrial Information* (Published by the Associated Industries of Massachusetts)
MM	*Morning Mercury* (New Bedford)
NBT	*New Bedford Times* (New Bedford)
NYT	*New York Times*
PBN	*Providence Business News*
SS	*Sunday Standard* (New Bedford)
ST	*Standard-Times* (New Bedford)
WP	*Washington Post*
WSJ	*Wall Street Journal*
WSLMT	*Whalemen's Shipping Log and Merchants' Transcript* (New Bedford)

INTRODUCTION

1. "Samuel Aj" is a pseudonym. See Knauer, "From Post-Conflict Guatemala to Post-Immigration Raid New Bedford."

2. Knauer, "The Maya of New Bedford," 176; Al-Khazraji and Al-Khazraji, *The Puerto Rican Journey to New Bedford.*

3. Juravich, *Altar of the Bottom Line*, 61.

4. Knauer, "The Maya of New Bedford," 172.

5. Ibid., 176.

6. Brian Fraga, "Colleagues, Friends Say Raided Plant Owner Was Hard-Working Immigrant," *ST*, Mar. 26, 2007.

7. Michael Bonner, "Ten Years Later, Effects from Immigration Roundup at Michael Bianco Remain Fresh," *ST*, Mar. 4, 2017.

8. ICE, "New Bedford Manufacturer . . . Arrested . . . ," Mar. 6, 2007; Tirman, "'They Treated Us as if We Were Murderers.'"

9. ICE, "New Bedford Manufacturer . . . Arrested."

10. Tirman, "'They Treated Us as if We Were Murderers.'"

11. Ibid.; Yvonne Abraham and Brian Ballou, "350 Are Held in Immigration Raid," *BG*, Mar. 7, 2007; "Timeline of the New Bedford Raid," *BG*, Mar. 15, 2007; Juravich, *Altar of the Bottom Line*, 91.

12. Tirman, "'They Treated Us as if We Were Murderers.'"

13. ICE, "New Bedford Manufacturer . . . Arrested."

14. New Bedford, *Historic Mill Inventory*, 132.

15. Tirman, "'They Treated Us as if We Were Murderers.'"

16. New Bedford Department of Planning, "Staff Report . . . March 8, 2017"; Young, "Kilburn Mill, Mill Nos. 1 & 2," Map.

17. Lewis Hine, "Group Going Out at Noon from the Kilburn Mills," Aug. 1911, https://www.loc.gov/pictures/item/2018675375/.

18. See Google Maps, https://www.google.com/maps/@41.6138459,-70.9190291,3a, 75y,226.03h,91.62t/data=!3m6!1e1!3m4!1sAlAB4NfQ4adtIzFbqXJtcA!2e0!7i3 328!8i1664.

19. New Bedford, *Historic Mill Inventory*, 57; Office of Historic Preservation, New Bedford, Mass., "Wamsutta Mills," Form nos. 216, 218, 219, 220, 224, 225, 125, Area no. 78, Folder 37, Box 4, *UMASSD-NB1928*; Rehold Real Estate Navigator, "1 Wamsutta St., New Bedford, MA," https://rehold.com/New+Bedford+MA/ WAMSUTTA+ST/1.

20. Jill Radsken, "Maury Povich Launches Clothing Company in New Bedford," *BG*, Aug. 6, 2014.

21. Davis et al., *In Pursuit of Leviathan*, 4; "Top Capacitor Vendors Show Mixed Results," May 30, 2010, http://www.passivecomponentmagazine.com/top-capacitor-vend ors-show-mixed-results-in-march-2010-quarter/; AVX, "Tantalum Capacitors," accessed Apr. 27, 2016, http://www.avx.com/products/tantalum/.

22. Massachusetts Department of Revenue, Division of Local Services, "Data Analytics and Resources Bureau: DOR Income and EQV Per Capita," accessed Sep. 6, 2023, https://dlsgateway.dor.state.ma.us/reports/rdPage.aspx?rdReport=DOR_Income_EQV_Per_Capita .

23. On Massachusetts, New England, and the "deindustrialization" narrative, see Koistinen, *Confronting Decline*; Bluestone and Harrison, *The Deindustrialization of America*; Sugrue, *Origins of the Urban Crisis*, 127; English, *A Common Thread*; Forrant, *Metal Fatigue*, 9–13; Freeman, *Behemoth*, 78–79. On the larger narrative of nineteenth-century industrialization and twentieth-century de-industrialization, see Bell, *The Coming of Post-Industrial Society*; Hobsbawm, *The Age of Extremes*; Stein, *Running Steel*; Stein, *Pivotal Decade*; Brady et al., "The Consequences of Economic Globalization"; Skrabec, *Fall of an American Rome*; High and Lewis, *Corporate Wasteland*; Milkman, *Farewell to the Factory*; Minchin, *Empty Mills*; McKee, *Problem of Jobs*, 11–13.

24. Koistinen, *Confronting Decline*; Koistinen, "The Causes of Deindustrialization"; Hartford, *Where Is Our Responsibility?*

25. In offering this argument, I am also drawing on the countless economic theorists who have studied the cyclical process of capital accumulation and dispossession. See Marx, *Grundrisse*; Schumpeter, *Capitalism, Socialism and Democracy*; Harvey, *The Limits to Capital*; Harvey, *The Enigma of Capital*; Harvey, *Spaces of Capital*.

26. See essays in Temin, *Engines of Enterprise*; Koistinen, *Confronting Decline*; Neumann, *Remaking the Rust Belt*.

27. Krippner, *Capitalizing on Crisis*; Klein, *The Shock Doctrine*.

28. Schumpeter, *Capitalism, Socialism and Democracy*.

29. Douglass, *The Life and Times of Frederick Douglass*, 256; Pease, *History of New Bedford*, 30; Davis et al., *In Pursuit of Leviathan*, 4.

CHAPTER 1

1. Borden, *Our County and Its People*, 22.

2. Thomas Bennett, "From Mem. and Paper of Thos. Bennett, Jr. . . . The Wamsutta Mills," Folder 1, Box 2, Series E, NBWMRL-BFP.

3. McMullin, "Industrialization and Social Change," 16.

4. Bennett, "From Mem. and Paper of Thos. Bennett, Jr.," *NBWMRL-BFP*.

5. Ibid.

6. A No Water Man, Letter to the Editor, *ES*, Jul. 29, 1865.

7. "Statement of Dividends . . . Jan. 1, 1849 to Oct. 1., 1880," Folder 1, Series D, NBWMRL-BFP.

8. Bennett, "From Mem. and Paper of Thos. Bennett, Jr.," NBWMRL-BFP.

9. Ibid.

10. Olga Louise Garth, "A Historical Account of New Bedford Rayon Division," Sep. 19, 1966, Folder 1, Series G, NBWMRL-NBRR.

11. Beckert, *Empire of Cotton*, 69.

12. Kulik, "The Beginnings of the Industrial Revolution in America," 140–141; Jeremy, "Damming the Flood," 2; Freeman, *Behemoth*, 45.

13. Beckert, *Empire of Cotton*, 139, 145–146.

14. Jeremy, *Transatlantic Industrial Revolution*, 211; Laurie, *Artisans into Workers*, 30; Engerman and Sokoloff, "Technology and Industrialization, 1790–1914," 373; Conrad, " 'Drive That Branch,' " 5.

15. *Massachusetts Spy* (Worcester), Oct. 30, 1822, quoted in Tucker, "The Merchant, the Manufacturer, and the Factory Manager," 310.

16. *Plebian and Milbury Workingman's Advocate*, Jan. 25, 1832, quoted in Tucker, "The Merchant, the Manufacturer, and the Factory Manager," 310.

17. Tucker, *Samuel Slater*, 86.

18. Dublin, *Women at Work*, 15.

19. Goldin and Sokoloff, "Women, Children, and Industrialization."

20. Rothenberg, "Invention of American Capitalism," 87; Dublin, *Women at Work*, 3; Clark, *Roots of Rural Capitalism*, 70.

21. Rothenberg, "Invention of American Capitalism," 79.

22. Ibid., 87; Barron, *Those Who Stayed Behind*, 29.

23. Barron, *Those Who Stayed Behind*, 29; Dublin, *Women at Work*, 76.

24. Hardt, "Jefferson and Democracy," 55; Jefferson, *Notes on the State of Virginia*, 274–275.

25. McCoy, *The Elusive Republic*, 185–188.

26. Blake, "And Did Those Feet in Ancient Time," 125.

27. William Appleton to Eben Appleton, Jul. 24, 1802, Appleton Family Papers, MHS, quoted in Dalzell, *Enterprising Elite*, 12.

28. Appleton, *Introduction of the Power Loom*, 7; Dalzell, *Enterprising Elite*, 6.

29. Francis Cabot Lowell to William Cabot, Jan. 2, 1812, Francis C. Lowell Papers, MHS, quoted in Dalzell, *Enterprising* Elite, 12.

30. Kasson, *Civilizing the Machine*, 55–61.

31. James Kirke Paulding, *A Sketch of Old England, by a New England Man* (New York: 1822), I, 144, 149, quoted in Kasson, *Civilizing the Machine*, 59.

32. C. Edwards Lester, *The Glory and Shame of England* (New York: 1850), I, 47, quoted in Kasson, *Civilizing the Machine*, 60.

33. Appleton, *Introduction of the Power Loom*, 15.

34. Kasson, *Civilizing the Machine*, 71; Freeman, *Behemoth*, 59.

35. Gross, *The Course of Industrial Decline*, 9; Prude, "Capitalism, Industrialization," 253–254.

36. Appleton, *Introduction of the Power Loom*, 16.

37. Lawrence Manufacturing Company, "General Regulations"; Lawrence Manufacturing Company, "Regulations to be Observed."

38. Middlesex Company, "Regulations for the Boarding Houses of the Middlesex Company," ca. 1850, reproduced in Eisler, *The Lowell Offering*, 27; *Handbook to*

Lowell (1848), 45–46, reproduced in Commons et al., *Documentary History of American Industrial Society*, 137.

39. Lowell, "Patrick Tracy Jackson," 565.

40. Merrimack Mfg. Co: Directors' Minutes, 1822–1843, 17, Vol. 1, BLHC-MMC.

41. Estimate based on Dublin, *Women at Work*, 76.

42. Gross, *The Course of Industrial Decline*, 11; Dalzell, *Enterprising Elite*, 67; *The Lowell Offering*, no. 1 (Oct. 1840), http://nrs.harvard.edu/urn-3:FHCL:4214878.

43. Dublin, *Women at Work*; Prude, "Capitalism, Industrialization," 251–254; Temin, "Product Quality," 900.

44. Rothenberg, "The Invention of American Capitalism," 102.

45. Lawrence Manufacturing Company, Payroll Record, Dec. 14, 1833–Dec. 13, 1834, 2–11, Vol. GA-1, BLHC-LMC.

46. Ibid.

47. Ibid.

48. Dublin, *Women at Work*, 66.

49. Dalzell, *Enterprising Elite*, 50.

50. Dalzell, *Enterprising Elite*, 50, 30; Boston Manufacturing Company [BMC], Dividend Record, Vol. 7, BLHC-BMC.

51. This claim is central to Dalzell, *Enterprising Elite*.

52. Davis, "Stock Ownership." On the claim of "merchant" decline fueling the rise of the textile industry, see Ware, *Early New England Cotton Manufacture*, 141.

53. Beckert, *Empire of Cotton*, 147; Temin, "Product Quality," 906.

54. Amos Lawrence to George Shattuck, Jul. 2, 1833, quoted in Dalzell, *Enterprising Elite*, 67.

55. Dalzell, *Enterprising Elite*, 10.

56. Francis Cabot Lowell to Patrick Johnson, Nov. 16, 1811, Francis C. Lowell Papers, MHS, quoted in Dalzell, *Enterprising* Elite, 8–9.

57. Lawrence, *Extracts*, 81.

58. Dalzell, *Enterprising Elite*, 65.

59. Dalzell, *Enterprising Elite*, 11–12; Rosenberg, *Life and Times of Francis Cabot Lowell*, 41, 47.

60. Abbott, *Cotton & Capital*, 24; Howe, *Political Culture of the American Whigs*, 96–108; Dalzell, *Enterprising Elite*, 165.

61. Appleton, *Selections from the Diaries*, 142, 234; Appleton, *Memoir of the Hon. Abbott Lawrence*, 8–9.

62. Rothenberg, "The Invention of American Capitalism," 101.

63. See Schakenbach Regele, *Manufacturing Advantage*, esp. 89–98.

64. NPS, "Boston Manufacturing Company"; Hurd, *History of Middlesex County*, 752; Gross, *The Course of Industrial Decline*, 5.

65. Miles, *Lowell*, 56.

66. Dalzell, *Enterprising Elite*, 225.

67. Lawrence, *Extracts*, 90.

68. Lawrence, "Memoir," 131.

69. BMC, Dividend Records, Apr. 15, 1828–Oct. 16, 1852, Vol. 7, Series I, BLHC-BMC; BMC, Dividend Records, Apr. 5, 1853–Oct. 2, 1871, Vol. 8, Series I, BLHC-BMC; BMC, Dividend Records, Jun. 15, 1889–Apr. 28, 1905, Vol. 9, Series I, BLHC-BMC; BMC, Directors' Records, Oct. 5, 1825–Dec. 20, 1909, 81, Vol. 3, Series I, BLHC-BMC; "Boston Manufacturing Co.," AWCR 36, no. 7, section 2 (Feb. 16, 1922): 524, https://books.google.com/books?id=D_ZYAAAYAAJ.

70. BMC, Directors' Records, Oct. 5, 1825–Dec. 20, 1909, 67, 77, Vol. 3, Series I, BLHC-BMC.

71. BMC, Directors' Records, Oct. 5, 1825–Dec. 20, 1909, 74, Vol. 3, Series I, BLHC-BMC.

72. Dalzell, *Enterprising Elite*, 225; Maggor, *Brahmin Capitalism*, 23–26.

73. Clipping, Dec. 8, 1881, Vol. 3, Series I, BLHC-BMC.

74. Report, Jun. 27, 1881, Vol. 3, Series I, BLHC-BMC.

75. "To the Stockholders of the Boston Manufacturing Company," Oct. 14, 1901, Vol. 3, Series I, BLHC-BMC.

76. Ibid.

77. "Hamilton Mfg. Co," AWCR 36, no. 7, section 2 (Feb. 16, 1922): 412, https://books.google.com/books?id=D_ZYAAAAYAA; "Tremont Mills," AWCR 36, no. 7, section 2 (Feb. 16, 1922): 422, https://books.google.com/books?id=D_ZYAAAAYAAJ.

78. Dalzell, *Enterprising Elite*, 38, 51.

79. This argument is central to Maggor, *Brahmin Capitalism*.

80. Morse, "Memoir," 116.

81. Adams, *Selected Letters*, 87–88.

82. Maggor, *Brahmin Capitalism*, chs. 1, 3.

83. Coolidge, *Autobiography*, 9–10.

84. Ayer, *Uses and Abuses*, 9; Gross, *The Course of Industrial Decline*, 29.

85. Gross, *The Course of Industrial Decline*, 30–33.

86. Thomas Jefferson Coolidge, Stock Ledger, 1858–1898, 20–27, Vol. 22, BLHC-CFBR.

87. Thomas Jefferson Coolidge, Stock Ledger, 1858–1898, 217, 341, 219, 219, 23, 24, 26, Vol. 22, BLHC-CFBR.

88. Thomas Jefferson Coolidge, Stock Ledger, 1858–1898, 34, 36, 44–45, 44, 46, 46, 51, 52, 56, 65, 68, 26, 260, 275, Vol. 22, BLHC-CFBR.

89. Amoskeag, *Amoskeag Manufacturing*, 216–218.

90. Lawrence, "Memoir," 132.

91. Nelson, *Nation of Deadbeats*, 140; Serda, "Boston Investors."

92. Stock Ledger of J.E. Thayer, 1836–1858 and N. Thayer, 1858–1869, Vol. 2, BLHC-KPCP.

93. Investigating Committee Report, Jun. 11, 1867, Folder "General Administrative Records," AO-1, BLHC-LMC.

94. "The Product of the Mills in the Year Ending . . ." ca. 1867, AO-1, BLHC-LMC.

95. Ibid.; Investigating Committee Report, 1867, 3, 21, BLHC-LMC.

96. Investigating Committee Report, 1867, 3-15, BLHC-LMC.

97. Report, Jun. 27, 1881, Vol. 3, BLHC-BMC.

98. Gross, *The Course of Industrial Decline*, 35.

99. Ibid., 45.

100. John Wright to Henry V. Ward, Feb. 8, 1862, quoted in Vernon-Wortzel, *Lowell*, 82.

101. Investigating Committee Report, 1867, 3, 21, BLHC-LMC; Vernon-Wortzel, *Lowell*, 113; Brown, "Decline and Fall," 155.

102. Dalzell, *Enterprising Elite*, 56.

103. Brown, "Decline and Fall," 143.

104. Ayer, *Uses and Abuses*, 9.

105. Ibid.

106. Dublin, *Lowell*, 67.

107. Cowley, *Illustrated History of Lowell*, 60-61.

108. Cowley, *Illustrated History of Lowell*, 60-61; Cowley, *Reminiscences*, 42.

109. Vernon-Wortzel, *Lowell*, 182-183.

110. *Boston Daily Evening Traveller*, Jul. 29, 1863, quoted in Vernon-Wortzel, *Lowell*, 108.

111. Appleton, *Introduction of the Power Loom*, 30.

112. Dublin, *Women at Work*, 133; US Bureau of the Census, *Manufactures of the United States in 1860*, xix.

113. US Bureau of the Census, *Reports of the Immigration Commission*, 38.

CHAPTER 2

1. Melville, *Moby-Dick*, 36.

2. Sweetser, *New England*, 91.

3. *The Boston Journal*, Jan. 27, 1872, reproduced in Nason, *Gazetteer of . . . Massachusetts*, 363.

4. Heath, *Patina of Place*, 192; Davis et al., *In Pursuit of Leviathan*, 4.

5. Creighton, *Rites and Passages*, 16.

6. Vickers, "Nantucket Whalemen in the Deep-Sea Fishery."

7. Ibid., 286–287.

8. Zallen, *American Lucifers*, 20; Creighton, *Rites and Passages*, 19; Hitchcock, *Down and Out*, 25.

9. Byers, *Nation of Nantucket*, 144.

10. Creighton, *Rites and Passages*, 23; Arato and Eleey, *Safely Moored at Last*, 7.

11. Arato and Eleey, *Safely Moored at Last*, 7; Bullard, *The Rotches*, 12–13.

12. Ricketson, *The History of New Bedford*, 23–24.

13. Pease, *History of New Bedford*, 14, 58.

14. Bullard, *The Rotches*, 15.

15. "Notes on New Bedford," 19.

16. Petition, Nov. 26, 1813, reproduced in Macy, *The History of Nantucket*, 176–177.

17. Ibid.

18. Davis et al., *In Pursuit of Leviathan*, 19.

19. Ibid., 6–7, 379.

20. Ibid. 14; Creighton, *Rites and Passages*, 28–30.

21. Davis et al., *In Pursuit of Leviathan*, 158, 15.

22. Ibid., 173, 194; Creighton, *Rites and Passages*, 93–95, 144; Warrin, *So Ends This Day*, 131–136.

23. Diary of Richard Boyenton, *Bengal*, Feb. 28, 1834, PEM, quoted in Creighton, *Rites and Passages*, 46.

24. Davis et al., *In Pursuit of Leviathan*, 15.

25. Creighton, *Rites and Passages*, 47.

26. Warrin, *So Ends This Day*, 40.

27. Lawrence Manufacturing Company, Payroll Record, Dec. 14, 1833–Dec. 13, 1834, 2–11, Vol. GA-1, BLHC-LMC.

28. Vickers, "Nantucket Whalemen in the Deep-Sea Fishery," 295.

29. Jared Gardner to Harriet Gardner, Jun. 1841, American Antiquarian Society, Worcester, Massachusetts, quoted in Creighton, *Rites and Passages*, 48; Diary of Ambrose Waldron, *Bowdick*, Jun. 1, 1847, Nicholson Whaling Collection, Providence Public Library, Providence, Rhode Island, quoted in Creighton, *Rites and Passages*, 48.

30. Diary of Lewis Williams, *Gratitude*, Apr. 8, 1859, *PEM*, quoted in Creighton, *Rites and Passages*, 48.

31. Diary of John Joplin, *Ann Parry*, Apr. 25, 1848, *PEM*, quoted in Creighton, *Rites and Passages*, 48.

32. Creighton, *Rites and Passages*, 43.

33. Jonathan Bourne Jr. [hereafter JB] to Edw. Fisher, Jan. 13, 1852, Vol. 2, NBWMRL-JBBR; JB to Thomas Beveridge, Mar. 30, 1853, Vol. 2, NBWMRL-JBBR; JB to Gilbert Hathaway, Apr. 14, 1857, Vol. 2, NBWMRL-JBBR; JB to Mary Haskell, Jun. 4, 1855, Vol. 2, NBWMRL-JBBR; JB to Frances Willard, Jan. 18, Oct. 28, 1857, Vol. 3, NBWMRL-JBBR; JB to Abby S. Reed, Apr. 9, 1858, Vol. 3, NBWMRL-JBBR.

34. JB to Edw. Fisher, Jan. 13, 1852, Vol. 2, NBWMRL-JBBR.

35. Grover, *Fugitive's Gibraltar*; Farr, "A Slow Boat to Nowhere," 164.

36. AFASS, *Annual Report . . . 1853*, 143.

37. Douglass, *My Bondage and My Freedom*, 342, 346–347.

38. McFeely, *Frederick Douglass*, 83–84.

39. Juravich et al., *Commonwealth of Toil*, 34–35.

40. Almanac Singers, *Deep Sea Chanteys and Whaling Ballads*; Barnes, *I Hear America Singing*, 159.

41. Creighton, *Rites and Passages*, 217.

42. Elisha Dexter, *Narrative of the Loss of the William and Joseph Whaling Brig* . . . (Boston: Samuel N. Dickenson, 1842), 6, quoted in Warrin, *So Ends This Day*, 57.

43. Joseph Silva, Journal, bark *George and Mary*, Oct. 5, 1852, Log 615, NBWMRL, quoted in Warrin, *So Ends This Day*, 44.

44. Bark *Zone*, Fairhaven, Massachusetts, Oct. 17, 1855, Log 278, *I*, quoted in Warrin, *So Ends This Day*, 61.

45. Ibid., 115, 173–174.

46. Ibid., 178.

47. Percentages based on Fall River crew lists of reasonable completeness as found in National Maritime Digital Library, "Fall River Crew List," https://web.archive. org/web/20131127165046/http://www.nmdl.org/frc/frcindex.cfm.

48. National Maritime Digital Library, "Crew List for the Aerial, bark of Fall River. Voyage (1851 May 12–1852 June 1) to Atlantic, Indian," https://web.archive.org/web/20151203222736/http://www.nmdl.org/frc/frcrew.cfm?voyage=309.

49. Ibid.

50. Nicholas, *VC*, 11.

51. JB to C. B. H. Fessenden, May 26, 1852, Vol. 2, NBWMRL-JBBR; Herringshaw, *Herringshaw's Encyclopedia of American Biography*, 132; Hurd, *History of Bristol County*, 144.

52. Pease, "The Story of the Building of the Bourne Whaling Museum."

53. Noel, *Jonathan Bourne*, 3.

54. Ibid. 3; Pease, "The Building of the Bourne Whaling Museum."

55. Noel, *Jonathan Bourne*, 4–5.

56. Ibid., 5–6.

57. Ibid., 15; Mulderink, *New Bedford's Civil War*, 149.

58. Mulderink, *New Bedford's Civil War*, 138–163, 187; Davis et al., *In Pursuit of Leviathan*, 427–428.

59. JB to Elbridge G. Peirce, Dec. 4, 1851, Vol. 2, NBWMRL-JBBR.

60. Mulderink, *New Bedford's Civil War*, 187.

61. JB to Mrs. John D. Willard, Mar. 6, 1858, Vol. 3, NBWMRL-JBBR.

62. Davis et al., *In Pursuit of Leviathan*, 427–428.

63. Joseph Dias, "New Bedford Whaling Ships, 1783–1906," 114, Series II, BLHC-ABNB.

64. Davis et al., *In Pursuit of Leviathan*, 427–428.

65. Dias, "New Bedford Whaling Ships," 6, BLHC-ABNB.

66. Davis et al., *In Pursuit of Leviathan*, 239.

67. Ibid., 240.

68. Ibid., 239; Dias, "New Bedford Whaling Ships," BLHC-ABNB.

69. Davis et al., *In Pursuit of Leviathan*, 152.

70. Affidavit, "Consulate of the United States of America at Saint Helena, Oct. 18, 1879," Logbook, *Marcella*, F6870.53, HLHU-DFLC.

71. JB to Capt. F. A. Weld, Aug. 6, 1860, Vol. 3, NBWMRL-JBBR.

72. Ibid.; JB to Mr. Elridge, Aug. 6, 1860, Vol. 3, NBWMRL-JBBR.

73. JB to Weston A. Briggs, Apr. 10, 1849, Vol. 1, NBWMRL-JBBR; JB to Unknown, Oct. 21, 1851, Vol. 2, NBWMRL-JBBR; JB to George Simmons, Oct. 22, 1851, Vol. 2, NBWMRL-JBBR.

74. JB to Capt. Z. A. Devoll, Aug. 2, 1852, Vol. 2, NBWMRL-JBBR; JB to Capt. John Willard, Jan. 19, 1857, Vol. 3, NBWMRL-JBBR.

75. JB to Capt. Augustus Hale, Mar. 11, 1850, Vol. 1, NBWMRL-JBBR; JB to Capt. Augustus Hale, Apr. 10, 1850, Vol. 1, NBWMRL-JBBR; JB to Capt. Augustus Hale, Jul. 12, 1850, Vol. 1, NBWMRL-JBBR; JB to Capt. Martin Palmer, Jul. 26, 1853, Vol. 2, NBWMRL-JBBR; JB to Capt. B. B. Lamphier, Jul. 18, 1855, Vol. 2, NBWMRL-JBBR; JB to Capt. Z. A. Devoll, Aug. 2, 1852, Vol. 2, NBWMRL-JBBR; JB to Capt. F. A. Weld, Aug. 6, 1860, Vol. 3, NBWMRL-JBBR.

76. JB to Capt. Augustus Hale, Jul. 12, 1850, Vol. 1, NBWMRL-JBBR.

77. JB to Capt. Augustus Hale, Mar. 11, 1850, Vol. 1, NBWMRL-JBBR; JB to William & Barnes, Dec. 18, 1851, 21, Vol. 2, NBWMRL-JBBR; JB to Capt. John Holt, Jan. 6, 1852, Vol. 2, NBWMRL-JBBR; JB to Capt. B. B. Lamphier, Jul. 18, 1855, Vol. 2, NBWMRL-JBBR.

78. JB to James Hunewell, May 23, 1849, 31–32, Vol. 1, NBWMRL-JBBR.

79. Ibid.

80. JB to R. L. Finch, Sep. 13, 1850, Vol. 1, NBWMRL-JBBR.

81. JB to Capt. John Holt, Jan. 6, 1852, 26–27, Vol. 2, NBWMRL-JBBR.

82. JB to Capt. Martin Palmer, Jul. 18, 1855, Vol. 2, NBWMRL-JBBR; JB to Capt. Richard Holley, Aug. 3, 1855, Vol. 2, NBWMRL-JBBR; JB to Capt. Martin Palmer, Aug. 4, 1857, Vol. 2, NBWMRL-JBBR; JB to Capt. John Willard, Aug. 4, 1857, Vol. 2, NBWMRL-JBBR; JB to Capt. John Willard, Jan. 18, 1858, Vol. 2, NBWMRL-JBBR.

83. Diary of William A. Abbe, *Atkins Adams*, Sep. 26, 1859, Jan. 14, 1859, Log 485, NBWMRL, quoted in Creighton, *Rites and Passages*, 131.

84. Diary of Benjamin Neal, *Reaper*, Mar. 11, 1839, PEM, quoted in Creighton, *Rites and Passages*, 133.

85. Diary of Samuel Winegar, *Julian*, Sep. 9, 1859, David Wagstall Collection, Yale University Library, New Haven, CT, quoted in Creighton, *Rites and Passages*, 85.

86. Davis et al., *In Pursuit of Leviathan*, 436–440.

87. Blewett, *Constant Turmoil*, 24.

88. Ibid.

89. JB to Capt. John Willard, Jan. 18, 1858, Vol. 3, NBWMRL-JBBR.

90. "Review of the Whale Fishery for 1872," *WSLMT*, Feb. 4, 1873.

91. JB to Capt. Martin Palmer, Jul. 18, 1855, Vol. 2, NBWMRL-JBBR; JB to Capt. Richard Holley, Aug. 3, 1855, Vol. 2, NBWMRL-JBBR; JB to Capt. Martin Palmer, Aug. 4, 1857, Vol. 3, NBWMRL-JBBR; JB to Capt. John Willard, Jan. 18, 1858, Vol. 3, NBWMRL-JBBR.

92. JB to Capt. Alden Besse, Nov. 20, 1860, Vol. 3, NBWMRL-JBBR.

93. McMullin, "Industrialization and Social Change," 12; Mulderink, *New Bedford's Civil War*, 139–141, 147.

94. Mulderink, *New Bedford's Civil War*, 146.

95. Ellis, *History of New Bedford*, 374.

96. Zallen, *American Lucifers*, 243.

97. Davis et al., *In Pursuit of Leviathan*, 363.

98. JB to David Floyd, Feb. 4, 1861, Vol. 3, NBWMRL-JBBR.

99. Ibid.

100. Mulderink, " 'We Want a Country,' " 160.

101. Creighton, *Rites and Passages*, 36.

102. McMullin, "Industrialization and Social Change," 13.

103. Davis et al., *In Pursuit of Leviathan*, 426–427.

104. Ibid.

105. Davis et al., *In Pursuit of Leviathan*, 426–427; New Bedford Whaling Museum, " 'Lagoda'—The Largest Ship Model in Existence," https://web.archive.org/web/20160307054635/http://www.whalingmuseum.org/explore/exhibitions/current/lagoda.

106. Ellis, *History of New Bedford*, 374.

107. Mulderink, "We Want a Country," 121.

108. McMullin, "Industrialization and Social Change," 70.

109. "Report of the Joint Special Committee of the City Council of New Bedford on the Introduction of Water," Dec. 21, 1861, 5, in New Bedford, *City Documents . . . 1861–1862*.

110. "Address of Isaac C. Taber . . . January 6th, 1862," in New Bedford, *City Documents . . . 1861–1862*.

111. "Address of George Howland, Jr. . . . January 5th, 1863," 4, in New Bedford, *City Documents . . . 1862–1863*.

112. McMullin, "Industrialization and Social Change," 7–8.

113. Ellis, *History of New Bedford*, 307; Mulderink, "We Want a Country," 29–30.

114. Aldrich, "New Bedford," 441.

115. Coggeshall, "The Development of the New Bedford Water Supplies," 11; "Address of George Howland, Jr. . . . January 5th, 1863," in New Bedford, *City Documents . . . 1862–1863*.

116. "Inaugural Address of Andrew G. Pierce . . . January 6, 1868," 4, in New Bedford, *City Documents . . . 1867–1868*; "Inaugural Address of Andrew G. Pierce . . . January 5, 1869," in New Bedford, *City Documents . . . 1868–1869*.

117. "Inaugural Address of George B. Richmond . . . January 3, 1870," 3, in New Bedford, *City Documents . . . 1869–1870*.

118. "Inaugural Address of George B. Richmond . . . January 3, 1870," 5, in New Bedford, *City Documents . . . 1869–1870*.

119. Wood, "The Development of the New Bedford Water Works System."

120. Mulderink, *New Bedford's Civil War*, 178.

121. A No Water Man, Letter to the Editor, *ES*, Jul. 29, 1865.

122. Main Street, "The Water Question," *ES*, Jul. 27, 1865.

123. Ibid.

124. Amor Patrie, "The Water Question," *ES*, Jul. 29, 1865.

125. "Address of Isaac C. Taber . . . January 6th, 1862," in New Bedford, *City Documents . . . 1861–1862.*

126. Ibid.

127. New Bedford, *Report of the Joint Special Committee* (1865), 6.

128. "Report of the Joint Special Committee of the City Council of New Bedford on the Introduction of Water," Dec. 21, 1861, in New Bedford, *City Documents . . . 1861–1862.*

129. William J. Potter, "A Pulpit View of the Business Interests of Our City," Jan. 18, 1863, 3–4, Sermon 98, Box 1, NBFPL-WPS.

130. William J. Potter, "A Pulpit View of the Business Interests of Our City," Jan. 18, 1863, 4, Sermon 98, Box 1, NBFPL-WPS.

131. William J. Potter, "A Pulpit View of the Business Interests of Our City," Jan. 18, 1863, 9, Sermon 98, Box 1, NBFPL-WPS.

132. William J. Potter, "A Pulpit View of the Business Interests of Our City," Jan. 18, 1863, 15, Sermon 98, Box 1, NBFPL-WPS.

133. William J. Potter, "A Pulpit View of the Business Interests of Our City," Jan. 25, 1863, 13, Sermon 99, Box 1, NBFPL-WPS.

134. Address of George Howland, Jr. . . . January 2d, 1865," 13, in New Bedford, *City Documents . . . 1864–1865.*

135. New Bedford, *Forty-Fourth Annual Report of the New Bedford Water Board*, 64; Pease, *History of New Bedford*, 203.

136. Pease, *History of New Bedford*, 204.

137. Crapo, "The Story of Cotton . . . in New Bedford."

138. New Bedford, *Ordinances and Rules . . . of New Bedford* (1884), 96; Pease, *History of New Bedford*, 205; "Inaugural Address of George B. Richmond . . . January 3, 1870," in New Bedford, *City Documents . . . 1869–1870*; New Bedford, *Inaugural Address of George B. Richmond . . . Jan. 1, 1872*; "Inaugural Address of Alanson Borden . . . January 1, 1877," in New Bedford, *New Bedford City Documents* (1877).

139. "Inaugural Address of Abraham H. Howland, Jr. . . . January 3, 1876," 11, in *City Documents of New Bedford* (1876).

140. McMullin, "Industrialization and Social Change," 82.

141. Ibid, 18.

142. Letterbook, 1833–1837, Vol. 4, BLHC-CMBR.

143. Mulderink, " 'We Want a Country,' " 153.

144. "Inaugural Address of George B. Richmond . . . January 3, 1870," 4, in *City Documents . . . 1869–1870.*

145. Ledger Clipping, "New Bedford Steam Mill," Folder 11, Box 1, BLHC-CMBR; Hough, *Wamsutta of New Bedford*, 9, 19; Hough and New Bedford Board of Trade, *New Bedford, Massachusetts*, 62.

146. Crapo, "The Story of Cotton . . . in New Bedford"; Beers and Company, *Representative Men and Old Families of Rhode Island*, 1459; Hurd, *History of Bristol County*, 131; Hall, *America's Successful Men of Affairs*, 372; Matthew Howland Letter Book, 1858–1879, Series II, BLHC-ABNB; Pease, *History of New Bedford*, 244. Crapo also mentions a "Henry F. Thayer" as director, but there is no record of him in the New Bedford City Directory of 1871.

147. Crapo, "The Story of Cotton . . . in New Bedford"; Pease, *History of New Bedford*, 402; National Archives Project, *Ship Registers of New Bedford*, 191; Davis et al., *In Pursuit of Leviathan*, 77.

148. United States House of Representatives, *Hearings on General Tariff Revision*, 2278.

149. JB to E. L. Anthony, Sep. 1888, Vol. 4, NBWMRL-JBBR; JB to Wm. Geo. F. Morgan, Nov. 2, 1888, Vol. 4, NBWMRL-JBBR; JB to J. A. Baker, Mar. 30, 1889, Vol. 4, NBWMRL-JBBR; JB to Maj. Durfee, Apr. 8, 1889, Vol. 4, NBWMRL-JBBR.

150. JB to Capt. Fisher, Nov. 11, 1887, Vol. 4, NBWMRL-JBBR.

151. Ibid.

152. Dias, "New Bedford Whaling Ships," 90, 154, 166, 165, 202, 179, BLHC-ABNB.

153. Noel, *Jonathan Bourne*, 27.

154. Catling, *The Spinning Mule*, 154–157.

155. Hahn, "Failures and Fairytales"; Freeman, *Behemoth*, 48.

156. Webber, *Manual of Power for Machines, Shafts, and Belts*, 53; Foster, *Lamb's Textile Industries of the United States*, 61; Lazonick, *Competitive Advantage on the Shop Floor*, 26; Blewett, *Constant Turmoil*, 35–26.

157. Webber, *Manual of Power for Machines, Shafts, and Belts*, 53.

158. Annawan Mill Payroll Record, 1858–1870, Apr. 1858, Vol. G-1, BLHC-AMS-FRIW.

159. Ibid.; Lawrence Manufacturing Company, Payroll Record, Dec. 14, 1833–Dec. 13, 1834, 2–11, Vol. GA-1, BLHC-LMC.

160. Lawrence Manufacturing Company, Payroll Record, Dec. 14, 1833–Dec. 13, 1834, 2–11, Vol. GA-1, BLHC-LMC.

161. Long, *Wages and Earnings*, 94.

162. Dublin, *Lowell*, 66.

163. Of the factory's 289 total workers, only 52 were men. Dataset developed from Lawrence Manufacturing Company, Payroll Record, May 14, 1850–Apr. 13, 1861, Vol. GA-18, BLHC-LMC.

164. Ibid.

165. Dataset developed from Metacomet Mill, Payrolls, 1881, week ending Jan. 8, 1881, Vol. KE-1, Case 13, BLHC-AMS-FRIW.

166. Ibid.

167. Annawan Mill Payroll Record, 1858–1870, Jan. 3, 1870, Vol. G-1, BLHC-AMS-FRIW.

168. "A Industria Textil de New Bedford," *DDN*, May 5, 1942.

169. Grieve, *New Bedford Semi-Centennial Souvenir*, 1.

170. Appleby, "The Popular Sources of American Capitalism," 457; Temin, "The Industrialization of New England," 110.

CHAPTER 3

1. MBSL, *Thirteenth Annual Report . . . 1882*, 195, 201–202.

2. Ibid., 201, 206, 341.

3. Ibid., 206–207.

4. MBSL, *Twelfth Annual Report . . . January, 1881*, 469–470.

5. MBSL, *Thirteenth Annual Report . . . 1882*, 92, 369.

6. Ibid., 191, 411–413.

7. For a sampling of works highlighting how America's "divided" working class hindered efforts at meaningful labor reform, see Roediger, *Wages of Whiteness*; Gutman, "Work, Culture, and Society"; Cohen, *Making a New Deal*, chs. 1–2; Saxton, *Indispensable Enemy*.

8. Barrett, "Americanization from the Bottom Up"; Gerstle, *Working-Class Americanism*; Cumbler, *Working-Class Community in Industrial America*, 175–178.

9. Bodnar, *The Transplanted*.

10. Beckert, *Empire of Cotton*, 242–273.

11. Aldrich, "New Bedford," 439.

12. Phalen, *The Consequences of Cotton in Antebellum America*, 167; Beckert, *Empire of Cotton*, 246–248.

13. United States, *Reports of the Immigration Commission*, 7; "Art. IV, Review," 363.

14. "Art. IV, Review," 363; "How the Distress Is Relieved in Preston," 443.

15. "Lancashire in 1862," 229–230.

16. F. W. Seward to Lorenzo Sabine, Apr. 1, 1863, reproduced in Boston Board of Trade, *Tenth Annual Report*, 16; Erickson, *American Industry and the European Immigrant*, 8–9; Blackett, *Divided Hearts*, 136; Letter to the Editor, "American Emigrant Company," *NYT*, Sep. 6, 1863; Laslett, *Colliers Across the Sea*, 67.

17. Williams, *Immigration*, 7.

18. Ibid., 2.

19. Erickson, *American Industry and the European Immigrant*, 11, 17, 19.

20. Ibid.

21. Cohen, *American Management and British Labor*, 98.

22. The Operative Cotton Spinners' Provincial Association, Bolton and District, *The Seventh Annual Report for the Year Ending Dec. 31st . . . 1886* (Bolton: 1887), 6, BCS 1/1/1:1884–1886, RYLANDS-OCSTB.

23. The Operative Cotton Spinners' Provincial Association, Bolton and District, *The Thirteenth Annual Report for the Year Ending Dec. 31st . . . 1892* (Bolton: 1893), BCS 1/1/3:1890–1892, RYLANDS-OCSTB.

24. *Rules to be Observed by the Amalgamated Association of Operative Cotton Spinners, Self-Actor Minders, Twiners, and Rovers of Lancashire and Adjoining Counties* (Manchester: 1870), 4, Vol. 94, LSE-WEBB.

25. Ibid.

26. *Rules of the Power-Loom Carpet Weavers' Mutual Defence and Provident Association* (Kidderminster, [established 1866]), 3, Vol. 101, LSE-WEBB.

27. Watts, *The Facts of the Cotton Famine*, 215.

28. Amalgamated Association of Operative Cotton Spinners, Minders, and Twiners of Lancashire and Adjoining Counties, *Annual Report for the Year Ending December 31st, 1879* (Manchester: Jas. Andrew), 26, ACS1/1/(1), RYLANDS-OCSL.

29. Amalgamated Association of Operative Cotton Spinners, etc. of Lancashire and Adjoining Counties, *Annual Report for the Year Ending December 31st, 1882* (Manchester: James Andrew), 40, ACS1/1/(1), RYLANDS-OCSL.

30. Erickson, "The Encouragement of Emigration," 257.

31. Ibid., 266.

32. Ibid., 267.

33. Ibid., 265.

34. Cohen, *American Management and British Labor*, 91.

35. Ibid., 98.

36. Blewett, *Constant Turmoil*, 197–198.

37. McMullin, "Industrialization and Social Change," 32.

38. Blewett, *Constant Turmoil*, 149; Cohen, *American Management and British Labor*, 96.

39. Cumbler, *Working-Class Community in Industrial America*, 149, 157.

40. Ibid.

41. Brierley, *Ab-o'th'-yate in Yankeeland*, 135.

42. Parliamentary Papers, 1889, X, *Report from the Select Committee on Colonization*, 92–93, quoted in Cohen, *American Management and British Labor*, 100.

43. *Rules to be Observed by the Operative Cotton Spinners', Self-Actor Minders', Twiners' and Rovers' Provincial Association of Oldham & Surrounding Districts* (Oldham: 1870), 18, Vol. 94, LSE-WEBB.

44. *Rules & Regulations for the Government of the Oldham Operative Cotton Spinners, Self-Actor Minders, and Twiners' Provincial Association* (Oldham: 1880), 32, Vol. 94, LSE-WEBB.

45. *Rules to be Observed by the Amalgamated Association of Operative Cotton Spinners, Self-Actor Minders, Twiners, and Rovers of Lancashire and Adjoining Counties* (Oldham: 1873), 26, Vol. 94, LSE-WEBB.

46. *Rules and Regulations to be Observed by the Friendly Associated Operative Cotton Spinners and Self-Acting Minders of Hyde and Surrounding Neighbourhood* (Hyde: 1866), 5, Vol. 95, LSE-WEBB.

47. *Rules and Regulations for the Government of the Operative Self-Actor Minders and Hand-Mule Spinners' Association of Bolton and Its Neighborhood* (Bolton: 1876), 14, Vol. 94, LSE-WEBB; *Rules and Regulations to be Observed by the Members of the Operative Cotton Spinners' & Twiners' Association of Bradford District* (Bradford: 1890), 11, Vol. 94, LSE-WEBB; *Rules and Regulations to be Observed by the Members of the Operative Cotton Spinners' & Twiners' Association, of Halifax District* (Halifax: 1886), 11, Vol. 94, LSE-WEBB; *Rules of the Operative Cotton Spinners, Self-Acting Minders and Twiners' Association of Lees and District* (Lees: n.d.), 11, Vol. 94, LSE-WEBB; *Rules and Regulations of the Operative Cotton Spinners' Association of Manchester and Its Vicinities* (Manchester: 1880), 12, Vol. 94, LSE-WEBB; *Rules of the Cotton Spinners' Association, Pendlebury District* (Pendlebury: 1884), Vol. 94, LSE-WEBB; *Rules of the Association of Operative Cotton Spinners of Preston and its Vicinity* (Preston: 1887), 18–19, Vol. 94, LSE-WEBB; *Rules and Regulations to be Observed by the Friendly Associated Operative Self-Actor Minders of Rochdale and Neighbourhood* (Rochdale: 1873), 15, Vol. 95, LSE-WEBB; *Rules to be Observed by the Self-Actor Mule Spinners of Ashton and Neighbourhood* (Ashton: 1886), 7, Vol. 95, LSE-WEBB; *Rules and Regulations to be Observed by the Members of the Operative Cotton Spinners and Twiners Association of Stockport and Neigbourhood* (Stockport: 1890), 10, Vol. 95, LSE-WEBB; *Rules and Regulations to be Observed by the Bury and Elton Operative Cotton Spinners' Association* (Bury: 1891), 15, Vol. 95, LSE-WEBB; *Rules & Regulations to be Observed by the Members of the Operative Cotton Spinners' & Twiners' Association, of Brighouse District* (Halifax: 1891), Vol. 95, LSE-WEBB; *Rules and Regulations to be Observed by the Operative Cotton Spinners of Hyde, Hadfield, Glossop, and Surrounding Neighbourhood* (Hyde: 1889), 7, Vol. 94, LSE-WEBB.

48. MBSL, *Thirteenth Annual Report . . . 1882*, 201.

49. "A Good Send-Off," Mar. 23, 1893, in Silvia, *Victorian Vistas . . . 1886–1900*, 378–380; Lincoln, *City of the Dinner-Pail*, 54-56; Blewett, *Constant Turmoil*, 1; Silvia, "The Spindle City," 464.

50. John Norris to the *Voice of Industry*, Apr. 7, 1848, quoted in Blewett, *Constant Turmoil*, 85.

51. "Meeting of the Weavers at City Hall," Feb. 1, 1868, in Silvia, *Victorian Vistas . . . 1865–1885*, 123–127; Blewett, *Constant Turmoil*, 130, 279; Cumbler, *Working-Class Community in Industrial America*, 157.

52. "John Golden Dead After Breakdown," *NYT*, Jun. 10, 1921; Cohen, *American Management and British Labor*, 102.

53. "The Troubles of Labor: Testimony Before the Senate Committee Yesterday," *NYT*, Aug. 26, 1883; "Big Success," Jul. 11, 1892, in Silvia, *Victorian Vistas . . . 1865–1885*, 323–326; Blewett, *Constant Turmoil*, 311.

54. Cohen, *American Management and British Labor*, 102.

55. *Lawrence Journal and Citizen*, May 9, 1874, quoted in Blewett, *Constant Turmoil*, 134.

56. Berthoff, *British Immigrants in Industrial America*, 96.

57. MBSL, *Thirteenth Annual Report . . . 1882*, 195.

58. Ibid., 369.

59. Blewett, *Constant Turmoil*, 307–308.

60. Ibid., 133, 220; "The Fall River Strike," *NYT*, Sep. 28, 1875; "Importation of Social Troubles," *Globe* (Toronto), Oct. 25, 1875; "Labor Riots: Fall River Ablaze with Excitement . . . Communistic Principles Rampant Throughout the City," *BDG*, Sep. 28, 1875.

61. Blewett, *Constant Turmoil*, 252–253.

62. See, for example, "Disgraceful Disturbance of the Peace," Aug. 24, 1870, in Silvia, *Victorian Vistas . . . 1865–1885*, 181; "The Shooting Near Slade Mill," Jul. 28, 1879, in Silvia, *Victorian Vistas . . . 1865–1885*, 350–351; "A 'Knobstick' Assaulted," Aug. 11, 1879, in Silvia, *Victorian Vistas . . . 1865–1885*, 355; "Shameful Outrage," Sep. 18, 1879, in Silvia, *Victorian Vistas . . . 1865–1885*, 366–367.

63. "The First Disturbance," Mar. 23, 1889, in Silvia, *Victorian Vistas . . . 1886–1900*, 160.

64. Blewett, *Constant Turmoil*, 256.

65. "Meeting of the Weavers at City Hall," Feb. 1, 1868, in Silvia, *Victorian Vistas . . . 1865–1885*, 123–127; Cumbler, *Working-Class Community in Industrial America*, 166.

66. McMullin, "Industrialization and Social Change," 214.

67. Jack Rubinstein, interview by Daniel Georgianna, Dumont, NJ, Sep. 2, 1980, transcript, Folder 8, Box 1, UMASSD-NB1928.

68. Jack Rubinstein, interview by "Gale," Aug. 19, 1980, transcript, Folder 8, Box 1, UMASSD-NB1928.

69. Blewett, *Constant Turmoil*, 242, 320; McMullin, "Industrialization and Social Change," 235.

70. "Meeting of the Weavers at City Hall," Feb. 1, 1868, in Silvia, *Victorian Vistas . . . 1865–1885*, 123–127.

71. "The Fall River Strike," Feb. 6, 1875, in Silvia, *Victorian Vistas . . . 1865–1885*, 253–255.

72. Berthoff, *British Immigrants in Industrial America*, 19–20; "Immigrants, by country of last residence–Europe: 1820–1997," Table Ad106–120 in Carter et al., *Historical Statistics of the United States.*

73. See, for example, "Meeting of the Weavers at City Hall," Feb. 1, 1868, in Silvia, *Victorian Vistas . . . 1865–1885*, 123–127; Bradlaugh, "Hints to Emigrants to the United States," 21; McMullin, "Industrialization and Social Change," 221; Cohen, *American Management and British Labor*, 178.

74. Great Britain, Gold and Silver Commission, *Second Report*, 97.

75. T. M. Young, *The American Cotton Industry* (London: 1902), 17–18, quoted in Berthoff, *British Immigrants in Industrial America*, 138.

76. MBSL, *Thirteenth Annual Report . . . 1882*, 206.

77. Wade, "The Acadian Background," 20; Leblanc, "The Acadian Migrations."

78. Leblanc, "The Acadian Migrations," 167, 170–171.

79. Legislative Assembly of Canada, *Rapport du comité spécial de l'Assemblée législative nommé pour s'enquérir des causes et de l'importance de l'émigration qui a lieu tous les ans du Bas-Canada vers les États-Unis* (Montréal: 1849), 5, Loc. S406, MCGILL-CC.

80. A small number of French Canadians were also brought to the United States to alleviate Civil War labor shortages. See Mulderink, *New Bedford's Civil War*, 161; Cowley, "The Foreign Colonies of Lowell," 175; Silvia, "Spindle City," 56.

81. Cumbler, *Working-Class Community in Industrial America*, 7, 173.

82. MBSL, *Thirteenth Annual Report. . . 1882*, 13, 17.

83. "Shameful Outrage," Sep. 18, 1879, in Silvia, *Victorian Vistas . . . 1865–1885*, 366–367; MBSL, *Eleventh Annual Report . . . 1880*, 55.

84. Roby, *The Franco-Americans of New England*, 59.

85. Hamelin, *Les premières années du parlementarisme québécois*, 73–117.

86. Legislative Assembly of Canada, *Rapport du comité spécial de l'Assemblée législative . . .* , 3–4, CC-MGILL.

87. Laurent-Olivier David, "Triste Bilan," *L'Opinion Publique* (Montréal, Québec), Nov. 2, 1871, quoted in Roby, *The Franco-Americans of New England*, 30.

88. Nive Voisine, *Louis-François Laflèche. deuxième évêque de Trois-Rivières* (Saint-Hyacinthe, Edisem, 1980), 106, quoted in Roby, *The Franco-Americans of New England*, 32.

89. Dugré, "Mgr. LaFleche," 171; Roby, *The Franco-Americans of New England*, 41.

90. Rumilly, *Histoire des Franco-Américains*, 41; Laflamme, "Les Canadiens aux États-Unis," 487.

91. Anctil, "The Franco-Americans of New England," 35.

92. Robidoux, *Conventions nationales des Acadiens*, 123.

93. *Le Moniteur Acadian*, Jan. 4, 1889, quoted in Fernand Arsenault, "Acadians and Emigration," in Quintal, *Steeples and Smokestacks*, 31.

94. McCallum, *Unequal Beginnings*, 35–38, 51–52; Chandler, *The Visible Hand*, 209–215.

95. Canada Department of Agriculture, *Reports of Tenant Farmers' Delegates*, 45; Ramirez, *Crossing the 49th Parallel*, 6.

96. Neil Boucher, "Acadians and Emigration: The Case of the Acadians of Southwest Nova Scotia," in Quintal, *Steeples and Smokestacks*, 56.

97. Zoël Richard, interview, Fitchburg, Dec. 12, 1983, quoted in Paul D. LeBlanc, "From Farm to Factory: Acadians in Fitchburg, Massachusetts (1880–1910)," in Quintal, *Steeples and Smokestacks*, 182.

98. Bernard, *Le travail et l'espoir*, 77–78.

99. Canada, *Reports of Tenant Farmers' Delegates*, 5, 132.

100. Ibid., 83.

101. Ibid., 39, 83.

102. Legislative Assembly of Canada, *Rapport du comité spécial de l'Assemblée législative . . .* , 12, MCGILL-CC.

103. "Elmire Boucher: 'C'était le besoin qui faisait travailler les femmes,'" 1981–1982, in Rouillard, *Ah les États!*, 87.

104. Yves Roby, "The Economic Evolution of Quebec and the Emigrant (1850–1929)," in Quintal, *Steeples and Smokestacks*, 11; Pierre Anctil, "The Franco-Americans of New England," 49.

105. "Credit Foncier," *Gazette des Campagnes* (Kamouraska, Bas-Canada), Dec. 2, 1861; Roby, "The Economic Evolution of Quebec," in Quintal, *Steeples and Smokestacks*, 11.

106. Roby, "The Economic Evolution of Quebec," in Quintal, *Steeples and Smokestacks*, 12.

107. MBSL, *Thirteenth Annual Report . . . 1882*, 60.

108. On "chain migration," see Tilly, "Transplanted Networks."

109. Hémon, *Maria Chapdelaine*, 73–74.

110. Ducharme, *The Shadows of the Trees*, 47–48; Frances Early, "The Settling-In Process: The Beginnings of the Little Canada in Lowell, Massachusetts, in the Late Nineteenth Century," in Quintal, *Steeples and Smokestacks*, 91.

111. Martha J. Cayer, Oral History Survey by Josephine Perrault, Nov. 3, 1981, FIAC-OHJP; Marie Delina Bernie, Oral History Survey by Josephine Perrault, Apr. 3, 1984, FIAC-OHJP; Roland Aime Pion, Oral History Survey by Josephine Perrault, Aug. 25, 1983, FIAC-OHJP.

112. Roby, *The Franco-Americans of New England*, 12.

113. Ibid., 24.

114. Takai, *Gendered Passages*, 24.

115. Brooks, "Canada-United States Relations," 381.

116. Roby, *The Franco-Americans of New England*, 19.

117. Jos Marin, interview by Pierre Anctil, Jan. 16, 1978, quoted in Anctil, "Aspects of Class Ideology in a New England Ethnic Minority," 65.

118. Joseph Maltais, interview, Aug. 9, 1964, J. Tape 17-B, NBWMRL-POHC.

119. The figure comes from Biddeford, Maine. See Roby, *The Franco-Americans of New England*, 86; Michael J. Guignard, "The Franco-Americans of Biddeford, Maine," in Quintal, *Steeples and Smokestacks*, 128.

120. MBSL, *Twelfth Annual Report . . . 1881*, 469.

121. "Béatrice Mandeville: 'Aux États-Unis, il y avait de l'argent . . . ; au Canada, c'était la pauvreté,'" 1981–1982, in Rouillard, *Ah les États!*, 121.

122. Ibid., 123.

123. "Alma Ouelette: 'Peu importe où on est on fait notre chez-nous,'" 1981–1982, in Rouillard, *Ah les États!*, 139.

124. "Évelyne Desruisseaux: 'Ils nous conseillaient tous de s'en aller aux États-Unis . . . ,'" in Rouillard, *Ah les États!*.

125. Ibid., 107, 111.

126. "Béatrice Mandeville: 'Aux États-Unis, il y avait de l'argent,'" 129.

127. LeBlanc, "Regional Competition," 112; Roby, *The Franco-Americans of New England*, 38.

128. *Canada: Journals House of Commons 1874*, Vol. 8, Appendix no. 7, Report of the Commission on Immigration and Colonization, 3, quoted in Leblanc, "Regional Competition," 113.

129. Little, *Nationalism, Capitalism, and Colonization*, 158–173; Rumilly, *Histoire des Franco-Américains*, 77.

130. "Meeting of French Residents Yesterday," Mar. 1, 1875, in Silvia, *Victorian Vistas...1865–1885*, 225.

131. Quebec, *General Report of the Commissioner of Agriculture... 1876*, 8.

132. Ferdinand Gagnon to Pierre Garneau, Jul. 1, 1875, reproduced in Rumilly, *Histoire des Franco-Américains*, 78.

133. MBSL, *Thirteenth Annual Report... 1882*, 26–32

134. Ferdinand Gagnon, "Discours sur la naturalisation et le rapatriement, prononcé à Worcester, Mass., en septembre, 1871," in Gagnon, *Gagnon*, 64–82.

135. Roby, *The Franco-Americans of New England*, 132.

136. *Canada: Sessional Papers*, 28, 9 (1895), Report of the Department of Interior (1894): 87, quoted in LeBlanc, "Colonisation et rapatriement," 390.

137. Société générale de colonisation, *Rapport annuel de l'agent général*; LeBlanc, "Regional Competition," 117.

138. LeBlanc, "Colonisation et rapatriement," 383, 389.

139. MBSL, *Thirteenth Annual Report... 1882*, 32.

140. Hamilton, "Migration of Population Between Canada and the United States," 38–39.

141. *Canada: Sessional Papers*, 29, 10 (1896). Report of the Department of Interior (1895): 54–56, quoted in LeBlanc "Colonisation et rapatriement," 392.

142. "Child Labor," Sep. 27, 1887, in Silvia, *Victorian Vistas . . . 1886–1900*, 85–95; Gunton, *Wealth and Progress*, 362.

143. Arthur Baribault, ed., *Congrès nationaux: Histoire et statistiques des Canadiens-Américains du Connecticut, 1885–1898* (Worcester: 1899), 203, quoted in Roby, *The Franco-Americans of New England*, 88.

144. MBSL, *Report of the Bureau of Statistics of Labor... 1870*, 248.

145. MBSL, *Twelfth Annual Report . . . 1881*, 469–470; MBSL, *Thirteenth Annual Report... 1882*, 206–207; Philip T. Silvia Jr., "Neighbors from the North vs. Trade Unionism in Fall River, Massachusetts," in Quintal, *Steeples and Smokestacks*, 151–160.

146. Philip T. Silvia Jr., "Neighbors from the North vs. Trade Unionism in Fall River, Massachusetts," in Quintal, *Steeples and Smokestacks*, 151–160; Blewett, *Constant Turmoil*, 356–357.

147. McMullin, "Industrialization and Social Change," 217.

148. Eva Valesh, "Strike Inquiry Now Assured," Jan. 20, 1898, Vol. 1, WLHU-HBH.

149. *Boston Traveler*, Jan. 26, 1898, Vol. 1, WLHU-HBH.

150. MBSL, *Thirteenth Annual Report... 1882*, 12.

151. Gerstle, *Working-Class Americanism*; Petrin, *French Canadians in Massachusetts Politics*, 18, 26–74.

152. Roby, *The Franco-Americans of New England*, 102, 190–194.

153. Thérèse Bealieu, oral history survey by Josephine Perrault, Aug. 23, 1983, FIAC-OHJP.

154. D'Arles, "Ferdinand Gagnon et la Survivance."

155. MBSL, *Thirteenth Annual Report . . . 1882*, 44–45.

156. "Shameful Outrage," Sep. 18, 1879, in Silvia, *Victorian Vistas . . . 1865–1885*, 366–367; Blewett, *Constant Turmoil*, 275–277.

157. "Religious Meeting Disturbed," Aug. 19, 1872, in Silvia, *Victorian Vistas . . . 1865–1885*, 207; "We Regret to Hear . . . ," May 12, 1873, in Silvia, *Victorian Vistas . . . 1865–1885*, 220–221; "A Scene in Church," Mar. 13, 1887, in Silvia, *Victorian Vistas . . . 1886–1900*, 56–57; Gerstle, *Working-Class Americanism*, 40; Silvia, "Spindle City," 381–428.

158. "Row in the School," May 10, 1895, in Silvia, *Victorian Vistas . . . 1886–1900*, 509–510.

159. "Court Chronicles," Dec. 28, 1894, in Silvia, *Victorian Vistas . . . 1886–1900*, 498–499.

160. Ibid.

161. Açores, *A Ilha no Mundo*.

162. MBSL, *Forty-Third Annual Report . . . 1912*, 36–38.

163. Wheeler, *Republican Portugal*, 7, 21.

164. Schwartzman, *The Social Origins of Democratic Collapse*, 30; Wheeler, *Republican Portugal*, 26, 30.

165. Wheeler, *Republican Portugal*, 28; Schwartzman, *The Social Origins of Democratic Collapse*, 31.

166. Wheeler, *Republican Portugal*, 24.

167. Kay, *Salazar and Modern Portugal*, 26.

168. Ministério do Interior, *Boletim da Junta da Emigração* (1969), 12–15, BNPL; Williams, *In Pursuit of Their Dreams*, 25–26.

169. *Problema Social Emigração: Discurso proferido na Camara dos Dignos pares do Rein em Sessão de 4 de Julho 1891 pelo Conde do Casal Ribeiro* (Lisboa: Imprensa Nacional, 1891), SC-7731, BNPL; Thomaz Riberio, *Questões sobre Emigração: Projecto de Lei* (Lisboa: Imprensa Nacional, 1891), SC-7563, BNPL.

170. Wheeler, *Republican Portugal*, 7.

171. See *Regulamento da Policia de Emigração Clandestina: Decretos de 3 de Julho de 1896 e 3 de Outubro de 1903 e Regulamento Geral da Policia para o Transito no Continente e Ilhas* (Angra do Heroismo: Imprensa Municipal, 1904), SC-7711, BNPL; Portugal, *Annuario da Direcção Geral de Administração Politica e Civil*, 431–433; "Emigração para os Estados Unidos do Norte," *AO*, May 7, 1892; Fairbank, "Iberian Emigration Law"; Pereira, "Algumas Observações Complementares Sobre a Política de Emigração Portuguesa," 736.

172. Sociedade de Geographia de Lisboa, *Programma dos Trabalhos da Commissão D'Emigração* (Lisboa: 1894), 9, Item 11, Box 84, BPARPD-FPEC; Martins,

Projecto de Lei de Fomento Rural; "A Questão Imigratoria," *DDA*, Oct. 7, 1912; "Emigração," *DDA*, Nov. 6, 1912; "As Miserias da Emigração," *AO*, Jun. 4, 1892.

173. "Emigração para o Ultramar," 1881, Cota 1.2.27, Doc. 0746, BPARPD-FPER.

174. Williams, *In Pursuit of Their Dreams*, 15; Pacheco, "É para Sair de Portugal a Todos os Custos," 23–31.

175. Pacheco, "É para Sair de Portugal a Todos ss Custos," 23–31; Walker, *The Azores*, 111.

176. Walker, *The Azores*, 111.

177. Dias, "A Economia ao Sabor das Circunstâncias," 35.

178. Ruy Moraes, "A Emigração," *AO*, Jan. 12, 1918.

179. Directive, Alfândega de Ponta Delgada, Oct. 15, 1874, Cota 1666.35, UI 0090, Series 7, BPARPD-AGCDPD.

180. *Boletim Oficial de Cabo Verde*, no. 40, 1880, 254, quoted in Carreira, *Migrações nas Ilhas de Cabo Verde*, 249–250; Warrin, *So Ends This Day*, 105.

181. Pap, *The Portuguese-Americans*, 38.

182. Manuel Sylvia, interview, Apr. 21, 1981, Tape 26, NBWMRL-POHC.

183. Da Rosa and Trigo, *Azorean Emigration*, 43; Dias, "A Economia ao Sabor das Circunstâncias," 37; Nelson, *A Nation of Deadbeats*, 169.

184. Costa, *Azores*, 304–305; Costa et al., *An Economic History of Portugal*, 87.

185. Costa, *Azores*, 283–284.

186. Williams, *In Pursuit of Their Dreams*, 11; Carreiro da Costa, "Tradições, Costumes e Turismo: Do Antigo Comércio da Laranja nos Açores," *AO*, Mar. 3, 1970.

187. Carreiro da Costa, "Tradições, Costumes e Turismo"; Dias, "A Economia ao Sabor das Circunstâncias," 40.

188. A Sociedade Promotora da Agricultura Micaelense, Meeting Minutes, Feb. 9, 1874, Atas da Direção, 1873–1887, Item 6, BPARPD-ASPAM; "Communicado: Ponta-Delgada 24 de Janeiro," *AO*, Jan. 25, 1862.

189. "Communicado: Ponta-Delgada 23 de Maio," *AO*, May 24, 1862.

190. "The Foreign Demand for American Breadstuffs," *American Agriculturist* 21 (Oct. 1862): 296; Great Britain, *Reports from Her Majesty's Consuls on . . . Manufactures*, 227.

191. On market disruptions and recurrent crisis in the Azores, see the following articles from the *Açoriano Oriental* newspaper: "Communicado: Ponta-Delgada 7 de Fevereiro," Feb. 8, 1862; "Communicado: Ponta-Delgada 7 de Março," Mar. 8, 1862; "Ponta Delgada: 26 de Junho," Jun. 26, 1869; "Ponta Delgada: 31 de Julho," Jul. 31, 1869; "Communicado: P.D. 29 de Julho," Jul. 31, 1869; "Communicado: P.D. 27 de Agosto," Aug. 28, 1869; "Ponta-Delgada," Jun. 3, 1876; "Miseria," Sep. 2, 1876; "Triste!," Jul. 8, 1893; "Miseria," Sep. 26, 1903; "Miseria," Oct. 17, 1903; "Miseria," Oct. 24, 1903; "Milho," Jun. 11, 1904; "Crise," Mar. 7, 1908; "Milho," Apr. 25, 1908; "Milho," Jun. 27, 1908; "Crise," Jun. 27, 1908; "Farinha Americana," Mar. 3, 1918; "Pão," May 18, 1918.

192. "Por Portugal e pelos Açores: Verdades Amargas," *AO*, Jan. 25, 1919; "Inauguração de um Caminho de Ferro na Ilha de S. Miguel," *AO*, Dec. 15, 1900; Costa, *Para a História da Emigração*, 27

193. "Industria Michaelense," *AO*, Jun. 22, 1901; "Triste!," *AO*, Jul. 8, 1893; "Os Autonomista dos Açores," *AO*, Dec. 1, 1894; Enes, "Uma Economia em Transformação," 201.

194. "A Miseria" in Camara, *Almanach . . . para 1895*, 11; J. Gomes Jr., "Abandonada," in *Almanach . . . para 1895*, 21; Joaquim Candido Abranches, "O Suicidio," in Camara, *Almanach . . . para 1894*, 17.

195. Williams, *In Pursuit of Their Dreams*, 14.

196. Enes, "Uma Economia em Transformação," 190–191.

197. Tax Assessment, Predio 394, Matriz 1052, BPARD-VP-AACL. For basis of alqueires to acres conversion, see Walker, *The Azores*, 79.

198. Tax Assessment, Predio 928, Matriz 1055, BPARD-VP-AACL; Tax Assessment, Predio 929, Matriz 1056, BPARD-VP-AACL.

199. See Verbetes de Rendimento Colectável, 1862, BPARD-VP-AACL.

200. See "Inauguração de um Caminho de Ferro na Ilha de S. Miguel," *AO*, Dec. 15, 1900; Williams, *In Pursuit of Their Dreams*, 9.

201. "A Fome," *AO*, Sep. 27, 1919.

202. Silva, *A Emancipação Dos Açores*, 16.

203. Reproduced in MBSL, *Twenty-Seventh Annual Report . . . 1897*, 69–70.

204. Oral History 47, interview by Olivia Silva, May 5, 1987, UMASSD-FMPAA-OHP.

205. Pap, *The Portuguese-Americans*, 47.

206. Massachusetts, *Report of the Massachusetts Board to Investigate the Subject of the Unemployed*, lvi.

207. *Textile Worker* 16 (May 1928): 80, quoted in Hartford, *Where Is Our Responsibility?*, 35.

208. Golden, "Pay of Labor in New England Cotton Mills," 78.

209. On advertisements for steamship service to the United States, see "Para Boston," *AO*, Jan. 2, 1875; "Empreza Insulana de Navegação," *AO*, Jan. 27, 1900; White Star Line, "De Ponta Delgada directamente para Boston em menos de 6 dias," *AO*, Jan. 16, 1915; "Empreza I. De Navegação," *AO*, Feb. 4, 1905; "White Star Line: Vapores Para Boston," *DDA*, Aug. 30, 1912; Pap, *The Portuguese-Americans*, 39; Williams, *In Pursuit of Their Dreams*, 33. It was easy for Azoreans to keep up with events in Fall River and New Bedford. Most newspapers carried regular columns to keep readers up to date on events such as festivals, deaths, and even the weather. See, for instance, "Noticias da America," *DDA*, Nov. 16, 1912, Nov. 18, 1912, Dec. 4, 1912, Dec. 6, 1912, Dec. 9, 1912; "Fall River," *AO*, Aug. 9, 1913, Sep. 20, 1913, Oct. 4, 1913, Oct. 18, 1913; "Em Fall River," *AO*, Jun. 1, 1912; "Noticias de America," *AO*, Mar. 3, 1917, Mar. 17, 1917, Mar. 24, 1917, May 5, 1917, May 26, 1917.

210. Baganha, *Portuguese Emigration to the United States*, 332.

211. Ministerio das Obras Publicas, *Commercio e Industrial, Movimento da Populaçáo: Estado Civil–Emigraçáo* (Lisboa: Imprensa Nacional, 1887), 157, 176–179, BPARD-FPTB.

212. Administração do Concelho da Povoação, "No. 2: Registo de processos d'emigrantes de 3 de Janeiro de 1917 a [19 de Set. 1922]," Emigrant Register, Item 140, BPARD-AACP.

213. Ibid.

214. Ibid.

215. See Maria Candida Pereira, "Two Women Conversation with Mrs. Linhares & Mrs. Pereira," in McCabe et al., *Portuguese Spinner*; Bela Feldman-Bianco and Donna Huse, "The Construction of Immigrant Identity," in McCabe et al., *Portuguese Spinner*, 64.

216. Williams, *In Pursuit of Their Dreams*, 45.

217. United States, *2009 Yearbook of Immigration Statistics*, 6-9.

218. Baganha, *Portuguese Emigration*, 333.

219. Ibid., 332

220. Mulcahy, "The Portuguese of the U.S.," 152.

221. MBSL, *Forty-Third Annual Report . . . 1912*, 36.

CHAPTER 4

1. Miernyk, *Inter-Industry Labor Mobility*, 104–105.

2. See Blewett, *Constant Turmoil*, 14; Hartford, *Where Is Our Responsibility?*, 3; Beckert, *Empire of Cotton*, 383, 392; English, *A Common Thread*.

3. Lamphere, *From Working Daughters to Working Mothers*, 33.

4. Hareven and Langenbach, *Amoskeag*, 34–38; Beckert, *Empire of Cotton*, 69; United States, *Job Descriptions for the Cotton Textile Industry*; Cumbler, *Working-Class Community in Industrial America*, 124.

5. Cumbler, *Working-Class Community in Industrial America*, 124.

6. "Mill Life in this City," Oct. 22, 1898, in Silvia, *Victorian Vistas . . . 1886–1900*, 671–676; Job Description, Picker Tender, Folder 1, Sub-Series 1, Series D, NBWMRL-PMCR; Mary Alves, interview by Dora Bastarche, Aug. 31, 1981, Folder 12, Box 1, UMASSD-NB1928.

7. "The Back Boy," Dec. 31, 1885, in Silvia, *Victorian Vistas . . . 1865–1885*, 460–462.

8. William Isherwood, Oral History, Jan. 23, 1980, Folder 9, Box 1, UMASSD-NB1928.

9. MBSL, *Sixth Annual Report . . . 1875*, 291.

10. US Senate, *Reports of the Immigration Commission*, 114.

11. Letter to the Editor, Sep. 25, 1867, in Silvia, *Victorian Vistas . . . 1865–1885*, 110–111.

12. Joseph Maltais, interview, Aug. 9, 1964, Tape 17-B, NBWMRL-POHC; United States, *Report of the Committee . . . Relations between Labor and Capital*, Vol. 1, 69; Cumbler, *Working-Class Community in Industrial America*, 124.

13. Ensign, *Compulsory School Attendance*, 57; Joseph Maltais, interview, Aug. 9, 1964, Tape 17-B, NBWMRL-POHC.

14. Joseph Maltais, interview, Aug. 9, 1964, Tape 17-B, NBWMRL-POHC.

15. Oral History 67, interview by Patricia Hunter, ca. 1987–1991, UMASSD-FMPAA-OHP; William Isherwood, Oral History, Jan. 23, 1980, Folder 9, Box 1, UMASSD-NB1928; Mary Alves, Oral History, interview by Dora Bastarche, Aug. 31, 1981, Folder 12, Box 1, UMASSD-NB1928.

16. Lazonick, *Competitive Advantage on the Shop Floor*, 83; "Factory Life as Seen Here by Wool and Cotton Reporter," Aug. 26, 1898, in Silvia, *Victorian Vistas . . . 1886–1900*, 666–668.

17. "Factory Life as Seen Here by Wool and Cotton Reporter," Aug. 26, 1898, in Silvia, *Victorian Vistas . . . 1886–1900*, 666–668; "Labor's Problems: Industrial Commissioners in this City Listen to Testimony of Union Secretaries at Mellen House," Feb. 23, 1901, in Silvia, *Victorian Vistas . . . 1901–1911*, 68–84.

18. Fall River Loom Fixers Association, Executive Committee Minutes, 1900–1901, 23, 25–26, 37, Box 1, UMASSA-FRLFA; Fall River Loom Fixers Association, Executive Committee Minutes, 1911–1917, Box 1, 104–105, UMASSA-FRLFA; Fall River Loom Fixers Association, Dues Book, 1907, Box 2, UMASSA-FRLFA; MBSL, *Forty-First Annual Report . . . 1910*, 302.

19. Oral History 9 and 10, interview by Leslie Fernandes, 1987–1988, Fall River, MA, UMASSD-FMPAA-OHP.

20. United States, *Report of the Committee . . . Relations between Labor and Capital*, Vol. 3, 451, 453.

21. Record Book, "Insurance, Cloth + Cotton . . . 884–1895 . . . Metacomet Manufacturing Co.," Vol. GE-1, Box 3, BLHC-MS-FRIW.

22. "From Our Extra This Morning: Another Terrible Fire," Dec. 16, 1967, in Silvia, *Victorian Vistas . . . 1865–1885*, 115–118; Phillips, *The Phillips History of Fall River*, Vol. 2, 142; Rosenberg, *Child Labor in America*, 163; Blewett, *Constant Turmoil*, 135; "Destructive Fire," Jun. 30, 1876, in Silvia, *Victorian Vistas . . . 1865–1885*, 289–291; "The Fire This Morning," Nov. 17, 1877, in Silvia, *Victorian Vistas . . . 1865–1885*, 311.

23. Tuttle, *Hard at Work*, 130.

24. Untitled Article, Feb. 15, 1867, in Silvia, *Victorian Vistas . . . 1865–1885*, 84–86.

25. "Serious Accident . . . ," Apr. 25, 1873, in Silvia, *Victorian Vistas . . . 1865–1885*, 219.

26. "Probably Fatal Accident," Jan. 24, 1879, in Silvia, *Victorian Vistas . . . 1865–1885*, 332.

27. "Elevator Boy Killed," Oct. 20, 1880, in Silvia, *Victorian Vistas . . . 1865–1885*, 380.

28. "Entangled in Shafting," Jan. 1, 1903, in Silvia, *Victorian Vistas . . . 1901–1911*, 159.

29. Cumbler, *Working-Class Community in Industrial America*, 104.

30. United States, *History of Wages in the United States*, 90; Pearce, *Recollections of a Long and Busy Life*, 43; Joseph Maltais, interview, Aug. 9, 1964, Tape 137-B, NBWMRL-POHC; Mrs. Stanley Curylo, Oral History, July 4, 1964, Tape 15, NBWMRL-POHC.

31. MBSL, *Thirteenth Annual Report . . . 1882*, 228; Blewett, *Constant Turmoil*, 128–140; Whittelsey and Hadley, "Massachusetts Labor Legislation"; "Big Success," Jul. 11, 1892, in Silvia, *Victorian Vistas . . . 1886–1900*, 323–326.

32. McMullin, "Industrialization and Social Change," 227; United States, *Report of the Committee . . . Relations between Labor and Capital*, Vol. 1, 55, 631; United States, *Report of the Committee . . . Relations between Labor and Capital*, Vol. 3, 493; "Three Strong Unions In New Bedford . . . ," Vol. 1, WLHU-HBH; "Joint Convention of Labor Organizers to Be Held Tomorrow—Call Issued," in Silvia, *Victorian Vistas . . . 1865–1885*, 385; "Big Strike Is Ordered," Jul. 21, 1904, in Silvia, *Victorian Vistas . . . 1901–1911*, 212–214.

33. MBSL, *Thirteenth Annual Report . . . 1882*, 359; "New Bedford's Warring Factions: Starvation Wages and Destitution . . . ," *Boston Sunday Post*, Jan. 16, 1898, WLHU-HBH.

34. United States, *Report of the Committee . . . Relations between Labor and Capital*, Vol. 3, 488.

35. Ibid., 411.

36. "Odors of Fall River," Aug. 31, 1867, in Silvia, *Victorian Vistas . . . 1865–1885*, 102–104.

37. William Hale, "The Importance of Churches in a Manufacturing Town," *Forum* 18 (Sep. 1884–Feb. 1895): 295, quoted in Cumbler, *Working-Class Community in Industrial America*, 117.

38. Heath, *The Patina of Place*, 166.

39. MBSL, *Thirteenth Annual Report . . . 1882*, 220, 342.

40. Ibid., 412.

41. "The New Slavery of the North: By an Ex-Slave . . ." Jan. 1898, Vol. 2, WLHU-HBH.

42. "Three Strong Unions in New Bedford . . . ," Vol. 1, WLHU-HBH.

43. Jack Rubinstein, interview by Daniel Georgianna, Sep. 2, 1980, 19–20, Folder 8, Box 1, UMASSD-NB1928.

44. United States, *Report of the Committee . . . Relations between Labor and Capital*, Vol. 1, 655–656.

45. "They Like the Place: Southern Operatives Satisfied with Conditions Here," May 26, 1900, in Silvia, *Victorian Vistas . . . 1886–1900*, 740–742.

46. "Labor Hearing: Local Delegates Before the Legislative Committee," Feb. 1, 1901, in Silvia, *Victorian Vistas . . . 1901–1911*, 53–57.

47. "Strong Opposition Put Up Against the Proposed Overtime Bill," Feb. 8, 1901, in Silvia, *Victorian Vistas . . . 1901–1911*, 61–67.

48. "New Bedford: Cotton Yarn Changes the Cause of a Stir," Oct. 4, 1903, Vol. 20, NBFPL-MAS.

49. *Fall River News*, Apr. 16, 1875, quoted in Blewett, *Constant Turmoil*, 207.

50. "Some Excitement: Flint Village the Scene of a Miniature Riot," Mar. 23, 1889, in Silvia, *Victorian Vistas . . . 1886–1900*, 159–160.

51. "Labor's Problems: Industrial Commissioners in this City Listen to Testimony of Union Secretaries at Mellen House," Feb. 23, 1901, in Silvia, *Victorian Vistas . . . 1901–1911*, 68–84.

52. "Operatives Meeting at City Hall," Jan. 1, 1868, in Silvia, *Victorian Vistas . . . 1865–1885*, 119–123.

53. On working-class resistance to market "encroachment," see Wilentz, *Chants Democratic*, 17; Glickman, *Living Wage*, 35; Cook, *Pricing of Progress*, 193–203.

54. MBSL, *Thirteenth Annual Report . . . 1882*, 239.

55. Ibid., 329.

56. Hartford, *Where Is Our Responsibility?*, 23.

57. Philip T. Silvia Jr., "Introduction," in Silvia, *Victorian Vistas . . . 1901–1911*.

58. "Deferring the F. R. Strike," Mar. 1, 1881, in Silvia, *Victorian Vistas . . . 1865–1885*, 386.

59. Montgomery, *Fall of the House of Labor*, 163.

60. Ibid.

61. Hartford, *Where Is Our Responsibility?*, 29.

62. United States, *Report of the Committee . . . Relations between Labor and Capital*, Vol. 1, 632, 638.

63. "Labor's Problems . . . ," Feb. 23, 1901, in Silvia, *Victorian Vistas . . . 1901–1911*, 68–84.

64. "Meeting of the Weavers at City Hall," Feb. 1, 1868, in Silvia, *Victorian Vistas . . . 1865–1885*, 123–127; Blewett, *Constant Turmoil*, 213, 268.

65. "Mills Have Made Grand Showing," Oct. 26, 1906, in Silvia, *Victorian Vistas . . . 1901–1911*, 394–395; "Five Per Cent Advance in Wages," Nov. 19, 1906, in Silvia, *Victorian Vistas . . . 1901–1911*, 406.

66. "Full Advance of Wages Granted: Manufacturers Grant Operatives Demands After Unions Had Voted to Strike . . . ," Nov. 23, 1906, in Silvia, *Victorian Vistas . . . 1901–1911*, 407–410; "New Wage Scale in Effect Today," May 27, 1907, in Silvia, *Victorian Vistas . . . 1901–1911*, 487.

67. *ST*, Jan. 22, 1877, quoted in Blewett, *Constant Turmoil*, 239.

68. "Eternal Infamy Their Reward . . . A Talk with Rev. Mr. Acornley," *Boston Traveler*, Feb. 3, 1898, Vol. 2, WLHU-HBH; Georgianna and Aaronson, *The Strike of '28*.

69. Silvia, "The Spindle City," 90–91.

70. Ibid.

71. Blewett, *Constant Turmoil*, 323.

72. "More Variety in Industry Needed," Jun. 25, 1877, in Silvia, *Victorian Vistas . . . 1865–1885*, 307.

73. McMullin, "Industrialization and Social Change," 208–209.

74. Ibid., 225.

75. Hartford, *Where Is Our Responsibility?*, 38.

76. Fall River Yarn Finishers Union, Yarn Finishers Union Minutebook, 1919–1922, UMASSA-FRYFU; Yarn Finishers Union Contribution Book, 1920–1922, UMASSA-FRYFU.

77. Mary Alves, interview by Dora Bastarche, Aug. 31, 1981, Folder 12, Box 1, UMASSD-NB1928.

78. "Notable Day for Spinners' Union," Jan. 18, 1908, in Silvia, *Victorian Vistas . . . 1901–1911*, 557–558.

79. Blewett, *Constant Turmoil*, 209.

80. Cumbler, *Working-Class Community in Industrial America*, 192.

81. Ibid., 193.

82. "In One Union: Textile Workers Agree to Amalgamate," May 13, 1901, in Silvia, *Victorian Vistas . . . 1901–1911*, 98–101.

83. Hartford, *Where Is Our Responsibility?*, 15.

84. Ibid., 22–23; Daniel, *Culture of Misfortune*, 17–18.

85. Hartford, *Where Is Our Responsibility?*, 40.

86. "Promise Aid: Lancashire Only Waiting for the Call . . . ," *New Bedford Standard*, Jan. 21, 1898, Vol. 1, WLHU-HBH.

87. Blewett, *Constant Turmoil*, 193.

88. "Saxon," Letter to the Editor, Feb. 3, 1875, in Silvia, *Victorian Vistas . . . 1865–1885*, 252–253.

89. *Providence Sun*, Jan. 30, 1875, quoted in Blewett, *Constant Turmoil*, 194.

90. Baxter, *History of the Fall River Strike*, 25–26.

91. MBSL, *Thirteenth Annual Report . . . 1882*, 363.

92. "New Bedford's Joan of Arc," Jan. 20, 1898, Vol. 1, WLHU-HBH.

93. Ibid.

94. Ibid.; Eva Macdonald [Valesh], "Journal Woman with Strikers," Jan. 18, 1898, Vol. 1, WLHU-HBH; Blewett, *Constant Turmoil*, 349–356.

95. Eula Papandreu, interview by Penn Reeve and Jack Stauder, Jul. 2, 1987, Folder 16, Box 1, UMASSD-NB1928; Sterne, "Patchwork of Protest," 57–58; Chomsky, *Linked Labor Histories*, 76–77.

96. Harris, "New England's Decline."

97. "Frauds Not Failures," Oct. 11, 1879, in Silvia, *Victorian Vistas . . . 1865–1885*, 367–368; "The Seven Family Frauds," Jan. 3, 1880, in Silvia, *Victorian Vistas . . . 1865–1885*, 375; Hartford, *Where Is Our Responsibility?*, 7.

98. McMullin, "Industrialization and Social Change," 57.

99. "Death of Col. Richard Borden," Feb. 25, 1974, in Silvia, *Victorian Vistas . . . 1865–1885*, 229–234.

100. "Col. Borden Dead," Nov. 22, 1902, in Silvia, *Victorian Vistas . . . 1901–1911*, 153–156.

101. For instance, see Obituary, Nathan Durfee, Apr. 10, 1876, in Silvia, *Victorian Vistas . . . 1865–1885*, 282–284; "Death Claims Richard B. Borden," Oct. 13, 1906, in Silvia, *Victorian Vistas . . . 1865–1885*, 390–391; Noel, *Jonathan Bourne*.

102. "Old Love Renewed," Sep. 11, 1897, in Silvia, *Victorian Vistas . . . 1886–1900*, 623–625.

103. Ibid.

104. Blewett, *Constant Turmoil*, 389.

105. Smith, *The Cotton Textile Industry*, 28, 33; Silvia, "Spindle City," 10.

106. Blewett, *Constant Turmoil*, 341; United States, *Report of the Committee . . . Relations between Labor and Capital*, Vol. 1, 54.

107. United States, *Report of the Committee . . . Relations between Labor and Capital*, Vol. 3, 495.

108. MBSL, *Thirteenth Annual Report . . . 1882*, 349; United States, *Report of the Committee . . . Relations between Labor and Capital*, Vol. 3, 501.

109. "New Bedford: Governmental Inquiry as to Cotton Mills," Feb. 24, 1901, Vol. 15, NBFPL-MAS.

110. Minutes of meetings, including balance sheets and accounts, 1892–1935, Vol. 1, Sub-Series 1, Series A, NBWMRL-PMCR.

111. Ibid.

112. "Notices Up Announcing the Wage Reduction of 12 1/2 per cent," Jul. 14, 1904, in Silvia, *Victorian Vistas . . . 1901–1911*, 211–212; "All Are in Line: Bourne the Last Mill to Post the Cutdown Notices," Nov. 12, 1903, in Silvia, *Victorian Vistas . . . 1901–1911*, 181–182.

113. English, *A Common Thread*, 130; Zonderman, *Aspirations and Anxieties*, 32.

114. Koistinen, *Confronting Decline*, 12, 29, 31, 33.

115. "A Strike Decreed," Feb. 1, 1884, in Silvia, *Victorian Vistas . . . 1865–1885*, 415–419.

116. Ibid.

117. Annawan Mill Weekly Statement, 1882–1884, Vol. N-1, BLHC-AMS-FRIW; Tortora and Johnson, *Fairchild Books Dictionary of Textiles*, 456.

118. Barkin, "Management and Ownership"; Chen, "Regional Differences."

119. "Cotton Mills in the Cotton States," *NYT*, Apr. 2, 1880.

120. "Manufacturing in the South," *NYT*, Nov. 25, 1881; Galenson, "The Migration of the Cotton Textile Industry," 84–85.

121. Morris, "Cotton and Wool Textiles"; Roberts, "The South Marches Onward to a New Place in the Cotton Textile Field," *Dry Goods Economist*, Oct. 21, 1922; Massachusetts, Department of Labor and Industries, *Report of a Special Investigation*, 2, 11, quoted in English, *A Common Thread*, 116.

122. "The Hours of Labor," *NYT*, Nov. 14, 1897.

123. E. N. Hurley, "Overcapacity: Problem or Opportunity," *IWJ*, Sep. 17, 1927, 4.

124. English, *A Common Thread*, 14–15; Galenson, "The Migration of the Cotton Textile Industry," 103–106.

125. "The Year's Business in the Country Along the Kansas City Southern Railroad," *Port Arthur Route Agricultural and Industrial Bulletin* 7, no. 11 (Oct. 1926): 3; Manufacturer's Association of New Jersey, *Manufacturers Association Bulletin* 14 (1926): 30.

126. Koistinen, "The Causes of Deindustrialization."

127. English, *A Common Thread*, 127.

128. Bernstein, *The Lean Years*, 2.

129. Gabrielan, *Rumson*, 41–42; Seebohm and Cook, *Cottages and Mansions of the Jersey Shore*, 19.

130. *The Lancet-Clinic* 122, no. 5 (Aug. 1914): 133.

131. "Official and Personal," *Amherst Graduates' Quarterly* 12, no. 48 (Aug. 1923): 283.

132. Ibid.; Brayton, *Brayton Family History*, 329–330; "Alice Brayton, Author Is Dead," *Nashua Telegraph*, Dec. 13, 1972; Holly Collins, "Living Art: A Singular Expression of Portuguese-American Cultural Traditions and Values," Preservation Society of Newport County, Jan. 28, 2004, https://web.archive.org/web/20180424185850/http://www.newportmansions.org/documents/green_animals_living_art.pdf.

133. Crapo, "The Story of Cotton . . . in New Bedford."

134. "Announcement," Apr. 9, 1928, Vol. 119, NBFPL-MAS.

135. "The Strike at a Glance," Apr. 1928, Vol. 119, NBFPL-MAS; Georgianna and Aaronson, *The Strike of '28*, 57.

136. Georgianna and Aaronson, *The Strike of '28*, 51.

137. "No Excuse," Apr. 12, 1928, Vol. 119, NBFPL-MAS.

138. Georgianna and Aaronson, *The Strike of '28*, 52.

139. Ibid., 51.

140. "Acushnet Mill Earnings Gain," *ES*, Nov. 17, 1927; "Loss in 1926 Turned to Gain," Nov. 1927, Vol. 117, NBFPL-MAS; "Grinnell Mill Earns $162,866," Vol. 117, NBFPL-MAS; "Kilburn Mill Earns $67,809," *ES*, Nov. 28, 1927; "Bristol Gain is $61,473," Nov. 1927, Vol. 117, NBFPL-MAS; "More Mill Gains," Feb. 19, 1928, NBFPL-MAS; "Butler Mill Profit for 1927 Reaches $111,000," Feb. 1928, NBFPL-MAS; "Taber Earns $9.63 on Share," Feb. 1928, NBFPL-MAS.

141. "Boosters Hear State Budget Expert Speak," *MM*, Dec. 1, 1927.

142. Georgianna and Aaronson, *The Strike of '28*, 45–46.

143. "Twenty Per Cent Curtailment by Fine Cotton Goods Mills," Jan. 1927, Vol. 117, NBFPL-MAS.

144. Chomsky, *Linked Labor Histories*, 37.

145. Pease, *History of New Bedford*, Vol. 3, 512–514; Walter Langshaw, "Press Clippings," 375, quoted in Georgianna and Aaronson, *The Strike of '28*, 73; "Declares Wage Cut Is Not Remedy," Aug. 1928, Vol. 123, NBFPL-MAS; "Langshaw Urges Junking Old Mills, Liquidation, Curtailment, to Cure Ills," Aug. 1928, Vol. 123, NBFPL-MAS.

146. Untitled, *MM*, Apr. 10, 1928, Vol. 119, NBFPL-MAS.

147. Georgianna and Aaronson, *The Strike of '28*, 68.

148. Ibid., 63.

149. Blanshard, "New Bedford Carries On," 692–693; "'Consider Mill Wages First, Profits Later,' Plead Pastors," May 1928, Vol. 120, NBFPL-MAS; Georgianna and Aaronson, *The Strike of '28*, 69–72.

150. "Textile Weekly Blames Mills for Own Plight," Apr. 1928, Vol. 119, NBFPL-MAS.

151. "Lack of Faith," Apr. 1928, Vol. 119, NBFPL-MAS.

152. "Lack Courage!," *NBT*, ca. Apr. 10, 1928, Vol. 119, NBFPL-MAS.

153. "More Millmen Not So Eager for Pay Slash," *NBT*, Apr. 1928, Vol. 119, NBFPL-MAS; "Expert Declares Wage Cut Cannot Stimulate Demand," Apr. 21, 1928, Vol. 119, NBFPL-MAS.

154. Beal, *Proletarian Journey*.

155. "Rival Strike Leaders Present Sharp Contrast of Attitudes," May 1928, Vol. 120, NBFPL-MAS.

156. "Murdoch Thinks Police had no Right to Interfere," May 1928, Vol. 120, NBFPL-MAS.

157. Georgianna and Aaronson, *The Strike of '28*, 122; Clara Sharpe Hough, "Rival Strike Leaders Present Sharp Contrast of Attitudes," May 1928, Vol. 120, NBFPL-MAS.

158. "Got Out a Fair Crowd, but Few Took T.M.C. Cards," Apr. 1928, Vol. 119, NBFPL-MAS.

159. "The T.M.C. Group Held Open Air Meeting on Scott Street," May 1928, Vol. 120, NBFPL-MAS.

160. " 'You Can't Win Fight in Bed,' Murdoch Aid Tells Strikers," May 1928, Vol. 120, NBFPL-MAS.

161. Beal, *Proletarian Journey*.

162. Sterne, "Patchwork of Protest," 52; Moran, *The Belles of New England*, 227.

163. Eula Pompandreau [Papandreu], interview by Dan Georgianna, Aug. 1, 1985, Folder 16, Box 1, UMASSD-NB1928.

164. "Mrs. Figueiredo Seized by U.S. Immigration Unit," Mar. 16, 1950, Folder 17, Box 1, UMASSD-NB1928.

165. Sterne, "Patchwork of Protest," 43; Georgianna and Aaronson, *The Strike of '28*, 84; "Children March in Picket Line as Batty, Murdoch Argue Issue," Apr. 1928, Vol. 119, NBFPL-MAS.

166. Sterne, "Patchwork of Protest," 1.

167. Ibid., 57

168. "Murdoch Thinks Police Had no Right to Interfere," May 1928, Vol. 120, NBFPL-MAS; "The Seven AIMS of the T.M.C.," Jul. 31, 1928, Vol. 123, NBFPL-MAS.

169. Alfred L. Botelho, Letter to the Editor, Apr. 21, 1928, Vol. 119, NBFPL-MAS.

170. Georgianna and Aaronson, *The Strike of '28*, 126.

171. Ibid., 137.

CHAPTER 5

1. Oral History 14, interview by Cara Connelly, 1987–1988, UMASSD-FMPAA-OHP.

2. Oral History 47, interview by Olivia Silva, May 1, 1987, UMASSD-FMPAA-OHP; "Sweatshops Fall River and New Bedford, Confidential Report, 1938," Folder 482, Box 28, AESL-CLMR; "City to Send 3 to Azores for Sum of $35," Jul. 1932, NBFPL-MAS.

3. Hartford, *Where Is Our Responsibility?*, 54.

4. Wolfbein, *The Decline of a Cotton Textile City*, 156.

5. "Unemployment Registration to Start Here, U.T.W. In Charge," *ES*, Oct. 28, 1930; "500 More File Pleas for Jobs as Bodfish Offers Work for 40," *ES*, Oct. 31, 1930; "Responses Are Still Coming," *SS*, Nov. 2, 1930; "Two Get Jobs in Registration," *ES*, Nov. 3, 1930.

6. Wolfbein, *The Decline of a Cotton Textile City*, 9–10, 156.

7. Adamic, "Tragic Towns of New England," 748.

8. "Textile Shutdown Visioned by Curley," *NYT*, Apr. 15, 1935. On New England as the opening salvo in northern deindustrialization, see Sugrue, *Origins of the Urban Crisis*, 127; Koistinen, *Confronting Decline*. Many others study deindustrialization as a postwar phenomenon. See Bluestone and Harrison, *Deindustrialization of America*; Harvey, *Spaces of Capital*; Shermer, "Take Government Out of Business."

9. Cumbler, *Working-Class Community in Industrial America*; Silvia, "The Spindle City"; Wolfbein, *The Decline of a Cotton Textile City*; Smith, *The Cotton Textile Industry of Fall River*; Fosler, *The New Economic Role of American States*, 9.

10. For a significant exception, see Keyssar, *Out of Work*.

11. Wolfbein, *The Decline of a Cotton Textile City*, 45.

12. Cumbler, *Working-Class Community in Industrial America*, 105; Bernstein, *The Lean Years*, 256.

13. Oral History 23, interview by Angela King, Oct. 8, 1987, UMASSD-FMPAA-OHP; Keyssar, *Out of Work*, 288–290.

14. Georgianna and Aaronson, *The Strike of '28*, 130–131.

15. "Free Gardens Ask for Help," *ES*, Apr. 16, 1932; "Garden Plots Allotted to More than 150 Applicants," *MM*, Apr. 19, 1932; "Garden Committee Receives Last Applications Today" *MM*, Apr. 23, 1932; "Free Gardens Now Assured 513 Jobless," *ES*, May 9, 1932; "600 Gardens Aid Jobless," *SS*, Jul. 17, 1932.

16. "The Local Unemployment Committee Discuss Problem," *MM*, Jan. 3, 1931.

17. "Effort to Bring New Industry Here Traces Back to '27," *ST*, May 11, 1954; "Reviews Work of Industrial Development," *ST*, Jan. 16, 1938; Greater New Bedford Industrial Foundation, Advertisement, "Partners in Progress," *ST*, Jan. 30, 1966.

18. "Campaign to Raise Industrial Development Fund Announced," Mar. 1931, Vol. 139, NBFPL-MAS.

19. "City May Get Shirt Factory: Prominent New York Manufacturer Looks Over Local Sites," Jan. 24, 1928, Vol. 118, NBFPL-MAS; "New Company May Come Here," Feb. 1928, Vol. 118, NBFPL-MAS; "Excellent Development," May 1928, Vol. 120, NBFPL-MAS; "New Industry Coming Here," Dec. 31, 1930, Vol. 138, NBFPL-MAS.

20. Cumbler, *Working-Class Community in Industrial America*, 140–141.

21. "Sweatshops Fall River and New Bedford, Confidential Report, 1938," Folder 482, Box 28, AESL-CLMR.

22. MDIC, *In Black and White*.

23. Ibid., 1.

24. Ibid., 3.

25. Ibid., 8.

26. Ibid., 13, 64.

27. Ibid., 17.

28. MDIC, *The Facts Concerning Industrial Advantages in Massachusetts* (1940); MDIC, *The Facts Concerning Industrial Advantages in Massachusetts* (1945).

29. W. A. Greenough, . . . *New Bedford and Fairhaven Directory . . . 1930* . . . ; Manning, . . . *New Bedford and Fairhaven (Massachusetts) Directory . . . 1936*, 1038–1041; Manning, . . . *New Bedford and Fairhaven (Massachusetts) Directory . . . 1941*, 935–938, 977.

30. Manning, . . . *New Bedford and Fairhaven (Massachusetts) Directory . . . 1945*, 1024–1027, 1068.

31. Editorial, *Boston American*, May 16, 1933; Corinna R. Marsh, "Shops That Pass in the Night," *The Rotarian* 63, no. 5 (Nov. 1933); "Sweatshops Fall River and New Bedford, Confidential Report, 1938," Folder 482, Box 28, *AESL-CLMR*.

32. "Sweatshops Fall River and New Bedford, Confidential Report, 1938."

33. Helfgott, "Women and Children's Apparel"; Fraser, "Combined and Uneven Development."

34. "Legislators Visit Newer Industries in this City," May 1931, Vol. 140, NBFPL-MAS.

35. Edwin Smith, "Statement of Wages in New Bedford," Folder 478, Box 28, AESL-CLMR; Edwin Smith, "Statement of Wages in Fall River," Folder 478, Box 28, AESL-CLMR.

36. "Sweatshops Fall River and New Bedford, Confidential Report, 1938," Folder 482, Box 28, AESL-CLMR.

37. Ibid.; "Joan Lowell Finds Girls Shamed and Ridiculed in Fall River by Unscrupulous New York Sweatshop Operators," *BDR*, Jan. 30, 1932.

38. Oral History 23, interview by Angela King, Oct. 8, 1987, UMASSD-FMPAA-OHP.

39. Oral History 44, interview by Susan Moniz, 1988, UMASSD-FMPAA-OHP.

40. "Sweatshops Fall River and New Bedford, Confidential Report, 1938," Folder 482, Box 28, AESL-CLMR.

41. Robert J. Watt to Helen Morton, Dec. 9, 1932, Folder 478, Box 28, AESL-CLMR; Skocpol, *Protecting Soldiers and Mothers*, 352–353.

42. "Joan's Expose Stirs Up Probers: Sweatshop Visited by College Girls," *BDR*, Jan. 30, 1932, Folder 406, Box 25, AESL-CLMR.

43. Ibid.

44. "The Right Idea," *Boston Daily Record*, Jan. 30, 1932, Folder 406, Box 25, AESL-CLMR.

45. Consumers' League of Massachusetts, "Sunday, October 1," Press Release, Folder 478, Box 28, AESL-CLMR.

46. Cohen, *A Consumers' Republic*, 54–56.

47. Citizens' Committee for the Ladies' Garment Industry, "Statement of Purpose," Folder 423, Box 25, AESL-CLMR.

48. "Starvation Wage Charge Here Vigorously Denied by Leary," Mar. 1931, Vol. 139, NBFPL-MAS.

49. "Labor Attacks Acts of Police," *ES*, Aug. 7, 1931; "Let's Have the Facts," Editorial, *ES*, Mar. 6, 1931; "Leary Replies to Councilman on 48 Hours," Jul. 1932, NBFPL-MAS; "Smith Criticizes Needle Pay," Jun. 1932, NBFPL-MAS.

50. Stock Brochure, "New Bedford Rayon Co.: Class A Stock," Folder 1, Series A, NBWMRL-NBRR.

51. "Starvation Wage Charge Here Vigorously Denied by Leary," Mar. 1931, Vol. 139, NBFPL-MAS.

52. Ibid.

53. "Says Industry Depends upon Liberalization," Jun. 1932, Vol. 145, NBFPL-MAS; "Leary Replies to Councilman on 48 Hours," Jul. 1932, Vol. 145, NBFPL-MAS. On larger struggle over labor legislation amid the textile crisis, see Koistinen, *Confronting Decline*, 26–66.

54. "Industrial Head Says the City Cannot Support Jobless in Idleness," Jun. 1932, Vol. 145, NBFPL-MAS.

55. Ibid.

56. See Hartford, *Where Is Our Responsibility?*, 20.

57. Faue, *Community of Suffering and Struggle*, 13; Zieger and Gall, *American Workers, American Unions*, 44.

58. See Hartford, *Where Is Our Responsibility?*, 20.

59. "Allege Conditions Are Below [Standard]: Labor Leaders Speak at Meeting in Interest of Garment Workers," Feb. 1937, Folder 2, Box 221, KCLA-ACWA; Flyer, "Join the Crusade Against Sweatshops," Feb. 7, [1937], Folder 15, Box 59, KCLA-ACWA.

60. "O Movimento a Favor da Industria Textil," *DDN*, Apr. 1, 1935.

61. "'Crusading' for Better Conditions in Garment Industry," *Boston Evening American*, Jan. 14, 1936, Folder 407, Box 25, AESL-CLMR; Crone and Gingold, *35 Northeast*, 17.

62. Crone and Gingold, *35 Northeast*, 17.

63. Dubofsky, *State and Labor in Modern America*, 111–112; Fraser, *Labor Will Rule*, 302–304.

64. William Ross to David Dubinsky, Nov. 16, 1934, Folder 4, Box 95, KCLA-ILGWU-DD; Ross to Dubinsky, Jun. 9, 1934, Folder 4, Box 95, KCLA-ILGWU-DD.

65. Ross to Dubinsky, Jan 8. 1935, Folder 4, Box 95, KCLA-ILGWU-DD.

66. Ibid.

67. Assistant General President to A. J. Morrow, Harwood Underwear Co., Feb. 1, 1937, Folder 15, Box 59, KCLA-ACWA.

68. On the collapse of the NIRA/NRA, see Brinkley, *The End of Reform*, 18.

69. Ross to Dubinsky, Aug. 27, 1935, Folder 4, Box 95, KCLA-ILGWU-DD.

70. "Workers of Sopkin Bros., Fall River, Mass." to "Sopkin Workers in Chicago," Nov. 7, 1936, Folder 4, Box 95, KCLA-ILGWU-DD.

71. Ross to Dubinsky, Aug. 27, 1934, Folder 4, Box 95, KCLA-ILGWU-DD; Ross to Dubinsky, Jun. 9, 1934, Folder 4, Box 95, KCLA-ILGWU-DD.

72. Ross to Dubinsky, Sep. 5, 1934, Folder 4, Box 95, KCLA-ILGWU-DD; Ross to Dubinsky, Jan. 8, 1935, Folder 4, Box 95, KCLA-ILGWU-DD; Ross to Dubinsky, Aug. 27, 1935, Folder 4, Box 95, KCLA-ILGWU-DD.

73. Ross to Dubinsky, Jun. 9, 1934, Folder 4, Box 95, KCLA-ILGWU-DD; "Har-Lee Tricks Fail," *Garment Worker* 1, no. 2, Mar. 1936, Folder 1, Box 25, KCLA-ILGWU-FU.

74. Oral History 56, interview by Judy Knox, Mar. 23, 1988, UMASSD-FMPAA-OHP; Oral History 46, interview by Julie Landry, Nov. 17, 1987, UMASSD-FMPAA-OHP; Miernyk, *Inter-Industry Labor Mobility*, 104.

75. Crone and Gingold, *35 Northeast*, 4, 22.

76. Ross to Elias Reisberg, Oct. 21, 1936, Folder 4, Box 95, KCLA-ILGWU-DD.

77. Crone and Gingold, *35 Northeast*, 4, 22.

78. Ibid.

79. "Strikes in Fall River and Vicinity, 25 Years Ago," Jan. 1960, Folder 8, Box 58, KCLA-ACWA.

80. Ibid.

81. Eula Papandreu, interview by Penn Reeve and Jack Stauder, Jul. 2, 1987, Folder 16, Box 1, UMASSD-NB1928.

82. "President Led into Wage Fight by Girl's Tears," *New York World Telegram*, Feb. 10, 1937, Folder 15, Box 59, KCLA-ACWA.

83. Ibid.

84. Herman Wolf to J. S. Potofsky, Memo, Feb. 10, 1937, Folder 2, Box 221, KCLA-ACWA; Edith Christensen to Jacob Potofsky, Jan. 9, 1937, Folder 15, Box 59, KCLA-ACWA; Clipping, *New Republic*, Feb. 17, 1937, Folder 15, Box 59, KCLA-ACWA; Pamphlet (Proof), "13 Letter Addressed to You . . . From Three Unlucky Girls," Folder 2, Box 221, KCLA-ACWA.

85. "O Vosso Interesse na Eleição Har-Lee," Advertisement, *DDN*, Feb. 14, 1941.

86. Fall River ILGWU, "Sit Down Sister!," Unpublished Play, KCLA.

87. Ibid.

88. Ibid.

89. "ILGWU Radio Serial Turns the Trick in Fall River Labor Strife," Feb. 13, 1941, Folder 7, Box 317, KCLA-ILGWU-DD; Ruby-Frye, *Double or Nothing*, 128–130.

90. Fones-Wolf, *Waves of Opposition*, 51–52.

91. Oral History 14, interview by Cara Connelly, 1987–1988, UMASSD-FMPAA-OHP; Oral History 23, interview by Angela King, Oct. 8, 1987, UMASSD-FMPAA-OHP.

92. "ILGWU Radio Serial Turns the Trick in Fall River Labor Strife," KCLA-ILGWU-DD.

93. Fones-Wolf, *Waves of Opposition*, 52.

94. Cohen, *Making a New Deal*, 256, 287–288.

95. Ross to Dubinsky, Oct. 21, 1936, Folder 4, Box 95, KCLA-ILGWU-DD.

96. Cohen, *Making a New Deal*, 302; Bernstein, *The Turbulent Years*, 775; Brinkley, *The End of Reform*, 12; Cobble, *The Other Women's Movement*, 110.

97. Harley, "When Your Work Is Not Who You Are," 51.

98. Dubinsky to Unknown, Telegram, Mar. 17, 1941, Folder 7, Box 317, KCLA-ILGWU-DD.

99. Fones-Wolf, *Waves of Opposition*, 52.

100. Election Results, United States of America National Labor Relations Board, Folder 7, Box 317, KCLA-ILGWU-DD.

101. "Station WSAR—Fall River, Mass.," Radio Script, Folder 7, Box 317, KCLA-ILGWU-DD.

102. Max D. Danish, Press Release, Mar. 17, 1941, Folder 7, Box 317, KCLA-ILGWU-DD.

103. Ross to Dubinsky, Telegram, Mar. 22, 1941, Folder 7, Box 317, KCLA-ILGWU-DD.

104. "Aumento de Salarios na Fábrica Har-Lee," *DDN*, Aug. 9, 1941.

105. "Sweatshops Fall River and New Bedford, Confidential Report, 1938," Folder 482, Box 28, AESL-CLMR.

106. Union Contract, ACWA 377 [New Bedford, MA] and Massachusetts Shirt Manufacturing Corp., Nov. 13, 1945, Folder 19, Box 3, Series 2, UMASSA-ACWA-NE; Union Contract, ACWA 177 [Fall River, MA] and C & D Sportswear, Jan. 12, 1946, Folder 25, Box 4, Series 2, UMASSA-ACWA-NE; Union Contract, ACWA 377 and Youth-Craft Clothing Company, Jul. 31, 1941, Folder 88, Box 7, Series 2, UMASSA-ACWA-NE; Union Contract, ACWA 177 and Dunmar Mfg. Co., Jul. 24, 1941, Folder 34, Box 4, Series 2, UMASSA-ACWA-NE; Union Contract, ACWA 177 and Freedman + Soloff, Apr. 10, 1946, Folder 111, Box 9, Series 2, UMASSA-ACWA-NE.

107. Pamphlet, New Bedford Joint Board, *Silver Anniversary*, Feb. 8, 1964, Folder 3, Box 1, Series 1, UMASSA-TWUA-NBJB.

108. Crone and Gingold, *35 Northeast*, 61, 98; "ILGWU local to mark 50th Year," *FRHN*, Mar. 3, 1984.

109. Oral History 14, interview by Cara Connelly, 1987–1988, UMASSD-FMPAA-OHP. On union benefits achieved by 1950s and 1960s, see Union Contract, ACWA 177 and Kay Bee Sportswear, May 1947, Folder 62, Box 6, Series 2, UMASSA-ACWA-NE; ACWA 177, Press Release, Dec. 15, 1960, Folder 86, Box 7, Series 2, UMASSA-ACWA-NE.

110. Harris, "New England's Decline"; Harris, *The Economics of New England*; Harrison and Kluver, "Deindustrialization and Regional Restructuring in Massachusetts," 104.

111. "Needle Trade Shops Observe Their 30 Year Here," *ST*, Jan. 18, 1953.

112. Estall, *New England*, 171, 176; "Alabama Concern to Use Massachusetts Spindles," *IWJ*, Aug. 16, 1930, 5.

113. "The L.G. Balfour Company Grows from Eight to 539 Employees," *IWJ*, Apr. 26, 1930, 6; Doug Robarchek, "The Attleboros: New Expression on a Familiar Face," *IND*, May 1968, 11.

114. Hartford, *Where Is Our Responsibility?*, 99.

115. See the following oral histories: "Leo and Theresa Dufault," in Lima, *America's Voices*, 158; "Frank Pontes," in Lima, *America's Voices*, 454; "James Henry Wray," in Lima, *America's Voices*, 538. Also see "Robert Kitchen," in Lima, *America's Voices*, 279; "Valentine Samuel Palmer Jr.," in Lima, *America's Voices*, 431; "Robert Eaton Vernon," in Lima, *America's Voices*, 509–510.

116. "Needle Trade Shops Observe Their 30 Year Here," *ST*, Jan. 18, 1953; Marc Munroe Dion, "Male Stitchers, Orthodox Russians and a Population of 111,963," *HN*, Sep. 18, 2012.

117. Hartford, *Where Is Our Responsibility?*, 169.

118. "Record of the IDC," *ST*, May 29, 1954.

119. "$5,000 in Daily Gifts Required," *ST*, Mar. 3, 1938.

120. Melvin F. LaBrode, "Old IDL Set Good Outline for Bringing Industry Here," *ST*, Sep. 23, 1954.

121. "New Industry is Installed in Nashawena," *ST*, Oct. 13, 1938.

122. "Effort to Bring New Industry Here Traces Back to '27," *ST*, May 11, 1954; Melvin F. LaBrode, "Surge of Industrial Payrolls in City Was Sparked by IDL," *ST*, Sep. 24, 1954; "Haish Reports on Work of the Industrial Legion," *MM*, Oct. 25, 1938.

123. "Haish Reports on Work of the Industrial Legion," *MM*, Oct. 25, 1938.

124. Ibid.

125. Levin and Grossman, *Employment and Economic Trends in Southeastern Massachusetts*, 36.

126. "IDC Surveys Jobs Potential," *ST*, Sep. 1, 1950

127. Estall, *New England*, 91.

128. Bookman, "The Process of Political Socialization."

129. On membership of industrial development boards, see "Reviews Work of Industrial Development," *ST*, Jan. 16, 1938; Greater New Bedford Industrial Foundation, Advertisement, "Partners in Progress," *ST*, Jan. 30, 1966.

130. Stanton, *Berkshire Hathaway*, 15–16.

131. Hund, "Electronics," 256.

132. William Zink, "Increased Job Openings Seen Reducing Unemployment Levels to New Low," *ST*, Jan. 18, 1953.

133. Miernyk, *Inter-Industry Labor Mobility*, 96, 114.

134. Ibid., 23.

135. Ibid., 101.

136. Robert H. Cain, Editorial, *IND*, Feb. 1975, 4.

137. Miernyk, *Inter-Industry Labor Mobility*, 3.

138. New Bedford Industrial Directory for New Bedford and the Metropolitan Area, 1968–1969, Folder 6, Series D, NBWMRL-NBRR-CC; Jeannette J. Lambert, "Fall River's Apparel Industry, 1920–1986," 10–11, AFKLFR.

139. Schumpeter, *Capitalism, Socialism and Democracy*.

140. A similar dynamic is explored in Cowie, *Capital Moves*, 4.

CHAPTER 6

1. "A Manifestação de Protesto da Colónia Portugueza de New Bedford," *AA*, Mar. 24, 1924.
2. Taft, *Two Portuguese Communities in New England*.
3. Ibid., 17.
4. Ibid., 192.
5. Ibid., 17.
6. Ibid., 193.
7. Park, "Review," 272.
8. "O Livro do Professor Taft," *AA*, Mar. 19, 1924.
9. Ibid.
10. Ibid.
11. "A Manifestação de Protesto da Colónia Portugueza de New Bedford," *AA*, Mar. 24, 1924.
12. Ibid.
13. Ibid.
14. Historians have shown increasing interest in the "transnational" connections of immigrants. See Jacobson, "More 'Trans-,' Less 'National'"; Waldinger and Green, "Introduction."
15. Ngai, *Impossible Subjects*, 28–29.
16. Ibid.
17. Ibid., 230; Reimers, "An Unintended Reform."
18. Handlin, *The Uprooted*; Barrett and Roediger, "The Irish and the 'Americanization' of the 'New Immigrants'"; Cohen, *Making a New Deal*; Gerstle, *American Crucible*; Kazal, "Revisiting Assimilation," 437.
19. Rischin, *The Promised City*, 95; Levitt, "Impossible Assimilations," 813.
20. There is a tremendous amount of literature addressing the fragmentation, lack of political power, and apparent "Americanization" of Portuguese Americans in the mid-twentieth century. See Rogers, "The Portuguese Experience in the United States," 3–4, 12–13; Ussach, "The New England Portuguese," 50, 55; Smith, "Portuguese Enclaves," 6, 10–11; Bloemraad, "Citizenship, Naturalization and Electoral Success," 27; Williams, *In Pursuit of Their Dreams*, 108, 112–113.
21. United States, *2009 Yearbook of Immigration Statistics*, 6–9.
22. Wheeler, *Republican Portugal*, 5.
23. Feldman-Bianco, "Multiple Layers of Time and Space," 67.
24. Higham, *Strangers in the Land*; Jacobson, *Whiteness of a Different Color*; Saxton, *The Indispensable Enemy*; Ngai, *Impossible Subjects*.
25. Immigration Restriction League, "Constitution of the Immigration Restriction League," WLHU-OC.
26. Halter, *Between Race and Ethnicity*, 7; Jacobson, *Whiteness of a Different Color*, 76.
27. Fairchild, "The Literacy Test and Its Making."

28. "Os Productos de Portugal nos Estados Unidos," *DDN*, Jul. 6, 1933.

29. Ibid.

30. Meneses, *Salazar*, 4–6, 10, 17, 21; Ferreira and Marshall, *Portugal's Revolution*, 6; Kay, *Salazar and Modern Portugal*, 39, 48.

31. Pinto, "Twentieth-Century Portugal," 36.

32. Kay, *Salazar and Modern Portugal*, 3, 75.

33. Pinto and Monteiro, "Cultural Myths and Portuguese National Identity," 212.

34. Cairo, " 'Portugal Is Not a Small Country.' "

35. Teixeira, "Between Africa and Europe," 63.

36. The Portuguese word "colónia" is ambiguous as to whether it refers to a formal colony—"a territory in which colonists are subject to the government of the metropole"—or merely any "group of compatriots that settle outside of their country." See "colónia," *Dicionário Priberam da Língua Portuguesa*, accessed Apr. 6, 2016, http://www.priberam.pt/DLPO/colonia.

37. Pinto, "Twentieth-Century Portugal," 34.

38. "O 'Preview' do Pavilão de Portugal," *DDN*, May 2, 1939. On Ferro's tireless efforts to advertise Portugal's place at the World's Fair, see "Discurso do Snr. António Ferro . . . ," *DDN*, Apr. 2, 1938; "O 'Preview' do Pavilão de Portugal," *DDN*, May 2, 1939; "Foi Oficialmente Inaugurado o Pavilhão de Portugal na Feira Mundial de New York," *DDN*, May 11, 1939; "A Recepção a António Ferro pelo Cônsul e Consuleza de New Bedford," *DDN*, Jun. 5, 1939; "Propaganda de Portugal," *DDN*, Jul. 18, 1939; "Portugal Celebra os Centenarios," *DDN*, Sep. 30, 1939; "António Ferro discursando no 'Dia de Portugal' na Feira," *DDN*, Nov. 29, 1939.

39. Portugal, *Portugal*, 11; "Opiniões que muito Honram o Pavilhão de Portugal na Exposicão de Nova York," *DDN*, Nov. 29, 1939.

40. Salazar did not actually deliver his speech in person. Notorious for his disdain for air travel, he had the speech delivered for him. See Pinto, "Twentieth-Century Portugal," 27.

41. "Mensagem do Doutor Oliveira Salazar aos Portugueses na America," *DDN*, Jul. 18, 1939.

42. "Discurso do Snr. António Ferro . . . ," *DDN*, Apr. 2, 1938.

43. Ibid.

44. "Propaganda de Portugal," *DDN*, Jul. 18, 1939.

45. Ibid.

46. See L. de Teixeira Machado, "Politica Portugueza: A Falencia da Ditadura," *O Colonial* (Fairhaven, MA), Sep. 19, 1930, Mç. 465, [pt. 27/1], File 54, Subseries 44, Series 4, Subfundo: Gabinete do Ministro 1917/1977, Code PT/TT/MI-GM/4-44/54, ANTT-MI. On other ways Portugal tracked the American press, see Silva Dias, Secretariat da Propaganda Nacional to Secretario de sua Excelencia o Presidente do Conselho, Feb. 28, 1941, cx. 662, pt.4, PC-12E, Document 4, UI 6, Series 31, Subsection M, Section D, Code PT/TT/AOS/D-M/31/6/4, ANTT-AS.

47. "Opiniões que muito Honram o Pavilhão . . . ," *DDN*, Nov. 29, 1939.

48. "Pela Feira: Criticas e Criticos . . . ," *DDN*, Sep. 30, 1939.

49. Ibid.

50. "Secção Editorial: Portuguesismo no Estrangeiro," *DDN*, Nov. 29, 1939.

51. "Casa de Portugal," *DDN*, May 9, 1945.

52. "A Grande Obra de Propaganda Portuguesa no Estrangeiro," *DDN*, Nov. 29, 1939.

53. Secretariado da Propaganda Nacional to Presidente do Concelho, May 21, 1935, cx. 662, pt.1, PC-12E, Document 1, UI 6, Series 31, Subsection M, Section D, Code: PT/TT/AOS/D-M/31/6/1, ANTT-AS.

54. Silva Dias, Secretariat da Propaganda Nacional to Secretario de sua Excelencia o Presidente do Conselho, Feb. 28, 1941, cx. 662, PC-12E, File/pt. 4, UI 6, Series 31, Subsection M, Section D, Code: PT/TT/AOS/D-M/31/6/4, ANTT-AS.

55. Rosa and Trigo, *Azorean Emigration*, 33.

56. See *Nós, os Emigrantes* (Lisboa: Junta da Emigração, 1954), 5, S.C. 16897, BNPL; *Canadá: Intruções Para Uso dos Emigrantes* (Junta da Emigração, 1955), S.C. 16858, BNPL; *Guia Prático para uso dos Trabalhadores Portugueses que se Destinam à República Federal da Alemanha* (Junta da Emigração, 1969), S.C. 23641, BNPL; *Instruções para uso dos Portugueses que se destinam a França* (Junta da Emigração, 1961), S.C. 20768, BNPL.

57. João Rocha to António Ferro [Confidencial], Feb. 18, 1939, cx. 661, PC-12D, File/pt. 12, UI 5, Series 31, Subsection M, Section D, Code: PT/TT/AOS/D-M/31/5/12, ANTT-AS.

58. On the request for financial assistance, see João Rocha to António Ferro, Feb. 18, 1939, cx. 661, PC-12D, File/pt. 12, UI 5, Series 31, Subsection M, Section D, Code: PT/TT/AOS/D-M/31/5/12, ANTT-AS. Rocha also corresponded personally with Salazar, see João Rocha to Senhor Presidente do Conselho, Feb. 18, 1939, cx. 661, PC-12D, File/pt. 12, UI 5, Series 31, Subsection M, Section D, Code: PT/TT/AOS/D-M/31/5/12, ANTT-AS; João Rocha to Oliveira Salazar, Feb. 17, 1959, PC-1D, cx. 572, pt. 35, UI 5, Series 21, Subsection M, Section D, Code: PT/TT/AOS/D-M/21/5/35, ANTT-AS.

59. Andrews, *Proceedings of the Vanderbilt Invitational Conference on High School Portuguese*, 130; Laurinda C. Andrade, *The Open Door*, 215.

60. António Ferro, "Plano duma Campanha de Lusitanidade em Toda a América, em Especial no Brasil," cx. 662, PC-12E, File/ pt. 17, UI 6, Series 31, Subsection M, Section D, Code: PT/TT/AOS/D-M/31/6/17, ANTT-AS.

61. Ibid.

62. See Advertisement, "Casa De Portugal," *DDN*, Dec. 22, 1948; "A Marinha de Guerra Portuguesa em New York," *DDN*, Jun. 16, 1958.

63. "Vai Ser um Facto O Dia da Raça Portuguesa nos E.U.," *DDN*, Apr. 3, 1957.

64. See, for example, Portuguese Alliance Benevolent Association of Massachusetts, *The Alliance Bulletin, April 1939*, Folder 18, Box 2, UMASSD-FMPAA-ABAP;

Portuguese Alliance Benevolent Association of Massachusetts, *Annual Book of Portuguese American Activities, Year of 1943*, Folder 10, Box 1, UMASSD-FMPAA-ABAP.

65. Ferreira and Marshall, *Portugal's Revolution*, 7; Meneses, *Salazar*, 223.

66. Portuguese Alliance Benevolent Association of Massachusetts, Annual Book of Portuguese American Activities, Year of 1943, Folder 10, Box 1, UMASSD-FMPAA-ABAP.

67. Pereira, "Portuguese Migrants and Portugal," 61, 68.

68. António Ferro, "Plano duma Campanha de Lusitanidade em Toda a América, em Especial no Brasil," cx. 662, PC-12E, File/ pt. 17, UI 6, Series 31, Subsection M, Section D, Code: PT/TT/AOS/D-M/31/6/17, ANTT-AS.

69. Rosa and Trigo, *Azorean Emigration*, 95; Marcos, *The Capelinhos Eruption*, 35; Lobão, "Capelinhos, Fifty Years Later . . . The Chronology of the Volcano," in Goulart, *Capelinhos*, 48.

70. Rosa and Trigo, *Azorean Emigration*, 95.

71. *Providence Journal*, May 28, 1958, quoted in Marcos, *Capelinhos Eruption*, 49–50.

72. Ibid., 67; "Fayal Aid Drive Raises $1,500," *ST*, 1958, reproduced in Oliveira, "Emotional Ties and Humanitarian Support by the Azorean Communities," in Goulart, *Capelinhos*, 103.

73. Marcos, *Capelinhos Eruption*, 47–50.

74. Advertisement, "Nós Luso-Americanos Precisamos de Joe Martin," *DDN*, Nov. 1, 1956; "Um Grupo de Portugueses de Fall River Apoia o Congressista Martin," *DDN*, Nov. 1, 1956; "Carta Aberta aos Eleitores Luso-Americanos de Mass," Advertisement, *DDN*, Oct. 29, 1952; Dallek, *An Unfinished Life*, ch. 5; Cronin, *Election Statistics*, 353.

75. Meneses, *Salazar*, 265; Kay, *Salazar and Modern Portugal*, 162, 168–170; Pap, *The Portuguese-Americans*, 49.

76. Marcos, *Capelinhos Eruption*, 47.

77. *O Télégrafo*, Oct. 25, 1958, in Marcos, *Capelinhos Eruption*, 90.

78. Marcos, *Capelinhos Eruption*, 69–70.

79. Official Letter no. 67 from the Consulate of Portugal, San Francisco to the Ministro dos Negócios Estrangeiros, Maço 232, Armário 59, ANTT-AHMNE, quoted in Marcos, *Capelinhos Eruption*, 69.

80. Telegram no. 159 from the Embassy of Portugal in Washington, Maço 232, Armário 59, ANTT-AHMNE, quoted in Marcos, *Capelinhos Eruption*, 71–72.

81. Report No. 2558, "For the Relief of Certain Distressed Aliens," 85th cong., 2nd sess., House of Representatives, reproduced in Marcos, *Capelinhos Eruption*, 147–157.

82. Maria da Gloria Mulcahy, "The Immigrants Assistance Center," in McCabe et al., *Portuguese Spinner*, 104.

83. Lamphere et al., "Kin Networks and Family Strategies," 226–227, 242–243.

84. Goulart, *Capelinhos*, 112–113; Kennedy, "The Immigration Act of 1965."

85. John F. Kennedy, "Letter to the President of the Senate and to the Speaker of the House on Revision of the Immigration Laws," Jul. 23, 1963, Gerhard Peters and John T. Woolley, *The American Presidency Project*, https://www.presidency.ucsb.edu/node/237245.

86. Lawrence F. O'Brien to João Rocha, Oct. 2, 1965, Folder 5, Box 1, UMASSD-FMPAA-JRP; Ted Kennedy to João Rocha, Jan. 24, 1969, Folder 5, Box 1, UMASSD-FMPAA-JRP; Framed pen that signed H.R. 2580, An Act to Amend the Immigration and Nationality Act, 1965, Box 2, UMASSD-FMPAA-JRP.

87. Fascist Italy developed similar programs. See Choate, *Emigrant Nation*; Douki, "The 'Return Politics' of a Sending Country."

88. Cabral, *Tradition and Transformation*.

89. United States, *2009 Yearbook of Immigration Statistics*.

90. Ibid., 6–9.

91. Medeiros and Madeira, *Emigração e Regresso*, 28; Williams, *And Yet They Come*, 100.

92. Pap, *The Portuguese-Americans*, 80.

93. Aguiar, *Alguns Dados sobre a Emigração Açoriana*, 20.

94. Rosa and Trigo, *Azorean Emigration*, 92.

95. Carvalho, *Possibilidade de Deslocação*.

96. Rosa and Trigo, *Azorean Emigration*, 40.

97. Enes, "Uma Economia em Tranformação," 190–191.

98. Ibid.

99. Ribeiro, *O Emigrante Açoreano*, quoted in Rosa and Trigo, *Azorean Emigration*, 66–67.

100. Serpa, *A Gente dos Açores*, 132–133.

101. Baptista, "A Agricultura e a Questão da Terra," 908.

102. Baganha, "From Closed to Open Doors"; Ngai, *Impossible Subjects*, 19, 24.

103. Marcos, *Capelinhos Eruption*, 45.

104. Circular, Ministério do Interior, Junta da Emigração, "Informações que Interessam aos Colonos que Pretendam Fixar-se em Qualquer dos Seguintes Colonatos," Colonos 1956, Cota 1771, BPARPD-AGCDPD.

105. Circular, João Nunes da Silva, Junta da Emigração, Lisbon, Portugal, Sep. 26, 1956, Colonos 1956, Cota 1771, BPARPD-AGCDPD.

106. Report, Secretaria do Governo Civil do Distrito Autónomo de Ponta Delgada, Oct. [20?], 1958, Colonos 1956, Cota 1771, BPARPD-AGCDPD.

107. Saul Tavares de Chaves to Governador Civil, Ponta Delgada, Oct. 22, 1956, Colonos 1956, Cota 1771, BPARPD-AGCDPD.

108. Antonio da Costa to Governador Civil do Distrito de Ponta Delgada, Oct. 26, 1956, Colonos 1956, Cota 1771, BPARPD-AGCDPD.

109. Manuel Medeiros Cabral to Governador Civil do Distrito de Ponta Delgada, Nov. 13, 1956, Colonos 1956, Cota 1771, BPARPD-AGCDPD.

110. Antonio Manuel Baptista to Governador do Distrito . . . de Ponta Delgada, Nov. 27, 1958, Colonos 1956, Cota 1771, BPARPD-AGCDPD.

111. For instance, see Secretaria, Câmara Municipal de Vila Franca do Campo, "Declaração," Dec. 30, 1958 [João Furtado Soares], Colonos 1956, Cota 1771, BPARPD-AGCDPD.

112. Presidente, Junta da Emigração to Governador do Distrito Autónomo de Ponta Delgada, Jun. 11, 1959, Colonos 1956, Cota 1771, BPARPD-AGCDPD.

113. Williams, *In Pursuit of Their Dreams*, 140.

114. Beth Negus, "The Smell of Ink Interview with Raymond Canto e Castro," in McCabe et al., *Portuguese Spinner*, 119

115. Joseph Thomas, "The Man from Santa Maria Interview with Miguel de Figueiredo Côrte-Real," in McCabe et al., *Portuguese Spinner*, 52. On return migration, see Lewis and Williams, "Portugal," 178–182; Medeiros and Madeira, *Emigração e Regresso . . . Nordeste*; Medeiros and Madeira, *Emigração e Regresso . . . Povoação*.

116. This factor distinguishes these Azorean migrants from the millions of "internal" urban-rural migrants across the world—in nations like China, Thailand, and the Philippines—who migrate to the city precisely to escape the "boredom" of rural life. See Harzig, "Domestics of the World (Unite?)," 58; Mills, "Contesting the Margins of Modernity," 37; Abad, "Internal Migration"; Henninger, "Poverty, Labour, Development," 295.

117. Oral History 44, interview by Susan Moniz, UMASSD-FMPAA-OHP.

118. Kathy Hackett, "Two Worlds Interview with Dineia Sylvia," in McCabe et al., *Portuguese Spinner*, 88.

119. Elizabeth Figueiredo, Oral History 28, interview by Michael Balenger, Mar. 9, 1988, UMASSD-FMPAA-OHP.

120. Paula Beech, "Coming to America Interview with Maria Tomasia" in McCabe et al., *Portuguese Spinner*, 76

121. Fatima Martin, "The Letter Interview with Fernanda DeSousa," in McCabe et al., *Portuguese Spinner*, 96.

122. Hackett, "Two Worlds Interview," in McCabe et al., *Portuguese Spinner*, 88.

123. Bela Feldman-Bianco and Donna Huse, "Saudade: Memory and Identity," in McCabe et al., *Portuguese Spinner*, 60.

124. Ibid., 67–68, 75; Paul Pinto, "The Long Journey Interview with Maria de Jesus," in McCabe et al., *Portuguese* Spinner, 32; Maria Candida Pereira, "Two Women Conversation with Mrs. Linhares & Mrs. Pereira," in McCabe et al., *Portuguese Spinner*, 35.

125. Moser and Tosta, *Luso-American Literature*, ix–x.

126. Pinto, "The Long Journey," in McCabe et al., *Portuguese Spinner*, 33

127. Pereira, "Two Women Conversation," in McCabe et al., *Portuguese Spinner*, 39; Negus, "The Smell of Ink," in McCabe et al., *Portuguese Spinner*, 118. See also Philip Rackley, "The New Immigrant Interview with Jorge Manuel Pereira," in McCabe et al., *Portuguese Spinner*, 86.

128. Susan Porter Benson, Notes, "Week of December 4 [1979]," Folder 35, Box 3, Series 1, UMASSA-ACTWU-NERJB.

129. Rackley, "The New Immigrant," 87, 85.
130. Smith, "A Tale of Two Cities," 70.
131. Smith, "Portuguese Enclaves," 86.
132. Wolforth, *The Portuguese in America*, 2, 46.

CHAPTER 7

1. Briggs, "Mass Immigration, Free Trade."
2. Harvey, "Neoliberalism as Creative Destruction"; Phillips-Fein, *Invisible Hands*; Burgin, *The Great Persuasion*; Fairbrother, "Economists, Capitalists, and the Making of Globalization."
3. Economic nationalism is, for instance, central to historian Andrew Wender Cohen's narrative of the ideological development of the American working class. Although other historians, such as Nelson Lichtenstein and Aviva Chomsky, have recognized the support free trade enjoyed among workers in the postwar era, they nevertheless argue that workers pursued such policies merely in the name of expanding the United States' global hegemony, seeking cheaper prices and further market penetration abroad. See Cohen, "Unions, Modernity, and the Decline of American Economic Nationalism," 16; Minchin, *Empty Mills*, 48; Chomsky, *Linked Labor Histories*, 133; Lichtenstein, *State of the Union*, 236–237.
4. See Ferguson et al., *Shock of the Global*.
5. Linden, *Workers of the World*, 269.
6. Dubofsky, *We Shall Be All*.
7. David Dubinsky, "Rift and Realignment in World Labor," Folder 6, Box 24, KCLA-ILGWU-PUB.
8. *Report of the CIO Delegates to the World Trade Union Conference* (London: Feb. 1945), 14, Folder 3, Box 213, KCLA-ACWA; Fraser, *Labor Will Rule*, 545–547.
9. "Report: Answers by Mr. Sidney Hillman of CIO to Questions of Mr. Jean Robert of La Tribune Economique, Paris 1945," Folder 3, Box 213, KCLA-ACWA.
10. Iron and Steel Trades Confederation to David Dubinsky, Jan. 19, 1949, Folder 2A, Box 173, KCLA-ILGWU-DD; Carew, "A False Dawn," 169.
11. ICFTU, *Official Report of the Free World Labour Conference . . . 1949*.
12. "Report of International Labor Relations Committee on Our Program of Action," Sep. 24, 1951, Folder 5104, IISH-ICFTU.
13. Parmet, *The Master of Seventh Avenue*, 234.
14. Dubinsky, "World Labor's New Weapon," 462.
15. Schrecker, "McCarthyism's Ghosts"; Carew, *American Labour's Cold War Abroad*, 84, 105.
16. Delton, *Rethinking the 1950s*.
17. Memo, Richard Rohmen to Jacob Potofsky, Jun. 14, 1951, "Notes for Milan Speech," Folder 2, Box 174, KCLA-ACWA; "ICFTU Is Best Hope for Peace, Democracy, Security, Says Potofsky," *CIO News*, Jul. 16, 1951, Folder 3, Box 238, KCLA-ACWA.

18. "The Crisis in Asia and Africa . . . Resolution by the Executive Council of the American Federation of Labor, Adopted Feb. 2, 1952, Miami Beach, Fla.," Folder 5104, IISH-ICFTU. On AFL, CIO, and AFL-CIO support for international development, see American Federation of Labor, Press Release, May 3, 1955, Folder 5104, IISH-ICFTU; Proceedings, Second Constitutional Convention of the American Federation of Labor and Congress of Industrial Organizations, Dec. 11, 1957, 38, Folder 5016, IISH-ICFTU; "Labor Reshapes Foreign Policies," *NYT*, Dec. 9, 1957, Folder 5106, IISH-ICFTU; "AFL-CIO Votes Foreign Aid Fund," *NYT*, Dec. 10, 1957, Folder 5106, IISH-ICFTU.

19. Pamphlet, New Bedford Joint Board, Silver Anniversary, Feb. 8, 1964, Folder 3, Box 1, Series 1, UMASSA-TWUA-NBJB.

20. Address by Sol Stetin, CIO Convention, Nov. 8, 1951, included in Sol Stetin to Francis K. Eady, Nov. 20, 1951, Folder 5105, IISH-ICFTU.

21. For a fuller explanation of the relationship between American labor unions and free trade, see Sheehan, "Opportunities Foregone."

22. ICFTU, *Official Report of the Free World Labour Conference . . . 1949*, 243.

23. "Partners in Progress: The Report of the International Development Advisory Board . . . ," Mar. 1951, Folder 1, Box 53, KCLA-ACWA; Alben, "GATT and the Fair Wage."

24. Borgwardt, *A New Deal for the World*, 4, 7.

25. Fraser, *Labor Will Rule*, 542.

26. Statement by Stanley H. Ruttenberg, AFL-CIO Director of Research, submitted to the Subcommittee on Foreign Trade Policy of the House Ways and Means Committee, Sep. 4, 1957, Folder 5106, IISH-ICFTU.

27. Ibid.

28. ICFTU, Committee on Fair Labour Standards in International Trade, Report, 1961, Folder 1387, IISH-ICFTU; ICFTU, "Report of the First Meeting of the Committee on Fair Labour Standards in International Trade," 1961, Folder 1387, IISH-ICFTU.

29. Walter Reuther, "Free Trade, or an Economic Rat-Race?," *Free Labour World* (Aug. 1961), Folder 1391, IISH-ICFTU.

30. Ibid.

31. Ibid; Lichtenstein, *Walter Reuther*, 327–345.

32. Sheehan, "Opportunities Foregone," 41–42.

33. "Labour's Cold War," *The Economist*, Jun. 18, 1966, Folder 5108, IISH-ICFTU.

34. Jacob Potofsky, form letter, "To Be Sent to All International Presidents," ca. 1954, Folder 4, Box 214, KCLA-ACWA.

35. Courtney Ward and Thomas Wilson, "Committee for A.F. of L. Participation in a World Trade Union Federation," Sep. 6, 1945, Folder 2B, Box 173, KCLA-ILGWU-DD.

36. *News from the AFL-CIO*, Oct. 17, 1957, Folder 5106, IISH-ICFTU.

37. ICFTU, Committee on Fair Labour Standards in International Trade, 1961, Folder 1387, IISH-ICFTU; ICFTU, "Draft ICFTU Memorandum to the

United Nations Conference on Trade and Development," 1964, Folder 1389, IISH-ICFTU; ICFTU, Committee on International Trade Questions, "Guiding Lines for the Free Trade Union Position in the United Nations Trade and Development Machinery," 1964, Folder 1390, IISH-ICFTU; Speech by Harm G. Buiter to AFL-CIO Convention, Dec. 7–13, 1967, Folder 5108C, IISH-ICFTU. On the push of Asian trade unionists for increased capital mobility, see Agenda Item 7, "Problems of Economic Development in Asia and the Far East," Asian Regional Conference, May 28–31, 1951, Folder 1236, IISH-ICFTU; ICFTU, Asian Regional Organisation, Fourth Asian Regional Conference, Kuala Lumpur, Malaya, Aug. 30–Sep. 6, 1958, Agenda Item No. 7B: "The Free Trade Union Movement of Asia in the Face of Advancing Industrialisation," Folder 1240, IISH-ICFTU. On ICFTU support for increased international aid and foreign investment, see ICFTU, "Statement on the Necessity of International Aid to Under-Developed Countries," 1953, Folder 1228, IISH-ICFTU; ICFTU, Asian Regional Organisation, "International Trade and Development," 1956, Folder 1246, IISH-ICFTU; Resolutions adopted by the ICFTU Third Asian Regional Conference, Mar. 30–Apr. 4, 1957, Folder 1238, IISH-ICFTU; ICFTU, Committee on International Trade Questions, Draft Resolution on the Foreign Trade Problems of Developing Countries, circa 1962, Folder 1388, IISH-ICFTU; ICFTU, Draft Memorandum to the United Nations Conference on Trade and Development, 1964, Folder 1389, IISH-ICFTU.

38. ICFTU, *The Need for a Dynamic World Economy*, 11.

39. American Federation of Labor, Press Release, May 3, 1955, Folder 5104, IISH-ICFTU; "Partners in Progress," Mar. 1951, Folder 1, Box 53, KCLA-ACWA.

40. ICFTU, *Training the World's Trade Unionists*, 9. On AFL-CIO support of the trade union college, see R. Deverall to Harry Goldberg, Mar. 23, 1961, Folder 5107, IISH-ICFTU.

41. Carew, "A False Dawn," 215; ICFTU, *Training the World's Trade Unionists*, 9.

42. ICFTU, *Training the World's Trade Unionists*, 32, 58; Ervin Dyer, Obituary, "Maida Springer Kemp," *Pittsburgh Post-Gazette*, Mar. 31, 2005.

43. ICFTU *Training the World's Trade Unionists*, 91–92; ICFTU, *Asian Trade Union College* (1960), Pamphlet, IISG Int 2333/6, IISH.

44. ICFTU *Training the World's Trade Unionists*, 90.

45. Windmuller, "Cohesion and Disunity in the ICFTU," 357.

46. Memo, "ICFTU Developments Highlight AFL-CIO Convention in Atlantic City," Dec. 16, 1957, Folder 5106, IISH-ICFTU; Address by President Arne Geijer of the ICFTU to AFL-CIO Convention, San Francisco, Sep. 22, 1959, Folder 5106, IISH-ICFTU; "AFL-CIO Votes Foreign Aid Fund," *NYT*, Dec. 10, 1957, Folder 5106, IISH-ICFTU.

47. Proceedings, Third Regional Conference, International Confederation of Labor Asian Regional Organisation, New Delhi, Mar. 30–Apr. 4, 1957, 29, 31, 33–39, Folder 1238, IISH-ICFTU.

48. "The Free Trade Union Movement of Asia in the Face of Advancing Industrialisation," 3.

49. Agenda, ICFTU, Asian Regional Organisation, Fourth Asian Regional Conference, Folder 1240, IISH-ICFTU.

50. International Textile and Garment Workers' Federation, "Statement of Policy Concerning International Trade in Textiles and Apparel," Oct. 18, 1960, Folder 52, IISH-ITGLWF; International Textile, Garment and Leather Workers' Federation, "Financial Assistance Given by the International to Affiliates," Jan. 11, 1972, Folder 63, IISH-ITGLWF.

51. General Secretary [J. Greenhalgh] to Jacob Potofsky, Nov. 30, 1964, Folder 21, Box 130, KCLA-ACWA; General Secretary [J. Greenhalgh] to Colleague [Jacob Potofsky], Jul. 12, 1966, Folder 21, Box 130, KCLA-ACWA; J. Greenhalgh to David Dubinsky, Feb. 21, 1964, Folder 2B, Box 262, KCLA-ACWA.

52. Fall River Amalgamated Clothing Workers Local 377, Minutebook, Jan. 17, 1962, Vol. 2, KCLA-ACTWU-FR.

53. Minute Book, [New Bedford TWUA] Board of Directors, 1949–50, Folder 6, Box 1, UMASSA-TWUA-NBJB.

54. Ibid.

55. Minute Book, [New Bedford TWUA] Board of Directors, 1947, Folder 4, Box 1, UMASSA-TWUA-NBJB; Minute Book, [New Bedford TWUA] Board of Directors, 1948, Folder 5, Box 1, UMASSA-TWUA-NBJB; Minute Book, [New Bedford TWUA] Board of Directors, 1949–1950, Folder 6, Box 1, UMASSA-TWUA-NBJB.

56. John Dyer, "The Real Reasons for a Break," *WFTU Monthly*, Folder 5109, IISH-ICFTU; Carew, *American Labour's Cold War Abroad*, 7, 84, 105.

57. George Meany to Mr. Omer Becu and JH Oldenbrook, Jun. 25, 1956, Folder 5106, IISH-ICFTU; Executive Council, AFL-CIO, "Guiding Lines for American Overseas Economic Policy," Jun. 7, 1956, Folder 5106, IISH-ICFTU; George Meany, Editorial, *London Times*, Apr. 12, 1957, Folder 5106, IISH-ICFTU; "Meany's Attitude Toward the ICFTU," *John Herling's Labor Letter*, Jun. 15, 1967, Folder 5106, IISH-ICFTU.

58. Dan Kurzman, "Lovestone Now at Odds with Free Trade Unions," *WP*, Dec. 31, 1965, Folder 5108, IISH-ICFTU; "Meany Explains 'Fairy' Rap to World Labor Group," *WP*, Mar. 17, 1965, Folder 5111, IISH-ICFTU. The ICFTU archive contains multiple folders filled with articles from all over the world covering the Meany "fairy" incident. See Folders 5111, 5112A, 5112B, and 5112C, IISH-ICFTU.

59. Windmuller, "Internationalism in Eclipse," 525; Windmuller, "Cohesion and Disunity in the ICFTU," 357–358.

60. Windmuller, "Cohesion and Disunity in the ICFTU," 357–358; "Labour's Cold War," *The Economist*, Jun. 18, 1966, Folder 5108, IISH-ICFTU; Dan Kurzman, "Lovestone's Cold War: The AFL-CIO Has Its Own CIA," *New Republic*, Jun. 25, 1966, Folder 5108D, IISH-ICFTU; Dan Kurzman, "Lovestone's Aid Program

Bolsters U.S. Foreign Policy," *WP*, Jan. 2, 1966, Folder 5108, IISH-ICFTU; John P. Windmuller, "Internationalism in Eclipse," 525; Carew, *American Labour's Cold War Abroad*, 85–87, 264. There is a sizable literature on the often-baleful consequences of AFL-CIO (and United States) involvement in Latin America in this era. See, for instance, Grandin, *The Last Colonial Massacre*; Levenson-Estrada, *Trade Unionists Against Terror*; Chomsky, *Linked Labor Histories*; Bergquist, *Labor and the Course of American Democracy*, 81–117; Scipes, *AFL-CIO's Secret War*; Hughes, *In the Interest of Democracy*.

61. George Meany, Editorial, *London Times*, Apr. 12, 1957, Folder 5106, IISH-ICFTU.

62. Address by Sol Stetin, CIO Convention, Nov. 8, 1951, included in Sol Stetin to Francis K. Eady, Nov. 20, 1951, Folder 5105, IISH-ICFTU.

63. On Reuther's criticism of Meany, see "Meany, Reuther End Policy Rift," *NYT*, Jun. 8, 1956, Folder 5106, IISH-ICFTU; "Meany's Attitude Toward the ICFTU," *John Herling's Labor Letter*, Jun. 15 1957, Folder 5106, IISH-ICFTU; John Herling, "Meany-Reuther Rift," *Washington Daily News*, Feb. 12, 1957, Folder 5106, IISH-ICFTU; Bernard D. Nossiter, "Meany Holdup of $200,000 Check Perils Anti-Red Confederation," *WP*, Jan. 10, 1961, Folder 5107, IISH-ICFTU.

64. "U.S. Labor's Iron Curtain," *NYT*, Feb. 6, 1966, Folder 5108B, IISH-ICFTU; Walter Reuther to George Meany, Jun. 9, 1966, Folder 5108B, IISH-ICFTU; George Meany to Walter Reuther, Jun. 10, 1966, Folder 5108B, IISH-ICFTU; "AFL-CIO Body Backs Meany Over Reuther in Vote on Walkout of Geneva Delegation," Jun. 17, 1966, Folder 5108B, IISH-ICFTU; "Labour's Cold War," *The Economist*, Jun. 18, 1966, Folder 5108B, IISH-ICFTU; "The Adamant Mr. Meany," *The Nation*, Jun. 27, 1966, Folder 17, Box 113, KCLA-ACWA. On Jacob Potofsky's support, see "The Walkout in ILO," Folder 17, Box 113, KCLA-ACWA.

65. Carew, *American Labour's Cold War Abroad*, 264–267.

66. The Meany-Reuther rift received much international attention. See Eiichi Ochiai to A. Braunthal, Feb. 10, 1967, Folder 5108C, IISH-ICFTU; Ohta, "[UAW to Withdraw its Members from AFL-CIO Executive Board]," *Nihon Keizai*, Feb. 4, 1967, trans. and reproduced by Eiichi Ochiai, Folder 5108C, IISH-ICFTU; Sekiguchi, "[Crack in AFL-CIO: Reuther Resigns as Vice President]," *The Tokyo* [Shimbun], Feb. 5, 1967, trans. and reproduced by Eiichi Ochiai, Folder 5108C, *IISH-ICFTU*; Ogawa, "AFL-CIO in Danger of Split-Up," *The Yomiuri*, Feb. 5, 1967, trans. and reproduced by Eiichi Ochiai, Folder 5108C, IISH-ICFTU.

67. Bill Hancock, "[USA's National Centre Threatens to Leave ICFTU. Result: Straighter Course]," *Stockholms-Tidningen*, Mar. 13, 1965, Folder 5111, IISH-ICFTU.

68. Lichtenstein, *Walter Reuther*, 407; Boyle, *The UAW*, ch. 10.

69. Walter Reuther to Bruno Storti, May 23, 1968, Folder 5113, IISH-ICFTU; Walter Reuther to Harm Buiter, Apr. 12, 1969, Folder 5113, IISH-ICFTU.

70. George Meany to Harm Buiter, Nov. 8, 1968, Folder 5113, IISH-ICFTU; General Secretary to George Meany, Mar. 14, 1969, Folder 5113, IISH-ICFTU; Windmuller, "Internationalism in Eclipse," 512–25.

71. Carew, "Towards a Free Trade Union Centre," 238–241, 305.

72. Alben, "GATT and the Fair Wage"; Chomsky, *Linked Labor Histories*, 132–134; ICFTU, Committee on Fair Labour Standards in International Trade, 1961, Folder 1387, IISH-ICFTU; Jacob Potofsky, Statement on Imports, Aug. 26, 1959, Folder 5, Box 238, KCLA-ACWA.

73. Jacob Potofsky, Statement on Imports, Aug. 26, 1959, Folder 5, Box 238, *KCLA-ACWA*.

74. Editorial, "Has the Amalgamated Turned Protectionist?," *The Advance*, Apr. 15, 1961, Folder 3, Box 283, KCLA-ACWA.

75. Paul Auerbach to Joe Salerno, Jun. 30, 1970, Folder 17, Box 3, Series 3, UMASSA-ACWA-NE.

76. Arbitration Record, Auerbach Bathrobe Co. Inc. and ACWA, Local 177, Sep. 1971, Folder 17, Box 3, UMASSA-ACWA-NE.

77. Much of the activism of clothing workers in the late 1960s and 1970s was done to demand import restriction. See Amalgamated Clothing Workers of America, Boston Joint Board, Scrapbook, 1965–1971, Box 12, Series 4, UMASSA-ACWA-BJB; Marvin M. Fooks to Manuel William, Apr. 20, 1982, Folder 20, Box 7, Series 3, UMASSA-ACTWU-NERJB; Department of Labor, Delton Shirtmakers, Inc. New Bedford, Certification Regarding Eligibility to Apply for Worker Adjustment Assistance, Folder 4, Box 6, Series 3, UMASSA-ACTWU-NERJB.

78. United States, *Jobs and Prices in Fall River*, 21.

79. Glenn Fowler, "Sol C. Chaikin, 73, Ex-Organizer Who Led Garment Workers, Dies," *NYT*, Apr. 3, 1991; Minchin, *Empty Mills*, 45–65.

80. Sol C. Chaikin, "The Impact of Exports on the American Economy," *USA Today*, Jan. 1979, Folder 9, Box 48, KCLA-ILGWU-SC; "Questions and Answers . . . February 4, 1977," Folder 37, Box 47, KCLA-ILGWU-SC; Chaikin, "Free Trade or Fair Trade for America," Feb. 5, 1979, Folder 10, Box 48, KCLA-ILGWU-SC; Address of Sol Chaikin, Symposium on International Trade and the American Economy, Nov. 30, 1981, Folder 9, Box 49, KCLA-ILGWU-SC; Chaikin, "Summary of Principal Points . . . Before the . . . Senate Committee on Finance . . . ," Apr. 21, 1982, Folder 16, Box 49, KCLA-ILGWU-SC; Chaikin, Speech, Jun. 18, 1982, Box 49, KCLA-ILGWU-SC; Chaikin, "Trade, Investment, and Deindustrialization: Myth and Reality," *Foreign Affairs* (Spring 1982), Folder 31, Box 49, KCLA-ILGWU-SC; Chaikin, "Toward a Rational Development Policy," May 17, 1983, Folder 37, Box 49, KCLA-ILGWU-SC; Chaikin, "Testimony of Sol C. Chaikin . . . Before the . . . House Committee on Banking, Finance, and Urban Affairs," Jan. 31, 1984, Folder 52, Box 49, KCLA-ILGWU-SC; Chaikin to President Jimmy Carter, Apr. 9, 1980, Folder 25, Box 41, KCLA-ILGWU-SC; ACTWU and ILGWU, "An Open Letter to the American Public," Folder 26, Box 41, KCLA-ILGWU-SC; Chaikin, "Statement Submitted to the United States International Trade Commission . . . ," Apr. 17, 1975, Folder 27, Box 41, KCLA-ILGWU-SC; Chaikin to Cyrus R. Vance, Secretary of State, Jan. 12, 1978, Folder 1, Box 42, KCLA-ILGWU-SC.

81. Victor Riesel, "Inside Labor: Japanese Textiles Posing Problem of U.S. Labor," *Buffalo Courier-Express*, Aug. 16, 1961; Clipping, "Amalgamated Bows to Kennedy Request, Lifts Stop Order on Japanese Fabric Cutting," *The Advance* 47, no. 9 (May 1961), Folder 3, Box 283, KCLA-ACWA.

82. Jacob Potofsky, "Statement on Imports," Aug. 26, 1959, Folder 4, Box 238, KCLA-ACWA.

83. Sheehan, "Opportunities Foregone," 50.

84. For contrasting narratives that focus on business owners and policymakers as the prime movers in the globalization of the American economy and the ascent of free trade political economy, see Harvey, "Neoliberalism as Creative Destruction"; Jones, *Entrepreneurship and Multinationals*, 7–8; Jones, "Globalization," 147–152; Frieden, *Global Capitalism*, 378–382, 400–405.

85. Max Klonsky to Sol Chaikin, [1983], Folder 4, Box 31, KCLA-ILGWU-SC. On Klonsky biographical note, see "Guide to the Robert Klonsky Papers ALBA.219," http://dlib.nyu.edu/findingaids/html/tamwag/alba_219/.

86. Sol Chaikin to Max Klonsky, May 10, 1983, Folder 4, Box 31, KCLA-ILGWU-SC.

CHAPTER 8

1. "A Inauguração da Energia Eléctrica na Freguesia das Calhetas," *AO*, Jul. 28, 1973.

2. Ibid.; MacQueen and Oliveira, " 'Grocer Meets Butcher' "; Pinto, "The Transition to Democracy."

3. Philip J. Rackley, "The New Immigrant Interview with Jorge Manuel Pereira," in McCabe et al., *Portuguese Spinner*, 81–82.

4. James Howell, "Fewer Capital Dollars for '78," *IND*, Feb. 1978, 13.

5. Edwin Campbell, "Lesson of the '60's," *IND*, Feb. 1968, 4; Barbara Sullivan, "Manufacturers Maintain Capital Spending Pace," *IND*, Mar. 1968, 10.

6. C. Philip Gilmore, "Capital Expenditures Raise the Roof," *IND*, Feb. 1967, 12.

7. Ibid., 13.

8. Sullivan, "Manufacturers Maintain Capital Spending Pace," 11.

9. Howell, "Fewer Capital Dollars for '78," 13.

10. Paul Gauvin, "Defense Products Stand Ready as Viet-Nam Orders Increase," *ST*, Jan. 30, 1966.

11. Howell, "Fewer Capital Dollars for '78," 13.

12. Lawrence Novick, "City Opens Its Doors to 600 a Month," *ST*, May 25, 1966.

13. "Schools Here Adapt to Flood of Immigrants," *ST*, May 14, 1966.

14. Gilbert, *Recent Portuguese Immigrants to Fall River*, 65.

15. Virginia Rodgers, "Immigration Tide Is Rising Rapidly," *ST*, Oct. 9, 1966.

16. Rodgers, "Immigration Tide Is Rising Rapidly."

17. Lawrence Novick, "City Opens Its Doors to 600 a Month," *ST*, May 25, 1966.

18. "Total Industrial Employment at Hand, Mayor Says," *ST*, Feb. 9, 1969.

19. Rodgers, "Immigration Tide Is Rising Rapidly."

20. Ibid.

21. Jeannette J. Lambert, "Fall River's Apparel Industry, 1920–1986," 10–11, AFKLFR.

22. Paul Mindus, "Garment Industry Employment Nears 8,000," *ST*, Feb. 9, 1969.

23. Lamphere, *From Working Daughters to Working Mothers*, 233.

24. Walter Klein, "The Changing Fabric of the Textile Industry," *AIM*, Jul. 1968.

25. Jim Sledd, "The Massachusetts Merger Merry-Go-Round," *IND*, Mar. 1969, 19; "Merger Merry-Go-Round Slows" *INR*, Feb. 1970; "Merger Carrousel Starts to Wind Down," *IND*, March 1971, 79.

26. "Merger Merry-Go-Round Winds Down," *IND*, Feb. 1974, 15.

27. Little, *How to Lose $100,000,000*, xv–xvii, 12–14; Sobel, *Rise and Fall of the Conglomerate Kings*, 24–26.

28. Little, *How to Lose $100,000,000*, 14.

29. Sobel, *Rise and Fall of the Conglomerate Kings*, 26–29; Hartford, *Where Is Our Responsibility?*, 92.

30. Little, *How to Lose $100,000,000*, 137, 142–146.

31. Hartford, *Where Is Our Responsibility?*, 176.

32. Little, *How to Lose $100,000,000*, 120–121, 134–135, 149, 152–153, 155, 157, 164, 166–167.

33. United States, *Hearings Before the Subcommittee on Antitrust and Monopoly*, 152.

34. Leontiades, "Another Look at Conglomerates," 81.

35. Rumelt, "Diversification Strategy and Profitability"; BCG, "The Power of Diversified Companies During Crises."

36. Little, *How to Lose $100,000,000*, 119.

37. Ibid., 119–120.

38. David Warsh, "Milking the Cash Cow: Is This It?," *BG*, May 23, 1982.

39. Little, *How to Lose $100,000,000*, 119–120.

40. Hyman, "Rethinking the Postwar Corporation," 203.

41. Ibid.

42. Khurana, *From Higher Aims to Hired Hands*, 3–4, 116, 296–297, 304–5.

43. Wallace B. Donham, "The Social Significance of Business," *Harvard Business Review* (July 1927), quoted in Khurana, *From Higher Aims to Hired Hands*, 116.

44. Englander and Kaufman, "The End of Managerial Ideology," 408.

45. Friedman, "Social Responsibility of Business."

46. TBR, *Statement on Corporate Responsibility*, 5–7, 14; on the Business Roundtable, see Waterhouse, *Lobbying America*, ch. 3.

47. TBR, "Statement on Corporate Governance," 1, 3.

48. Massachusetts, *The Six-District Plan*, ii; Armedio 'Al' Armenti, Oral History, interview by Renee Garrelick, Sep. 10, 2001, https://web.archive.org/web/2022113 0172618/https://concordlibrary.org/special-collections/oral-history/Armenti; Massachusetts, *Route 128*.

49. Walter H. Palmer, "The Job Ahead I: Urban Unrest Forces a New, Hard Look at National Priorities," *IND*, Aug. 1967, 29; Walter H. Palmer, "The Job Ahead—II: It's Time to Get Serious," *IND*, Jan. 1968, 14.

50. Edwin Campbell, "Black Power: Destructive or Constructive?," *IND*, Apr. 1968, 4.

51. Edwin Campbell, "S. 1175—Promise for Our Cities," *IND*, Mar. 1969, 6.

52. Joe McCarthy, "Michael Paul Feeney: The Complete State Legislator," *IND*, Jun. 1970, 10.

53. Milton Lauenstein Jr., "Contagious Effects of Trade Barriers," *IND*, Apr. 1971, 25; Elden L. Auker, "World Trade: A New Policy of Fairness," *IND*, Nov. 1971, 6.

54. Richard Nenneman, "Economic Illiteracy in U.S.—Political Opportunism," *IND*, Mar. 1974, 8.

55. "An Introduction to Free Enterprise," *IND*, Jul. 1977, 34.

56. Waterhouse, *Lobbying America*, 66–71.

57. A. L. Bolton, Editorial, *IND*, Apr. 1978, 6.

58. Phillips-Fein, *Invisible Hands*; Brinkley, *The End of Reform*, 173; Smith, "The Liberal Invention of the Multinational Corporation," 109.

59. Eleventh Quarterly Report to the Stockholders, Apr. 1931, Folder 2, Series A, NBWMRL-NBRR; Twelfth Quarterly Report to the Stockholders, Jul. 31, 1931, Folder 2, Series A, NBWMRL-NBRR; Thirteenth Quarterly Report to the Stockholders, Sep. 30, 1931, Folder 2, Series A, NBWMRL-NBRR; Stockholder Report, Feb. 15, 1932, Folder 2, Series A, NBWMRL-NBRR; Sixth Annual Report, Covering the Year 1934, Folder 2, Series A, NBWMRL-NBRR.

60. Annual Report to Stockholders, Dec. 31, 1951, Mohawk Carpet Mills, Inc., Folder 5, Series A, NBWMRL-NBRR; Lewis R. Jones, "Through the Mill," *Tomohawk* [*sic*], Sep. 1951, Folder 2, Series G, NBWMRL-NBRR; Olga Louise Garth, "A Historical Account of New Bedford Rayon Division," Sep. 19, 1966, 29, Folder 1, Series G, NBWMRL-NBRR; *Mohasco Industries: Annual Report, 1956*, Folder 4, Series A, NBWMRL-NBRR.

61. *Mohasco Industries: Annual Report: 1957*, Folder 4, Series A, NBWMRL-NBRR; "Notice of Special Meeting of Stockholders, Dec. 31, 1955," Folder 14, Series A, NBWMRL-NBRR; Gasbarre et al., "Mohawk Industries, Inc.," 258–263.

62. *Mohasco Industries, Inc., Annual Report, 1958*, Folder 4, Series A, NBWMRL-NBRR; *Mohasco Industries, Inc., Annual Report, 1959*, Folder 5, Series A, NBWMRL-NBRR; *Mohasco Industries, Inc., Annual Report, 1961*, Folder 5, Series A, NBWMRL-NBRR; *Annual Report to Stockholders, Dec. 31, 1951, Mohawk Carpet Mills, Inc.*, Folder 5, Series A, NBWMRL-NBRR.

63. Leo F. St. Aubin [hereafter Aubin] to Robert Steiger, Jul. 9, 1969, Folder 6, Sub-Series 2, Series F, NBWMRL-NBRR.

64. Harold Unterberg to Aubin, Memo, Jul. 11, 1969, Folder 17, Series A, NBWMRL-NBRR; Aubin to Robert Chadbourne, Aug. 11, 1969, Folder 7, Sub-Series 2, Series F, NBWMRL-NBRR; Letter to Edward Roberts, Aug. 11, 1970, Folder 12, Sub-Series 2, Series F, NBWMRL-NBRR; Form Letter, Aug. 12, 1970, Folder 12, Sub-Series

2, Series F, NBWMRL-NBRR; Olga Louise Garth, "A Historical Account of New Bedford Rayon Division," Sep. 19, 1966 [last page addendum, 1970], Folder 1, Series G, NBWMRL-NBRR.

65. Aubin to Arthur Brown, Oct. 15, 1968, Folder 3, Sub-Series 2, Series F, NBWMRL-NBRR.

66. Aubin to Arthur Brown, Oct. 29, 1969, Folder 8, Sub-Series 2, Series F, NBWMRL-NBRR.

67. Ibid.

68. Ibid.; Aubin to Adalberth S. Rozario, Onboard Inc., Dec. 29, 1969, Folder 9, Sub-Series 2, Series F, NBWMRL-NBRR.

69. Aubin to Frank Dixon, Oct. 7, 1969, Folder 8, Sub-Series 2, Series F, NBWMRL-NBRR.

70. For a sampling of Aubin's 1969 and 1970 lobbying letters, see Aubin to Edward Coury, Aug. 11, 1969, Folder 7, Sub-Series 2, Series F, NBWMRL-NBRR; Aubin to Hastings Keith, Telegram, Aug. 1969, Folder 7, Sub-Series 2, Series F, NBWMRL-NBRR; Aubin to George C. Mendonca, Jan. 26, 1970, Folder 9, Sub-Series 2, Series F, NBWMRL-NBRR; Aubin to Hastings Keith, Aug. 19, 1970, Folder 12, Sub-Series 2, Series F, NBWMRL-NBRR.

71. Aubin to Hastings Keith, Aug. 19, 1970, Folder 12, Sub-Series 2, Series F, *NBWMRL-NBRR.*

72. Aubin to Armand Boudreau, "United Fund of Greater New Bedford," Feb. 4, 1969, Folder 4, Sub-Series 2, Series F, NBWMRL-NBRR; Aubin to Armand Boudreau, Jul. 28, 1969, Folder 6, Sub-Series 2, Series F, NBWMRL-NBRR.

73. Edward Rigney, "PAACM: A Link with Political Reality," *IND*, Feb. 1977, 4.

74. Massachusetts et al., *An Evaluation of Massachusetts' Changing Attitude Toward Industry*; United States, *Industrial Policy*, 129; Berman, "Future Trends in Economic Development"; Plaut and Pluta, "Business Climate, Taxes and Expenditures," 99; Berkman, *The State Roots of National Politics*, 90–91; Friedman, "A Trail of Ghost Towns," 28.

75. "Rhode Island: Industry's Ideal State," Advertisement, *ID*, Oct. 1956; "Your New Plant Will Grow in the Erie Area," Advertisement, *ID*, Oct. 1956; "Put Your Plant Where Others are Thriving," Advertisement, *ID*, Oct. 1956.

76. "More Than 5000 Groups at Your Service," *ID*, Oct. 1956, 45.

77. New Bedford Industrial Development Commission, Advertisement, "Plant Location Facts of New Bedford, Massachusetts," *ID*, Oct. 1958.

78. Harrison and Bluestone, "The Incidence and Regulation of Plant Closings," 3–4.

79. Thomas, *Historical and Functional Aspects of State Industrial Development Organizations*, 41–42.

80. Ibid.

81. Ibid., 65–66.

82. Jacobs, *Bidding for Business*, 4, 12–13.

83. AIM, *The Move to New Hampshire*, 3.

84. Historians with a more local focus tend to be more positive in their appraisals of these development schemes. See, for instance, McKee, *Problem of Jobs*, ch. 2.

85. Carroll Sheehan, "Wage, Money Policies Incompatible," *IND*, Feb. 1971, 54–55.

86. Rosen, *Making Sweatshops*, 44.

87. Campaign for a Democratic Foreign Policy, "Background Report: U.S. Foreign Aid and U.S. Job Loss: Textiles in South Korea," Folder 3, Box 1, Series 1, UMASSA-ACTWU-NERJB.

88. Frieden, *Global Capitalism*, 421; Chaudhuri, "Government and Economic Development in South Korea."

89. Rosen, *Making Sweatshops*, 47; Fitting, "Export Processing Zones," 732.

90. Sasada, *The Evolution of the Japanese Developmental State*, 127; Johnson, *MITI and the Japanese Miracle*; Caldentey, "The Concept and Evolution of the Developmental State," 28–29.

91. Frieden, *Global Capitalism*, 421.

92. ILO, "Globalization Changes the Face of Textile, Clothing and Footwear Industries."

93. Bluestone and Harrison, *The Deindustrialization of America*, 42.

94. Bolton and ITGLWF, *The MNCs in the Textile, Garment, and Leather Industries*, xi–xii.

95. ACWA, ILGWU, Campaign for a Democratic Foreign Policy to Senator Brooke, May 4, 1976, Folder 3, Box 1, Series 1, UMASSA-ACTWU-NERJB.

96. Rosen, *Making Sweatshops*, 41.

97. AAMA, *Focus*, 9.

98. Ibid., 13.

99. AAMA, *The MFA and the American Apparel Industry*; Allison, *The Impact of Imports*, 18.

100. Allison, *The Impact of Imports*, 11.

CHAPTER 9

1. Kris Hudson and Das Anupreeta, "Mayor Tries to Save Warren Buffett's Old Berkshire Hathaway Headquarters," *WSJ*, Dec. 1, 2013.

2. Hathaway, *A New Bedford Merchant*, xi–xiii, 3; Beers, *Representative Men . . . of Southeastern Massachusetts*, 1309–1313; Pease, *History of New Bedford*, 75; Day Book, 1821–1825, Vol. 2, Box 1, Sub-series 1, Series A, NBWMRL-HFBR.

3. Taber, "Condensed Data"; Davis et al., *In Pursuit of Leviathan*, 77.

4. Stanton, *Berkshire Hathaway*, 15.

5. Ibid., 23.

6. This was the attitude of many workers: see Henry, "Workplace in Exile," 196; Georgianna, "The Call for Capital." See also Kilpatrick, *Of Permanent Value*, 105–114; Schroeder, *The Snowball*, ch. 27.

7. Numbers go to the end of 2022. Berkshire Hathaway, "Shareholder Letters," 2022, Feb. 25, 2023, https://www.berkshirehathaway.com/letters/2022ltr.pdf.

8. Hudson and Anupreeta, "Mayor Tries to Save Warren Buffett's Old Berkshire Hathaway Headquarters."

9. DeCosta, "Historic Berkshire Hathaway Mill Is Torn Down," *ST*, Jan. 14, 2014.

10. Ferguson et al., *The Shock of the Global*; Cowie, *Stayin' Alive*, esp. 72–73; Hobsbawm, *The Age of Extremes*, ch. 14.

11. Schumpeter, *Capitalism, Socialism and Democracy*; Bell, *Coming of Post-Industrial Society*; Brady et al., "The Consequences of Economic Globalization for Affluent Democracies"; Kollmeyer, "Explaining Deindustrialization."

12. Sugrue, *Origins of the Urban Crisis*; Self, *American Babylon*; Bluestone and Harrison, *Deindustrialization of America*; Stein, *Running Steel*.

13. Harrison and Kluver, "Deindustrialization and Regional Restructuring," 104.

14. Astakhov, *Drills*, 293; Biggs, "Twist Drill," 304.

15. Lawrence Green to "Fellow Employee," May 17, 1976, Folder "General Notices," Box 1, UPASC-UE277; William King to Lawrence Green, "Vacation Survey," Jan. 24, 1972, Folder "General Notices," Box 1, UPASC-UE277.

16. Robert Barcellos, "Council Irked by Morse Parent Firm's Hands-Off Attitude," *ST*, May 28, 1982, Folder "S-T Article—2nd City Council Meeting," Box 1, UPASC-UE277.

17. "Hayes Epitomizes New Bedford's Industrial Leadership," *IND*, May 1969, 32.

18. Korda, "Annals of Tycoonery," 82.

19. Sobel, *Conglomerate Kings*, 102, 106; Korda, "Annals of Tycoonery"; Anson, "Hurricane Charlie."

20. Welles, "Charles Bluhdorn," 43; Sobel, *Conglomerate Kings*, 118.

21. Sobel, *Conglomerate Kings*, 118.

22. Korda, "Annals of Tycoonery," 85; Anson, "Hurricane Charlie"; Doherty, *The Struggle to Save Morse*, 10.

23. Brooks, *Silent Movie*.

24. Bluhdorn's own larger-than-life personality certainly played a role in G+W's chaotic and sprawling growth trajectory. "We got more deals, even bigger deals coming up that I can't talk about yet," Bluhdorn grandstanded during a 1967 interview with *Life* magazine. He then pulled out a drawing of the planned Gulf+Western skyscraper on Columbus Circle in New York: "It will be a landmark, a LANDMARK! . . . It will make the General Motors Building look like peanuts!" he proclaimed. See Welles, "Charles Bluhdorn," 50.

25. Korda, "Annals of Tycoonery," 84.

26. Ibid.

27. Ibid., 85.

28. Doherty, *The Struggle to Save Morse*, 2.

29. ICA, "Investment & Strategy," 28; Harrison, "Gulf + Western," 20.

30. ICA "Investment & Strategy," 28.

31. Swinney, "UE Local 277's Strike," 7.

32. ICA, "Investment & Strategy," 26.

33. David Warsh, "Milking the Cash Cow: Is This It?," *BG*, May 23, 1982.

34. Harrison, "Gulf + Western," 21; Doherty, *The Struggle to Save Morse*, 8.

35. Elmer Rodrigues, "Morse Contract Talks Remain at a Standstill," *ST*, Jun. 10, 1982, Folder "S-T," Box 1, UPASC-UE277.

36. ICA, "Investment & Strategy"; "Morse Union, Officials Argue Strike Claims," *ST*, Jun. 12, 1982, Folder "S-T June 12," Box 1, UPASC-UE277; Rod Poineau, "UE Labor News," Jun. 10, 1982, Folder "Press Statement—G&W Presentation," Box 1, UPASC-UE277; Elmer Rodrigues, "Morse Strikers Seek 'People' Support," *ST*, May 30 1982.

37. UE Local 277, "Statement to the Press," May 26, 1982, Folder "Press Conference," Box 1, UPASC-UE277.

38. Swinney, "UE Local 277's Strike," 11.

39. William Serrin, "In New Bedford, Union Efforts Keep a Plant Alive," *NYT*, Jun. 15, 1986.

40. Doherty, *The Struggle to Save Morse*, 11–13.

41. Lucien Rhodes, "Against All Odds," *Inc*, Nov. 1986, Folder 17, Box 9, UPASC-UEDIST2; Doherty, *The Struggle to Save Morse*, 14–17.

42. Arthur Buchsbaum, Arthur Haft, Douglas L. Parker, and the Institute for Public Representation, "Memorandum: Power of New Bedford, Massachusetts, to Acquire the Morse Cutting Tools Plant Through Eminent Domain," May 18, 1984, Box 4, UPASC-UE284; Eisinger, *Rise of the Entrepreneurial State*, 326; Massachusetts Constitution, https://malegislature.gov/laws/constitution.

43. Rhodes, "Against All Odds"; Serrin, "In New Bedford, Union Efforts Keep a Plant Alive."

44. Serrin, "In New Bedford, Union Efforts Keep a Plant Alive."

45. Advertisement, *ST*, Oct. 3, 1984, quoted in Doherty, *The Struggle to Save Morse*, 16.

46. Local 277 UER&MW of A to The Commandant, 1st Naval District, Nov. 2, 1942, Folder 39, Box 14, UPASC-UEDIST2; Serrin, "In New Bedford, Union Efforts Keep a Plant Alive."

47. Rhodes, "Against All Odds"; Lucien Rhodes, "Update: Morse Tool 'We Really Could've Made It,'" *Inc.*, Jun. 1987.

48. "New Bedford Tool Plant in New Battle over Jobs," *NYT*, May 31, 1987; "Ruling Saves Jobs at New Bedford Tool Plant," *NYT*, Jun. 14, 1987.

49. John Doherty and Monica Allen, "Final Act of Morse Tools in City Runs like Tragedy," *ST*, Apr. 19, 1999.

50. Ibid.

51. Simón Rios, "'Serenity Gardens' Will See 'No Trespass' Order," *ST*, Jan. 9, 2014.

52. Ibid.

53. "Dog Park Discussion Continues in New Bedford," *WBSM*, http://wbsm.com/dog-park-discussion-continues-in-new-bedford/.

54. Doherty and Allen, "Final Act of Morse Tools in City Runs like Tragedy."

55. Jennette Barnes, "Outdoor Air Re-tested at Morse Site in New Bedford," *ST*, Nov. 2, 2017.

56. MBSL, *The Annual Statistics of Manufactures: 1891*, 313; "United Shoe Machinery Co.," *Commercial & Financial Chronicle* 80 (Jun. 17, 1905): 2456.

57. "United Shoe Machinery Co.," *Commercial & Financial Chronicle* 80 (Jun. 17, 1905): 2456.

58. Chandler, *Visible Hand*, 12.

59. Ibid., 315.

60. Dreier, *Story of Three Partners*, 13.

61. United States v. United Shoe Machinery Corp., 110 F. Supp. 295, D. Mass., (1953); David Wessel, "After 26 Years, PCI Group Is Back with Emhart," *BG*, Feb. 2, 1982.

62. "Rope Producers Act to Diversify," *NYT*, Jun. 16, 1956.

63. "Victor Muscat Dies at Age of 56," *NYT*, Oct. 6, 1975.

64. "Defiance Defied: American Hardware Holds the Key to a Financial Empire," *BNBFW*, Dec. 3, 1962.

65. Ibid.; "B.S.F Co. Goes to Court in Fight for American Hardware Control," *NYT*, Sep. 22, 1962.

66. "American Hardware Is Seeking More Plymouth Cordage Stock," *NYT*, Dec. 13, 1962

67. "Hardware Firm Names Directors," *NYT*, Mar. 5, 1963; "Emhart Stands to Reap Sizable Merger Benefits," *BNBFW*, Oct. 26, 1964.

68. "Emhart Stands to Reap Sizable Merger Benefits," *BNBFW*, Oct. 26, 1964; "Emhart Company Sets Acquisition," *NYT*, Jan. 29, 1964; "Emhart Appears Poised for Earnings Upswing," *BNBFW*, Dec. 25, 1967.

69. "J.C. Rhodes: Last Link in a Broken Chain," *ST*, Apr. 24, 1996; "Rhodes Now Part of Massive Emhart Corp.," *ST*, Feb. 9, 1969; Jeff McLaughlin, "Old Library a Link to Past: Plymouth Hopes to Find a New Home for Structure Displaced by Superstore," *BG*, Sep. 24, 1995.

70. Elmer Rodrigues, "More Area Firms Trim Work Week, Cut Staffs," *ST*, Nov. 22, 1974; Robert Lenzner, "Unfriendly to Whom? New Wave of Tender Offers May Benefit Shareholder," *BNBFW*, Sep. 22, 1975.

71. Carl R. Anderson to United Electrical Radio & Machine Workers of America, Feb. 20, 1975, Folder 120, Box 14, UPASC-UEDIST2; Steven Anreder and Frank Campanella, "Investment News & Views: Solid Backlog Brighten Emhart Profits Outlook," *BNBFW*, Jun. 2, 1975.

72. Wood and Anderson, "The Politics of U.S. Antitrust Regulation," 22; Wessel, "After 26 Years, PCI Group Is Back with Emhart."

73. William Doherty, "USM Faces Pollution Charges," *BG*, Nov. 11, 1986; William Doherty, "Firm Is Fined $1M for Discharging Toxic Pollutants," *BG*, Dec. 31, 1986.

74. Liberty Mutual Insurance Co. v. Black Decker Corp., Civil Action No. 96-10804-DPW (D. Mass. Dec. 5, 2003).

75. Patricia O'Connor, "J.C. Rhodes' Fate Still Uncertain," *ST*, Apr. 19, 1996.

76. Appelbaum and Batt, *Private Equity at Work*, 42; Knafo and Dutta, "The Myth of the Shareholder Revolution," 12.

77. Appelbaum and Batt, *Private Equity at Work*, 2, 24, 43.

78. Kaufman and Englander, "Kohlberg Kravis Roberts," 59; Englander and Kaufman, "The End of Managerial Ideology," 423.

79. Kaufman and Englander, "Kohlberg Kravis Roberts," 69–70.

80. Englander and Kaufman, "The End of Managerial Ideology," 423.

81. Knafo and Dutta, "The Myth of the Shareholder Revolution," 13.

82. Davis, *Managed by the Markets*, 81; Baker and Smith, *The New Financial Capitalists*, 17.

83. Lazonick and O'Sullivan, "Maximizing Shareholder Value," 15; Appelbaum and Batt, *Private Equity at Work*, 18; Baker and Smith, *The New Financial Capitalists*, 16.

84. Anders, *Merchants of Debt*, 5.

85. Englander and Kaufman, "The End of Managerial Ideology," 67. Kohlberg was also trying to serve the owners of successful family firms who were heading to retirement and looking to "cash out," but not necessarily eager to go public or hand over the management of their firm to a conglomerate giant. See Kaufman and Englander, "Kohlberg Kravis Roberts," 66.

86. While this may not sound particularly attractive for acquired firms, it did have certain advantages: owners got their payouts and management got to stay in charge and retain some semblance of firm autonomy. See Appelbaum and Batt, *Private Equity at Work*, 24–26; Winch, *Pensions and Leveraged Buyouts*, 36.

87. Anders, *Merchants of Debt*, xv.

88. Appelbaum and Batt, *Private Equity at Work*, 24–25.

89. Ibid., 25–26; Anders, *Merchants of Debt*, 197.

90. All acquisition costs were covered by outside debt, which ensured that investors were only minimally "on the hook" for an acquired firm's failure. The risk of failure was further mitigated by the "advisory fees" charged to those acquired (often amounting to 14–21 percent of total firm revenue), as well as the further 2 percent "management fee" charged to investors in the private equity firm itself. Private equity investors also profited on the dividend yield of their shares in the acquired firm. Unlike most conglomerates, all profits could be continually dispersed to shareholders, since there was no need to retain earnings for future purchases. Finally, enviable tax advantages came with debt financing, since the acquired firm's gargantuan interest payments became tax deductible expenses. See Anders, *Merchants of Debt*, xvi; Appelbaum and Batt, *Private Equity at Work*, 51, 54.

91. Appelbaum and Batt, *Private Equity at Work*, 27.

92. Kaufman and Englander, "Kohlberg Kravis Roberts," 79.

93. Appelbaum and Batt, *Private Equity at Work*, 20.

94. Anders, *Merchants of Debt*, 153.

95. Covell, "Scovill Fasteners," 433–436.

96. Holly Edwards, "Well Users Wonder Which Companies to Sue for Pollution," *The Tennessean* (Nashville, TN), Oct. 7, 2003.

97. Ibid.; "First City Raises Offer," *BG*, Jan. 5, 1985; John D. Williams, "The Restructuring Phenomenon," *WSJ*, Aug. 12, 1985; David Smith, "Westport,

Conn. Manufacturer Asks Court for More Time to Reorganize," *Knight Ridder Tribune Business News*, Dec. 7, 2004.

98. United States Bankruptcy Court, Southern District Of New York, "Memorandum Decision and Order on Objection of Alper Holdings USA, Inc.," Sep. 10, 2008, https://web.archive.org/web/20170511043448/http://www.nysb.uscourts.gov/sites/default/files/opinions/158534_276_opinion.pdf; Scovill Holdings, Inc., Scovill Fasteners, Inc., "Form S-1 Registration Statement . . . As Filed with the Securities and Exchange Commission on December 24, 1997," https://www.sec.gov/Archives/edgar/data/1051885/0000950109-97-007732.txt.

99. Ibid.

100. Carl Olsen to Sen. Edward Kennedy, Apr. 10, 1996, Box 4, UPASC-UE284; Patricia O'Connor, "J.C. Rhodes to Close Up, Head South," *ST*, Mar. 28, 1996.

101. Patricia O'Connor, "J.C. Rhodes Urged to Help Find Buyer," *ST*, Mar. 29, 1996.

102. Ibid.

103. Executive Board of UE Local 284 to Mayor Rosemary Tierney, May 15, 1996, Box 4, UPASC-UE284; Patricia O'Connor, "Scovill Says No Deal," *ST*, Apr. 26, 1996.

104. Bob Brown to Barney Frank, Apr. 26, 1996, Box 4, UPASC-UE284; Carl Olsen to Edward Kennedy, Apr. 10, 1996, Box 4, UPASC-UE284; Barney Frank to David Barrett, Mar. 27, 1996, Box 4, UPASC-UE284; John Kerry to Jerome Kohlberg Jr., Apr. 11, 1996, Box 4, UPASC-UE284; UE Local 284, Press Release: "****UPDATE**** . . ." Apr. 26, 1996, UPASC-UE284; Patricia O'Connor, "Kennedy, Kerry Join Fight to Save J.C. Rhodes Workers," *ST*, Apr. 17, 1996; Patricia O'Connor and John Estrella, "Fighting to Survive," *ST*, Apr. 2, 1996; Patricia O'Connor, "City Delegation to Pressure Owners to Spare J.C. Rhodes," *ST*, Apr. 9, 1996; Patricia O'Connor, "Frank Vows National Fight for J.C. Rhodes," *ST*, Apr. 11, 1996.

105. William Weld to William Andrews, Apr. 3, 1996, Box 4, UPASC-UE284.

106. Patricia O'Connor, "J.C. Rhodes Owners Will Listen to Offers," *ST*, Apr. 10, 1996.

107. Patricia O'Connor, "Rhodes Official: No Chance for Plant, Jobs," *ST*, Mar. 30, 1996; Patricia O'Connor, "Scovill Says No Deal," *ST*, Apr. 26, 1996.

108. Jerry Ackerman, "Pack Up and Stop," *BG*, Apr. 18, 1996.

109. Dick White, "Slip-sliding Down the Rhodes to Ruin," *ST*, Apr. 7, 1996.

110. O'Connor, "Rhodes Official."

111. Scovill Fasteners, Inc., "Form 10-K/A, for the Fiscal Year Ended December 31, 1998," https://www.sec.gov/Archives/edgar/data/1051860/000093176399001852/0000931763-99-001852.txt; United States, *1990 Census . . . Georgia*, 3.

112. It is also possible Scovill's lawyer said "extant": i.e., that there was already a waiting factory in Georgia. See "Meeting with Company, 3–25–96," Handwritten Meeting Notes, Box 4, UPASC-UE284.

113. Patricia O'Connor, "Union Officials Accuse Scovill of Insincerity," *ST*, Apr. 26, 1996.

114. Patricia O'Connor, "The Faces of a Plant Closing," *ST*, Apr. 7, 1996.

115. Ric Oliveira, "Politicians, Unions Rally for J.C. Rhodes," *ST*, Apr. 27, 1996.

116. O'Connor, "The Faces of a Plant Closing."

117. Scovill Fasteners, "NOTICE," May 24, 1996, Box 4, UPASC-UE284; Anonymous to George Rogers, "I Am a Tax Payer in New Bedford . . . ," Box 4, UPASC-UE284; Executive Board of UE Local 284 to Mayor Rosemary Tierney, May 15, 1996, Box 4, UPASC-UE284; UE Local 284, "City Council Vote is . . . On!," Press Release, May 21, 1996, Box 4, UPASC-UE284; UE Local 284, "Mayor Tierney Vetos [*sic*] ordinance on Eminent Domain . . . ," Press Release, May 30, 1996, Box 4, UPASC-UE284.

118. Leslie Broberg, "New Bedford Battles over J.C. Rhodes Jobs," *PBN*, May 20, 1996.

119. Patricia O'Connor, "Businessman's Lament: Profit, not Jobs, Are Key," *ST*, Apr. 28, 1996.

120. Ibid.

121. Russell Sinclair, "Hands Off; Rhodes Is Private Property," *ST*, May 6, 1996; Elizabeth G. Sinclair, Obituary, Dec. 31, 2005, https://www.hathawayfunerals.com/obituary/Elizabeth-Sinclair.

122. Christian Berg, "Defection Dooms Plan to Save N. Bedford Plant," *Providence Journal*, May 31, 1996.

123. Ibid.

124. Patricia O'Connor, "J.C. Rhodes Workers Start Phasing Out," *ST*, Jun. 26, 1996.

125. Don Abood, "Industry Works Hard to Fill Gap of J.C. Rhodes," *PBN*, Jul. 15, 1996.

126. Ibid.

127. "Effort to Bring New Industry Here Traces Back to '27," *ST*, May 11, 1954; Melvin F. LaBrode, "Surge of Industrial Payrolls in City Was Sparked by IDL," *ST*, Sep. 24, 1954; "Haish Reports on Work of the Industrial Legion," *MM*, Oct. 25, 1938.

128. AVX, "Global Manufacturing/R&D Locations," Apr. 2, 2023, https://web.archive.org/web/20230402203820/https://www.kyocera-avx.com/contact-us/avx-locations/; Dinger and Gjertsen, "AVX Corporation"; United States Securities and Exchange Commission, "Aerovox Incorporated: Annual Report Pursuant to Section 13 Or 15(D) of The Securities Exchange Act Of 1934," Form 10-K405, http://www.sec.gov/Archives/edgar/data/856164/0001021408000001377/0001021408-00-001377.txt.

129. United States Securities and Exchange Commission, "Aerovox Incorporated: Annual Report"; "Aerovox History," *ST*, Mar. 31, 2011; Aerovox, "Company Information: Aerovox," accessed Jun. 4, 2013, https://web.archive.org/web/20130604112449/http://www.aerovox.com/AboutAerovox.aspx; Norman Butterworth, Aerovox Industries Inc. to Jeffrey Miller, Director, Enforcement Division Environmental Protection Agency, Sep. 29, 1975, U.S. Environmental Protection Agency, New Bedford Site (New Bedford Harbor Superfund Site), http://www.epa.gov/region1/superfund/sites/newbedford/59586.pdf; "L.I. Concern in PCB's Settlement," *NYT*, Mar. 5, 1987; Beth Daley and Katheleen

Conti, "$366m Accord Reached to Clean Up New Bedford Harbor," *BG*, Oct. 11, 2012; U.S. Environmental Protection Agency, "Aerovox Mill Site, New Bedford, MA: Site Update," Feb. 2011, http://www.epa.gov/region1/superfund/sites/aero vox/480701.pdf.

130. On traditional structure of garment production firms, see Scranton, *Endless Novelty*, 21, 94–95.

131. "Company News: Sale of Palm Beach," *NYT*, Dec. 16, 1988; Merwin Sigale, "Cincinnati-Based Palm Beach Inc.: Only Name Same," *Palm Beach Post*, Nov. 21, 1988; Ross Hetrick, "J. Schoeneman's Owner Buys Men's Clothing Business, *Baltimore Sun*, Oct. 21, 1992; "New Bedford Apparel Plant May Close," *The Day* (New London, CT), Jul. 20, 1994; Grant B. Southward, "The Bay State Boys Grow Up," *Daily News Record*, Jun. 20, 1977, Folder 4, Box 1, Series 1, UMASSA-ACTWU-NERJB.

132. Grant B. Southward, "The Bay State Boys Grow Up"; Asher B. Lans to Joseph Salerno, Feb. 15, 1968, Folder 19, Box 3, Series 2, UMASSA-ACWA-NE; NLRB-859 Form, Order to Reschedule Hearing, Nov. 14, 1967, Folder 85, Box 7, Series 2, UMASSA-ACWA-NE; Harold B. Rotiman to Jacob Sheinkman, Jul. 31, 1967, Folder 85, Box 7, Series 2, UMASSA-ACWA-NE; Form NLRB-4479, NLRB Decision, Fall River Clothing Mfg. Co. . . . and ACWA, Case No. 1-Rc-9488, Jul. 7, 1967, Folder 85, Box 7, Series 2, UMASSA-ACWA-NE.

133. Grant Welker, "Anderson-Little Is Back in Fashion," *HN*, Jul. 16, 2008; Beth Perdue, "Reuse: Housing Developments Planned for New Bedford's Cliftex Mills," *Southcoast Business Bulletin*, Nov. 18, 2011; Aaron Nicodemus, "Manager's Financial Problems Drive Cliftex Demolition," *ST*, Aug. 6, 2007; David Rising, "Cliftex Closing Stores," *ST*, Nov. 17, 1996; "Cliftex Lofts Launch," Oct. 28, 2011, https://web.archive.org/web/20111029052814/http://www.mass.gov/governor/pressoffice/pressreleases/2011/111028-cliftex-landing-launch.html; Pederson, "Woolworth Corporation," 528–532; Auditi Guha, "Cliftex Mill That Was Almost Demolished Is Reborn as Manomet Place," *ST*, May 29, 2013.

134. Auditi Guha, "Cliftex Mill That Was Almost Demolished Is Reborn as Manomet Place."

135. Frederick Rubin, "A One-Industry City No Longer," *IND*, Dec. 1978, 26.

136. On similar dynamics in other New England cities, see Lamphere, *From Working Daughters to Working Mothers*, 39, 224, 292; Nash, *From Tank Town to High Tech*; Kirsch, *In the Wake of the Giant*; Forrant, *Metal Fatigue*, 3–4.

137. Bluestone and Harrison, *The Deindustrialization of America*, 42.

CHAPTER 10

1. Hobsbawm, *The Age of Extremes*, 405.

2. Minchin, *Empty Mills*, 69–70.

3. Rosegrant and Lampe, *Route 128*, 129.

4. Charles Stein, "Record Recession? Massachusetts Downturn Approaches the Great Slump of '74," *BG*, Nov. 4, 1990.

5. Jimmy Carter, "Crisis of Confidence," Jul. 15, 1979, https://web.archive.org/web/20230301152255/https://pbs.org/wgbh/americanexperience/features/carter-crisis/.

6. Robert Cain, "The 'Plus' Side of a Crisis," *IND*, Feb. 1974, 6.

7. Edward Rigney, Editorial, *IND*, Oct. 1975, 4.

8. Lampe, *Massachusetts Miracle*, 9–10; Ferguson and Ladd, "Massachusetts," in Fosler, *The New Economic Role of American States*, 40–41.

9. Massachusetts, *Massachusetts Business Incentives*.

10. Harrison and Kluver, "Deindustrialization and Regional Restructuring in Massachusetts," 284.

11. Geismer, *Don't Blame Us*, 255.

12. Rosegrant and Lampe, *Route 128*, 126.

13. Massachusetts High Technology Council, "A New Social Contract for Massachusetts," Feb. 1977, in Lampe, *Massachusetts Miracle*, 155.

14. Ibid.

15. Geismer, *Don't Blame Us*, 262.

16. Massachusetts High Technology Council, "A New Social Contract for Massachusetts," 156.

17. Interview with Edson de Castro, Oct. 10, 1985, quoted in Rosegrant and Lampe, *Route 128*, 125–126.

18. Tracy Kidder, *Soul of a New Machine* (Boston: Little, Brown, 1981), 72–73, quoted in Geismer, *Don't Blame Us*, 260.

19. Massachusetts High Technology Council, "A New Social Contract for Massachusetts," 160; Nancy S. Dorfman, "Route 128: The Development of a Regional High Technology Economy," Dec. 1983, in Lampe, *The Massachusetts Miracle*, 253.

20. Harrison and Kluver, "Deindustrialization and Regional Restructuring in Massachusetts," 104; Kuhn, *Computer Manufacturing*, 2. On the similar transformation of Pittsburgh, see Neumann, *Remaking the Rustbelt*, 3, 88–89.

21. Rosegrant and Lampe, *Route 128*, 11, 6.

22. Hamilton William, "Hard Times Not New to New Bedford," *BG*, Mar. 2, 1975.

23. Massachusetts, *Massachusetts in Perspective*, 3; Massachusetts, *Make It in Massachusetts*, 3.

24. Dukakis, *Creating the Future*, 44–53; Carroll P. Sheehan, "Wage, Money Policies Incompatible," *IND*, Feb. 1971, 17.

25. Massachusetts, *Massachusetts . . . Creating the Future*.

26. Ferguson and Ladd, "Massachusetts," 32.

27. Doherty, "Spindle City Blues."

28. Atkins, *There Is More Than One Massachusetts Economy*, vii.

29. Patricia Flynn, "Lowell: A High Tech Success Story," Sep. 1984, in Lampe, *The Massachusetts Miracle*, 281; Rosegrant and Lampe, *Route 128*, 11.

30. Bluestone and Stevenson, "The Industrial Revolution," 68–70; Frederic Biddle and Josh Hyatt, "Word of Departures by Digital and Stride Rite Shakes Roxbury," *BG*, Dec. 18, 1992.

31. Harrison and Kluver, "Deindustrialization and Regional Restructuring in Massachusetts," 106; Brenner, "The Economy," 14–18.

32. Peter Greenough, "Education Key to Unemployment," *BG*, Jul. 13, 1964; Wilfrid Rodgers, "The Old Statistics Are Changing: Influx of Modern Industry Gives New Bedford a Boost," *BG*, Jun. 9, 1980; Neville S. Lee, "The Economic Outlook for the Tri-City Area in Southeastern Massachusetts: New Bedford, Fall River, and Taunton," Oct. 14, 1983, in Fall River Office of Economic Development, Binder, Box 1, UMASSD-FMPAA-CVP.

33. Rachelle Patterson, "Dukakis Shifts Focus from Suburbia," *BG*, Mar. 18, 1975; Anthony J. Yudis, "Massachusetts: Optimistic Outlook," *BG*, Mar. 11, 1980; Ben Bradlee, "New Bedford Tour Guide: Dukakis," *BG*, Jun. 16, 1982; James Risen, "Dukakis' State Miracle: Long on Jawboning," *Los Angeles Times*, Aug. 7, 1988; Thaddeus Herrick, "Steering Mill Towns Closer to Tech-Boom Riches," *WSJ*, Feb. 26, 2007.

34. The "Bay State Project" was intended to do just this. See Nick King, "Kariotis Likes Challenge," *BG*, Jan. 30, 1980.

35. Ian Menzies, "High-Tech Offers High Reward for State's Jobless," *BG*, Mar. 24, 1980.

36. Gifun, *UMass Dartmouth*.

37. Rosenberg, "Techno-Bytes: Come East, High Tech," *BG*, Apr. 6, 1982.

38. Southeastern Massachusetts Economic Development Committee, Advertisement, *IND*, Apr. 1982, 18–19, Folder 7, Box 2, UMASSD-FMPAA-CVP.

39. Fall River Office of Economic Development, *Decade for Progress: The First 2000 Days* (ca. 1983), 6, Fall River Office of Economic Development, Binder, Box 1, UMASSD-FMPAA-CVP.

40. Rosenberg, "Techno-Bytes: Come East, High Tech."

41. Southeastern Massachusetts Economic Development Committee, *Southeastern Massachusetts: The Golden Connection* (ca. 1982), Folder 6, Box 2, UMASSD-FMPAA-CVP.

42. Stephen C. Smith, "South Coast—On the Verge of the Breakthrough," *ST*, Aug. 15, 2013.

43. Southeastern Regional Planning and Economic Development District, *Dawn of the 80's for Southeastern Massachusetts* (Jun. 1980), Folder 1, Box 4, Series IV, UMASSD-SMREDC; "Economic Overview," *Economic Update for Southeastern Massachusetts* 1, no. 1 (Jan. 15, 1985), Folder 40, Box 3, Series III, UMASSD-SMREDC.

44. Saxenian, *Regional Advantage*, ch. 1; Al Larkin, "Whither High Tech," *BG*, Jan. 11, 1981.

45. Bluestone and Stevenson, "The Industrial Revolution," 60.

46. Ibid., 62.

47. Rosegrant and Lampe, *Route 128*, 79, 93.

48. Bluestone and Stevenson, "The Industrial Revolution," 65.

49. Moussouris, "The Higher Education-Economic Development 'Connection,'" 91.

50. Linda Frankel and James Howell, "Economic Revitalization and Job Creation in America's Oldest Industrialized Region," Oct. 1985, in Lampe, *Massachusetts Miracle*, 304, 306.

51. Florida and Smith, "Venture Capital Formation," 441, 446.

52. Ibid., 434.

53. Jack Bush, interview with Rosegrant and Lampe, Dec. 11, 1985, quoted in Rosegrant and Lampe, *Route 128*, 117.

54. Rosegrant and Lampe, *Route 128*, 111–113.

55. William Foster, interview with Rosegrant and Lampe, Oct. 7, 1985, quoted in *Route 128*, 160.

56. Jack Bush, interview with Rosegrant and Lampe, Dec. 11, 1985, quoted in *Route 128*, 158–159.

57. Kenneth Fisher, interview with Rosegrant and Lampe, Nov. 19, 1985, quoted in *Route 128*, 161.

58. Brenner, "The Economy," 23.

59. United States, *1970 Census . . . New Bedford*, P–1.

60. Grover, *Fugitive's Gibraltar*.

61. Ibid.; Margery Eagan, "Subtle Bigotry Halted Black Progress," *ST*, Feb. 21, 1980.

62. Model Cities, "1972 Third Year Action Plan," Nov. 1971, IV-3, Vol. 9, Subseries I, Series III, UMASSD-SMREDC; C.F. Seales, Letter to the Editor, *ST*, Jul. 25, 1970.

63. Roger Martin, "Councillors Appalled After West End Tour," *ST*, Apr. 12, 1967.

64. Roger Martin, "Negroes' New Bedford: City of Rat-Infested, Drafty Tenements," *ST*, Apr. 9, 1967.

65. Richard J. Ward and Donald H. James, "Employment and Training Survey: New Bedford, Massachusetts Consortium," Dec. 1976, 5, Folder 7, Box 1, Subseries I, Series II, UMASSD-SMREDC; Halter, *Between Race and Ethnicity*, 4.

66. Halter, *Between Race and Ethnicity*, 5.

67. Ibid., 39.

68. Colin Nickerson, "Black, White or Cape Verdean?," *BG*, Sep. 30, 1983, quoted in Halter, *Between Race and Ethnicity*, 146; Ribeiro, *This Path I Took*, 7.

69. Ramos and Reardon, "Black, White or Portuguese?," 64.

70. Edward Rogers Sousa, Letter to the Editor, *ST*, Nov. 15, 1965.

71. Joaquim A. Custodio, interview by Marilyn Halter, Jul. 28, 1988, quoted in Halter, *Between Race and Ethnicity*, 166.

72. Van Sauter, "Many Puerto Ricans Go Back in Winter," *ST*, Jan. 2, 1960; Thomas et al., *A Picture History of New Bedford*, 293.

73. Don McClay, "City's 800 Puerto Ricans Find Friend in ONBOARD," *ST*, Sep. 7, 1965; Van Sauter, "Puerto Ricans Find Better Life in New Bedford," *ST*, Dec. 30, 1959.

74. Van Sauter, "Puerto Ricans Find Better Life in New Bedford," *ST*, Dec. 30, 1959; Van Sauter, "Puerto Ricans Make Good Citizens Here," *ST*, Jan. 1, 1960.

75. "Aid for City Puerto Ricans Planned," *ST*, Oct. 18, 1967.

76. Roger Martin, "Renewal: Blueprint for Progress—I: 5 Projects in 2-Mile Belt Make Up City's Program," *ST*, May 17, 1965; "State Agency Moves in Favor of West End Housing," *New Bedford Redevelopment Authority News*, no. 5 (Mar. 31, 1972), Folder 21, Box 2, Subseries I, Series III, UMASSD-SMREDC; Eagan, "Subtle Bigotry"; City of New Bedford Model Cities, "1972 Third Year Action Plan," Nov. 1971, II-14, Vol. 9, Subseries I, Series III, UMASSD-SMREDC.

77. Halter, *Between Race and Ethnicity*, 164; Lazerow, "'A Rebel All His Life,'" 114.

78. Lazerow, "'A Rebel All His Life,'" 118; Ramos, "Black, White or Portuguese?," 66; Ribeiro, *This Path I Took*, 9.

79. Ribeiro, *This Path I Took*, 13.

80. Dick Bigos and Dave Branco, "Three Are Arrested in West End Fracas," *ST*, July 9, 1970; "16 Hurt in New Bedford's 2d Night of Violence," *BG*, July 10, 1970.

81. Lazerow, "The Black Panthers at the Water's Edge," 95.

82. Ibid., 103.

83. Lazerow, "'A Rebel All His Life,'" 121.

84. Bigos and Branco, "Three Are Arrested"; Atkins, "Report and Recommendations," 1; Lazerow, "Black Panthers at the Water's Edge," 96.

85. Lazerow, "Black Panthers at the Water's Edge," 96; Bigos and Branco, "Three Are Arrested"; Paul Drolet, "Communication: The Way to Calm," *ST*, Jul. 11, 1970; Alan Sheehan and Daniel Juda, "Mayor Clamps Curfew to Calm New Bedford," *BG*, Jul. 13, 1970; Atkins, "Report and Recommendations," 7–13; Greg Stone, "Disorders Erupt Again in New Bedford; 23 Hurt," *ST*, Jul. 10, 1970.

86. Lazerow, "Black Panthers at the Water's Edge," 109, 131; Kavanaugh, *Race, Politics, and Basketball*, 16–17; Thom Shepard, "Black Youth Killed, 3 Hurt in New Bedford," *BG*, Jul. 12, 1970.

87. Kavanaugh, *Race, Politics, and Basketball*, 16–17.

88. Ibid.; Dick Bigos and Don Fraser, "Youth Slain, 3 Hurt by Gunfire from Car," *ST*, Jul. 12, 1970.

89. Atkins, "Report and Recommendations," 2.

90. F.B. Taylor Jr., "N. Bedford Feels Acquittal Effects," *BG*, May 22, 1971.

91. Dick Bigos, "Blacks Halt Meeting with City, Vow Revolt," *ST*, Jul. 13, 1970.

92. Atkins, "Report and Recommendations," 4.

93. Ibid.; "Atkins Scoffs at Outside Agitation: City Trouble Blamed on Officials," *ST*, Aug. 18, 1970; "Shooting, Fires Flare in New Bedford," *BG*, Jul. 30, 1970.

94. Roger Martin, "Learning to Learn—Monster or Salvation?—IV: Critics Include Most of City Council," *ST*, Aug. 19, 1970.

95. Daniel Juda, "Compromise Called Key to New Bedford Progress," *BG*, Jul. 26, 1970.

96. "Shooting, Fires Flare in New Bedford," *BG*, Jul. 30, 1970.

97. David Taylor and Daniel Juda, "Brooke, Blacks, City Agree on New Bedford Peace Plan," *BG*, Jul. 14, 1970; "Sen. Brooke Expresses Hope, Asks Cooperation," *ST*, Jul. 14, 1970; Tillman, "New Bedford."

98. Juda, "Compromise Called Key."

99. David Branco, "Public Funds Asked to Build Plants," *ST*, Jul. 13, 1970.

100. Roger Martin, "Jobs Available for All, Front Told," *ST*, May 15, 1968.

101. Ibid.; Don Fraser, "Job Information Trailer Planned Here," *ST*, May 22, 1968.

102. New Bedford Consortium, *Employment & Training Survey*, Dec. 1976, V, Folder 7, Box 1, Subseries I, Series II, UMASSD-SMREDC.

103. Brenda Payton, "Cape Verdean Becomes Plumber; Bias Charges Fly," *ST*, Aug. 28, 1975.

104. Lazerow, "Black Panthers at the Water's Edge," 86.

105. Tillman, "New Bedford."

106. "Work Program Failure Blamed for City Fracas," *ST*, Jul. 14, 1970.

107. Tillman, "New Bedford."

108. Kessel, "The Impact of the Work Incentive Program," 174.

109. Yvonne Levesque, "The Senator Interview with Mary Fonseca," in McCabe et al., *Portuguese Spinner*, 122; Everett Allen, "Employment: New Bedford's No. 1 Problem—XIX: SMU Grads Forced to Leave Area," *ST*, Nov. 30, 1971.

110. Gavin Hymes, "A Man of Steel: Interview with Emidio Raposo," in McCabe et al., *Portuguese Spinner*, 250.

111. William A. Davis, "Unemployment a Way of Life in New Bedford," *BG*, Jul. 27, 1970.

112. Ibid.

113. Roger Martin and Doreen Martin, "City Has Spent $43.9 Million in Aid," *ST*, Jul. 26, 1970.

114. United States, *Jobs and Prices in Fall River*, 17.

115. Elden Auker, "Prescribing for the 'Job Paradox,'" *IND*, Jan. 1973, 6.

116. Everett Allen, "Employment: New Bedford's No. 1 problem—XII: City's Old Ways Conflict with New Technology," *ST*, Nov. 24, 1971.

117. United States, *Jobs and Prices in Fall River*, 36.

118. Everett Allen, "Employment: New Bedford's No. 1 Problem—XXVIII: Many Businessmen Feel Jobs Not Greatest Question," *ST*, Dec. 9, 1971; On "Jobs Paradox," see Ken Botwright, "Massachusetts Needs Jobs—and More Jobs: State Lags as Nation Recovers," *BG*, Oct. 26, 1975.

119. United States, *Jobs and Prices in Fall River*, 13.

120. Ibid., 37.

121. Ibid., 18.

122. Lamphere, *From Working Daughters to Working Mothers*, 274.

123. Ibid., 277.

124. Ibid., 278.

125. Ibid., 298.

126. Lazerow, "'A Rebel All His Life,'" 114–115.

127. United States, *Extent of Subversion in the 'New Left,'* 878.

128. Bennie DiNardo, "Apparel Manufacturers Fighting Back," *Boston Business Bureau*, Aug. 1989.

129. Southeastern Massachusetts Partnership, *The High Skills Path for Southeastern Massachusetts: A Framework for Decisionmakers*, 1991, Folder 51, Box 3A, Subseries III, Series III, UMASSD-SMREDC.

130. DiNardo, "Apparel Manufacturers Fighting Back."

131. Hollander, *An Ordinary City*, 68.

132. On the inevitable tendency for affluent, "pioneering" industrial nations to deindustrialize, see Hobsbawm, *Industry and Empire*, 166; Kollmeyer, "Explaining Deindustrialization"; Brady et al., "The Consequences of Economic Globalization."

CONCLUSION

1. George C. Butts, Holmes Mfg. Co., Inc., Historic Building Survey, Nov. 29, 1977, in Office of Historic Preservation, *New Bedford Mills (Textile and Non-Related Industries)* (New Bedford: 1977–1978), NBFPL; "Leary Elected Vice-President," *ST*, Jan. 11, 1959.

2. Google Maps, https://goo.gl/maps/Vf58uvTXWfBsHq3eA; Brittany Global Technologies, https://www.brittanyusa.com/.

3. Kilburn Mill at Clarks Cove, https://kilburnmill.com/.

4. New Bedford, *Historic Mill Inventory*, 7.

5. Ben Berke, "Regulators See Hard Years Ahead for the Scallop Fishery, New Bedford's Cash Cow," *Public's Radio*, Dec. 8, 2022, https://thepublicsradio.org/article/regulators-see-hard-years-ahead-for-the-scallop-fishery-new-bedford-s-cash-cow.

6. Ibid.; David Abel, "Sector of New Bedford Fishing Industry Sees Rapid Decline," *BG*, Jun. 18, 2014; Will Sennott, "Investigation: How Foreign Private Equity Hooked New England's Fishing Industry," *New Bedford Light*, Jul. 6, 2022, https://newbedfordlight.org/investigation-how-foreign-private-equity-hooked-new-englands-fishing-industry/.

7. Will Sennott, "Investigation: How Foreign Private Equity Hooked New England's Fishing Industry."

8. Ibid.

9. Janelle Nanos and Tim Logan, "On the Street: New Bedford Is a Shining Sea of Possibilities," *BG*, Nov. 10, 2021.

10. Ibid.; Kathryn Gallerani, "New Bedford Fishing Industry Considers Compensation for Offshore Wind's Impact," *ST*, Jan. 19, 2023.

11. New Bedford Economic Development Council, "Creative Economy Task Force Report," Feb. 2008, https://web.archive.org/web/20170712082744/http://www.nbedc.org/wp/wp-content/uploads/2014/02/NBEDC-Creative-Economy-Task-Force-Final-Report.pdf ; Ken Hartnett, " 'Whither Is Fled the Visionary Gleam?' Look to the Arts," *ST*, Oct. 5, 2008.

12. Natalie Myers, "Betting on the Arts to Revitalize the City," Jul. 25, 2007, http://www.nbedc.org/news/betting-on-the-arts-to-revitalize-the-city/.

13. In contrast to the generally dismal media coverage of these cities, New Bedford received a very positive 2022 appraisal in the "Travel" section of the *New York Times*, highlighting its arts and tourism rebirth. See Elisabeth Goodridge, "The Old Whaling Capital of New Bedford Looks Ahead," *NYT*, Jun. 29, 2022.

14. US Bureau of Labor Statistics, "Economy at a Glance: New Bedford, MA," accessed Nov. 2022, http://www.bls.gov/eag/eag.ma_newbedford_mn.htm; US Bureau of Labor Statistics, "May 2022 Metropolitan and Nonmetropolitan Area Occupational Employment and Wage Estimates, New Bedford, MA," https://www.bls.gov/oes/current/oes_75550.htm. Also see Winant, *The Next Shift*, 2–7, 16–19.

15. Fall River Office of Economic Development, "City Overview," accessed Aug. 19, 2018, https://web.archive.org/web/20180819015833/http://froed.org/city-overview/.

16. James Murdock, "A Red Carpet for Amazon in Fall River, Mass., and Hopes for More," *NYT*, Mar. 29, 2016.

17. Fall River Office of Economic Development, "Welcome to the Official FROED Website," accessed Aug. 19, 2018, https://web.archive.org/web/20180819001211/http://froed.org/.

18. Murdock, "A Red Carpet for Amazon in Fall River, Mass."

19. Ibid.

20. Harry August and Julia Rock, "Working at an Amazon Warehouse is a Tough Job: It's the First of Many Problems Facing Injured Workers," *BG*, Jul. 24, 2021; Jodi Reed, "Amazon Fulfillment Center in Fall River Says It Prepares all Year for Cyber Monday," Nov. 25, 2022, https://turnto10.com/news/local/amazon-fulfillment-center-in-fall-river-says-its-been-preparing-all-year-for-cyber-monday.

21. Job Advertisement, "Amazon Fulfillment Center Warehouse Associate," Nov. 29, 2022, https://web.archive.org/web/20230323070329/https://www.salary.com/job/amazon-warehouse/amazon-fulfillment-center-warehouse-associate/j202210082017135608138; August and Rock, "Working at an Amazon Warehouse."

22. Data from 2018. See August and Rock, "Working at an Amazon Warehouse."

23. Kevin O'Connor, "Financing Falls into Place for Commonwealth Landing Apartments," *HN*, Nov. 10, 2015.

24. Sean Murphy, "Commission Extends Time for Southeastern Mass. Casinos," *BG*, Mar. 19, 2015; Mike Lawrence, "Promise of Jobs Central to New Bedford Casino Debate," *ST*, Jun. 6, 2015; Sean Murphy, "New Bedford Voters Overwhelmingly Back Casino Proposal," *BG*, Jun. 23, 2015.

25. Sean Murphy, "New Bedford Voters Overwhelmingly Back Casino Proposal."

26. Lawrence, "Promise of Jobs."

27. Knauer, "The Maya of New Bedford," 182; Juravich, *At the Altar of the Bottom Line*, 59.

28. Elizabeth Teitz, "Fall River's Reputation a Challenge in Effort to Attract Younger Crowds at Night," *HN*, Aug. 21, 2015.

29. Steve Urbon, "Worst? Buddy, You Don't Know the Meaning of Worst," *ST*, Jul. 16, 2015; Kyle Scott Clauss, "This '10 Worst Places to Live in Mass.' Ranking Is Just Silly: Is New Bedford Really that Bad?," *Boston Magazine*, Aug. 7, 2015; Nick James, "These Are the 10 Worst Places to Live in Massachusetts," Jul. 9, 2015, http://www.roadsnacks.net/places-in-massachusetts-that-need-a-hug/.

30. Thomas C. Frohlich and Samuel Stebbins, "50 Worst Cities to Live In: 24/7 Wall St.," Jun. 30, 2016, https://www.usatoday.com/story/money/2016/06/30/50-worst-cities-to-live-24-7-wallst/86480244/; Ben Berke, "Find Brockton on this Extremely Detailed Map of Massachusetts' Opioid Crisis," *The Enterprise* (Brockton, MA), Dec. 14, 2020, https://www.enterprisenews.com/story/news/drugs/opioid-crisis/2020/12/14/opioids-massachusetts-2020-brockton-detailed-map-crisis-epidemic/6448407002/; Michael Silvia, "New Bedford and Fall River Ranked in Top Ten Most Dangerous Cities in Massachusetts," Mar. 11, 2023, https://www.newbedfordguide.com/new-bedford-ranked-3rd-most-dangerous-city-massachusetts/2023/03/11.

31. Donald J. Trump, "Remarks on Signing the National Manufacturing Day Proclamation," Oct. 6, 2017, https://www.presidency.ucsb.edu/documents/remarks-signing-the-national-manufacturing-day-proclamation.

32. Barack Obama, "Blueprint for an America Built to Last," Jan. 24, 2012, https://obamawhitehouse.archives.gov/blueprint; Barack Obama, "Remarks by the President in State of the Union Address," Jan. 24, 2012, https://www.whitehouse.gov/the-press-office/2012/01/24/remarks-president-state-union-address.

33. "The Biden Plan to Ensure the Future Is 'Made in All of America' by all of America's Workers," accessed Nov. 3, 2020, https://web.archive.org/web/20201103001712/https://joebiden.com/made-in-america/#.

34. Cowie and Salvatore, "The Long Exception"; Jefferson Cowie and Joseph Heathcott, "Introduction: The Meanings of Deindustrialization," in Cowie and Heathcott, *Beyond the Ruins*, 14–15.

35. On the "ideological" explanation of the origins of "modern economic growth," see Rostow, *Stages of Economic Growth*; Mokyr, "The Intellectual Origins of Modern Economic Growth." On the "institutional" explanation, see Acemoglu et al., "The Rise of Europe." On the "cultural" explanation, see Ashton, *The Industrial Revolution*; Clark, *A Farewell to Alms*. On the "technological" explanation, see Landes, *The Unbound Prometheus*. On the "resource" explanation, see Pomeranz, *The Great Divergence*.

36. Bell, *The Coming of Post-Industrial Society*; Brady et al., "The Consequences of Economic Globalization"; Kollmeyer, "Explaining Deindustrialization."

Bibliography

All translations by author unless otherwise noted.

MANUSCRIPT COLLECTIONS

Arthur and Elizabeth Schlesinger Library on the History of Women in America, Radcliffe Institute for Advanced Study, Harvard University, Cambridge, Massachusetts
  Consumers' League of Massachusetts Records, 1891–1955

Ambrose F. Keeley Library, Fall River, Massachusetts

Arquivo Nacional Torre do Tombo, Lisbon, Portugal
  Arquivo Histórico do Ministério dos Negócios Estrangeiros, Repartição dos Negócios Políticos
  Arquivo Salazar
  Fundo: Ministério do Interior 1910/1983

Baker Library Historical Collections, Harvard Business School, Boston, Massachusetts
  Account Books and Other Material Relating to the Whaling Industry Chiefly from New Bedford and Nantucket, Mass., 1774–1922, MSS 252
  Annawan Manufactory Series, Fall River Iron Works Collection, MSS 5
  Boston Manufacturing Company Records, MSS 442
  Coolidge Family Business Records, 1857–1938, MSS 8993
  Charles W. Morgan Business Records, MSS 252
  Kidder, Peabody & Co. Papers, MSS 783
  Lawrence Manufacturing Company Records, 1831–1955, MSS 442
  Merrimack Mfg. Co. Papers, MSS 442
  Metacomet Series, Fall River Iron Works Collection, MSS 5

Biblioteca Nacional de Portugal, Lisbon, Portugal

Biblioteca Pública e Arquivo Regional de Ponta Delgada, Ponta Delgada, São Miguel, Açores
Arquivo da Administração do Concelho de Povoação
Arquivo da Administração do Concelho de Lagôa
Arquivo do Governo Civil do Distrito de Ponta Delgada
Arquivo da Sociedade Promotora da Agricultura Micaelense
Fundo Particular de Eugénio do Canto
Fundo Particular de Ernesto Rodolfo Hintze Ribeiro
Fundo Particular de Teófilo Braga

French Institute, Emmanuel d'Alzon Library, Assumption College, Worcester, Massachusetts
Oral History Project Coordinated by Josephine Perrault, 1981–1984

Houghton Library, Harvard University, Cambridge, Massachusetts
Daniel B. Fearing Logbook Collection, 1816–1882

International Institute of Social History, Amsterdam, Netherlands
International Confederation of Free Trade Union Archives, 1949–1993
International Textile, Garment and Leather Workers' Federation Collection

Kheel Center for Labor-Management Documentation and Archives, Cornell University Library, Ithaca, New York
ACTWU Fall River Local Minute Books on Microfilm, 1949–1977, Coll. No. 5665 mf
Amalgamated Clothing Workers of America Records, 1914–1980, Coll. No. 5619
International Ladies' Garment Workers' Union: David Dubinsky, President's Records, 1932–1966, Coll. No. 5780/002
International Ladies' Garment Workers' Union, Frederick F. Umhey, Executive Secretary, Collection, Coll. No. 5780/005
International Ladies' Garment Workers' Union Publications, Coll. No. 5780 PUBS
International Ladies' Garment Workers' Union: Sol Chaikin Papers, 1940–1986, Coll. No. 5780/083

Archives and Special Collections, London School of Economics and Political Science, London, United Kingdom
[Sidney and Beatrice] Webb Trade Union [Collection]

Rare Books and Special Collections, McGill University Library, Montréal, Canada
Canadien Collection

Massachusetts Historical Society, Boston, Massachusetts

New Bedford Free Public Library, New Bedford, Massachusetts
  Mayor Ashley Scrapbooks
  William J. Potter Sermons

New Bedford Whaling Museum Research Library, New Bedford, Massachusetts
  Thomas Bennett Jr. Papers, Bennett Family Papers, MSS 9
  Hathaway Family Business Records, MSS 8
  Jonathan Bourne Jr. Business Records, MSS 18
  New Bedford Rayon, Inc., Records, 1926–1974, MSS 25
  New Bedford Area Chamber of Commerce Records, 1961–1969, New Bedford
  Rayon, Inc. Records, MSS 25
  Pierce Manufacturing Corporation Records, 1892–1944, MSS 3
  Purrington Oral History Collection

Peabody Essex Museum, Salem, Massachusetts

John Rylands Library, University of Manchester, Manchester, United Kingdom
  Archive of the Amalgamated Association of Operative Cotton Spinners and
  Twiners [of Lancashire and Adjoining Counties], GB 133 ACS
  Archives of the Operative Cotton Spinners and Twiners' Provincial Association of
  Bolton and Surrounding Districts, GB 133 BCS

University of Massachusetts Amherst Special Collections, Amherst, Massachusetts
  ACTWU: New England Regional Joint Board, MS 241
  Amalgamated Clothing Workers of America, Boston Joint Board, MS 2
  Amalgamated Clothing Workers of America, New England Joint Board, MS 193
  [Fall River] Loom Fixers Association Records, 1895–1917, MS 3
  Yarn Finishers Union (Fall River, Mass.) Records, 1919–1922, MS 6
  Textile Workers Union of America, New Bedford Joint Board Records, MS 134

Ferreira-Mendes Portuguese-American Archives, University of Massachusetts
Dartmouth, Dartmouth, Massachusetts
  Portuguese Alliance Benevolent Association (Associação Beneficente Aliança
  Portuguesa) Records, 1924–2004, MC 50/PAA
  The Carlton M. Viveiros Papers, MC 86/PAA
  João Rocha Papers, MC 100/PAA
  Oral History Project, 1987–1990, MC 24/PAA

Claire T. Carney Library Archives and Special Collections, University of Massachusetts
Dartmouth, Dartmouth, Massachusetts
  New Bedford Textile Worker's Strike of 1928 Oral History Interviews and Research
  Collection, MC 9
  Southeastern Massachusetts Regional Economic Development Collection, MC 196

Archives and Special Collections, University of Pittsburgh Library System, Pittsburgh, PA

  UE [United Electrical, Radio and Machine Workers of America] Local 277 Records [New Bedford, MA], Coll. No. UE.16.277

  Records of United Electrical, Radio and Machine Workers of America Local 284, New Bedford, Massachusetts, 1970s–1990s, Coll. No. US-PPiU-UE16-284

  UE [United Electrical, Radio and Machine Workers of America] District 2 Records, 1950s–1980s, Coll. No. UE.15.2

Widener Library, Harvard University, Cambridge, Massachusetts

  Henry Beetle Hough Scrapbook, 1898 Textile Strike in New Bedford, Massachusetts Open Collections Program

NEWSPAPERS AND PERIODICALS

A Alvorada (New Bedford)
AIM Industrial News (Published by the Associated Industries of Massachusetts)
Açoriano Oriental (Ponta Delgada, Açores)
American Wool and Cotton Reporter
Boston Daily Globe
Boston Daily Reporter
Boston Globe
Barron's National Business and Financial Weekly
Diario Dos Açores (Ponta Delgada, Açores)
Diário de Notícias (New Bedford)
Evening Standard (New Bedford)
Fall River Herald News (Fall River)
Herald News (Fall River)
Industrial Development: National Magazine of Area Analysis and Business Site Selection
Industry (Published by the Associated Industries of Massachusetts)
Industrial News Reporter
Industry: A Weekly Journal of Industrial Information (Published by the Associated Industries of Massachusetts)
Morning Mercury (New Bedford)
New Bedford Times (New Bedford)
New York Times
Providence Business News
Sunday Standard (New Bedford)
Standard-Times (New Bedford)
Washington Post
Wall Street Journal
Whalemen's Shipping Log and Merchants' Transcript (New Bedford)

PUBLISHED PRIMARY SOURCES

AAMA, American Apparel Manufacturers Association. *The MFA and the American Apparel Industry*. Arlington, VA: American Apparel Manufacturers Association, 1978.

AAMA, American Apparel Manufacturers Association, and Carl Priestland. *Focus: Economic Profile of the Apparel Industry*. Arlington, VA: American Apparel Manufacturers Association, 1976.

Açores, Região Autónoma dos. *A Ilha no Mundo: Exposição sobre a Emigração Açoriana*. Angra do Heroísmo, 1989.

Adamic, Louis. "Tragic Towns of New England." *Harper's Magazine*, May 1931.

Adams, Henry. *Henry Adams, Selected Letters*. Edited by Ernest Samuels. Cambridge, MA: Harvard University Press, 1992.

AFASS, American and Foreign Anti-Slavery Society. *The Thirteenth Annual Report of the American and Foreign Anti-Slavery Society: Presented at New York, May 11, 1853*. New York, 1853.

Aguiar, Cristóvão de. *Alguns Dados sobre a Emigração Açoriana*. Coimbra: Vértice, 1976.

AIM, Associated Industries of Massachusetts. *The Move to New Hampshire, 1950 to 1970*. Boston: AIM, 1977.

Almanac Singers, Woody Guthrie, Peter Seeger, Peter Hawes, Lee Hays, and Millard Lampbell. *Deep Sea Chanteys and Whaling Ballads*. New York: General Records, 1941.

Amoskeag Manufacturing Company. *The Amoskeag Manufacturing Co. of Manchester, New Hampshire: A History*. Manchester, NH: Amoskeag Manufacturing Company, 1915.

Andrade, Laurinda C. *The Open Door*. New Bedford: Reynolds-De Walt, 1968.

Andrews, Norwood Jr. "Proceedings of the Vanderbilt Invitational Conference on High School Portuguese." US Department of Health, Education, and Welfare, Jan. 1970. https://web.archive.org/web/20200711173318/http://files.eric.ed.gov/fulltext/ED035868.pdf.

Anson, Robert Sam. "Hurricane Charlie." *Vanity Fair*, Apr. 2001. https://www.vanityfair.com/magazine/2015/02/archive-march-2015-charlie-bluhdorn.

Appleton, Nathan. *Introduction of the Power Loom and Origin of Lowell*. Lowell: B. H. Penhallow, 1858.

Appleton, Nathan. *Memoir of the Hon. Abbott Lawrence: Prepared for the Massachusetts Historical Society*. Boston: J. H. Eastburn's Press, 1856.

Appleton, William. *Selections from the Diaries of William Appleton, 1786–1862*. Boston: Merrymount Press, 1922.

"Art. IV, Review." *British Quarterly Review* 41 (Apr. 1864).

Atkins, Chester G. *There Is More Than One Massachusetts Economy: A Study of Massachusetts Private Sector Employment*. [Boston]: Massachusetts Senate Committee on Ways and Means, 1984.

Atkins, Thomas Irving. "Report and Recommendations of Boston City Councilor, Thomas Atkins, to Governor Sargent Re: Racial Problems in New Bedford," 1970. Typewritten Manuscript, Harvard Law School Library, Cambridge, Massachusetts.

Ayer, James Cook. *Some of the Uses and Abuses in the Management of Our Manufacturing Corporations.* Lowell: C. M. Langley and Co., 1863.

Barnes, Ruth, ed. *I Hear America Singing: An Anthology of Folk Poetry.* Chicago: John C. Winston, 1937.

Baxter, C. H. *History of the Fall River Strike: Being a Full and Complete Report of the Labor Troubles from 1873, to April 5th, 1875.* Edited by "John Smith." Fall River: Clark and Co., 1875.

BCG, Boston Consulting Group. The Power of Diversified Companies During Crises, 2012. https://web.archive.org/web/20190713105741/https://image-src.bcg.com/Images/BCG_The_Power_of_Diversified_Companies_During_Crises_Jan_12_t cm9-106136.pdf.

Beal, Fred Erwin. *Proletarian Journey: New England, Gastonia, Moscow.* New York: Hillman-Curl, 1937.

Beers, J. H. and Company. *Representative Men and Old Families of Rhode Island.* Chicago: J. H. Beers and Company, 1908.

Beers, J. H. and Company. *Representative Men and Old Families of Southeastern Massachusetts.* Vol. 3. Chicago: J. H. Beers and Company, 1912.

Berman, Norton L. "Future Trends in Economic Development." *Vital Speeches of the Day* 51, no. 22 (1985): 691–94.

Blake, William. "And Did Those Feet in Ancient Time." In *Blake: Selected Poems,* edited by Mike Davis and Alan Pound. Oxford: Heinemen Educational, 1996.

Blanshard, Paul. "New Bedford Carries On." *Nation* 126, no. 3285 (Jun. 20, 1928): 692–693.

Bolton, Brian, and ITGLWF, International Textile, Garment, and Leather Workers' Federation. *The MNCs in the Textile, Garment, and Leather Industries.* Dublin: International Textile, Garment and Leather Workers' Federation, 1976.

Boston Board of Trade. *Tenth Annual Report of the Government . . . on the 13th January, 1864.* Boston: T. R. Marvin and Son, 1864.

Bradlaugh, Charles. "Hints to Emigrants to the United States." In *Miscellanies.* London: A. and H. Bradlaugh Bonner, 1899.

Brierley, Ben. *Ab-o'th'-Yate in Yankeeland: The Results of Two Trips to America.* Manchester: Abel Heywood and Son, 1885.

Brooks, Mel. *Silent Movie.* Crossbow Productions, 1976.

Camara, Manoel Jaçintho da. *Almanach do Campeão Popular para 1894.* Ponta Delgada, 1893.

Camara, Manoel Jaçintho da. *Almanach do Campeão Popular para 1895.* Ponta Delgada, 1894.

Canada, Department of Agriculture. *Reports of Tenant Farmers' Delegates on the Dominion of Canada as a Field for Settlement.* Liverpool: Turner and Dunnett, 1880.

Carvalho, Henrique Martins de. *Possibilidade de Deslocação de Mão-de-Obra Portuguesa para o Continente* . . . Lisboa: Centro de Estudos de Serviço e Desenvolvimento Comunitário, 1973.

Commons, John R., Ulrich B. Phillips, Eugene A. Gilmore, Helen L. Sumner, and John B. Andrews, eds. *A Documentary History of American Industrial Society*. Vol. 7. Cleveland: Arthur H. Clark, 1910.

Coolidge, Thomas Jefferson. *Autobiography of T. Jefferson Coolidge: Drawn in Great Part from His Diary and Brought Down to the Year MDCCCC*. Boston: Merrymount Press, 1901.

Cowley, Charles. *Illustrated History of Lowell*. Boston: Lee and Shepard, 1868.

Cowley, Charles. *Reminiscences of James C. Ayer*. Lowell: Penhallow Printing Company, 1880.

Cowley, Charles. "The Foreign Colonies of Lowell, by Charles Cowley . . . Read Feb. 15, 1881." *Contributions of the Old Residents' Historical Association* 2, no. 2 (1882).

Crone, Harry, and David Gingold. *35 Northeast: A Short History of the Northeast Department, International Ladies' Garment Workers' Union, AFL-CIO*. New York: Northeast Department, International Ladies' Garment Workers' Union, 1970.

Cronin, Edward. *Election Statistics: The Commonwealth of Massachusetts, 1952*. Office of Secretary of the Commonwealth, 1952. http://hdl.handle.net/2452/43444.

D'Arles, Henri. "Ferdinand Gagnon et la survivance fraçaise aux États-Unis." *L'Action française* 3, no. 4 (Apr. 1919).

Doherty, Barbara. *The Struggle to Save Morse Cutting Tool: A Successful Community Campaign*. North Dartmouth: Arnold M. Dubin Labor Education Center, Southeastern Massachusetts University, 1986.

Douglass, Frederick. *Life and Times of Frederick Douglass*. Boston: De Wolfe, Fiske and Co., 1892.

Douglass, Frederick. *My Bondage and My Freedom*. New York: Miller, Orton and Mulligan, 1855.

Dreier, Thomas. *The Story of Three Partners: United Shoe Machinery Company, Beverley, Mass. USA*. Boston: Barta Press, 1911.

Dubinsky, David. "Rift and Realignment in World Labor." *Foreign Affairs*, Jan. 1949.

Dubinsky, David. "World Labor's New Weapon." *Foreign Affairs*, Apr. 1950.

Dugré, Adélard. "Mgr. LaFleche: Le patriote." *L'Action française* 12, no. 3 (Sep. 1924).

Dukakis, Michael, and Rosabeth Kanter. *Creating the Future: The Massachusetts Comeback and Its Promise for America*. New York: Summit Books, 1988.

Eisler, Benita, ed. *The Lowell Offering: Writings by New England Mill Women, 1840–1845*. New York: Norton, 1977.

Fairchild, Henry Pratt. "The Literacy Test and Its Making." *Quarterly Journal of Economics* 31, no. 3 (May 1917): 447–460.

Foster, E. Everton. *Lamb's Textile Industries of the United States*. Boston: James H. Lamb, 1916.

Friedman, Milton. "The Social Responsibility of Business Is to Increase Its Profits." *New York Times Magazine*, Sep. 13, 1970. https://www.nytimes.com/1970/09/13/archives/article-15-no-title.html.

Gagnon, Ferdinand. *Ferdinand Gagnon, sa vie et ses œuvres . . .* Edited by Benjamin Sulte. Worcester, MA: O. Lawrence, 1886.

Golden, John. "Pay of Labor in New England Cotton Mills." *Annals of the American Academy of Political and Social Science* 33, no. 2 (1909): 77–82.

Great Britain, Foreign Office. *Reports from Her Majesty's Consuls on the Manufactures, Commerce, &c. of their Consular Districts.* Harrison and Sons, 1864.

Great Britain, Gold and Silver Commission. *Second Report of the Royal Commission Appointed to Inquire into the Recent Changes in the Relative Values of Precious Metals.* London, 1888.

Grieve, Robert, ed. *New Bedford Semi-Centennial Souvenir.* Providence: Journal of Commerce Co., 1897.

Gunton, George. *Wealth and Progress: A Critical Examination of the Wages Question.* 7th ed. New York: D. Appleton, 1897.

Hall, Henry, ed. *America's Successful Men of Affairs.* Vol. 2. [New York]: *New York Tribune*, 1896.

Harrison, Bennett. "Gulf + Western: A Model of Conglomerate Disinvestment." *Labor Research Review* 1, no. 1 (Sep. 1982). https://hdl.handle.net/1813/102404.

Hathaway, Horatio. *A New Bedford Merchant: Being Notes Taken from Records in the Office of the Late Thomas Schuyler Hathaway.* Boston, 1930.

Hémon, Louis. *Maria Chapdelaine.* Translated by W. H. Blake. New York: Macmillan, 1922.

Hough, George, and New Bedford Board of Trade. *New Bedford, Massachusetts: Its History, Industries, Institutions and Attractions.* Mercury Publishing Company, 1889.

Hough, Henry Beetle. *Wamsutta of New Bedford, 1846–1946: A Story of New England Enterprise.* New Bedford, 1946.

"How the Distress Is Relieved in Preston." *The Quiver*, March 21, 1863.

ICA, Industrial Cooperative Association. "Investment and Strategy at Morse Cutting Tool." *Labor Research Review* 1, no. 1 (Sep. 1982). https://hdl.handle.net/1813/102405.

ICE, Immigration and Customs Enforcement. "New Bedford Manufacturer and Managers Arrested on Charges of Conspiring." News Release, Mar. 6, 2007. https://www.aila.org/File/DownloadEmbeddedFile/51503.

ICFTU, International Confederation of Free Trade Unions and Free World Labour Conference. *Official Report of the Free World Labour Conference and the First Congress of the International Confederation of Free Trade Unions, London, November–December, 1949.* London: British Trades Union Congress, 1949.

ICFTU, International Confederation of Free Trade Unions. *The Need for a Dynamic World Economy: Report of the World Economic Conference of Free Trade Unions (Geneva 18–19 March 1959).* Brussels, 1959.

ICFTU, International Confederation of Free Trade Unions. *Training the World's Trade Unionists: A Survey of Five Years of ICFTU Educational Work.* Brussels: International Confederation of Free Trade Unions, 1956.

ILO, International Labour Organization. "Globalization Changes the Face of Textile, Clothing and Footwear Industries." Press Release, Oct. 28, 1996. http://www.ilo. org/global/about-the-ilo/newsroom/news/WCMS_008075/lang--en/index.htm.

Jacobs, Jerry. *Bidding for Business: Corporate Auctions and the 50 Disunited States.* Washington, DC: Public Interest Research Group, 1979.

Jefferson, Thomas. *Notes on the State of Virginia.* London: John Stockdale, 1787.

Kavanaugh, Gerry. *Race, Politics, and Basketball: A Cultural Education of Everyday Life.* Rotterdam: Sense Publishers, 2017.

Kennedy, Edward M. "The Immigration Act of 1965." *Annals of the American Academy of Political and Social Science* 367 (Sep. 1966): 137–49.

Korda, Michael. "Annals of Tycoonery: The Last Business Eccentric." *New Yorker*, Dec. 9, 1996. https://www.newyorker.com/magazine/1996/12/16/the-last-business-eccentric.

Laflamme, J. L. K. "Les Canadiens aux États-Unis." *La Revue Canadienne* 37 (Jun. 1901).

Lampe, David, ed. *The Massachusetts Miracle: High Technology and Economic Revitalization.* Cambridge, MA: MIT Press, 1988.

"Lancashire in 1862." *National Review* 16, no. 31 (Jan. 1863).

Lawrence Manufacturing Company. "General Regulations to Be Observed by Persons Employed by the Lawrence Manufacturing Company in Lowell," May 21, 1833. http://id.lib.harvard.edu/aleph/007330061/catalog.

Lawrence Manufacturing Company. "Regulations to Be Observed by All Persons Employed by the Lawrence Manufacturing Company," ca 1842. http://id.lib.harv ard.edu/aleph/007330061/catalog.

Lawrence, William, ed. *Extracts from the Diary and Correspondence of the Late Amos Lawrence.* Boston: Gould and Lincoln, 1856.

Lawrence, William, ed. "Memoir of Amos Adams Lawrence." In *Proceedings of the Massachusetts Historical Society*, Vol. 12. Boston, 1899.

Levin, Melvin R., and David A. Grossman. *Employment and Economic Trends in Southeastern Massachusetts, 1950–1970.* Boston: Southeastern Massachusetts Regional Planning Program, 1959.

Lima, Alfred J., ed. *America's Voices: An Oral History of Fall River Massachusetts, from 1900–1950.* Fall River: PearTree Press, 2014.

Lincoln, Jonathan Thayer. *The City of the Dinner-Pail.* Boston: Houghton Mifflin, 1909.

Little, Royal. *How to Lose $100,000,000 and Other Valuable Advice.* Boston: Little, Brown, 1979.

Lowell, John A. "Patrick Tracy Jackson." In *Lives of American Merchants*, edited by Freeman Hunt, Vol. 1. New York: Derby and Jackson, 1858.

Manning Company, H. A. *Manning's Greenough New Bedford and Fairhaven (Massachusetts) Directory . . . 1936.* Vol. 64. Boston: H. A. Manning, 1936.

Manning Company. *Manning's New Bedford and Fairhaven (Massachusetts) Directory . . . 1941.* Vol. 68. Boston: H. A. Manning, 1941.

Manning Company. *Manning's New Bedford and Fairhaven (Massachusetts) Directory . . . 1945.* Vol. 70. Boston: H. A. Manning, 1945.

Martins, J. P. Oliveira. *Projecto de Lei de Fomento Rural*. Lisboa: Imprensa Nacional, 1887.

Massachusetts, Advisory Committee to the United States Commission on Civil Rights. "The Six-District Plan. Integration of the Springfield, Mass., Elementary Schools," Mar. 1976. https://eric.ed.gov/?id=ED133389.

Massachusetts, Board to Investigate the Subject of the Unemployed. *Report of the Massachusetts Board to Investigate the Subject of the Unemploy*ed . . . *March 13, 1895*. Boston: Wright and Potter, 1895.

Massachusetts, Department of Commerce and Development. *Massachusetts Business Incentives: Creating a Better Economic Climate*. Boston: Massachusetts Department of Commerce and Development, 1977.

Massachusetts, Department of Commerce and Development. *Massachusetts . . . Creating the Future*. Boston, 1983.

Massachusetts, Department of Commerce and Development and Fantus Company. *An Evaluation of Massachusetts' Changing Attitude Toward Industry*. South Orange, NJ: Fantus, 1978.

Massachusetts, Department of Commerce and Development, Provandie and Chirurg, and Harbridge House. *Make It in Massachusetts*. Boston, 1979.

Massachusetts, Department of Commerce and Development. *Massachusetts in Perspective*. Boston, 1977. http://archive.org/details/massachusettsinpoomass.

MBSL, Massachusetts Bureau of Statistics of Labor. *Eleventh Annual Report . . . January, 1880*. Boston: Rand, Avery, and Co, 1880.

MBSL, Massachusetts Bureau of Statistics of Labor. *Forty-First Annual Report of the Statistics of Labor for the Year 1910*. Boston: Wright and Potter, 1911.

MBSL, Massachusetts Bureau of Statistics of Labor. *Forty-Third Annual Report . . . 1912*. Boston: Wright and Potter, 1913.

MBSL, Massachusetts Bureau of Statistics of Labor. *Report of the Bureau of Statistics of Labor . . . from August 2, 1869, to March 1, 1870* . . . Boston: Wright and Potter, 1870.

MBSL, Massachusetts Bureau of Statistics of Labor. *Sixth Annual Report of the Bureau of Statistics of Labor, March, 1875*. Boston: Wright and Potter, 1875.

MBSL, Massachusetts Bureau of Statistics of Labor. *The Annual Statistics of Manufactures: 1891*. Boston: Wright and Potter, 1892.

MBSL, Massachusetts Bureau of Statistics of Labor. *Thirteenth Annual Report . . . March, 1882*. Boston: Rand, Avery, and Co, 1882.

MBSL, Massachusetts Bureau of Statistics of Labor. *Twelfth Annual Report . . . January, 1881*. Boston: Rand, Avery, and Co, 1881.

MBSL, Massachusetts Bureau of Statistics of Labor *Twenty-Seventh Annual Report . . . 1897*. Boston: Wright and Potter, 1897.

McCabe, Marsha, Joseph D. Thomas, Tracy A. Furtado, and Jay Avila, eds. *Portuguese Spinner, an American Story: Stories of History, Culture, and Life from Portuguese Americans in Southeastern New England*. New Bedford: Spinner, 1998.

MDIC, Massachusetts Development and Industrial Commission. *In Black and White: The Facts Concerning Industrial Advantages in Massachusetts*. Boston, 1937.

MDIC, Massachusetts Development and Industrial Commission. *The Facts Concerning Industrial Advantages in Massachusetts*. Boston, 1940.

MDIC, Massachusetts Development and Industrial Commission. *The Facts Concerning Industrial Advantages in Massachusetts*. Boston, 1945.

Melville, Herman. *Moby-Dick*. New American Library, 1892.

Miernyk, William. *Inter-Industry Labor Mobility: The Case of the Displaced Textile Worker*. Boston: Bureau of Business and Economic Research, Northeastern University, 1955.

Miles, Henry A. *Lowell, as It Was. And as It Is*. Lowell: Powers and Bagley, 1845.

Morse, John T. Jr. "Memoir of Henry Lee Higginson." In *Proceedings of the Massachusetts Historical Society*. Vol. 3. Boston, 1920.

Nason, Elias. *A Gazetteer of the State of Massachusetts*. Boston: B. B. Russell, 1874.

National Archives Project, Works Project Administration. *Ship Registers of New Bedford, Massachusetts*. Vol. 2. Boston: National Archives Project, 1940.

New Bedford, Department of Planning, Housing and Community Development. "Staff Report: Planning Board Meeting, March 8, 2017," 2017. https://web.archive.org/web/20230920204955/http://s3.amazonaws.com/newbedford-ma/wp-content/uploads/sites/46/20191219214451/Case-03-17-and-Case-04-17-Apartments-on-the-Cove-Staff-Reports-Attachments.pdf.

New Bedford, Massachusetts. *1872—City Document No. 1, Inaugural Address of George B. Richmond . . . Jan. 1, 1872*. New Bedford: E. Anthony and Sons, 1872.

New Bedford, Massachusetts. *City Documents: Mayor's Address to the City Council; City Government; and Reports of Committees . . . For the Year 1861–1862*. New Bedford: Fessenden and Baker, 1862.

New Bedford, Massachusetts. *City Documents of New Bedford*. New Bedford: E. Anthony and Sons, 1876.

New Bedford, Massachusetts. *City Documents . . . 1862–1863*. New Bedford: Fessenden and Baker, 1863.

New Bedford, Massachusetts. *City Documents . . . 1864–1865*. New Bedford: Fessenden and Baker, 1865.

New Bedford, Massachusetts. *City Documents . . . 1867–1868*. New Bedford: E. Anthony and Sons, 1868.

New Bedford, Massachusetts. *City Documents . . . 1868–1869*. New Bedford: Fessenden and Baker, 1869.

New Bedford, Massachusetts. *City Documents . . . 1869–1870*. New Bedford: E. Anthony and Sons, 1870.

New Bedford, Massachusetts. *Forty-Fourth Annual Report of the New Bedford Water Board to the City Council*. New Bedford, 1914.

New Bedford, Massachusetts. Historic Mill Inventory, 2008. https://web.archive.org/web/20220401153819/http://s3.amazonaws.com/newbedford-ma/wp-content/uploads/sites/46/20191219215803/NB_MillInventory08.pdf.

New Bedford, Massachusetts. *New Bedford City Documents*. New Bedford: Mercury Publishing Company, 1877.

New Bedford, Massachusetts. *Ordinances and Rules and Orders of the City of New Bedford*. New Bedford: E. Anthony and Sons, 1884.

"Notes on New Bedford." In *Collections of the Massachusetts Historical Society*, Vol. 3. Series 2. Boston: Freeman and Bolles, 1815.

NPS, National Park Service. "National Register of Historic Places . . . Boston Manufacturing Company," Jun. 1977. https://web.archive.org/web/20170222205 733/https://npgallery.nps.gov/pdfhost/docs/NHLS/Text/77001412.pdf.

Park, Robert E. "Review: Two Portuguese Communities in New England." *American Journal of Sociology* 31, no. 2 (1925): 272.

Pearce, Benjamin Wood. *Recollections of a Long and Busy Life, 1819–1890*. Newport, RI: B. W. Pearce, 1890.

Portugal. *Annuario da Direcção Geral de Administração Politica e Civil*. Lisboa: Imprensa Nacional, 1896.

Portugal, Secretariado da Propaganda Nacional. *Portugal: The New State in Theory and in Practice*. Lisboa: Editorial Império Limitada, 1939.

Quebec. *General Report of the Commissioner of Agriculture and Public Works of the Province of Quebec, For the Year Ending on the 30th of June 1876*. Quebec: Charles Fraçois Langlois, 1876.

Ramos, Lucy, and John C. Reardon. "Black, White or Portuguese? A Cape Verdean Dilemma." *Spinner: People and Culture in Southeastern Massachusetts* 1 (1981).

Ribeiro, Gerald. *This Path I Took*. Edited by Robert French. iUniverse, 2005.

Ribeiro, Luís da Silva. *O Emigrante Açoreano*. Ponta Delgada, 1940.

Ricketson, Daniel. *The History of New Bedford, Bristol County, Massachusetts . . .* New Bedford: Published by the Author, 1858.

Robidoux, Ferdinand J., ed. *Conventions nationales des Acadiens: recueil des travaux et délibérations des six premières conventions*. Shédiac, NB, 1907.

Rouillard, Jacques. *Ah les États! Les travailleurs canadiens-français dans l'industrie textile de la Nouvelle-Angleterre d'après le témoignage des derniers migrants*. Montréal: Boréal Express, 1985.

Ruby-Frye, Thelma. *Double or Nothing: Two Lives in the Theatre: The Autobiography of Thelma Ruby and Peter Frye*. London: Janus, 1997.

Rumelt, Richard P. "Diversification Strategy and Profitability." *Strategic Management Journal* 3, no. 4 (1982): 359–369.

"Say Brother." New Bedford. Boston, MA: WGBH, 1970. https://search.alexanderstr eet.com/view/work/bibliographic_entity%7Cvideo_work%7C2785687.

Silva Junior, Francisco José da. *A Emancipação dos Açores*. Lisboa: Typographia Universal, 1871.

Silvia, Philip T. Jr., ed. *Victorian Vistas: Fall River, 1865–1885: As Viewed Through Its Newspaper Accounts*. Fall River: R. E. Smith Print. Co., 1987.

Silvia, Philip T. Jr., ed. *Victorian Vistas: Fall River, 1886–1900: As Viewed Through Its Newspaper Accounts*. Fall River: R. E. Smith Print. Co., 1988.

Silvia, Philip T. Jr., ed. *Victorian Vistas: Fall River, 1901–1911: As Viewed Through Its Newspaper Accounts*. Fall River: R. E. Smith Print. Co., 1992.

Société générale de colonisation et de rapatriement de la province de Québec. *Rapport annuel de l'agent général de la société générale de colonisation et de rapatriement de la province de Québec*. Ottawa, 1895. https://www.canadiana.ca/view/oocihm.8_00974_1/5.

Stanton, Seabury. *Berkshire Hathaway, Inc.: A Saga of Courage*. Newcomen Address, 1962. New York: Newcomen Society in North America, 1962.

Sweetser, M. F. *New England: A Handbook for Travellers . . .* 7th ed. Boston: James R. Osgood and Co., 1883.

Swinney, Dan. "UE Local 277's Strike at Morse Cutting Tool." *Labor Research Review* 1, no. 1 (Sep. 1982). https://hdl.handle.net/1813/102403.

Taft, Donald R. *Two Portuguese Communities in New England*. New York, 1923.

TBR, The Business Roundtable. "Statement on Corporate Governance," Sep. 1997. https://web.archive.org/web/20230128074353/http://www.ralphgomory.com/wp-content/uploads/2018/05/Business-Roundtable-1997.pdf.

TBR, The Business Roundtable. *Statement on Corporate Responsibility*. Business Roundtable, 1981.

United States, Bureau of the Census. *1970 Census of Population and Housing: Census Tracts: New Bedford, Mass., 1972*. https://www2.census.gov/library/publications/decennial/1970/phc-1/39204513p13ch10.pdf.

United States, Bureau of the Census. *1990 Census of Population: General Population Characteristics: Georgia*. Bureau of the Census, 1992.

United States, Bureau of the Census. *Manufactures of the United States in 1860*. Washington, DC: United States Government Printing Office, 1865.

United States, Congress, Joint Economic Committee. *Jobs and Prices in Fall River, Mass: Hearing Before the Joint Economic Committee, Congress of the United States . . . February 15, 1976*. Washington, DC: United States Government Printing Office, 1977.

United States, Department of Homeland Security. *2009 Yearbook of Immigration Statistics*. Washington, DC: United States Office of Immigration Statistics, 2010.

United States, Department of Labor. *History of Wages in the United States from Colonial Times to 1928*. Washington, DC: United States Government Printing Office, 1934.

United States, Department of Labor and United States, Employment Service. *Job Descriptions for the Cotton Textile Industry*. Washington, DC: United States Government Printing Office, 1939.

United States, House of Representatives. *Hearings on General Tariff Revision before the Committee on Ways and Means*. Part IV. Washington, DC: United States Government Printing Office, 1921.

United States, Joint Economic Committee, Congress of the United States. *Industrial Policy, Economic Growth, and the Competitiveness of U.S. Industry*. Washington, DC: United States Government Printing Office, 1983. https://www.jec.senate.gov/public/index.cfm/1984/12/report-b8014291-8dbd-4f1e-84fc-789f21ff4c35.

United States, Senate, Committee on Education and Labor. *Report of the Committee of the Senate upon the Relations Between Labor and Capital and Testimony Taken by the Committee*. Washington, DC: United States Government Printing Office, 1885.

United States, Senate, Committee on the Judiciary. *Extent of Subversion in the "New Left" (Fall River, Mass . . .* Washington, DC: United States Government Printing Office, 1970.

United States, Senate, Immigration Commission. *Reports of the Immigration Commission: Immigrants in Industries*. Vol. 3–4. Washington, DC: United States Government Printing Office, 1911. https://hdl.handle.net/2027/coo1.ark:/13960/t6n01qv9z.

United States, Senate, Subcommittee on Antitrust and Monopoly. *Hearings Before the Subcommittee on Antitrust and Monopoly . . . Appendix to Part 8: Staff Report of the Federal Trade Commission. Economic Report on Corporate Mergers*. Washington, DC: United States Government Printing Office, 1969.

W. A. Greenough Co. *W.A. Greenough Co.'s New Bedford and Fairhaven Directory for the Year Ending November, 1930 . . .* Boston: W. A. Greenough, 1930.

Walker, Walter Frederick. *The Azores: Or Western Islands: A Political, Commercial and Geographical Account . . .* London: Trübner and Co., 1886.

Wall, William Allen. *Wamsutta Mill*. ca. 1850. Painting. Acc. No. 1971.7. New Bedford Whaling Museum.

Watts, John. *The Facts of the Cotton Famine*. London: Simpkin, Marshall and Co., 1866.

Webber, Samuel. *Manual of Power for Machines, Shafts, and Belts: With the History of Cotton Manufacture in the United States*. New York: D. Appleton, 1879.

Welles, Chris. "Charles Bluhdorn: With a Multimillion Reach, Wall Street's 'Mad Austrian' Collects Companies." *Life* 62, no. 10 (Mar. 10, 1967).

Williams, John. *Immigration: A Letter to Peter Cooper, Esq*. New York: Office of Hardware Reporter, 1864.

Winch, Kevin F. *Pensions and Leveraged Buyouts*. Washington, DC: United States Government Printing Office, 1989. http://hdl.handle.net/2027/pst.000014990069.

Windmuller, John P. "Cohesion and Disunity in the ICFTU: The 1965 Amsterdam Congress." *Industrial and Labor Relations Review* 19, no. 3 (April 1966).

Windmuller, John P. "Internationalism in Eclipse: The ICFTU after Two Decades." *Industrial and Labor Relations Review* 23, no. 4 (July 1970): 510.

Young, G. W. "Kilburn Mill 'Mill Nos. 1 & 2' (Cotton Yarn), New Bedford, Mass." Map. Digital Commonwealth, 1933. https://www.digitalcommonwealth.org/search/commonwealth:ww72bz537.

SECONDARY SOURCES

Abad, Ricardo G. "Internal Migration in the Philippines: A Review of Research Findings." *Philippine Studies* 29, no. 2 (Jun. 1981): 129–143.

Abbott, Richard H. *Cotton & Capital: Boston Businessmen and Antislavery Reform, 1854–1868.* Amherst: University of Massachusetts Press, 1991.

Acemoglu, Daron, Simon Johnson, and James Robinson. "The Rise of Europe: Atlantic Trade, Institutional Change, and Economic Growth." *American Economic Review* 95, no. 3 (2005): 546–579.

Alben, Elissa. "GATT and the Fair Wage: A Historical Perspective on the Labor-Trade Link." *Columbia Law Review* 101, no. 6 (Oct. 2001): 1410–1447.

Aldrich, Herbert. "New Bedford." *New England Magazine and Bay State Monthly* 1, no. 5 (May 1886).

Al-Khazraji, Majid, and Emilie Al-Khazraji. *The Puerto Rican Journey to New Bedford, MA.* New Bedford: Action Research Project, 1971.

Allison, Elisabeth. *The Impact of Imports on the Men's Clothing Industry.* Boston: Graduate School of Business Administration, Harvard University, 1977.

Anctil, Pierre. "Aspects of Class Ideology in a New England Ethnic Minority: The Franco-Americans of Woonsocket, Rhode Island (1865–1929)." PhD diss., New School for Social Research, 1980.

Anctil, Pierre. "The Franco-Americans of New England." In *French America: Mobility, Identity, and Minority Experience Across the Continent,* edited by Dean Louder and Eric Waddell. Baton Rouge: Louisiana State University Press, 1993.

Anders, George. *Merchants of Debt: KKR and the Mortgaging of American Business.* New York: Basic Books, 1992.

Appelbaum, Eileen, and Rosemary Batt. *Private Equity at Work: When Wall Street Manages Main Street.* New York: Russell Sage Foundation, 2014.

Appleby, Joyce. "The Popular Sources of American Capitalism." *Studies in American Political Development* 9, no. 2 (Sep. 1995): 437–457.

Arato, Christine A., and Patrick Eleey. *Safely Moored at Last: Cultural Landscape Report for New Bedford Whaling National Historical Park.* Vol. 1. Boston: National Park Service, 1998.

Ashton, T. S. *The Industrial Revolution, 1760–1830.* 2nd ed. Oxford: Oxford University Press, 1998.

Astakhov, Viktor P. *Drills: Science and Technology of Advanced Operations.* Boca Raton, FL: CRC Press, 2014.

Baganha, Maria Ioannis. "From Closed to Open Doors: Portuguese Emigration under the Corporative Regime." *E-Journal of Portuguese History* 1, no. 1 (Summer 2003).

Baganha, Maria Ioannis. *Portuguese Emigration to the United States, 1820–1930.* New York: Garland, 1990.

Baker, George P., and George David Smith. *The New Financial Capitalists: Kohlberg Kravis Roberts and the Creation of Corporate Value.* Cambridge: Cambridge University Press, 1998.

Baptista, Fernando Oliveira. "A Agricultura e a Questão da Terra—Do Estado Novo À Comunidade Europeia." *Análise Social* 29, no. 128 (Jan. 1994): 907–921.

Barkin, Solomon. "Management and Ownership in the New England Cotton Textile Industry." *Journal of Economic Issues* 15, no. 2 (1981): 463–475.

Barrett, James R. "Americanization from the Bottom Up: Immigration and the Remaking of the Working Class in the United States, 1880–1930." *Journal of American History* 79, no. 3 (Dec. 1992): 996–1020.

Barrett, James R., and David R. Roediger. "The Irish and the 'Americanization' of the 'New Immigrants' in the Streets and in the Churches of the Urban United States, 1900–1930." *Journal of American Ethnic History* 24, no. 4 (Jul. 2005): 3–33.

Barron, Hal S. *Those Who Stayed Behind: Rural Society in Nineteenth-Century New England*. Cambridge: Cambridge University Press, 1984.

Beckert, Sven. *Empire of Cotton: A Global History*. New York: Knopf, 2014.

Bell, Daniel. *The Coming of Post-Industrial Society: A Venture in Social Forecasting*. New York: Basic Books, 1976.

Bergquist, Charles. *Labor and the Course of American Democracy: US History in Latin American Perspective*. London: Verso, 1996.

Berkman, Michael B. *The State Roots of National Politics: Congress and the Tax Agenda, 1978–1986*. Pittsburgh: University of Pittsburgh Press, 1994.

Bernard, Roger. *Le travail et l'espoir: Migrations, développement économique et mobilité sociale, Québec/Ontario, 1900–1985*. Hearst: Le Nordir, 1988.

Bernstein, Irving. *The Lean Years: A History of the American Worker, 1920–1933*. Reissue. Chicago: Haymarket Books, 2010.

Bernstein, Irving. *The Turbulent Years: A History of the American Worker, 1933–1940*. Reissue. Chicago: Haymarket Books, 2010.

Berthoff, Rowland. *British Immigrants in Industrial America, 1790–1950*. Cambridge, MA: Harvard University Press, 1953.

Biggs, Brenna. "Twist Drill." In *Technical Innovation in American History: An Encyclopedia of Science and Technology*, edited by Rosanne Welch and Peg A. Lamphier, Vol. 1. Santa Barbara, CA: ABC-CLIO, 2019.

Blackett, R. J. M. *Divided Hearts: Britain and the American Civil War*. Baton Rouge: LSU Press, 2001.

Blewett, Mary H. *Constant Turmoil: The Politics of Industrial Life in Nineteenth-Century New England*. Amherst: University of Massachusetts Press, 2000.

Bloemraad, Irene. "Citizenship, Naturalization and Electoral Success: Putting the Portuguese-American Experience in a Comparative Context." In *Community, Culture and the Makings of Identity: Portuguese-Americans Along the Eastern Seaboard*, edited by Kimberly da Costa Holton and Andrea Klimt. North Dartmouth: University of Massachusetts Dartmouth, Center for Portuguese Studies and Culture, 2009.

Bluestone, Barry, and Bennett Harrison. *The Deindustrialization of America: Plant Closings, Community Abandonment, and the Dismantling of Basic Industry*. New York: Basic Books, 1982.

Bluestone, Barry, and Mary Huff Stevenson. "The Industrial Revolution: From Mill-Based to Mind-Based Industries." In *The Boston Renaissance: Race, Space, and Economic Change in an American Metropolis*. New York: Russell Sage Foundation, 2000.

Bodnar, John. *The Transplanted: A History of Immigrants in Urban America*. Bloomington: Indiana University Press, 1985.

Bookman, Ann. "The Process of Political Socialization Among Women and Immigrant Workers: A Case Study of Unionization in the Electronics Industry." PhD diss., Harvard University, 1977.

Borden, Alanson. *Our Country and Its People: A Descriptive and Biographical Record of Bristol County, Massachusetts*. Vol. 2. Boston History Company, 1899.

Borgwardt, Elizabeth. *A New Deal for the World: America's Vision for Human Rights*. Cambridge, MA: Belknap Press of Harvard University Press, 2007.

Boyle, Kevin. *The UAW and the Heyday of American Liberalism 1945–1968*. Ithaca, NY: Cornell University Press, 1998.

Brady, David, Jason Beckfield, and Wei Zhao. "The Consequences of Economic Globalization for Affluent Democracies." *Annual Review of Sociology* 33 (Jan. 2007): 313–334.

Brayton, Clifford Ross. *Brayton Family History*. Vol. 2. Rochester, NY, 1982.

Brenner, Mark. "The Economy: A Growing Divide with Uneven Prospects." In *The Future of Work in Massachusetts*, edited by Tom Juravich. Amherst: University of Massachusetts Press, 2007.

Briggs, Vernon M. Jr. "Mass Immigration, Free Trade and the Forgotten American Worker." *In Defense of the Alien* 17 (Jan. 1994): 20–32.

Brinkley, Alan. *The End of Reform: New Deal Liberalism in Recession and War*. New York: Alfred A. Knopf, 1995.

Brooks, Stephen. "Canada-United States Relations." In *The Oxford Handbook of Canadian Politics*, edited by John C. Courtney and David E. Smith. New York: Oxford University Press, 2010.

Brown, Fidelia O. "Decline and Fall: The End of a Dream." In *Cotton Was King: A History of Lowell, Massachusetts*, edited by Arthur Eno. Somersworth: New Hampshire Publishing, 1976.

Bullard, John M. *The Rotches*. New Bedford: 1947.

Burgin, Angus. *The Great Persuasion: Reinventing Free Markets Since the Depression*. Cambridge, MA: Harvard University Press, 2012.

Byers, Edward. *The Nation of Nantucket: Society and Politics in an Early American Commercial Center, 1660–1820*. Boston: Northeastern University Press, 1987.

Cabral, Stephen L. *Tradition and Transformation: Portuguese Feasting in New Bedford*. New York: AMS Press, 1989.

Cairo, Heriberto. "'Portugal Is Not a Small Country': Maps and Propaganda in the Salazar Regime." *Geopolitics* 11, no. 3 (Sep. 2006): 367–395.

Caldentey, Esteban Pérez. "The Concept and Evolution of the Developmental State." *International Journal of Political Economy* 37, no. 3 (Oct. 2008): 27–53.

Carew, Anthony. "A False Dawn: The World Federation of Trade Unions (1945–1949)." In *The International Confederation of Free Trade Unions*, edited by Marcel van der Linden. New York: Peter Lang, 2000.

Carew, Anthony. *American Labour's Cold War Abroad: From Deep Freeze to Détente, 1945–1970*. Edmonton: AU Press, 2018.

Carew, Anthony. "Towards a Free Trade Union Centre: The International Confederation of Free Trade Unions (1949–1972)." In *The International Confederation of Free Trade Unions*, edited by Marcel van der Linden. New York: Peter Lang, 2000.

Carreira, António. *Migrações nas Ilhas de Cabo Verde*. 2nd ed. Instituto Caboverdeano do Livro, 1983.

Carter, Susan, Scott Sigmund Gartner, Michael Haines, Alan Olmstead, Richard Sutch, and Gavin Wright, eds. *Historical Statistics of the United States: Earliest Times to the Present*. New York: Cambridge University Press, 2006.

Catling, Harold. *The Spinning Mule*. Newton Abbot, UK: David and Charles, 1970.

Chandler, Alfred D. Jr. *The Visible Hand: The Managerial Revolution in American Business*. Cambridge, MA: Belknap Press of Harvard University Press, 1977.

Chaudhuri, Sudip. "Government and Economic Development in South Korea, 1961–79." *Social Scientist* 24, no. 11/12 (Nov. 1996): 18–35.

Chen, Chen-Han. "Regional Differences in Costs and Productivity in the American Cotton Manufacturing Industry, 1880–1910." *Quarterly Journal of Economics* 55, no. 4 (1941): 533–566.

Choate, Mark I. *Emigrant Nation: The Making of Italy Abroad*. Cambridge, MA: Harvard University Press, 2008.

Chomsky, Aviva. *Linked Labor Histories: New England, Colombia, and the Making of a Global Working Class*. Durham, NC: Duke University Press, 2008.

Clark, Christopher. *The Roots of Rural Capitalism: Western Massachusetts, 1780–1860*. Ithaca, NY: Cornell University Press, 1990.

Clark, Gregory. *A Farewell to Alms: A Brief Economic History of the World*. Princeton, NJ: Princeton University Press, 2009.

Clark, Victor S. *History of Manufactures in the United States, 1607–1860*. Washington, DC: Carnegie Institution of Washington, 1916.

Cobble, Dorothy Sue. *The Other Women's Movement: Workplace Justice and Social Rights in Modern America*. Princeton, NJ: Princeton University Press, 2004.

Coggeshall, R. P. "The Development of the New Bedford Water Supplies." *Old Dartmouth Historical Sketch*, no. 42 (Apr. 1915).

Cohen, Andrew Wender. "Unions, Modernity, and the Decline of American Economic Nationalism." In *The Right and Labor in America: Politics, Ideology, and Imagination*, edited by Nelson Lichtenstein and Elizabeth Tandy Shermer. Philadelphia: University of Pennsylvania Press, 2012.

Cohen, Isaac. *American Management and British Labor: A Comparative Study of the Cotton Spinning Industry.* New York: Greenwood Press, 1990.

Cohen, Lizabeth. *A Consumers' Republic: The Politics of Mass Consumption in Postwar America.* New York: Vintage, 2003.

Cohen, Lizabeth. *Making a New Deal: Industrial Workers in Chicago, 1919–1939.* 2nd ed. New York: Cambridge University Press, 2008.

Conrad, James L. "'Drive That Branch': Samuel Slater, the Power Loom, and the Writing of America's Textile History." *Technology and Culture* 36, no. 1 (1995): 1–28.

Cook, Eli. *The Pricing of Progress: Economic Indicators and the Capitalization of American Life.* Cambridge, MA: Harvard University Press, 2017.

Costa, Carreiro da. *Para a História da Emigração do Distrito de Ponta Delgada.* Ponta Delgada, 1972.

Costa, Leonor Freire, Pedro Lains, and Susana Münch Miranda. *An Economic History of Portugal, 1143–2010.* Cambridge: Cambridge University Press, 2016.

Costa, Susana Goulart. *Azores: Nine Islands, One History/ Açores: Nove Ilhas, Uma Historia.* Translated by Rosa Neves Simas. Berkeley: Institute of Governmental Studies Press, University of California, 2008.

Covell, Jeffrey. "Scovill Fasteners Inc." In *International Directory of Company Histories*, edited by J. Pederson, Vol. 24. Detroit: St. James Press, 1999.

Cowie, Jefferson, and Joseph Heathcott, eds. *Beyond the Ruins: The Meanings of Deindustrialization.* Ithaca, NY: ILR Press, 2003.

Cowie, Jefferson. *Capital Moves: RCA's 70-Year Quest for Cheap Labor.* New York: New Press, 2001.

Cowie, Jefferson. *Stayin' Alive: The 1970s and the Last Days of the Working Class.* New York: New Press, 2012.

Cowie, Jefferson, and Nick Salvatore. "The Long Exception: Rethinking the Place of the New Deal in American History." *International Labor and Working-Class History* 74, no. 1 (2008): 3–32.

Crapo, Henry H. "The Story of Cotton and Its Manufacture into Cloth in New Bedford." *Old Dartmouth Historical Sketch*, no. 67 (Nov. 1937).

Creighton, Margaret S. *Rites and Passages: The Experience of American Whaling, 1830–1870.* Cambridge: Cambridge University Press, 1995.

Cumbler, John T. *Working-Class Community in Industrial America: Work, Leisure, and Struggle in Two Industrial Cities, 1880–1930.* Westport, CT: Greenwood Press, 1979.

Dallek, Robert. *An Unfinished Life: John F. Kennedy, 1917–1963.* Boston: Little, Brown, 2003.

Dalzell, Robert F. *Enterprising Elite: The Boston Associates and the World They Made.* Cambridge, MA: Harvard University Press, 1987.

Daniel, Clete. *Culture of Misfortune: An Interpretive History of Textile Unionism in the United States.* Ithaca, NY: ILR Press, 2001.

Davis, Gerald F. *Managed by the Markets: How Finance Reshaped America.* New York: Oxford University Press, 2011.

Davis, Lance E., Robert E. Gallman, and Karin Gleiter. *In Pursuit of Leviathan: Technology, Institutions, Productivity, and Profits in American Whaling, 1816–1906.* Chicago: University of Chicago Press, 1997.

Davis, Lance Edwin. "Stock Ownership in the Early New England Textile Industry." *Business History Review* 32, no. 2 (Jul. 1958): 204–222.

Delton, Jennifer A. *Rethinking the 1950s: How Anticommunism and the Cold War Made America Liberal.* New York: Cambridge University Press, 2013.

Dias, Fátima de Sequeira. "A Economia ao Sabor das Circunstâncias: Produções, Agentes e Intercâmbios." In *Historia dos Açores: Do Descobrimento ao Século XX,* edited by Artur Teodoro de Matos, Avelino de Freitas de Meneses, and José Guilherme Reis Leite, Vol. 2. Angra do Heroísmo: Instituto Açoriano de Cultura, 2008.

Dinger, Ed, and Lee Gjertsen. "AVX Corporation." In *International Directory of Company Histories,* edited by Drew D. Johnson, 172:43–47. Farmington Hills, MI: St. James Press, 2016.

Doherty, Maura. "Spindle City Blues: The Impact of the Maturing Industrial Economy on the City of Lowell, Massachusetts, 1947–1978." PhD diss., New York University, 1998.

Douki, Caroline. "The 'Return Politics' of a Sending Country: The Italian Case, 1880s–1914." In *A Century of Transnationalism: Immigrants and Their Homeland Connections,* edited by Roger Waldinger and Nancy L. Green. Urbana: University of Illinois Press, 2016.

Dublin, Thomas. *Lowell: The Story of an Industrial City.* Washington, DC: US Department of the Interior, 1992.

Dublin, Thomas. *Women at Work: The Transformation of Work and Community in Lowell, Massachusetts, 1826–1860.* 2nd ed. New York: Columbia University Press, 1981.

Dubofsky, Melvyn. *The State and Labor in Modern America.* Chapel Hill: University of North Carolina Press, 1994.

Dubofsky, Melvyn. *We Shall Be All: A History of the Industrial Workers of the World.* Urbana: University of Illinois Press, 2000.

Ducharme, Jacques. *The Shadows of the Trees: The Story of French-Canadians in New England.* New York: Harper and Bros., 1943.

Eisinger, Peter K. *The Rise of the Entrepreneurial State: State and Local Economic Development Policy in the United States.* Madison: University of Wisconsin Press, 1988.

Ellis, Leonard Bolles. *History of New Bedford and Its Vicinity, 1602–1892.* Syracuse, NY: D. Mason and Co., 1892.

Enes, Carlos. "Uma Economia em Transformação, mas uma Pobreza que Persiste." In *Historia Dos Açores: Do Descobrimento ao Século XX,* edited by Artur Teodoro de Matos, Avelino de Freitas de Meneses, and José Guilherme Reis Leite, Vol. 2. Angra do Heroísmo: Instituto Açoriano de Cultura, 2008.

Engerman, Stanley, and Kenneth Sokoloff. "Technology and Industrialization, 1790–1914." In *The Cambridge Economic History of the United States*, edited by Stanley Engerman and Robert Gallman, Vol. 2. Cambridge: Cambridge University Press, 2000.

Englander, Ernie, and Allen Kaufman. "The End of Managerial Ideology: From Corporate Social Responsibility to Corporate Social Indifference." *Enterprise and Society* 5, no. 3 (2004): 404–450.

English, Beth. *A Common Thread: Labor, Politics, and Capital Mobility in the Textile Industry*. Athens: University of Georgia Press, 2010.

Ensign, Forest. *Compulsory School Attendance and Child Labor: A Study of the Historical Development of Regulations Compelling Attendance and Limiting the Labor of Children in a Selected Group of States*. Iowa City, IA: Athens Press, 1921.

Erickson, Charlotte. *American Industry and the European Immigrant, 1860–1885*. Cambridge, MA: Harvard University Press, 1957.

Erickson, Charlotte. "The Encouragement of Emigration by British Trade Unions, 1850–1900." *Population Studies* 3, no. 3 (1949): 248–273.

Estall, R. C. *New England: A Study in Industrial Adjustment*. New York: Praeger, 1966.

Fairbank, Rebekah. "Iberian Emigration Law: A Comparison Study of Liberalism in Nineteenth-Century Emigration Law of Spain and Portugal." *BYU Family Historian* 6, no. 1 (2007).

Fairbrother, Malcolm. "Economists, Capitalists, and the Making of Globalization: North American Free Trade in Comparative-Historical Perspective." *American Journal of Sociology* 119, no. 5 (Mar. 2014): 1324–1379.

Farr, James. "A Slow Boat to Nowhere: The Multi-Racial Crews of the American Whaling Industry." *Journal of Negro History* 68, no. 2 (1983): 159–170.

Faue, Elizabeth. *Community of Suffering and Struggle: Women, Men, and the Labor Movement in Minneapolis, 1915–1945*. Chapel Hill: University of North Carolina Press, 1991.

Feldman-Bianco, Bela. "Multiple Layers of Time and Space: The Construction of Class, Ethnicity, and Nationalism among Portuguese Immigrants." In *Community, Culture and the Makings of Identity: Portuguese-Americans Along the Eastern Seaboard*, edited by Kimberly da Costa Holton and Andrea Klimt. North Dartmouth, MA: University of Massachusetts Dartmouth, Center for Portuguese Studies and Culture, 2009.

Ferguson, Niall, Charles Maier, Manela Erez, and Daniel Sargent, eds. *The Shock of the Global: The 1970s in Perspective*. Cambridge, MA: Belknap Press of Harvard University Press, 2010.

Ferreira, Hugo Gil, and Michael W. Marshall. *Portugal's Revolution: Ten Years On*. Cambridge: Cambridge University Press, 2011.

Fitting, George. "Export Processing Zones in Taiwan and the People's Republic of China." *Asian Survey* 22, no. 8 (1982): 732–744.

Florida, Richard, and Donald F. Smith. "Venture Capital Formation, Investment, and Regional Industrialization." *Annals of the Association of American Geographers* 83, no. 3 (1993): 434–451.

Fones-Wolf, Elizabeth A. *Waves of Opposition: Labor and the Struggle for Democratic Radio*. Urbana: University of Illinois Press, 2006.

Forrant, Robert. *Metal Fatigue: American Bosch and the Demise of Metalworking in the Connecticut River Valley*. Amityville, NY: Baywood, 2009.

Fosler, R. Scott, ed. *The New Economic Role of American States: Strategies in a Competitive World Economy*. New York: Oxford University Press, 1988.

Fraser, Steven. "Combined and Uneven Development in the Men's Clothing Industry." *Business History Review* 57, no. 4 (1983): 522–547.

Fraser, Steven. *Labor Will Rule: Sidney Hillman and the Rise of American Labor*. Ithaca, NY: Cornell University Press, 1993.

Freeman, Joshua B. *Behemoth: A History of the Factory and the Making of the Modern World*. New York: W. W. Norton, 2018.

Frieden, Jeffry. *Global Capitalism: Its Fall and Rise in the Twentieth Century*. New York: W. W. Norton, 2006.

Friedman, Tami J. "'A Trail of Ghost Towns Across Our Land': The Decline of Manufacturing in Yonkers, New York." In *Beyond the Ruins: The Meanings of Deindustrialization*, edited by Jefferson Cowie and Joseph Heathcott. Ithaca, NY: ILR Press, 2003.

Gabrielan, Randall. *Rumson: Shaping a Superlative Suburb*. Charleston, SC: Arcadia, 2003.

Galenson, Alice Carol. "The Migration of the Cotton Textile Industry from New England to the South, 1880 to 1930." PhD diss., Cornell University, 1975.

Gasbarre, April Dougal, Candice Mancini, and Eric W. Novinson. "Mohawk Industries, Inc." In *International Directory of Company Histories*, edited by Drew D. Johnson, 135: 258–263. Detroit: St. James Press, 2012.

Geismer, Lily. *Don't Blame Us: Suburban Liberals and the Transformation of the Democratic Party*. Princeton, NJ: Princeton University Press, 2015.

Georgianna, Daniel. "The Call for Capital." *Spinner: People and Culture in Southeastern Massachusetts* 4 (1988).

Georgianna, Daniel, and Roberta Hazen Aaronson. *The Strike of '28*. New Bedford: Spinner, 2001.

Gerstle, Gary. *American Crucible: Race and Nation in the Twentieth Century*. Princeton, NJ: Princeton University Press, 2002.

Gerstle, Gary. *Working-Class Americanism: The Politics of Labor in a Textile City, 1914–1960*. 2nd ed. Princeton, NJ: Princeton University Press, 2002.

Gifun, Frederick V. *UMass Dartmouth, 1960–2000: Trials and Triumph*. Dartmouth, MA: University of Massachusetts Dartmouth, 2007.

Gilbert, Dorothy Ann. *Recent Portuguese Immigrants to Fall River, Massachusetts: An Analysis of Relative Economic Success*. New York: AMS Press, 1989.

Glickman, Lawrence B. *A Living Wage: American Workers and the Making of Consumer Society*. Ithaca, NY: Cornell University Press, 1997.

Goldin, Claudia, and Kenneth Sokoloff. "Women, Children, and Industrialization in the Early Republic: Evidence from the Manufacturing Censuses." *Journal of Economic History* 42, no. 4 (1982): 741–774.

Goulart, Tony P., ed. *Capelinhos: A Volcano of Synergies: Azorean Emigration to America*. San Jose: Portuguese Heritage Publications of California, 2008.

Grandin, Greg. *The Last Colonial Massacre: Latin America in the Cold War*. Chicago: University of Chicago Press, 2004.

Gross, Laurence F. *The Course of Industrial Decline: The Boott Cotton Mills of Lowell, Massachusetts, 1835–1955*. Baltimore: Johns Hopkins University Press, 2000.

Grover, Kathryn. *The Fugitive's Gibraltar: Escaping Slaves and Abolitionism in New Bedford, Massachusetts*. Amherst: University of Massachusetts Press, 2001.

Gutman, Herbert G. "Work, Culture, and Society in Industrializing America, 1815–1919." *American Historical Review* 78, no. 3 (Jun. 1973): 531–588.

Hahn, Barbara. "Failures and Fairytales: Innovative Losers of the Industrial Revolution." Paper presented at the Joint Meeting of the Business History Conference and European Business History Association, Miami, FL, Jun. 26, 2015.

Halter, Marilyn. *Between Race and Ethnicity: Cape Verdean American Immigrants, 1860–1965*. Urbana: University of Illinois Press, 1993.

Hamelin, Marcel. *Les premières années du parlementarisme québécois, 1867–1878*. Québec: Presses de l'Université Laval, 1974.

Hamilton, Andrew. "Migration of Population Between Canada and the United States." MA thesis, McGill University, 1930.

Handlin, Oscar. *The Uprooted: The Epic Story of the Great Migrations That Made the American People*. Boston: Little, Brown, 1952.

Hardt, Michael. "Jefferson and Democracy." *American Quarterly* 59, no. 1 (2007): 41–78.

Hareven, Tamara K., and Randolph Langenbach. *Amoskeag: Life and Work in an American Factory-City*. New York: Pantheon Books, 1978.

Harley, Sharon. "When Your Work Is Not Who You Are: The Development of a Working-Class Consciousness among Afro-American Women." In *Gender, Class, Race, and Reform in the Progressive Era*, edited by Noralee Frankel and Nancy Schrom Dye. Lexington: University Press of Kentucky, 1994.

Harris, Seymour E. "New England's Decline in the American Economy." *Harvard Business Review* 25, no. 3 (Spring 1947): 348–371.

Harris, Seymour E. *The Economics of New England: Case Study of an Older Area*. Cambridge, MA: Harvard University Press, 1952.

Harrison, Bennett, and Barry Bluestone. "The Incidence and Regulation of Plant Closings." In *Sunbelt/Snowbelt: Urban Development and Regional Restructuring*, edited by Larry Sawers and William K. Tabb. New York: Oxford University Press, 1984.

Harrison, Bennett, and Jean Kluver. "Deindustrialization and Regional Restructuring in Massachusetts." In *Deindustrialization and Regional Economic Transformation: The Experience of the United States*, edited by Lloyd Rodwin and Sazanami Hidehiko. Boston: Unwin Hyman, 1989.

Hartford, William F. *Where Is Our Responsibility? Unions and Economic Change in the New England Textile Industry, 1870–1960*. Amherst: University of Massachusetts Press, 1996.

Harvey, David. "Neoliberalism as Creative Destruction." *Annals of the American Academy of Political and Social Science* 610 (Mar. 2007): 22–44.

Harvey, David. *Spaces of Capital: Towards a Critical Geography*. New York: Routledge, 2001.

Harvey, David. *The Enigma of Capital: And the Crises of Capitalism*. Oxford: Oxford University Press, 2010.

Harvey, David. *The Limits to Capital*. London: Verso, 2007.

Harzig, Christiane. "Domestics of the World (Unite?): Labor Migration Systems and Personal Trajectories of Household Workers in Historical and Global Perspective." *Journal of American Ethnic History* 25, no. 2/3 (Winter-Spring 2006): 48–73.

Heath, Kingston Wm. *The Patina of Place: The Cultural Weathering of a New England Industrial Landscape*. Knoxville: University of Tennessee Press, 2001.

Helfgott, Roy B. "Women and Children's Apparel." In *Made in New York: Case Studies in Metropolitan Manufacturing*, edited by Max Hall and Roy B. Helfgott. Cambridge, MA: Harvard University Press, 1959.

Henninger, Max. "Poverty, Labour, Development: Towards a Critique of Marx's Conceptualisations." In *Beyond Marx: Theorising the Global Labour Relations of the Twenty-First Century*, edited by Marcel van der Linden and Karl Heinz Roth. Leiden: Brill, 2014.

Henry, Robert A. "Workplace in Exile." *Spinner: People and Culture in Southeastern Massachusetts* 4 (1988).

Herringshaw, Thomas William. *Herringshaw's Encyclopedia of American Biography of the Nineteenth Century ...* Chicago: American Publishers' Association, 1904.

High, Steven, and David Lewis. *Corporate Wasteland: The Landscape and Memory of Deindustrialization*. Ithaca, NY: ILR Press, 2007.

Higham, John. *Strangers in the Land: Patterns of American Nativism, 1860–1925*. New York: Atheneum, 1963.

Hitchcock, Tim. *Down and Out in Eighteenth-Century London*. London: Hambledon and London, 2004.

Hobsbawm, Eric. *Industry and Empire: The Birth of the Industrial Revolution*. New York: New Press, 1999.

Hobsbawm, Eric. *The Age of Extremes: A History of the World, 1914–1991*. New York: Vintage, 1996.

Hollander, Justin B. *An Ordinary City: Planning for Growth and Decline in New Bedford, Massachusetts*. Cham, Switzerland: Palgrave Macmillan, 2018.

Howe, Daniel Walker. *The Political Culture of the American Whigs*. Chicago: University of Chicago Press, 1984.

Hughes, Quenby Olmsted. *"In the Interest of Democracy"*: *The Rise and Fall of the Early Cold War Alliance Between the American Federation of Labor and the Central Intelligence Agency.* Bern: Peter Lang, 2011.

Hund, James M. "Electronics." In *Made in New York: Case Studies in Metropolitan Manufacturing,* edited by Max Hall and Roy B. Helfgott. Cambridge, MA: Harvard University Press, 1959.

Hurd, Duane Hamilton. *History of Bristol County, Massachusetts: With Biographical Sketches of Many of Its Pioneers and Prominent Men.* Philadelphia: J. W. Lewis and Company, 1883.

Hurd, Duane Hamilton. *History of Middlesex County, Massachusetts: With Biographical Sketches of Many of Its Pioneers and Prominent Men.* Philadelphia: J. W. Lewis and Company, 1890.

Hyman, Louis. "Rethinking the Postwar Corporation: Management, Monopolies, and Markets." In *What's Good for Business: Business and American Politics Since World War II,* edited by Kim Phillips-Fein and Julian E. Zelizer. New York: Oxford University Press, 2012.

Jacobson, Matthew Frye. "More 'Trans-,' Less 'National.'" *Journal of American Ethnic History* 25, no. 4 (Jul. 2006): 74–84.

Jacobson, Matthew Frye. *Whiteness of a Different Color: European Immigrants and the Alchemy of Race.* Cambridge, MA: Harvard University Press, 1999.

Jeremy, David. "Damming the Flood: British Government Efforts to Check the Outflow of Technicians and Machinery, 1780–1843." *Business History Review* 51, no. 1 (1977): 1–34.

Jeremy, David. *Transatlantic Industrial Revolution: The Diffusion of Textile Technologies Between Britain and America, 1790–1830s.* Cambridge, MA: MIT Press, 1981.

Johnson, Chalmers. *MITI and the Japanese Miracle: The Growth of Industrial Policy, 1925–1975.* Stanford: Stanford University Press, 1982.

Jones, Geoffrey. *Entrepreneurship and Multinationals: Global Business and the Making of the Modern World.* Cheltenham, UK: Edward Elgar, 2013.

Jones, Geoffrey. "Globalization." In *The Oxford Handbook of Business History,* edited by Geoffrcy Jones and Jonathan Zeitlin. Oxford: Oxford University Press, 2009.

Juravich, Tom. *At the Altar of the Bottom Line: The Degradation of Work in the 21st Century.* Amherst: University of Massachusetts Press, 2009.

Juravich, Tom, William F. Hartford, and James R. Green. *Commonwealth of Toil: Chapters in the History of Massachusetts Workers and Their Unions.* Amherst: University of Massachusetts Press, 1996.

Kasson, John F. *Civilizing the Machine: Technology and Republican Values in America, 1776–1900.* New York: Grossman, 1976.

Kaufman, Allen, and Ernest J. Englander. "Kohlberg Kravis Roberts & Co. and the Restructuring of American Capitalism." *Business History Review* 67, no. 1 (1993): 52–97.

Kay, Hugh. *Salazar and Modern Portugal.* New York: Hawthorn Books, 1970.

Kazal, Russell A. "Revisiting Assimilation: The Rise, Fall, and Reappraisal of a Concept in American Ethnic History." *The American Historical Review* 100, no. 2 (Apr. 1995): 437–71.

Kessel, Herbert Neil. "The Impact of the Work Incentive Program in Two Local Labor Markets." PhD diss., Boston University, 1981.

Keyssar, Alexander. *Out of Work: The First Century of Unemployment in Massachusetts.* Cambridge: Cambridge University Press, 1986.

Khurana, Rakesh. *From Higher Aims to Hired Hands: The Social Transformation of American Business Schools and the Unfulfilled Promise of Management as a Profession.* Princeton, NJ: Princeton University Press, 2007.

Kilpatrick, Andrew. *Of Permanent Value: The Story of Warren Buffett.* Birmingham: AKPE, 1994.

Kirsch, Max H. *In the Wake of the Giant: Multinational Restructuring and Uneven Development in a New England Community.* Albany: State University of New York Press, 1998.

Klein, Naomi. *The Shock Doctrine: The Rise of Disaster Capitalism.* New York: Picador, 2008.

Knafo, Samuel, and Sahil Jai Dutta. "The Myth of the Shareholder Revolution and the Financialization of the Firm." *Review of International Political Economy* 27, no. 3 (Aug. 7, 2019): 1–24.

Knauer, Lisa Maya. "From Post-Conflict Guatemala to Post-Immigration Raid New Bedford: Temporality, Violence and Alternative Citizenships," Jul. 16, 2004. http://blogs.southcoasttoday.com/massmigration/2014/07/16/from-post-confl ict-guatemala-to-post-immigration-raid-new-bedford-temporality-violence-and-alternative-citizenships/.

Knauer, Lisa Maya. "The Maya of New Bedford: Genesis and Evolution of a Community, 1980–2010." *Historical Journal of Massachusetts* 39, no. 1 and 2 (Summer 2011).

Koistinen, David. *Confronting Decline: The Political Economy of Deindustrialization in Twentieth-Century New England.* Gainesville: University Press of Florida, 2014.

Koistinen, David. "The Causes of Deindustrialization: The Migration of the Cotton Textile Industry from New England to the South." *Enterprise and Society* 3, no. 3 (Sep. 2002): 482–520.

Kollmeyer, Christopher. "Explaining Deindustrialization: How Affluence, Productivity Growth, and Globalization Diminish Manufacturing Employment." *American Journal of Sociology* 114, no. 6 (May 2009): 1644–1674.

Krippner, Greta R. *Capitalizing on Crisis: The Political Origins of the Rise of Finance.* Cambridge, MA: Harvard University Press, 2012.

Kuhn, Sarah. *Computer Manufacturing in New England: Structure, Location, and Labor in a Growing Industry.* Cambridge, MA: Joint Center for Urban Studies of MIT and Harvard University, 1982.

Kulik, Gary B. "The Beginnings of the Industrial Revolution in America: Pawtucket, Rhode Island, 1672–1829." PhD diss., Brown University, 1980.

Lamphere, Louise. *From Working Daughters to Working Mothers: Immigrant Women in a New England Industrial Community.* Ithaca, NY: Cornell University Press, 1987.

Lamphere, Louise, Filomena M. Silva, and John P. Sousa. "Kin Networks and Family Strategies: Working Class Portuguese Families in New England." In *The Versatility of Kinship: Essays Presented to Harry W. Basehart,* edited by Linda S. Cordell and Stephen Beckerman. New York: Academic Press, 1980.

Landes, David S. *The Unbound Prometheus: Technological Change and Industrial Development in Western Europe from 1750 to the Present.* 2nd ed. Cambridge: Cambridge University Press, 2003.

Laslett, John. *Colliers Across the Sea: A Comparative Study of Class Formation in Scotland and the American Midwest, 1830–1924.* Urbana: University of Illinois Press, 2000.

Laurie, Bruce. *Artisans into Workers: Labor in Nineteenth-Century America.* Urbana: University of Illinois Press, 1997.

Lazerow, Jama. "'A Rebel All His Life': The Unexpected Story of Frank 'Parky' Grace." In *In Search of the Black Panther Party: New Perspectives on a Revolutionary Movement,* edited by Jama Lazerow and Yohuru Williams. Durham: Duke University Press, 2006.

Lazerow, Jama. "The Black Panthers at the Water's Edge: Oakland, Boston, and the New Bedford 'Riots' of 1970." In *Liberated Territory: Untold Local Perspectives on the Black Panther Party,* edited by Yohuru Williams and Jama Lazerow, 52. Durham, NC: Duke University Press, 2009.

Lazonick, William. *Competitive Advantage on the Shop Floor.* Cambridge, MA: Harvard University Press, 1990.

Lazonick, William, and Mary O'Sullivan. "Maximizing Shareholder Value: A New Ideology for Corporate Governance." *Economy and Society* 29, no. 1 (Feb. 2000): 13–35.

LeBlanc, Robert G. "Colonisation et repatriement au Lac-Saint-Jean (1895–1905)." *Revue d'histoire de l'Amérique française* 38, no. 3 (1985).

LeBlanc, Robert G. "Regional Competition for Franco-Americans Repatriates, 1870–1930." *Quebec Studies* 1 (Apr. 1983).

LeBlanc, Robert G. "The Acadian Migrations." In *French America: Mobility, Identity, and Minority Experience Across the Continent,* edited by Dean R. Louder and Eric Waddell. Baton Rouge: Louisiana State University Press, 1993.

Leontiades, Milton. "Another Look at Conglomerates." *Financial Analysts Journal* 25, no. 3 (May 1969): 80–86.

Levenson-Estrada, Deborah. *Trade Unionists Against Terror: Guatemala City, 1954–1985.* Chapel Hill: University of North Carolina Press, 1994.

Levitt, Laura. "Impossible Assimilations, American Liberalism, and Jewish Difference: Revisiting Jewish Secularism." *American Quarterly* 59, no. 3 (2007): 807–832.

Lewis, Jim, and Allan Williams. "Portugal: The Decade of Return." *Geography* 70, no. 2 (Apr. 1985): 178–182.

Lichtenstein, Nelson. *State of the Union: A Century of American Labor*. Princeton, NJ: Princeton University Press, 2013.

Lichtenstein, Nelson. *Walter Reuther: The Most Dangerous Man in Detroit*. Urbana: University of Illinois Press, 1997.

Linden, Marcel van der. *Workers of the World: Essays Toward a Global Labor History*. Leiden, The Netherlands: Brill, 2008.

Little, J. I. *Nationalism, Capitalism and Colonization in Nineteenth-Century Quebec the Upper St. Francis District*. Kingston: McGill-Queen's University Press, 1989.

Long, Clarence D. *Wages and Earnings in the United States, 1860–1890*. Princeton, NJ: Princeton University Press, 1960.

MacQueen, Norrie, and Pedro Aires Oliveira. "'Grocer Meets Butcher': Marcello Caetano's London Visit of 1973 and the Last Days of Portugal's Estado Novo." *Cold War History* 10, no. 1 (Feb. 2010): 29–50.

Macy, Obed. *The History of Nantucket*. Boston: Hilliard, Gray, and Co., 1835.

Maggor, Noam. *Brahmin Capitalism: Frontiers of Wealth and Populism in America's First Gilded Age*. Cambridge, MA: Harvard University Press, 2017.

Marcos, Daniel da Silva Costa. *The Capelinhos Eruption: Window of Opportunity for Azorean Emigration*. Providence, RI: Gávea-Brown, 2008.

Marx, Karl. *Grundrisse: Foundations of the Critique of Political Economy*. Translated by Martin Nicolaus. London: Penguin Books, 1973. https://www.marxists.org/arch ive/marx/works/1857/grundrisse/.

McCallum, John. *Unequal Beginnings Agriculture and Economic Development in Québec and Ontario Until 1870*. Toronto: University of Toronto Press, 1980.

McCoy, Drew R. *The Elusive Republic: Political Economy in Jeffersonian America*. New York: W. W. Norton, 1980.

McFeely, William S. *Frederick Douglass*. New York: W. W. Norton, 1995.

McKee, Guian A. *The Problem of Jobs: Liberalism, Race, and Deindustrialization in Philadelphia*. Chicago: University of Chicago Press, 2008.

McMullin, Thomas Austin. "Industrialization and Social Change in a Nineteenth Century Port City: New Bedford, Massachusetts, 1865–1900." PhD diss., University of Wisconsin, Madison, 1977.

Medeiros, Octávio H. Ribeiro de, and Artur Boavida Madeira. *Emigração e Regresso no Concelho da Povoação*. Ponta Delgada: Câmara Municipal da Povoação, 2003.

Medeiros, Octávio H. Ribeiro de, and Artur Boavida Madeira. *Emigração e Regresso no Concelho de Nordeste*. Ponta Delgada: Câmara Municipal da Povoação, 2003.

Meneses, Filipe Ribeiro de. *Salazar: A Political Biography*. New York: Enigma Books, 2009.

Milkman, Ruth. *Farewell to the Factory: Auto Workers in the Late Twentieth Century*. Berkeley: University of California Press, 1997.

Mills, Mary Beth. "Contesting the Margins of Modernity: Women, Migration, and Consumption in Thailand." *American Ethnologist* 24, no. 1 (Feb. 1997): 37–61.

Minchin, Timothy. *Empty Mills: The Fight Against Imports and the Decline of the U.S. Textile Industry*. Lanham, MD: Rowman and Littlefield, 2013.

Mokyr, Joel. "The Intellectual Origins of Modern Economic Growth." *Journal of Economic History* 65, no. 2 (Jun. 2005): 285–351.

Montgomery, David. *The Fall of the House of Labor: The Workplace, the State, and American Labor Activism, 1865–1925*. Cambridge: Cambridge University Press, 1989.

Moran, William. *The Belles of New England: The Women of the Textile Mills and the Families Whose Wealth They Wove*. New York: Thomas Dunne Books, 2002.

Morris, James A. "Cotton and Wool Textiles—Case Studies in Industrial Migration." *Journal of Industrial Economics* 2, no. 1 (1953): 65–83.

Moser, Robert Henry, and Antonio Luciano de Andrade Tosta. *Luso-American Literature: Writings by Portuguese-Speaking Authors in North America*. New Brunswick: Rutgers University Press, 2011.

Moussouris, Linda. "The Higher Education-Economic Development 'Connection' in Massachusetts: Forging a Critical Linkage?" *Higher Education* 35, no. 1 (1998): 91–112.

Mulcahy, Maria Gloria. "The Portuguese of the U.S. from 1880 to 1990: Distinctiveness in Work Patterns Across Gender, Nativity and Place." PhD diss., Brown University, 2003.

Mulderink, Earl F. *New Bedford's Civil War*. New York: Fordham University Press, 2012.

Mulderink, Earl F. "'We Want a Country': African American and Irish American Community Life in New Bedford, Massachusetts, During the Civil War Era." PhD diss., University of Wisconsin, Madison, 1995.

Nash, June C. *From Tank Town to High Tech: The Clash of Community and Industrial Cycles*. Albany: State University of New York Press, 1989.

Nelson, Scott Reynolds. *A Nation of Deadbeats: An Uncommon History of America's Financial Disasters*. New York: Alfred A. Knopf, 2012.

Neumann, Tracy. *Remaking the Rust Belt: The Postindustrial Transformation of North America*. Philadelphia: University of Pennsylvania Press, 2016.

Ngai, Mae M. *Impossible Subjects: Illegal Aliens and the Making of Modern America*. Princeton, NJ: Princeton University Press, 2005.

Nicholas, Tom. *VC: An American History*. Cambridge, MA: Harvard University Press, 2019.

Noel, Hugh R. Jr. *Jonathan Bourne: Whaling Merchant/Tycoon*. New Bedford, MA: Old Dartmouth Historical Society, 1985.

Pacheco, Sonia Patricia da Silva. "É para Sair de Portugal a Todos os Custos! The Policia Repressiva De Emigração Clandestina (1896–1911) and the Politics of Azorean Emigration to the United States." MA thesis, University of Massachusetts Dartmouth, 2015.

Pap, Leo. *The Portuguese-Americans*. Boston: Twayne, 1981.

Parmet, Robert D. *The Master of Seventh Avenue: David Dubinsky and the American Labor Movement*. New York: New York University Press, 2005.

Pease, Zephaniah W. *History of New Bedford*. New York: Lewis Historical Publishing, 1918.

Pease, Zephaniah W. "The Story of the Building of the Bourne Whaling Museum with Reminiscences of Old Counting Rooms." *Old Dartmouth Historical Sketch*, no. 44 (Apr. 1916).

Pederson, Jay P., ed. "Woolworth Corporation." In *International Directory of Company Histories*, 20: 528–532. Detroit: St. James Press, 1998.

Pereira, Miriam Halpern. "Algumas Observações Complementares sobre a Política de Emigração Portuguesa." *Análise Social*, Terceira Série, 25, no. 108/109 (Jan. 1990): 735–739.

Pereira, Victor. "Portuguese Migrants and Portugal: Elite Discourse and Transnational Practices." In *A Century of Transnationalism: Immigrants and Their Homeland Connections*, edited by Roger Waldinger and Nancy L. Green. Urbana: University of Illinois Press, 2016.

Petrin, Ronald Arthur. *French Canadians in Massachusetts Politics, 1885–1915: Ethnicity and Political Pragmatism*. Philadelphia: Balch Institute Press, 1990.

Phalen, William J. *The Consequences of Cotton in Antebellum America*. Jefferson, NC: McFarland, 2014.

Phillips, Arthur Sherman. *The Phillips History of Fall River*. Fall River: Dover Press, 1945.

Phillips-Fein, Kim. *Invisible Hands: The Making of the Conservative Movement from the New Deal to Reagan*. New York: W. W. Norton, 2009.

Pinto, António Costa. "The Transition to Democracy and Portugal's Decolonization." In *The Last Empire: Thirty Years of Portuguese Decolonization*, edited by Stewart Lloyd-Jones and António Costa Pinto. Bristol, UK: Intellect, 2003.

Pinto, António Costa. "Twentieth-Century Portugal: An Introduction." In *Modern Portugal*, edited by António Costa Pinto. Palo Alto: Sposs, 1998.

Pinto, António Costa, and Nino G. Monteiro. "Cultural Myths and Portuguese National Identity." In *Modern Portugal*, edited by António Costa Pinto. Palo Alto: Sposs, 1998.

Plaut, Thomas R., and Joseph E. Pluta. "Business Climate, Taxes and Expenditures, and State Industrial Growth in the United States." *Southern Economic Journal* 50, no. 1 (1983): 99–119.

Pomeranz, Kenneth. *The Great Divergence: China, Europe, and the Making of the Modern World Economy*. Princeton, NJ: Princeton University Press, 2000.

Prude, Jonathan. "Capitalism, Industrialization, and the Factory in Post-Revolutionary America." *Journal of the Early Republic* 16, no. 2 (1996): 237–255.

Quintal, Claire, ed. *Steeples and Smokestacks: A Collection of Essays on the Franco-American Experience in New England*. Worcester: Assumption College, Institut Français, 1996.

Ramirez, Bruno. *Crossing the 49th Parallel: Migration from Canada to the United States, 1900–1930*. Ithaca, NY: Cornell University Press, 2001.

Reimers, David M. "An Unintended Reform: The 1965 Immigration Act and Third World Immigration to the United States." *Journal of American Ethnic History* 3, no. 1 (Oct. 1983): 9–28.

Rischin, Moses. *The Promised City: New York's Jews, 1870–1914*. Cambridge, MA: Harvard University Press, 1962.

Roby, Yves. *The Franco-Americans of New England Dreams and Realities*. Sillery, Québec: Septentrion, 2004.

Roediger, David. *The Wages of Whiteness: Race and the Making of the American Working Class*. New ed. London: Verso, 2007.

Rogers, Francis. "The Portuguese Experience in the United States: Double Melt or Minority Group?" *Journal of the American Portuguese* 10, no. 1 (Spring 1976).

Rosa, Victor Pereira da, and Salvato Trigo. *Azorean Emigration: A Preliminary Overview*. Translated by Margaret Butler. Porto: Fernando Pessoa University Press, 1994.

Rosegrant, Susan, and David R. Lampe. *Route 128: Lessons from Boston's High Tech Community*. New York: Basic Books, 1992.

Rosen, Ellen Israel. *Making Sweatshops: The Globalization of the U.S. Apparel Industry*. Berkeley: University of California Press, 2002.

Rosenberg, Chaim M. *Child Labor in America: A History*. Jefferson, NC: McFarland, 2013.

Rosenberg, Chaim M. *The Life and Times of Francis Cabot Lowell, 1775–1817*. Lanham, MD: Lexington Books, 2010.

Rostow, W. W. *The Stages of Economic Growth: A Non-Communist Manifesto*. Cambridge: Cambridge University Press, 1960.

Rothenberg, Winifred Barr. "The Invention of American Capitalism: The Economy of New England in the Federal Period." In *Engines of Enterprise: An Economic History of New England*, edited by Peter Temin. Cambridge, MA: Harvard University Press, 2000.

Rumilly, Robert. *Histoire des Franco-Américains*. Montréal: L'Union Saint-Jean-Baptiste d'Amérique, 1958.

Sasada, Hironori. *The Evolution of the Japanese Developmental State: Institutions Locked in by Ideas*. London: Routledge, 2012.

Saxenian, AnnaLee. *Regional Advantage: Culture and Competition in Silicon Valley and Route 128*. Cambridge, MA: Harvard University Press, 1996.

Saxton, Alexander. *The Indispensable Enemy: Labor and the Anti-Chinese Movement in California*. Berkeley: University of California Press, 1975.

Schakenbach Regele, Lindsay. *Manufacturing Advantage: War, the State, and the Origins of American Industry, 1776–1848*. Baltimore: Johns Hopkins University Press, 2019.

Schrecker, Ellen. "McCarthyism's Ghosts: Anticommunism and American Labor." *New Labor Forum*, no. 4 (1999): 6–17.

Schroeder, Alice. *The Snowball: Warren Buffett and the Business of Life*. New York: Bantam Books, 2008.

Schumpeter, Joseph A. *Capitalism, Socialism and Democracy*. Eastford, CT: Martino Fine Books, 2010.

Schwartzman, Kathleen C. *The Social Origins of Democratic Collapse: The First Portuguese Republic in the Global Economy*. Lawrence: University Press of Kansas, 1989.

Scipes, Kim. *AFL-CIO's Secret War Against Developing Country Workers: Solidarity or Sabotage?* Lanham, MD: Lexington Books, 2011.

Scranton, Philip. *Endless Novelty: Specialty Production and American Industrialization, 1865–1925*. Princeton, NJ: Princeton University Press, 1997.

Seebohm, Caroline, and Peter C. Cook. *Cottages and Mansions of the Jersey Shore*. New Brunswick, NJ: Rutgers University Press, 2007.

Self, Robert O. *American Babylon: Race and the Struggle for Postwar Oakland*. Princeton, NJ: Princeton University Press, 2005.

Serda, Daniel. "Boston Investors and the Early Development of Kansas City, Missouri." Midwest Research Institute, Jan. 23, 1992. https://web.archive.org/web/2015091 1221856/http://shs.umsystem.edu/kansascity/mcp/Serda-1-23-92.pdf.

Serpa, Caetano Valadão. *A Gente dos Açores: Identificação, Emigração e Religiosidade, Séculos XVI-XX*. Lisboa: Prelo, 1978.

Sheehan, Melanie. "Opportunities Foregone: US Industrial Unions and the Politics of International Economic Policy, 1949–1983." PhD diss., University of North Carolina at Chapel Hill, 2022.

Shermer, Elizabeth Tandy. "'Take Government Out of Business by Putting Business into Government': Local Boosters, National CEOs, Experts, and the Politics of Midcentury Capital Mobility." In *What's Good for Business: Business and American Politics Since World War II*, edited by Kim Phillips-Fein and Julian E. Zelizer. New York: Oxford University Press, 2012.

Silvia, Philip T. Jr. "The Spindle City: Labor, Politics, and Religion in Fall River, Massachusetts, 1870–1905." PhD diss., Fordham University, 1973.

Skocpol, Theda. *Protecting Soldiers and Mothers: The Political Origins of Social Policy in United States*. Cambridge, MA: Belknap Press of Harvard University Press, 1995.

Skrabec, Quentin R. *The Fall of an American Rome: Deindustrialization of the American Dream*. New York: Algora, 2014.

Smith, Jason Scott. "The Liberal Invention of the Multinational Corporation: David Lilienthal and Postwar Capitalism." In *What's Good for Business: Business and American Politics Since World War II*, edited by Kim Phillips-Fein and Julian E. Zelizer. New York: Oxford University Press, 2012.

Smith, M. Estellie. "A Tale of Two Cities: The Reality of Historical Differences." *Urban Anthropology* 4, no. 1 (Apr. 1975).

Smith, M. Estellie. "Portuguese Enclaves: The Invisible Minority." In *Social and Cultural Identity: Problems of Persistence and Change*, edited by Thomas K. Fitzgerald. Athens: University of Georgia Press, 1974.

Smith, Thomas Russell. *The Cotton Textile Industry of Fall River, Massachusetts: A Study of Industrial Localization*. New York: King's Crown Press, 1944.

Sobel, Robert. *The Rise and Fall of the Conglomerate Kings*. New York: Stein and Day, 1984.

Stein, Judith. *Pivotal Decade: How the United States Traded Factories for Finance in the Seventies*. New Haven, CT: Yale University Press, 2010.

Stein, Judith. *Running Steel, Running America: Race, Economic Policy and the Decline of Liberalism*. Chapel Hill: University of North Carolina Press, 1998.

Sterne, Evelyn. "Patchwork of Protest: Social Diversity and Labor Militancy in the New Bedford Strike of 1928." MA thesis, Duke University, 1994.

Sugrue, Thomas J. *The Origins of the Urban Crisis: Race and Inequality in Postwar Detroit*. Rev. ed. Princeton, NJ: Princeton University Press, 2005.

Taber, Edgar Jr, "Condensed Data Relating to the New Bedford Cotton Mills." *Old Dartmouth Historical Sketch*, no. 67 (Nov. 1937).

Takai, Yukari. *Gendered Passages: French-Canadian Migration to Lowell, Massachusetts, 1900–1920*. New York: Peter Lang, 2008.

Teixeira, Nuno Severiano. "Between Africa and Europe: Portuguese Foreign Policy, 1890–1986." In *Modern Portugal*, edited by António Costa Pinto. Palo Alto: Sposs, 1998.

Temin, Peter, ed.. *Engines of Enterprise: An Economic History of New England*. Cambridge, MA: Harvard University Press, 2000.

Temin, Peter. "Product Quality and Vertical Integration in the Early Cotton Textile Industry." *Journal of Economic History* 48, no. 4 (1988): 891–907.

Temin, Peter. "The Industrialization of New England, 1830–1880." In *Engines of Enterprise: An Economic History of New England*, edited by Peter Temin. Cambridge, MA: Harvard University Press, 2000.

Thomas, Joseph D., Alfred H. Saulniers, Natalie A. White, Marsha L. McCabe, and Jay Avila, eds. *A Picture History of New Bedford*. Vol. 2. New Bedford, MA: Spinner, 2016.

Thomas, William Ronald. *Historical and Functional Aspects of State Industrial Development Organizations*. Columbia: Division of Research, Bureau of Business and Economic Research, College of Business Administration, University of South Carolina, 1975.

Tilly, Charles. "Transplanted Networks." In *Immigration Reconsidered: History, Sociology, and Politics*, edited by Virginia Yans-McLaughlin. New York: Oxford University Press, 1990.

Tirman, John. "'They Treated Us as If We Were Murderers': The Trauma of an ICE Raid." *Salon*, April 5, 2015. https://www.salon.com/2015/04/05/they_treated_us_as_if_we_were_murderers_the_trauma_of_an_ice_raid/.

Tortora, Phyllis G., and Ingrid Johnson. *The Fairchild Books Dictionary of Textiles*. New York: Fairchild Books, 2013.

Tucker, Barbara M. *Samuel Slater and the Origins of the American Textile Industry, 1790–1860*. Ithaca, NY: Cornell University Press, 1984.

Tucker, Barbara M.. "The Merchant, the Manufacturer, and the Factory Manager: The Case of Samuel Slater." *Business History Review* 55, no. 3 (Oct. 1981): 297–313.

Tuttle, Carolyn. *Hard at Work in Factories and Mines: The Economics of Child Labor During the British Industrial Revolution*. New York: Westview Press, 1999.

Ussach, Steven Samuel. "The New England Portuguese: A Plural Society within a Plural Society." *Plural Societies* 6 (1975).

Vernon-Wortzel, Heidi. *Lowell: The Corporations and the City.* New York: Garland, 1992.

Vickers, Daniel. "Nantucket Whalemen in the Deep-Sea Fishery: The Changing Anatomy of an Early American Labor Force." *Journal of American History* 72, no. 2 (Sep. 1985): 277–296.

Waldinger, Roger, and Nancy L. Green. "Introduction." In *A Century of Transnationalism: Immigrants and Their Homeland Connections,* edited by Roger Waldinger and Nancy L. Green. Urbana: University of Illinois Press, 2016.

Ware, Caroline F. *The Early New England Cotton Manufacture: A Study in Industrial Beginnings.* Boston: Houghton Mifflin, 1931.

Warrin, Donald. *So Ends This Day: The Portuguese in American Whaling, 1765–1927.* North Dartmouth, MA: University of Massachusetts Dartmouth, 2010.

Waterhouse, Benjamin C. *Lobbying America: The Politics of Business from Nixon to NAFTA.* Princeton, NJ: Princeton University Press, 2014.

Wheeler, Douglas L. *Republican Portugal: A Political History, 1910–1926.* Madison: University of Wisconsin Press, 1998.

Whittelsey, Sarah Scovill, and Arthur Twining Hadley. "Massachusetts Labor Legislation, An Historical and Critical Study." *Annals of the American Academy of Political and Social Science* 17 (1901): 1–157.

Wilentz, Sean. *Chants Democratic: New York City and the Rise of the American Working Class, 1788–1850.* 20th anniversary ed. New York: Oxford University Press, 2004.

Williams, Jerry R. *And Yet They Come: Portuguese Immigration from the Azores to the United States.* Staten Island, NY: Center for Migration Studies, 1982.

Williams, Jerry R. *In Pursuit of Their Dreams: A History of Azorean Immigration to the United States.* North Dartmouth, MA: University of Massachusetts Dartmouth, Center for Portuguese Studies and Culture, 2005.

Wolfbein, Seymour Louis. *The Decline of a Cotton Textile City: A Study of New Bedford.* New York: Columbia University, 1944.

Wolforth, Sandra. *The Portuguese in America.* San Francisco: R and E Research Associates, 1978.

Winant, Gabriel. *The Next Shift: The Fall of Industry and the Rise of Health Care in Rust Belt America.* Cambridge, MA: Harvard University Press, 2021.

Wood, B. Dan, and James E. Anderson. "The Politics of U.S. Antitrust Regulation." *American Journal of Political Science* 37, no. 1 (1993): 1–39.

Wood, Edmond. "The Development of the New Bedford Water Works System." *Old Dartmouth Historical Sketch,* no. 48 (Oct. 1919).

Zallen, Jeremy. *American Lucifers: The Dark History of Artificial Light, 1750–1865.* Chapel Hill: University of North Carolina Press, 2019.

Zieger, Robert H., and Gilbert J. Gall. *American Workers, American Unions: The Twentieth Century.* Baltimore: Johns Hopkins University Press, 2002.

Zonderman, David A. *Aspirations and Anxieties: New England Workers and the Mechanized Factory System, 1815–1850.* New York: Oxford University Press, 1992.

Index

For the benefit of digital users, indexed terms that span two pages (e.g., 52–53) may, on occasion, appear on only one of those pages.

Acushnet Mills, 45–46, 186
Adams, Henry, 24–25
Ades, Samuel, 170–71
Aerial (whaling bark), 35
Aerovox, 124, 204–5
African Americans
  Black Power movement and, 177–78, 218
  in Boston, 177–78
  labor unions and, 121
  lack of opportunity in skilled jobs for, 221–22
  in New Bedford, 180–81, 216–17, 219–20, 221–22, 225–26
  racial hostility toward, 180–81, 220, 221
  whaling industry and, 34
agriculture in New England, 16–17, 62
Aguiar, Cristóvão, 142–43
Alexander Smith Carpet Mills, 179
Alex Coffin (whaling ship), 36–37
Allegheny Technologies, 229
Allen, Gilbert, 45–46
Alper Holdings, 200
Alves, Mary, 93
Amalgamated Clothing Workers of America (ACWA)

collective bargaining agreements and, 122
economic nationalism and, 164
labor internationalism and, 160, 163
obstacles to organizing encountered by, 118
trade policy and, 163
walkouts and, 118–19
Amazon (multinational technology company), 9–10, 231–32
American Emigrant Company (AEC), 54
American Federation of Labor (AFL), 154–56, 157–58. *See also* American Federation of Labor-Congress of Industrial Organizations (AFL-CIO)
American Federation of Labor-Congress of Industrial Organizations (AFL-CIO)
  anti-Communism during Cold War and, 161–62
  Central Intelligence Agency and, 161–62
  free trade and, 157
  International Confederation of Free Trade Unions and, 162, 166
  labor internationalism and, 159–60

American Hardware Co., 195–97

American Linen Company, 54, 61, 85

American Printing Company, 85, 100

American Research and Development
　　Corporation, 214–15

American South
　　anti-Black racism in, 218
　　consumer markets in, 123
　　cotton trade and, 27–28, 53
　　labor unions and, 94, 160–61
　　textile industry in, 81–82, 89, 92, 96,
　　　99–100, 105–6, 109, 124, 126–27
　　wages in, 89, 121

American Standard Companies, 179–80

American West, 7, 16–17, 24–25, 45, 62

American Woolen Company, 173

Amoskeag Manufacturing Company, 25

Anderson-Little, 205–6

Andrade, Laurinda, 137

Andrade, Richard, 202

Angola, 143–44, 168

Annawan Manufacturing Company,
　　47–49, 99

Antone, Peter, 219–20

Appleton, Nathan, 17–18, 22, 23, 28

Appleton, William, 22, 25

Arkwright Club, 89, 97

Associação Benificente Aliança
　　(Portuguese Mutual Aid Society), 138

Associated Industries of Massachusetts
　　(AIM), 171, 177–78

Associated Operative Cotton Spinners
　　of Lancashire, Cheshire, Yorkshire,
　　and Derbyshire, 55

Atkins, Thomas Irving, 220

Atlantic Charter (1941), 156

Attleboro (Massachusetts), 123, 224

Auerbach Bathrobe Co., 163

AVX, 4, 204–5

Ayer, J. C., 27–28

Azorean immigrants. *See also* Portuguese
　　immigrants

Azorean Refugee Acts (1958 and 1960)
　　and, 139–41
　　contact with families in Azores
　　　by, 142–43
　　economic conditions' impact on rate
　　　of immigration among, 126–27
　　educational opportunities prioritized
　　　by, 147–48
　　ethnic antagonism toward, 132
　　in garment industry, 146–47, 153
　　generational divisions among, 147–48
　　immigration levels among, 142, 169–
　　　71, 223–24
　　Massachusetts's economic
　　　development facilitated by presence
　　　of, 168–69, 170–71
　　return migration to the Azores by, 74,
　　　107, 145
　　as textile workers, 49, 85–86
　　women immigrants and, 75–76

The Azores
　　Africa resettlement initiative (1950s)
　　　targeting, 143–45
　　agriculture in, 71, 72–74, 143–44, 145
　　arrendamento rural tenancy system in,
　　　73–74, 143, 145
　　Capelinhos Volcano eruptions (1957–
　　　1958) in, 139–40
　　emigration restrictions in, 71–72, 143–44
　　military conscription and, 168
　　political repression in, 168
　　Portuguese economic policies
　　　in, 72–73
　　poverty in, 144, 145, 168
　　rural elites in, 143, 145
　　Second World War and, 138
　　whaling industry and, 34–35, 69, 71–72

Baliko, Barbara, 206

Barkin, Solomon, 157, 173–74

Barrett, David, 201

Bartholo, Alipio C., 129

Beacon Manufacturing Company, 100
Beal, Fred, 103–4
Bedford Shirtmakers, 205
Bennett Jr., Thomas, 13–15
Benson, Susan Porter, 147–48
Berkshire Hathaway Inc., 187–88, 189, 206, 229
Biden, Joe, 233
Birtles, William, 94
Blackburn Spinners (England), 55
Blacker Printer Incorporated, 187
Black Panther Party, 220
Black Power movement, 177–78, 218
Blake, William, 17–18
Blewett, Mary, 58
Bluhdorn, Charles, 189–90
Bolton (England), 54–55, 56–57
Booth Manufacturing Company building
    (New Bedford, MA), 229
Boott Mills, 22–23, 25, 26–28
Borden, Bertram, 100
Borden, Howard, 100
Borden, Lizzie, 58
Borden, Matthew, 97, 100
Borden, M. C. D., 97
Borden, Richard, 96–97
Borden, Thomas, 96–97
Borden Mills tenements, 87
Border City Mill fire (1877), 85
Boston (Massachusetts)
    African Americans in, 177–78
    federally funded research at
        universities in and around, 214
    as hub of "high-tech Massachusetts,"
        209, 211–16, 226–27
    supplier networks in, 215
    venture capital and, 214–15
"Boston Associates"
    cultural and political prestige sought
        by, 22–23
    mills owned by, 22–23, 27
    recruitment of women laborers to
        Massachusetts mills by, 18–19

salaries paid to mill
    management by, 20
sons of, 23, 25, 27–28, 62, 100
steady source of profits sought by, 21–
    22, 23, 24
Boston Consulting Group (BCG),
    175, 195
Boston Manufacturing Company, 18–19,
    20, 22–23, 24, 26–27
Botelho, Alfred, 105
Botelho, Maria, 95
Boucher, Elmire, 63
Bourne Jr., Jonathan
    biographical background of, 36
    Civil War (American) and, 40
    decline of whaling industry in 1860s
        and, 40–41, 46–47
    financial setbacks faced by, 36–37, 39–40
    ship captains hired by, 37–38
    textile industry and, 45–46
    wealth of, 36
    whaling industry successes of, 33–
        34, 35–36
Boyenton, Richard, 32–33
Brayton, John S., 100
Brayton, Thomas, 45–46
Brière, Dorothy, 120–21
British immigrants
    British labor movement's
        encouragement of, 54–57
    British laws barring textile workers
        from becoming, 16
    economic conditions' impact on rate
        of immigration among, 60
    Johnson-Reed Immigration Act
        quotas (1924) and, 130
    labor activism among, 51, 57–60, 77
    recruitment agents in Great Britain
        and, 54
    return migration to Great Britain
        among, 59, 123
Brittany Global Technologies, 229

Brown, Moses, 16

BSF (holding company), 195–97

B. Sopkin & Sons Company, 117–18, 121

Buffett, Warren, 187

Buraczynski, Alice, 160

Bush, Jack, 214–15

Bush, Vannevar, 214

Business Roundtable, 176

Buzzards Bay (Massachusetts), 31. *See also* New Bedford (Massachusetts)

Cabral, Manuel Medeiros, 144

Cabral, Maria, 75–76

Cabral, Rosalina, 75–76

Caetano, Marcello, 167–68

Calhetas (The Azores), 167–69

Calvin Clothing, 205

Camara, Antonio da, 144

Camara, Maria Jacinto da, 75–76

Canada. *See also* French Canadian immigrants

  Acadian expulsions (1750s-1760s) from, 60, 61–62

  farming in, 62–64, 65

  government's condemnation of emigration by French Canadians from, 61–62, 77

  independence rebellions (1837–1838) in, 60

  interest rates in, 63

  repatriation incentives offered to French Canadian emigrants in United States by, 65–67, 68, 77

  return migration by French Canadians to, 59, 64–68, 123

  US tariffs against, 62

Canto e Castro, Raymond, 145

Capacitores Unidos, 204–5

Capelinhos Volcano eruptions (Azores, 1957–1958), 139–40

Cape Verde, 34–35, 71–72

Cape Verdeans, 49, 71–72, 132, 217–18, 226

Carmo, William, 222

Carmona, Oscar, 132–33

Carter, Jimmy, 208

Cartier, George-Étienne, 61

Carvalho, Henrique Martins de, 142–43

Carver, Ron, 191–93

Casa de Portugal (New York City), 136–38

Castro, Edson de, 211

Catholic Church, 61, 68–69

Central Intelligence Agency (CIA), 161–62

Chace, S. B., 98–99, 106

Chaikin, Sol "Chick," 164, 165–66

Chandler Jr., Alfred, 194–95

Chase, Earl, 1–2

Cheshire (England), 53–54, 55

Chouinard, Barry, 203–4

Churchill, Winston, 156

Citizens' Committee for the Ladies Garment Industry, 114

Civil War (American)

  Azorean economy and, 72

  British immigration to Massachusetts during, 56

  Confederate trade and, 40

  cotton trade during, 24, 26, 53–54

  tariffs and, 62

  textile industry during, 24, 26–28

  whaling industry and, 40

Cliftex Corporation, 205–6

Clube Social Português, 139–40

Cold War, 125, 153–54, 155–56, 161–62

Collins, Jennie, 57–58

Commonwealth Landing Apartments (Fall River), 231

Communists

  business leaders' fears regarding, 114–15, 119–20

  as labor organizers, 103–4

  labor unions' opposition against, 153–54, 155–56, 161–62

Costa, Antonio da, 144

conglomeration
    anti-monopoly enforcement and, 172,
        174, 198
    cash liquidity and credit obtained
        through, 173, 174–75, 188–89, 190–
        91, 192*f*, 197
    electronics industry and, 168–69, 204–5
    emotional and financial investment
        in local communities lessened
        through, 171, 175–76, 177–81, 210
    garment industry and, 168–69, 205–6
    leveraged buyouts and, 199–200
    liquidation of factories under, 179, 188,
        193, 197
    Massachusetts as a center of, 4, 171,
        177, 188–89
    monopolies compared to, 194–95
    New Bedford Rayon and, 179–81
    private equity firms' displacement
        of, 198–99
    profits prioritized over all other
        business goals in, 176–77
    profits used for expansion of other
        ventures under, 9, 171, 172, 174–75,
        187, 188, 195
    "Shareholder Revolution" and, 176
    tax liabilities reduced via, 174
    tax loss carry-forwards and, 172–73
    textile industry and, 187
Congress of Industrial Organizations
    (CIO), 154–56, 157–58, 160–61.
    See also American Federation
    of Labor-Congress of Industrial
    Organizations (AFL-CIO)
Consumers' League of
    Massachusetts, 113–14
Conway Data, 182
Coolidge, Thomas Jefferson, 25–28
Cooper Industries, 204–5
Copeland, Joseph, 87–88
Cornell Dubilier, 229
Cornell Mills, 86*f*
Correia, Jose Salvador, 144

Costa, Mary, 95
"cotton famine" (1860s), 53–54
Cowley, Charles, 27–28
Crapo, Henry Howland, 45
Crapo, William, 45–46
Cusick, Gerald, 223
Custodio, Jack, 217

Dalzell Jr., Robert, 22
Dartmouth (Massachusetts).
    See University of
    Massachusetts-Dartmouth
Dartmouth Mill, 102
David, Laurent-Olivier, 61
Davis Sportswear Company, 205
Davol, William, 47–48
Defiance holding company, 195–96
deindustrialization of textile industry
    business owners' decisions amid, 96–101
    disinvestment and, 188
    economic theories regarding, 96
    electronics factories opened amid, 124,
        126, 189
    Fall River and, 107–8, 110–11, 125–26
    garment shops established during, 109,
        111, 113–14, 116, 126, 189
    labor unions' activism amid, 81–82, 89,
        105–6, 114–15, 118
    liquidation of factories and, 100, 109
    "masculine jobs" lost in, 125–26
    Massachusetts and, 4–5, 8, 107–9,
        110–11, 113–14, 126, 234
    New Bedford and, ix–x, 107, 109–12, 186
    unemployment and poverty amid,
        107–8, 109–10, 113
    US trade policy and, 153
Derbyshire (England), 53–54, 55
DeSousa, Fernanda, 146–47
Desruisseaux, Évelyne, 65
Dexter, Elisha, 34–35
Diário de Notícias (Portuguese
    newspaper in New Bedford),
    134, 136–38

Digital Equipment Corporation (DEC), 211, 212–13
Donham, Wallace B., 175–76
Doriot, George, 214–15
Douglass, Frederick, 34
Drake, Edwin, 40
Dubinsky, David, 155, 161
Dukakis, Michael, 193, 213
Durfee, Bradford, 47–48
Dwight Mills, 25

Eastern Avenue School (Fall River), 68–69
Eastern Sportswear, 225
electronics industry
  business owners' interests in, 125
  Cold War and, 125
  conglomeration in, 168–69, 204–5
  deindustrialization of textile industry and, 124, 126, 189
  expansion in Massachusetts after 1965 of, 169
  globalization and, 8–9, 183–84
  labor unions and, 124
  in New Bedford, 124–25, 183–84, 204–5
  Second World War and, 125
  women workers and, 125
Ellis, Leonard, 40
Emhart Company, 196–97
Emigrant Board (Portugal), 136–37
Empire Synthetics, 179–80, 181
England. *See* Great Britain
Erie Canal, 16–17
Escóbar, Amelia, 225
Evans, Thomas, 57

Fairhaven Mills, 112
Fair Labor Standards Act of 1938, 121
Fall River (Massachusetts)
  crime levels in, 232–33
  deindustrialization of textile industry in, 107–8, 110–11, 125–26

electronics industry in, 183–84
elite business families in, 97, 100
ethnic conflict among immigrant groups in, 53
fraternal organizations in, 56
French Village in, 61
garment industry in, 111–13, 117–19, 121–22, 146–47, 183–84, 205–6
"Great Vacation" of 1875 in, 58, 92
"high-tech Massachusetts" initiatives and, 209, 212, 213
housing conditions in, 87
immigrants during nineteenth century in, 7–8, 51–52, 53, 54, 56, 57–59, 60, 61, 64, 68–69, 76
incentives offered to businesses relocating to, 231
labor unions in, 57, 90, 93–95, 117, 118, 119, 121–22, 160
map of, 4*f*
Office of Economic Development (FROED) in, 213, 230–31
photo of, 108*f*
public money used to lure industry to, 183
strikes and labor activism in, 57–59, 61, 85, 88
textile industry in, 4, 28–29, 39, 46, 47–49, 51, 52, 54, 57–59, 61, 64, 81–82, 87–88, 89–91, 93–95, 96–97, 98–100, 118, 230–31
whaling industry's rise and decline in, 4, 33–34, 35
Fall River Clothing Mfg., 205
Fantus Factory Locating Service, 182
Farland, Alphonse, 68–69
Federalist Party, 17
Feeney, Michael Paul, 178
Ferro, António, 134–35, 137, 138–39
Figueiredo Côrte-Real, Miguel de, 145
Figueiredo, Elizabeth, 145–46
First City Properties, Inc., 200

First World War, 99–100
Fisher, Ken, 215
Fogarty, John, 141
Forand, Aime, 141
Forbes, John Murray, 26
Foreign Emigrant Society, 54
Foresters fraternal club, 56
Fortes, Gail, 71–72, 229–30
Foster, Bill, 215
Frank, Barney, 200–1, 203
free trade
  Atlantic Charter and, 156
  business owners' attitudes regarding,
    163, 178
  General Agreement on Tariffs and
    Trade and, 156, 163
  globalization and, 8–9, 153–54, 165
  labor unions and, 154, 156–58,
    163, 164–65
  US businesses' promotion of, 153–54
French Canadian immigrants. *See
  also* Canada
  anti-union attitudes and
    strikebreaking among, 52, 60, 67–
    68, 75
  Canadian government's condemnation
    of emigration by, 61–62, 77
  Catholicism among, 68–69
  child workers and, 84
  economic conditions' impact on rate
    of immigration among, 64, 65–67
  ethnic antagonism toward, 59,
    61, 67–69
  ethnic insularity among, 68
  family networks among, 63–64
  overall number (1840–1930) of, 64
  repatriation incentives offered to, 65–
    67, 68, 77
  return migration to Canada among,
    59, 64–68, 123
  textile industry and, 61, 64, 84, 85–86,
    87, 103–4

union organizing and participation
    among, 77, 103–4, 105, 119
  wages paid to, 52
Frye, Peter, 120–21

Gagnon, Ferdinand, 66–67
garment industry
  child workers in, 113
  conglomeration in, 168–69, 205–6
  deindustrialization of textile industry
    and, 109, 111, 113–14, 116, 126, 189
  in Fall River, 111–13, 117–19, 121–22,
    146–47, 183–84, 205–6
  globalization and, 180–81, 183–84
  labor unions and, 115–19, 121–
    22, 157–58
  Multi-Fibre Agreement (1974)
    and, 184
  in New Bedford, 111–13, 114–15, 117,
    118–19, 122–23, 170–71, 183–84, 205,
    218, 229–30
  in New York City, 111–12, 218
  reform movement addressing
    conditions in, 113–14, 116–22
  resiliency after 1970 of, 209
  training for World War II veterans for
    work in, 123
  wages in, 112, 113–15, 117, 119, 121–22
  women workers in, 115–16, 122–
    23, 146–47
  working conditions in, 112–13, 119
  working hours in, 117
Gaspé Peninsula (Canada), 60, 62
Gastonia (North Carolina), 28–29
Geijer, Arne, 158
Gendron, Samuel, 63
General Agreement on Tariffs and Trade
    (GATT), 156, 163
General Pike (whaling ship), 36
Gentlemen's Wearhouse, 205–6
George and Mary (whaling bark), 34–35
Gerwatowski, David, 203

Gerwatowski, Fred, 203
globalization
  East Asian countries' incentives to
    businesses under, 183–84
  electronics industry and, 8–9, 183–84
  free migration and, 8–9
  free trade and, 8–9, 153–54, 165
  garment industry and, 180–81, 183–84
  incentives offered by local and state
    governments in, 181–83
  industrial relocation firms and, 182
  labor unions and, 154, 165
  Massachusetts and, 4–5, 8–9, 165,
    168–69, 181–82, 184–85, 206, 210
  textile industry and, 4–5, 8–9, 82
Golconda (whaling ship), 33
Golden, John, 57, 75
Gomes, Luiz, 136
Grace, "Parky," 219, 225
Granite Mill fire (1867), 85
Gratitude (whaling ship), 33
Great Britain. *See also* British immigrants
  cotton supply for textile industry
    in, 53–54
  labor unions in, 54–57, 60, 94
  laws barring textile workers' immigration
    to United States from, 16
  Portugal and, 69–70, 167–68
  textile industry in, 17–18
  US Civil War's impact on economy
    of, 53–54
Greek immigrants, 76, 104–5
Green, James, 115–16
Grinnell, Joseph, 13–14
Guatemalan immigrants, 1–3
Guinea-Bissau, 168
Gulf+Western (G+W) corporation,
  189–93, 200–1. *See also* Morse Drill
  Company

Haish, T. A., 124
Hamilton, Alexander, 17

Hamilton Company, 20, 22–23, 25
Har-Lee factory (Fall River), 112, 117–18,
  119, 121–22
Harrington, Leo S., 170
Harris, Seymour, 96
Harrison, Bennett, 188
Hart-Celler Act (1965), 130, 141,
  145, 149
Harvard Business School, 175–76
Harwood Underwear Company, 118–19
Hathaway, Francis, 45–46, 186
Hathaway, Horatio, 45–46, 186
Hathaway, Humphrey, 186
Hathaway, Thomas Schuyler, 186
Hathaway Mills, 125, 186–87, 188
Haverhill (Massachusetts), 212
Heckler, Margaret, 170–71, 223, 224–25
Henderson, Bruce, 175–76
"high-tech Massachusetts"
  Boston as a hub for, 209, 211–
    16, 226–27
  educated workforce viewed as key to
    success of, 212, 222–23
  Fall River and, 209, 212, 213
  Massachusetts High Technology
    Council and, 210–11
  "Massachusetts Miracle" and,
    211, 222–23
  New Bedford and, 209, 212, 213
  New Social Contract for
    Massachusetts (1979) and, 210–11
  social welfare cuts and, 209, 210, 226
  state aid supporting establishment of,
    209, 210, 226
  tax incentives and, 210–11, 213–14
  venture capital and, 214–15
  worker training for, 209, 223
  World War II contracts and, 214
Hillman, Sidney, 154–55
Hine, Lewis, 3, 86*f*
Holmes, William, 48–49
Holmes Mill, 229

Honduran immigrants, 2–3
Houdaille Industries, 199
Houtman, Warren, 219
Howard, Robert, 57, 89, 91, 93–94, 97
Howland, Emily Summers, 36
Howland, John, 36
Howland, Matthew, 45–46
Howland, Weston, 40
Howland Jr., George, 41–43
Hunter (whaling ship), 47
Hyde Spinners (England), 56–57
Hyman, Louis, 175

Immigration and Customs Enforcement
    (ICE), x, 2–3
Immigration Restriction League, 132
In Black and White (Massachusetts
    Development and Industrial
    Commission), 110–11
Indonesia, 159–60, 183–84
Industrial Workers of the World
    (IWW), 154
Insolia, Francesco, 2–3
International Confederation of Free
    Trade Unions (ICFTU)
  American Federation of Labor-
      Congress of Industrial
      Organizations and, 162, 166
  anti-colonialism and, 155–56
  anti-Communism and, 155–56
  Cold War and, 161–62
  free trade and, 156, 158
  International Solidarity Fund
      and, 159–61
  labor internationalism and, 159–61,
      162, 166
  Manifesto (1949) of, 156
  Milan Convention (1951) and, 155–56
International Labor
    Organisation, 159–60
International Ladies' Garment Workers'
    Union (ILGWU)

  collective bargaining agreements
      and, 122
  economic nationalism and,
      164, 165–66
  at Har-Lee factory, 121–22, 126
  healthcare benefits for members of, 122
  immigration policy and, 164
  labor internationalism and, 154–55,
      160, 166
  obstacles to organizing encountered
      by, 117–18
  radio plays sponsored by, 120–21
  Roosevelt supported by, 121
  wages and, 117, 121–22
  working conditions and, 116–17
International Textile and Garment
    Workers' Federation, 160
International Workingmen's Association
    (First International), 154
Irish immigrants, 48, 51–52, 68–
    69, 83–84
Isherwood, William, 83

Japan, 138, 164, 180–81, 183–84
J.C. Rhodes Company
  anti-trust enforcement against United
      Shoe (1956) and, 195–96
  layoffs (1974) at, 196–97
  Emhart Company's takeover (1966)
      of, 196–97
  eminent domain proposed to
      save, 202–3
  Kohlberg & Co.'s purchase and
      liquidation (1996) of, 197, 200–2,
      203–4, 209–10
  Plymouth Cordage Company's
      purchase (1956) of, 195–96
  pollution at, 197
  United Shoe Machinery Company's
      takeover (1905) of, 194
  USM's takeover (1982) of, 196–97
Jefferson, Thomas, 17

Jesus, Maria de, 147
John E. Thayer and Brother, 26
Johnson-Reed Act (Immigration Act of
  1924), 130
Jonathan Logan Inc., 205
Julian (whaling ship), 39
"just wage" ideology, 91–92, 101, 102–
  3, 105–6

Karam, Robert, 213
Kariotis, George, 213
Kennedy, Edward, 141, 200–1
Kennedy, John F., 139–41
Kerry, John, 200–1
Kevelson, Kev, 203
Kilburn Mill, 3, 229
Kingfisher (whaling ship), 36–37
Klonsky, Max, 165–66
Kluver, Jean, 188
Knauer, Lisa, 1
Knights of Labor, 92–93
Kohlberg & Co., 199–202
Kohlberg Jr., Jerome, 199–200
Kohlberg Kravis Roberts (KKR),
  199–200
Korda, Michael, 190–91
Korean War, 186–87
Kyocera, 204–5

labor unions. *See also specific unions*
  African Americans and, 121
  anti-colonialism and, 155–56
  Cold War and, 153–54, 155–
    56, 161–62
  company unions and, 117–18
  deindustrialization and, 81–82, 89,
    105–6, 114–15, 118
  divisions along ethnic lines in, 92–93
  divisions along lines of geography and
    craft in, 92–94, 95, 101, 106
  economic nationalism and, 153–
    54, 163–66

  electronics industry and, 124
  Fair Labor Standards Act of 1938
    and, 121
  free trade and, 154, 156–58,
    163, 164–65
  garment industry and, 115–19, 121–
    22, 157–58
  globalization and, 154, 165
  in Great Britain, 54–57, 60, 94
  immigrants and, 93–94, 103–5
  immigration policy and, 164
  labor internationalism and, 154–56,
    157–61, 162–63, 164–66
  National Labor Relations Act (1935)
    and, 121–22
  National Recovery Administration's
    protections for, 116–17, 119
  in New Bedford, 88, 93–95, 114–16,
    117, 118–19, 122, 160–61, 191–93,
    200–1, 202
  in New York City, 111–12
  Norris-LaGuardia Act (1932) and, 121
  Roosevelt supported by, 121
  textile industry and, 81–82, 88, 90–91,
    92–93, 116, 118, 157–58
  "vacation" actions and, 92
  wages and, 90–91, 93–94, 95, 101–3,
    105, 115–16, 119, 121–22
  women workers and, 93–95, 104–5,
    115–16, 118–19, 121–22
  working hour demands and, 92–93
Laflèche, Louis-François Richer, 61
Lagoda (whaling ship), 40–41
Lambert, James, 193–94
Lambert Consolidated Industries
    Inc., 193–94
Lamphere, Louise, 225
Lancashire (England)
  "cotton famine" of 1860s and, 53–54
  emigration from, 55–57, 60
  labor activism in, 58–59, 61
Langshaw, Walter, 102, 106

La société de rapatriement du Lac-Saint-
  Jean, 66–67
Lawrence (Massachusetts)
  high-tech manufacturing in, 212
  obstacles to long-term success in
    mills at, 15
  textile industry in, 7, 26–27, 51, 90–91
Lawrence, A.A. (Amos Adams), 23, 26
Lawrence, Abbot, 22, 23
Lawrence, Amos, 19, 21–22, 23
Lawrence Manufacturing Company,
  20, 26, 48
Leary, Frank J., 110, 112, 114–15,
  124, 229
Lee, Joseph and Henry, 21–22
Leeman, Jerry, 229–30
Lees, Donna, 205
Lefebvre, Camille, 61–62
"Letter from João Valente"
  (Oliveira), 142–43
leveraged buyouts (LBOs), 199–
  200, 205
Lima, David, 231–32
Lima, Lester, 219–20
Little, Arthur D., 172
Little, Royal
  conglomeration practices of, 172–75,
    176, 195, 198
  Congressional probe (1948) of, 173–74
  family background of, 172
  Great Depression losses experienced
    by, 172, 190
Long Island (New York State), 31
Lord, Napoléon, 63–64
Lotus Software, 211
Lovestone, Jay, 161
Lowell (Massachusetts)
  boardinghouses for women textile
    workers in, 19
  high-tech manufacturing in, 212
  machines used in textile industry
    in, 47–48

obstacles to long-term success in
  textile industry in, 15–16, 49–50
Panic of 1857 and, 23
textile industry's rise and decline in, 7,
  19–20, 22–23, 24, 26–27, 28–29, 48,
  51, 87–88
wages for women textile workers in, 48
Lowell, Francis Cabot, 17–18, 20, 21–
  22, 23
Lowell, Joan, 113
Lowell Offering magazine, 19
Lyman Mills, 25
Lyon, Katie, 85–86

Machado, Jen, 232–33
Macon (Georgia), 28–29
Madureira, Castro, 129–30
Magnett, Jimmy, 222
The Maids cleaning service, 3
Maltais, Joseph, 64, 84
Manchester (England), 17–18, 41–
  42, 54
Mandeville, Beatrice, 65
Manville-Jenckes, 172–74
Marcella (whaling bark), 37
Marengo (whaling ship), 47
Maria Chapdelaine (Hémon), 63–64
Markson, Al, 170–71
Martin Jr., Joseph, 139–40
Massachusetts. *See also* "high-tech
  Massachusetts"; *specific cities*
  Acadian resettlements (1750s–
    1760s) in, 60
  Act to Regulate and Limit Municipal
    Indebtedness (1875) in, 44–45
  child labor law in, 84, 98
  conglomeration in, 4, 171, 177, 188–89
  corporate taxes in, 178
  "cotton famine" of 1860s and, 54
  deindustrialization of textile industry
    and, 4–5, 8, 107–9, 110–11, 113–14,
    126, 234

Massachusetts (*cont.*)
  Democratic Party in, 178
  Department of Commerce and
    Industrial Development in, 212
  Department of Workforce
    Development in, 2
  Development and Industrial
    Commission in, 110–11
  electronics industry in, 124,
    126, 168–69
  garment industry in, 113–14, 122–23,
    126, 153, 168–69
  globalization's impact on, 4–5, 8–9,
    165, 168–69, 181–82, 184–85,
    206, 210
  labor laws regarding work hours in,
    52, 114–15
  manufacturing expansion after 1965
    in, 169
  "Mass Incentives" legislation (1973)
    in, 210
  social spending cuts starting in 1970s
    in, 209, 210, 226
  state aid to businesses starting in 1970s
    in, 209, 210, 226
  textile industry in, 18–19, 24, 28, 46f
  unemployment during 1970s in, 208
  women and labor law in, 98
Massachusetts Emigrant Aid Society, 26
Massachusetts High Technology Council
  (MHTC), 210–11
Massachusetts Institute of Technology
  (MIT), 214
Massachusetts Manufacturing
  Company, 22–23
Massachusetts State Federation of
  Weavers, 94
Massasoit Mills, 100
McNeal, Annie, 85–86
Meany, George, 158, 161–62
Mellion, Robert A., 230–31
Mello, Phil, 200

Melville, Herman, 30
Mendes, Eula, 95, 104–5, 106, 118–19
Mendes, Maria Lídia, 225
Merrill Lynch, 205
Merrimack Manufacturing
  Company, 19, 27
Metacomet Mill, 48–49, 85
Michael Bianco Inc., 2–3
Mittleman, Aaron, 223–24
Moby-Dick (Melville), 30
Mohasco corporation, 179–80
Mohawk Carpet Manufacturers, 179
monopolies, 194–97
Montigny, Mark C., 201–2
Montreal (whaling ship), 33
Morgan, Charles, 45–46
Morin, Jos, 64
Morrisey, Matt, 230
Morse, Stephen Ambrose, 189
Morse Drill Company
  closure (1990) of, 193–94, 200–
    1, 209–10
  founding (1864) of, 189
  Gulf+Western Corporation's takeover
    (1968) of, 189–91
  Gulf+Western's sale (1984) of, 193
  site redevelopment failures after 2010
    at, 194
  as source of profit for Gulf+Western,
    191, 192f
  strike against Gulf+Western
    Corporation (1982) at, 191–
    93, 192f
  wages and benefits at, 189
Morse Jr., John T., 24–25
Mozambique, 144, 168
Mueller, Robert, 197
Multi-Fibre Agreement (1974), 184
Murdoch, William, 103–4
Murphy, Evelyn, 212
Murphy, Francis J., 170
Muscat, Victor, 195–96

Nantucket Island (Massachusetts), 31–32, 40
Napoleon (whaling bark), 47
Nashua Manufacturing Co., 173–74
National Defense Research Committee (NDRC), 214
National Indemnity Co., 187
National Labor Relations Act (1935), 121–22
National Recovery Administration (NRA), 116–17, 119
National Union of Textile Workers, 94
Needle Trades Workers' Industrial Union, 121
New Bedford (Massachusetts)
  affluence during early nineteenth century in, 30, 42
  African Americans in, 180–81, 216–17, 219–20, 221–22, 225–26
  anti-working-class sentiment during 1850s and 1860s in, 42
  Board of Commerce in, 110, 114, 115
  Cape Verdean community in, 217–18
  casino initiative in, 231–32
  Chamber of Commerce in, 180, 202–3
  City Council in, 42, 114–15, 123–24, 191–93, 194, 220
  Civil War (American) and, 40
  coexistence of unemployment and job openings after 1970 in, 221, 223–24
  conglomeration practices as a challenge for, 187, 191–93, 200–3, 206
  crime levels in, 232–33
  deindustrialization of textile industry in, ix–x, 107, 109–12, 186
  electronics industry in, 124–25, 183–84, 204–5
  elite business families in, 96–97, 100–1
  fishing industry in, 229–30
  garment industry in, 111–13, 114–15, 117, 118–19, 122–23, 170–71, 183–84, 205, 218, 229–30

  "high-tech Massachusetts" initiatives and, 209, 212, 213
  housing conditions in, 87
  Howland Street in, 42
  immigrants during nineteenth century in, 7–8, 56, 57–58, 59, 64, 68, 75, 76
  Immigration and Customs Enforcement raid (2007) in, x, 2–3, 229
  incorporation (1787) of, 31
  Industrial Development Commission in, 114–15, 123–24, 182
  Industrial Development Fund in, 110
  Industrial Development League in, 123–24
  labor unions in, 88, 93–95, 114–16, 117, 118–19, 122, 160–61, 191–93, 200–1, 202
  Latino population in, 1–2
  map of, 4*f*
  "Maya Alley" in, 1–2
  municipal improvements and debt during 1870s in, 44–45, 50
  municipal water system in, 42–44
  North End in, 1–2
  outmigration during 1990s from, 226
  photograph of, 146*f*
  pollution and environmental problems in, 194, 197, 205
  Portuguese community in, 34–35, 128–30, 135–38, 145–46, 148, 169–71
  public money used to lure industry to, 183
  Puerto Rican community in, 218–19, 226
  Quakers in, 34
  the "rebellion" (1970 "race riots") in, 180, 181, 216, 219–22
  renewable energy initiatives in, 229–30
  runaway slaves in, 34, 216–17
  service sector in, 230

New Bedford (Massachusetts) (*cont.*)
  South End of, 2, 217–18, 229
  strike of 1877 in, 91
  strike of 1898 in, 68, 88, 91, 123
  strike of 1928 in, 88, 91, 95, 101–6, 104*f*,
    123, 160–61
  Textile Council, 116
  textile industry in, 2–4, 15, 43–44, 45–
    46, 49–50, 59, 87–88, 89, 90–91,
    93–95, 96–97, 100, 101–6, 229–30
  urban renewal programs during 1960s
    in, 218
  Wall's painting (1853) of, 13, 14*f*
  West End neighborhood of, 216–20
  whaling industry's rise and decline in,
    4, 7, 30, 31–34, 35, 37, 39–44, 45,
    46*f*, 49–50, 71–72, 110, 186
New Bedford Rayon, 179–81
New Social Contract for Massachusetts
    (1979), 210–11
Nonquitt Mill, 204–5
Norris, John, 57
Norris-LaGuardia Act (1932), 121
Northern Light (whaling bark), 47

Obama, Barack, 233
O'Brien, Robert, 202
Odd Fellows fraternal organization, 56
O'Donnell, Thomas, 85
Office of Scientific Research and
    Development (OSRD), 214
oil crises (1973 and 1979), 187–88, 208
O Independente (Portuguese news
    weekly), 137
Oldham (England), 56–57
Oliveira, Álamo, 142–43
Organization of Petroleum Exporting
    Countries (OPEC), 187–88
Ouelette, Alma, 65

Pacheco, Joseph, 85–86, 202
Palmer, Walter H., 177–78

Panic of 1857, 23, 36
Panic of 1873, 45–46, 66–67
Panic of 1893, 66–67, 94
Pantheon (whaling bark), 47
Park, Robert, 129
Park Chung-hee, 183
Paulding, James, 18
Pereira, Jorge Manuel, 147–48, 168
Pickering, Harriet, 95
Pierce, Andrew G., 42, 45–46, 97–98
Pimental, Freitas, 140
Pino, María, 225
Plaid Clothing Group, 205
Plumbers and Steamfitters Union, 221
Plymouth Cordage Industries (PCI
    Group), 195–97, 200
Pocasset Mill (Fall River), 39
"Point Four" program (Truman
    Administration), 156
Polish immigrants, 103–5, 119
Portugal. *See also* The Azores; Portuguese
    immigrants
  Africa resettlement initiative (1950s)
    promoted by, 143–45
  conscription laws in, 70–71, 168
  Carnation Revolution (1974)
    in, 167–68
  emigration levels (1885–1930) from,
    70, 131
  emigration restriction laws in, 70–71,
    74, 131, 143–44
  Estado Novo fascist dictatorship (1933–
    1974) in, 131, 132–38, 133*f*, 167–68
  First Republic era (1910–1926) and,
    69–70, 132–34
  Great Britain and, 69–70, 167–68
  imperialism of, 70–71, 72–73, 133*f*,
    133–35, 136, 141–42, 143–45, 167–68
    (*See also specific territories*)
  Napoleonic Wars and, 69–70
  National Propaganda Secretariat in,
    134, 137

Policia Repressiva de Emigração
Clandestina in, 70
Portuguese immigrants' relationship
with the government of, 129–30,
132, 135–39, 149
Second World War and, 138
whaling industry and, 34–35
World's Fair in New York City (1939)
and, 134–36
Portugal Day celebrations (June 12),
134, 137–38
Portuguese-American Civic
League, 139–40
Portuguese-American Democrats of
Rhode Island, 139–40
Portuguese Educational Society of New
Bedford, 137
Portuguese immigrants. *See also* Azorean
immigrants; Cape Verdeans
anti-union attitudes among, 75
assimilation and, 52, 131
Azorean Refugee Acts (1958 and 1960)
and, 139–41
ethnic antagonism toward, 75, 112–13,
128–29, 132
as garment shop workers, 112–13
Hart-Celler Act (1965) and, 130
increased immigration to
Massachusetts after 1965
and, 169–70
infant mortality rates among, 128–29
Johnson-Reed Immigration Act
quotas (1924) and, 130
levels of immigration among, 76, 142
Portuguese government and, 129–30,
132, 135–39, 149
remittances to Portugal from, 138–39
return migration to Portugal among,
59, 74, 123
Salazar regime in Portugal (1933–1968)
and, 134–36, 137–39
saudade and, 146–47

Second World War and, 138
textile industry and, 75, 76, 83–84, 87,
103–4, 109, 225
unemployment among, 109–10
union organizing and participation
among, 77, 95, 103–5, 119
wages paid to, 75, 77, 83
whaling industry and, 71–
72, 74, 77
women immigrants and, 76, 77, 95,
104–5, 119
Portuguese Radio Club, 136–37
Potofsky, Jacob, 155–56, 157–58, 161, 162,
163, 164
Potomska Mill (New Bedford), 45–46
Potter, William J., 44
Povich, Maury, 3
Povoação (Azores), 75–76
Poyntz, Juliet, 103–4
Prince, John D., 20
private equity firms, 198–200, 229–30
Proposition 2 1/2 (Massachusetts,
1980), 210–11
Providence (Rhode Island), 231
Puerto Ricans, 1–2, 218–19, 226

Quaker Fabric Corp., 231
Quakers, 34
Québec, 62–63, 65–66

Raposa, Anita, 163–64
Raposo, Emidio, 222–23
Rau Fastener Company, 200
Raytheon, 211
Reagan, Ronald, 196–97
Reaper (whaling ship), 39
Rebello, Luis, 73
Reciprocal Tariff Act (1934), 163
Reuther, Victor, 162
Reuther, Walter, 157–58, 161, 162
Ribeiro, Gordon, 218
Ribeiro, Luís, 143

Richard, Kevin, 202
Richard, M. F., 61–62
Richman Brothers, 205–6
Richmond, George, 42, 45
"Rita Quill, Union Member" (radio
    program), 120–21
Robinson, James, 45–46
Rocha, João, 137, 141
Roderick, Mary, 160
Rodman, Samuel, 39
Rogers, George, 220
Roosevelt, Franklin D., 119, 121, 156, 214
Roscoe (whaling bark)*,* 36
Ross, Michael, 159–60
Ross, William, 117
Rotch, Joseph, 31–32
Rotch, William, 45–46
Roxbury (Massachusetts), 212–13
RTE Corporation, 204–5
Rubinstein, Jack, 59
Russell, Joseph, 31

Salazar, António de Oliveira
    Capelinhos Volcano refugees (1958)
        and, 140
    as dictator of Portugal (1933–
        1968), 132–33
    imperialism embraced by, 133–35, 140
    as minister of finance, 132–33
    Portuguese community in the United
        States and, 134–36, 137–39
    Second World War and, 138
    as university professor, 129–30, 132–33
    US consumer market as source of
        interest to, 138–39
    World's Fair (New York City, 1939)
        and, 134–35
Saltzman, William, 220
Salvadoran immigrants, 2–3, 232
Sapienza, Anthony R., 231–32
saudade (Portuguese concept for longing
    for what has passed), 146–47

Schumpeter, Joseph, 6
Scovill Fasteners, Inc., 200–3
Second World War, 125, 138, 186–87,
    214, 233
Segall, Samson, 170–71
Senna, John A., 221
"Shareholder Revolution," 176, 203
Shelburne Shirt Company, 118–
    19, 146–47
Shepard Clothing, 205
Silva Jr., Francisco José da, 74
Simas, Manuel C., 160–61
Simores, Christina, 104–5
Sinclair, Russell, 203
"Sit Down Sister!" (play), 119–20
Slater's Mill (Pawtucket, Rhode
    Island), 16
Smith, Edwin, 112
Smith, M. Estellie, 148
Snow Jr., Loum, 45–46
Southeastern Massachusetts Economic
    Development Committee, 213
Southeastern Massachusetts
    Partnership, 225–26
Southeastern Massachusetts University,
    222–23. *See also* University of
    Massachusetts-Dartmouth
Southeastern Regional Planning
    and Economic Development
    District, 220
South Korea, 183–84
Spellmen, Thomas, 102–3
Springer, Maida, 159
Stafford and Crescent Mills (Fall
    River), 61
Stanton, Seabury, 125, 186–87
Stark Mills, 25
St. Aubin, Leo F., 179–81
Stephania (whaling ship)*,* 47
Stetin, Sol, 155–56, 161–62
Stockport (England), 56–57
Stone, Gil, 136

Stratus Computer, 215
Suffolk Mills, 22–23, 26–27, 28
Sullivan, Michael, 2–3
sweatshops. *See* garment industry
Sylvia, Dineia, 145–47
Sylvia, Manuel, 71–72
Sylvia, Paul, 203

Taber, Isaac, 41, 43
Taft, Donald, 128–30
Taiwan, 163, 180–81, 183–84
Tansey, James, 91
Taylor, Emmanuel, 85–86
Teixeira, Antone, 202
textile industry. *See also* deindustrialization
    of textile industry
  in the American South, 81–82, 89, 92,
    96, 99–100, 105–6, 109, 124, 126–27
  Azorean immigrants in, 139–41
  boardinghouses for women
    workers in, 19
  British immigrants in, 54, 56, 57–
    59, 84
  business owners' decisions in, 96–101
  child workers in, 83–84, 85–87
  Civil War (American) and, 24, 26–28
  conglomeration and, 187
  Embargo Act of 1807 and, 21
  expansion during post-Civil War
    period in, 28–29
  expansion in Massachusetts after 1965
    of, 169
  family labor model and, 16, 83–84
  fires and industrial accidents in, 85–86
  former whaling industry workers in, 7,
    47, 48–50
  French Canadian immigrants in, 61,
    64, 84, 85–86, 87, 103–4
  globalization and, 4–5, 8–9, 82
  housing conditions among
    workers in, 87
  inconsistent availability of work in, 85

  labor unions and, 81–82, 88, 90–91,
    92–93, 116, 118, 157–58
  machines used in, 47–48, 84–85
  overproduction in, 98–100
  Portuguese immigrants in, 75, 76, 83–
    84, 87, 103–4, 109, 225
  profit levels in, 101–2
  resiliency after 1970 of, 209
  Second World War and stimulated
    demand for, 186–87
  strikes and labor activism in, 57–
    59, 85, 88
  wages in, 20, 48–49, 83–85, 90–91,
    98–100, 101–3, 105
  women workers in, 18–20, 47–
    48, 86–87
  workers' attitudes regarding jobs
    in, 224–26
  working conditions in, 83–89
  working hours in, 86–87
Textile Mill Committee (TMC), 103–6,
    104*f*, 118–19
Textile Workers of America, 122
Textile Workers Union of America
    (TWUA), 155–56, 160–61
Textron Inc., 172–74, 175
Thayer, Eli, 26
Thayer, Nathaniel, 26
Tiffany, Henry L., 3
Tirman, John, 3
Tomasia, Maria, 145–46
Trade Adjustment Act (1974), 163–64
Tremont Mill, 22–23, 28
Truman, Harry S., 156
Trump, Donald, 233
Tsoupreas, Angilina, 104–5

União Portuguesa Benificente, 139–40
United Auto Workers (UAW), 157–58, 162
United Electrical Workers, 191–93, 192*f*
United Shoe Machinery Co., 194–97
United Textile Workers (UTW), 93–94

University of Massachusetts-Dartmouth,
    213, 222–23, 230
US Industries, 205
USM (division of Emhart Corp.), 196–97

Valente, Mary, 95, 104–5
Valesh, Eva, 95
Verzina, Regis, 85–86
Vieira Jr., Jose, 144
Vietnam War, 169, 190–91, 218
Voisine, Ed, 202

Wagner Act (1935), 121–22
Wall, William Allen, 13, 14*f*, 14–15
Wallace, Henry, 156
Waltham (Massachusetts), 22–23, 24
Wampanoag Indians, 31
Wamsutta Mills (New Bedford)
    contemporary businesses located in, 3
    investors who financed, 45–46
    obstacles during nineteenth century at, 15
    opening (1849) of, 15
    photograph of, 5*f*
    strikes at, 91, 92–93
    Wall's painting (1853) of, 13, 14*f*
War of 1812, 32
Water Jr., Herbert, 219
Waterman, Fred, 89
Watkins, William, 45–46
Webb, Thomas, 57
Weld, Bill, 200–1
whaling industry
    African American workers in, 34
    Arctic ice disasters of 1871 and
        1876 in, 36
    bonanza payouts for workers in, 33, 35
    Cape Verdeans and, 217
    Civil War (American) and, 40
    decline during 1860s with emergence
        of petroleum of, 40–44, 45, 46*f*,
        46–47, 49–50, 186

economic volatility of, 36–38, 39–40
environmental crisis during nineteenth
    century affecting, 7, 15, 40
illuminants produced in, 31
labor needs of, 31, 33–35
"lay" system of labor contracts in,
    32–33, 35
in Nantucket, 31–32, 40
Native American workers in, 31
in New Bedford, 4, 7, 30, 31–34, 35,
    37, 39–44, 45, 46*f*, 49–50, 71–72,
    110, 186
ship captains and, 38–39
shipping agents in, 33–34
William and Joseph (whaling brig), 34–35
Williams, John, 54
Winegar, Samuel, 39
women
    Azorean immigrant women
        and, 75–76
    garment industry and, 115–16, 122–
        23, 146–47
    labor unions and, 93–95, 104–5, 115–
        16, 118–19, 121–22
    Portuguese women immigrants and,
        76, 77, 95, 104–5, 119
    as textile workers, 18–20, 47–
        48, 86–87
Wood, Charles L., 45–46
Woolworth Corporation, 205–6
World Federation of Trade
    Unions, 154–55
World's Fair (New York City,
    1939), 134–36
World War I. *See* First World War
World War II. *See* Second World War
W.W. Cross & Co., 195–96

Yarn Finishers union (Fall River), 93

Zink, William, 124

Printed in the USA/Agawam, MA
February 2, 2024

860510.174